PETERSON'S®

MASTER THE™ COMMERCIAL DRIVER'S LICENSE EXAMS

About Peterson's®

Peterson's has been your trusted educational publisher for more than 50 years. It's a milestone we're quite proud of as we continue to offer the most accurate, dependable, high-quality educational content in the field, providing you with everything you need to succeed. No matter where you are on your academic or professional path, you can rely on Peterson's for its books, online information, expert test-prep tools, the most up-to-date education exploration data, and the highest quality career success resources—everything you need to achieve your education goals. For our complete line of products, visit **www.petersons.com**.

For more information, contact Peterson's, 4380 S. Syracuse St., Suite 200, Denver, CO 80237; 800-338-3282 Ext. 54229; or visit us online at **www.petersons.com**.

ISBN-13: 978-0-7689-4588-1

Printed in the United States of America

10 9 8 7 6 5 4 3 2 1   24 23 22

First Edition

CONTENTS

CONTENTS

Peterson's Updates and Corrections:

Check out our website at **www.petersonsbooks.com/updates-and-corrections/** to see if there is any new information regarding the test and any revisions or corrections to the content of this book. We've made sure the information in this book is accurate and up to date; however, the test format or content may have changed since the time of publication.

BEFORE YOU BEGIN

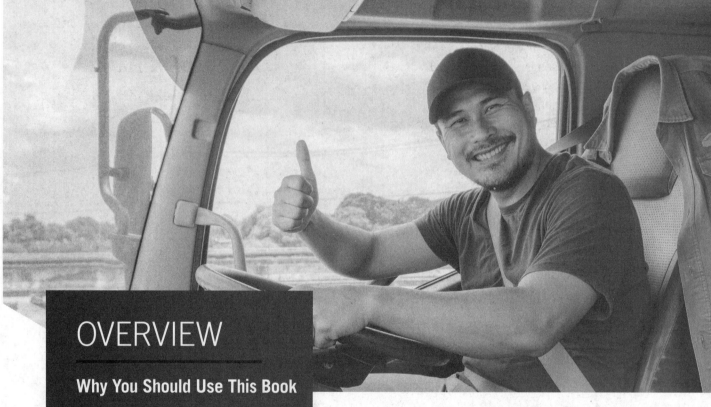

OVERVIEW

Why You Should Use This Book

How This Book Is Organized

How to Use This Book

Special Study Features

Helpful Study Tips

Tips for Test Takers

Test Day Strategies

Peterson's® Publications

You're Well on Your Way to Success

If you are looking to start a career as a commercial driver, you have several hurdles you must first overcome. Not only will you have to obtain a commercial learner's permit (CLP), but to earn your commercial driver's license (CDL), you will also have to pass a medical exam, a written test, a physical skills test, and take additional endorsement exams depending on the types of materials you plan to transport and the vehicles you plan to drive. With all that, the effort you put in is worth what you'll get out. Commercial drivers are (and will continue to be) in high demand, acting as a key component of commercial industries. And whether you're applying for your CDL for the first time, adding new endorsements, or renewing your license in another state, this book has the testing materials you need to build on and practice with the knowledge offered by the state CDL manuals and registered driver-training programs.

WHY YOU SHOULD USE THIS BOOK

Peterson's *Master the™ Commercial Driver's License Exams* is designed by subject-matter experts and educators to fully prepare you for success on the CDL written exams. This study guide contains the following:

TEST INFORMATION

This book contains the information on how the tests are structured, including registering for the exam, the number of questions, time limits, and what to bring on test day.

THOROUGH TEST TOPIC REVIEW

This study guide offers the information on the different topics of the exams, whether it is the general knowledge exam or any of the CDL endorsement tests.

REALISTIC PRACTICE QUESTIONS

Not only does every chapter have a full practice test for the relevant subtest, but this book also gives you multiple additional practice tests designed to simulate the types of questions that will appear on test day.

We know that a successful and satisfying career as a commercial driver depends on being ready for anything. Whether it's the basics of turning a large vehicle or the protocol for dealing with truck fires, practice and preparation are the best ways to guarantee success. With this study guide, you can prepare and practice for your exams. Whether it's a career as a bus driver or a transporter for hazardous materials, Peterson's is here to help you on your path to obtaining a CDL.

HOW THIS BOOK IS ORGANIZED

Divided into chapters for each of the CDL endorsements, this study guide introduces all elements of the CDL exams to help you organize your studies. Use Chapter 1 to learn important details about the CDL exam on a broader level, including registration information and what to expect on test day. Chapter 2 offers several diagnostic tests to assess where you stand with the exams required for a Class A CDL. Chapter 3 contains information about the general knowledge exam, which must be taken to obtain the CLP prior to obtaining any subsequent endorsements. Chapter 4 covers the air brakes exam, an essential test for avoiding an air brakes restriction on your CDL. Chapters 5 through 9 focus on specific endorsements and include a practice test for each. At the end of the book, you will find additional practice tests for the general knowledge and air brakes exams as well as each of the endorsements. There's also an appendix that contains a glossary of important commercial driving terms.

HOW TO USE THIS BOOK
Endorsement-Specific Test Method

One way to use this book is to only focus on the specific endorsements you seek to obtain. For example, if you are only interested in obtaining a CDL to drive a passenger vehicle, you would focus on studying the General Knowledge, Air Brakes (if you'll drive a vehicle equipped with air brakes), and the Passenger Vehicle chapters.

With this method, you can focus your study time on a few key areas. Read through the necessary chapters, take the practice tests, then repeat until you feel comfortable with the material. The practice tests will have sample questions like those you will find on the actual exams. These questions will show you where you might need to focus your test-prep efforts—identifying topics to review in the chapter or in your state CDL manual.

Once you've taken a practice test for the first time, use the answer key to check your answers and identify your strengths and weaknesses. Make a list of your strong and weak areas and rank them from best to worst. If you scored well in the general knowledge section, you would count that as a strength. If you didn't score so well with air brakes questions, that would be an area for you to brush up on. Rank the exams from your strongest to your weakest.

Use your scores to develop your study plan. Your study plan should prioritize working on your weaker skills first. Keep in mind that while you may not need to spend as much time on your strong areas, you should, however, still review these areas to keep them in shape for test day.

Front-to-Back Method

Another way to use this book is the "front-to-back" method. In this method, you work through the book the way it's organized.

Start with Chapter 1 and carefully read through the introductory information for the different exams. This will help you understand each exam, its format, and how it's scored. Next, take your diagnostic tests: General Knowledge, Air Brakes, and Combination Vehicles. These tests are often required for a Class A CDL. Then, study the content in Chapters 3 through 9. Focus on the exams that relate to your CDL plans. If you know your strengths, you might devote extra time to the tests where you need the most improvement.

After you've reviewed the content, take the practice tests at the end of each chapter and then those at the end of the book. Taking a practice test will help you be

more prepared for test day. Sometimes, just the process of taking the test itself can help you increase your score.

After you complete the test, review your answers with the explanations provided. If you still don't understand how to answer a certain question, you can always refer to the relevant chapter of the book and your state CDL manual for the relevant information.

The subject review in *Peterson's Master the™ Commercial Driver's License Exams* can help familiarize you with the unique content, structure, and format of the test.

SPECIAL STUDY FEATURES

You will find the following kinds of special study features scattered throughout this book.

Overview

Each chapter begins with an overview listing the topics covered in the chapter. These allow you to quickly target the areas in which you are most interested.

Summing It Up

Each chapter ends with a point-by-point summary that captures the most important points contained in the chapter. This provides a convenient way to review key points.

Tips, Notes, and Alerts

- Tips provide insight into key testing topics or exam standards.
- Notes identify additional pieces of information related to chapter structure or exam topics.
- Alerts signal potential pitfalls in the exam requirements or topic areas.

Glossary of Commercial Driving Terms

For those who do not have a background in commercial driving, we offer a glossary of common terms you should know. This is a general list, but there are terms listed that are broadly applicable to all areas of the CDL exams as well as terms related to specific endorsements.

HELPFUL STUDY TIPS

The following are study tips to help you prepare for the CDL exam.

1 **Set up a study schedule.** Assign yourself a period each day devoted to preparing for the exam. A regular schedule is best, but the important thing is to study daily, even if you can't do so at the same time every day.

2 **Study alone.** You will concentrate better if you work by yourself. Make a list of questions that you find puzzling and points of confusion. Later, discuss the items on the list with a friend who is preparing for the same exam. Exchange ideas and discuss more difficult questions at a joint review session shortly before the exam date.

3 **Eliminate distractions.** Choose a quiet, well-lit spot that is removed from distractions. Arrange your study area in a way that minimizes interruptions and allows you to concentrate.

4 **Read carefully and take notes.** Underline points that you consider significant. Make marginal notes. Flag the pages you think are especially important.

5 **Concentrate on the information and instructional chapters.** Get yourself psyched to enter the world of a commercial vehicle driver. Learn how to inspect, maintain, and operate commercial vehicles.

6 **Take a practice test.** Focus on eliminating wrong answers; this is an important method for answering all multiple-choice questions. Take the practice test in one sitting and time yourself.

TIP

Do not memorize questions and answers. You might see questions on your exam that are very similar to the ones provided, but you will not see any of the exact questions you encounter in this book.

TIPS FOR TEST TAKERS

Here's a list of general tips to help ensure that your score accurately reflects your understanding of the content on the exam.

- **Remain calm.** You know yourself best and which strategies or techniques will help you ease any test anxiety. Keep your mind calm and clear.

- **Read the directions, the entire question, and all answer choices before selecting your answer.** Multiple-choice questions on the CDL exam will only have one answer option that is correct. This is also the case for true/false questions. Pay attention to what the exam directions are asking you to do, and read the question carefully. Before selecting your answer, you should always read each answer choice.

- **Predict the answer.** For multiple-choice and true/false questions, you'll read the question then, before reading each answer choice, predict the answer. This will help you draw on what you know and avoid getting trapped by those "close but not quite right" answers.

- **Focus on the questions you know.** Struggling with a question? Skip it and focus on answering the questions you *do* know. As time permits, you can go back to the questions you skipped.

- **Eliminate answer options.** When you are unsure of the answer to a question, try eliminating the answers you know are incorrect. Then, guess using the remaining options.

- **Answer every question.** Remember, your score will be based on the number of questions you answer correctly. Any unanswered question will be marked as incorrect, so, if you're unsure, take a guess! If you have eliminated the answers you know to be incorrect, your chances of choosing the correct answer have increased dramatically.

- **If time permits, go back and check your answers.** More often than not, your first answer will be the correct answer. But, if you feel like you need to review certain questions again, and you have the time, go for it.

- **Mark your answer sheet correctly.** This applies mainly to a paper-based test and not a computer-based test. However, it goes without saying that you should make sure you are marking the answer on the correct question on the answer sheet. This is especially true if you skip a question.

TEST DAY PREPARATIONS

You may find it helpful to keep the following strategies in mind for the actual test day.

1 **Be prepared.** Research what you will need to bring with you on test day. The night before, make sure you have everything you need in one place. Decide on the outfit you will wear. Be comfortable and dress in layers to suit the temperature of the testing site.

2 **Eat smart.** Plan to eat a balanced meal before your CDL exams. Have something with a combination of healthy fats, protein, and carbs. Avoid caffeine if it makes you jittery, and avoid sugary items that will spike your energy level—it won't last, and you'll be worse for it as you complete your tests.

3 **Focus only on the test.** Don't plan any other activities on test day or attempt to squeeze the test in between appointments.

4 **Arrive rested, relaxed, and on time.** In fact, plan to arrive a little bit early. Leave plenty of time for traffic tie-ups or other complications that might upset you and interfere with your test performance.

5 **If the test is proctored, ask questions about any instructions you do not understand.** Make sure that you know exactly what to do. In the test room, the proctor will provide the instructions you must follow when taking the examination.

6 **Follow instructions exactly during the examination.** Do not begin until you are told to do so. Stop as soon as you are told to stop. Any infraction of the rules can be considered cheating.

7 **Maintain a positive attitude.** This will help ease any test anxiety. A can-do attitude creates confidence, and confidence is key.

PETERSON'S® PUBLICATIONS

Peterson's publishes a full line of books—career preparation, education exploration, test prep, and financial aid. Peterson's books are available for purchase online at **www.petersons.com**. Sign up for one of our online subscription plans and you'll have access to our entire test prep catalog of more than 150 exams *plus* instructional videos, flashcards, interactive quizzes, and more! Our subscription plans allow you to study as quickly as you can or as slowly as you'd like. For more information, go to **www.petersons.com/testprep/**. Peterson's publications can also be found at college libraries and career centers, and your local bookstore and library.

GIVE US YOUR FEEDBACK

We welcome any comments or suggestions you may have about this publication. Your feedback will help us make education dreams possible for you—and others like you.

YOU'RE WELL ON YOUR WAY TO SUCCESS

Remember that knowledge is power. By using this book, you're taking a big step toward preparing yourself for all that the CDL exams can throw at you.

We *know* you're eager to get to the practice tests and review, but remember that having a thorough understanding of the exam from top to bottom will give you a real advantage—and put you ahead of the test-taking competition. So take the time to learn about each exam, and work through each step so you'll be confident and prepared for test day success. Let's get started!

Good luck!

CHAPTER

**Introduction to
Commercial Driver's License**

INTRO TO CDL

OVERVIEW

Requirements

Endorsements

Testing Logistics

Physical Skills Test

Next Steps

Summing It Up

A commercial driver's license (CDL) is a license specifically for working drivers that allows them to operate commercial vehicles with or without trailers. Like a personal license, it requires a written test and a skills test. Unlike a personal license, however, a CDL comes in different classes and may be expanded to include various endorsements.

The CDL process encompasses both the initial licensing exam as well as any endorsements that expand the driver's capabilities for what they can transport. The initial CDL exam requires BOTH a written and skills test using the class of vehicle the driver intends to operate as a commercial driver. There are three basic vehicle classes for commercial drivers: Class A (combination vehicles with a GCWR of 26,001 or more pounds), Class B (heavy straight vehicles with a GVWR of 26,001 or more pounds), and Class C (small vehicles with a GVWR of less than 26,001 pounds).

There are eight exams in total, including endorsements, with a significant overlap between them. These exams include general knowledge, air brakes, combination vehicles, double and triple trailers, tankers, passenger vehicles, school buses, and hazardous materials.

You'll complete a slightly different test battery depending on the class of vehicle you plan to drive and the kinds of materials you plan to transport. For instance, default testing for a Class A CDL requires the general knowledge, air brakes, and combination vehicles exams. These three tests are taken first, followed by the physical skills test at a later date, and then any additional endorsement exams thereafter. Regardless of what class of CDL you're applying for, it is crucial to study each area closely when preparing for the tests, as even the essential tests may include questions relating to specific endorsements. All tests are composed of a combination of true/false and multiple-choice questions and require a passing rate of 80%.

REQUIREMENTS

Requirements exist at both the federal and state levels for who can acquire a CDL and when they can do so. The federal level creates a base consistency through all the states. However, some states add on to these base federal requirements, and some states make it so that certain situations require a CDL when circumstance wouldn't require one in other states. In California, for example, a passenger vehicle is recognized as such if it is carrying 10 passengers in a commercial setting. In other states, however, a passenger vehicle is one that carries 16 passengers. Familiarize yourself with local motor vehicle laws in the area to know if there are specific state requirements in addition to federal ones. Knowing the requirements is one of the first steps to obtaining a CDL. The following table shows basic requirements that all drivers must meet.

REQUIREMENTS FOR OBTAINING A CDL	
Age	18 for intrastate, 21 for interstate (except in NY where Class A is 21, and in HI where it is 21 for both). Different endorsements do have different age requirements.
Education	A high school diploma or a GED is not necessary to get a CDL at the federal or state level for many states. However, many trucking schools and private companies do require one to be enrolled or hired.
Citizenship	Proof of US-citizenship or permanent residency is needed. Social Security card, birth certificate, valid passport, and a green card are acceptable documentation. Applicants should bring one document verifying age and identity, a Social Security card (or document proving that the applicant has an SSN), two documents proving residency (issued by state or federally, like a vehicle registration card or property/income tax statement), and in some states proof of liability insurance coverage. For non-US citizens, a document issued by the US government proving legal presence is also required.
Driving Records	Applicants must possess a valid license that is non-commercial and have 1–2 years of driving experience (dependent on the state, so check with the local DMV) and have no disqualifications due to past offenses within the last 5 years, such as a conviction for a DUI.
Time and Experience	One to two years of previous driving experience is required (and as previously stated, this amount of time is dependent on the state, so check with the local DMV), and a commercial learner's permit (CLP) generally must be held for a minimum of 14 days (but can vary between states) after passing the written test and before applying for the CDL and taking the skills test.

As of February 7, 2022, certain applicants are now required to complete Entry Level Driver Training (ELDT) prior to taking a CDL exam. This training program includes instruction from a registered training provider listed on the Federal Motor Carrier Training Provider Registry. Applicants that are required to undergo this training include drivers seeking a vehicle class upgrade, a hazardous materials endorsement, a passenger endorsement, and a school bus endorsement. For more information on exemptions and where to find a registered training provider near you, visit the Federal Motor Carrier Training Provider Registry at **tpr.fmcsa.dot.gov**.

Medical Requirements

Physical health requirements are in place at the federal level to ensure that drivers are able to properly operate a commercial vehicle without posing significant risk to themselves or others. Working as a commercial driver can be exhausting and stressful and can require significant endurance. To ensure that commercial drivers can operate under these conditions, the Department of Transportation (DOT) requires a medical exam. The DOT medical exam will review the details of a driver's medical record, including things such as recent surgeries, health conditions, and any lost limbs. The frequency of required medical exams will vary based on the presence of specific health conditions. The most basic medical qualifications subject to review include vision, hearing, blood pressure, sleep apnea, epilepsy/seizure disorders, diabetes, and blood sugar.

VISION

Vision should be at least 20/40 in each eye with or without the use of corrective lenses. Each eye must have at least 70 degrees of peripheral vision for the horizontal meridian. Glasses/contacts can be used to meet these requirements.

HEARING

Hearing should be strong enough to hear, in at least one ear, a forced whisper from a distance of more than 5 feet away. Hearing aid devices can be used to meet this requirement.

BLOOD PRESSURE

Drivers with stage 3 high blood pressure that is greater than 180/110 will not meet the requirements for a CDL certification.

Drivers with stage 2 high blood pressure that is around 160–179/100–109 will only be allowed a temporary three-month certificate. However, this is left completely to the discretion of the examiner. An examiner can choose to exclude the person or permit the temporary certificate depending on other health concerns.

Drivers with stage 1 high blood pressure that is around 140–159/90–99 will be allowed a one-year certificate card.

Drivers with a blood pressure below 140/90 are provided a two-year certificate card.

SLEEP APNEA

Unless it can be proven to be under control from a recent annual sleep study and an approved release from a physician, drivers with sleep apnea cannot qualify to receive a CDL certification.

EPILEPSY AND SEIZURE DISORDERS

Drivers with epilepsy and seizure disorders are disqualified from operating a commercial motor vehicle in interstate commerce.

Exemptions do exist for those who have been seizure-free for certain periods of time, for single unprovoked seizures, and those with single provoked seizures with specific criteria. Regardless of the qualification for exemption, an application must be submitted to the Department of Transportation Federal Motor Carrier Safety Administration (FMCSA).

DIABETES

Drivers that take insulin through needle injections will not meet the requirements to receive a CDL certification unless they obtain a Medical Examiner's Certificate (MEC) that must be renewed annually. Drivers with insulin-treated diabetes mellitus (ITDM) must visit a treating clinician and provide an ITDM Assessment Form.

Permanent disqualifications exist for those with diabetic retinopathy.

BLOOD SUGAR

Hemoglobin A1C levels should be 8% or less, and if blood sugars are above 10%, it is the examiner's decision if a CDL certificate can be given to the driver. Depending on the results of such blood testing, a driver may be required to undergo more frequent medical exams to maintain qualifications for a CDL.

ENDORSEMENTS

The general knowledge test is not for a general knowledge endorsement but is simply the basic exam required to obtain a commercial learner's permit (CLP), paving the way to getting your CDL. Air brakes and combination vehicle endorsements are their own endorsements, but they do not have endorsement letter codes as they are required for specific classes of vehicles (you'll receive a restriction code for not passing the written test or driving a vehicle without air brakes during your skills test).

The following table lists all the endorsements that can be added to a CDL, their letter code, age required to receive them, what classes they can be obtained for, and what tests they require.

ENDORSEMENTS AND REQUIREMENTS

Endorsement	Definition	Letter Code	Minimum Age	Class Required	Tests Needed
Air Brakes	Drive a vehicle of any class equipped with air brakes	None	18 years old for intrastate (except for HI which requires an age of 21, and for a Class A in NY which requires an age of 21) and 21 for interstate	A, B, or C to avoid restriction code L	Written and skills
Combination Vehicles	Drive a Class A vehicle that uses a fifth-wheel connection	None	18 years old for intrastate (except for HI which requires an age of 21, and for a Class A in NY which requires an age of 21) and 21 for interstate	A to avoid restriction code O	Written and skills
Double and Triple Trailers	Drive a Class A vehicle to pull double or triple trailers	T	18 years old for intrastate (except for HI which requires an age of 21, and for a Class A in NY which requires an age of 21) and 21 for interstate	A	Written only
Tanker Trailers	Drive vehicles of any class designed to transport any liquid or gaseous materials with individual capacity of 119 gallons or aggregate 1,000 gallons	N	18 years old for intrastate (except for HI which requires an age of 21, and for a Class A in NY which requires an age of 21) and 21 for interstate	A, B, or C	Written only
Passenger Vehicles (excludes school buses)	Drive a vehicle in any class that is designed to carry 16 or more people	P	18 years old for intrastate (except for HI which requires an age of 21, and for a Class A in NY which requires an age of 21) and 21 for interstate	A, B, or C	Written and skills
Hazardous Materials	Drive a vehicle of any class designed to haul material deemed hazardous under 49 U.S.C. 5103 and that must be placarded under subpart F of 49 CFR part 172	H	21 for both intrastate and interstate	A, B, or C	Written only
School Bus	Drive a school bus vehicle in any class to transport passengers	S	Varies by state (age 18 or 21)	A, B, or C	Written and skills
Combination: Hazmat and Tanker	Drive tank vehicles that haul hazardous materials in amounts requiring placards	X	21 for all drivers	A	Written only (combines Tanker and HazMat exams)

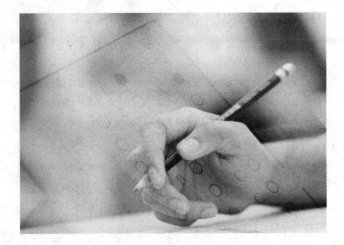

TESTING LOGISTICS

The written tests for obtaining a CDL and the corresponding endorsements are the first tests that the driver will take. There are variations in how many questions will be on each test, and each one will also have varying time limits in which it must be completed. If any tests (written or skills) are failed, then a driver has a chance to retake the test twice before paying the fee again (though this may vary by state). Tests can often be taken again after three days for the second attempt. In some cases, however, the third test will need a buffer of 90 days before it can be retaken. Check with your local motor vehicle department for the time limits between retaking a test and if there are any retesting fees.

CDL TEST SPECIFICATIONS		
Written Test	Number of Questions	Time for Testing
General Knowledge	50	90 minutes
Air Brakes	25	60 minutes
Combination Vehicles	20	60 minutes
Double and Triple Trailers	20	60 minutes
Tanker Vehicles	20	60 minutes
Passenger Vehicles	20	60 minutes
School Buses	20	60 minutes
Hazardous Materials	30	60 minutes

Scheduling

In most states the written portion of the initial CDL exam does not require scheduling. However, the skills portion (and endorsement specific testing) usually requires an appointment. This can be scheduled in the same fashion as the traditional driving test for a personal vehicle.

Cost

This varies dramatically from state to state with some fees being as low as $10 and others as high as $150. Check with your local DMV for costs related to the written and skills tests as well as CLP costs and endorsement fees.

Scoring

The following chart is a breakdown of all the tests, how many questions they will contain, and how many questions need to be answered correctly to pass at an 80 percent grade.

TEST-SPECIFIC PASSING REQUIREMENTS			
Written Test	Number of Questions	# of Correct Questions Needed (80%)	Skills Test Needed
General Knowledge	50	40	Yes
Air Brakes	25	20	Yes
Combination Vehicles	20	16	Yes
Double and Triple Trailers	20	16	No
Tanker Vehicles	20	16	No
Passenger Vehicles	20	16	Yes
School Buses	20	16	Yes
Hazardous Materials	30	24	No

Test Day

Once you have scheduled your exam, it is important to prepare for the actual day of the test as well. Although, by then, you have no doubt spent time studying through this guide and the practice tests provided, there are a few things to remember for day-of logistics that will help you feel prepared.

GET REST

It may seem obvious but restful sleep should be a top priority before the exam. You may feel pressure to get in one last study session, but sleep will act as a greater boon for your performance. Spend your time leading up to your testing to prepare but spare yourself the stress the day before.

WEAR COMFORTABLE CLOTHING

Wear layers that allow you to adjust easily based on the temperature of the testing room. Being too hot or too cold can prove distracting and decrease your score. For the skills test, wear comfortable clothing that is easy to move in and distraction free. Additionally, wear safe, closed-toe shoes.

LEAVE EARLY AND BLOCK OFF TIME

The initial CDL written exam is 90 minutes, and the skills exam is usually around 120 minutes. However, the DMV can be unpredictable. Plan to be there the entire day, avoiding any commitments before and beyond the exam. This will allow you to be fully present without worrying about other commitments, work shifts, etc. In addition, this extra time can help accommodate any possible technical difficulties or other delays that may prolong the actual exam process.

PHYSICAL SKILLS TEST

The physical skills test can be a daunting task, but proper preparation can not only increase the likelihood of doing well but also ease any anxiety and boost your confidence. Knowing what to bring and what is expected can help with that preparation on top of the standard studying and practice needed to pass.

The skills test is broken up into three segmented tests: pre-trip inspection, basic controls, and driving. All of these segments combined generally take around 2 hours.

1. **Pre-Trip Inspection:** This segment is just as important as the actual driving portion of the skills test. You must complete a point-by-point inspection of the vehicle. If completing the skills test in a vehicle equipped with air brakes, you must demonstrate the proper procedure for testing the air braking system. This segment usually has around a 30-minute time limit.

2. **Basic Controls:** This segment is focused on the skills needed within the parking lot, prior to driving on the open road. This includes knowledge about the interior of the cab as well as parking and reversing. This generally has around a 40-minute time limit.

3. **Driving:** This segment is where the driver will operate the vehicle with the test administrator present. Knowing the rules of the road, the proper operation of the vehicle, and the limitations that the vehicle has will allow for a smooth and safe ride. As always, practice is necessary for passing performance. However, never practice without a CDL driver in the vehicle while you hold your CLP. Time limits for this segment are set by local DMVs and can vary.

If ever there is a question or concern before going to the skills test, call the DMV location or test provider or go to their website for answers. Similarly, before or during the test, direct questions or concerns to the test administrator. The test administrator is present to observe and also ensure safety for everyone involved.

5

 NOTE -

Skills tests can be taken either at the local DMV or at an approved commercial driving school. If you require ELDT, check with your driving school or training program about testing options.

What to Bring

For your physical skills test, you must arrive prepared with the following:

- Required paperwork (e.g., proof of age, citizenship, insurance, social security number, etc.)
- The class vehicle you plan to drive commercially. If you bring a lower-class vehicle (or a vehicle without air brakes), restriction codes will be placed on your license that prohibit you from driving any other type of vehicle. For instance, the restriction "M" means that the driver can only operate Class B or C passenger vehicles. The restriction "N" means that the driver can only operate Class C passenger vehicles.

Automatic Fails

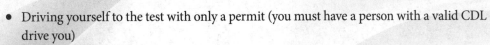

The following list provides common reasons for automatic fails during the course of the skills test:

- Driving yourself to the test with only a permit (you must have a person with a valid CDL drive you)
- Not wearing a seatbelt
- Stopping on railroad tracks
- Running a stop sign or red light
- Speeding
- Braking too hard
- Driving onto a curb or sidewalk
- Forgetting to do the pre-trip inspection
- Other major safety infractions (check your local CDL manual for further details)

NEXT STEPS

After you have passed your written and skills tests for your CDL, you are ready to look for employment within the commercial driving field! Although it may take up to 30 days for you to receive your hard copy license, your printed test results can often be used when applying for employment.

License Terms

As with any driver's license, a CDL is valid for five years (though this may vary by state). It is your responsibility to renew your license BEFORE it expires. This is a simple process that does not entail repeat testing. If you do let it lapse, fines and retesting may apply based on state guidelines.

Reciprocity

If you move to another state, your CDL will NOT transfer. You will be required to surrender your old state's CDL and obtain a new one in the new state. This is different from state to state and can include the following steps:

- Contact the local DMV to schedule a CDL transfer
- Provide proof of your new state residency
- Present a medical DOT exam within your new state
- Get fingerprinted and go through a background check (if you had the HazMat endorsement in the prior state)
- Retake portions of the original CDL and/or endorsement exams
- Complete the process within 30–60 days of residency

NOTES

SUMMING IT UP

- The commercial driver's license process encompasses both the initial licensing exam as well as multiple endorsements that expand the driver's capabilities for what they can transport. The initial CDL exam requires BOTH a written and skills test using the class of vehicle the driver intends to operate as a commercial driver.

- There are requirements that are provided on the federal level in order to keep a base consistency through all the states. However, some states add on to these base federal requirements, and some of them make it so that certain situations require a CDL when they wouldn't require one in other states. Familiarize yourself with local motor vehicle laws to know if there are specific state requirements in addition to federal ones.

  - In California, for example, a passenger vehicle is recognized as such if it is carrying 10 passengers in a commercial setting. In other states, however, a passenger vehicle is one that carries 16 people.

- To ensure that commercial drivers can successfully operate under strenuous conditions, the Department of Transportation (DOT) requires a medical exam. The DOT medical exam will review many factors of a driver's medical record including things such as recent surgeries, health conditions, and any lost limbs.

- All CDL applicants take the general knowledge exam. Other exams will be required depending on the class of license for which you apply. For instance, air brakes and combination vehicles are the base endorsements for Class A CDL holders. All other endorsements require a separate endorsement exam.

- All endorsement exams require 80% of the answers to be correct for a passing grade, regardless of the number of questions on each exam.

- In addition to the written portion of the exam, there is also a physical skills test. The skills test is broken up into three segmented tests: pre-trip inspection, basic controls, and driving. All of these segments combined generally take around 2 hours.

- Once you have scheduled your exam, be sure to prepare for exam day. This includes getting enough rest, wearing comfortable clothing, and making sure your day is clear of other engagements.

CHAPTER

Diagnostic Tests

DIAGNOSTIC TESTS

DIAGNOSTIC TESTS

These diagnostic tests are designed to help you recognize your strengths and weaknesses. The questions cover information from the the three exams that are commonly required for a Class A commercial driver's license: General Knowledge, Air Brakes, and Combination Vehicles. For each of the questions, choose the correct answer and then fill in the corresponding circle on the answer sheet. Check your answers using the answer keys and explanations that follow each test.

ANSWER SHEET: CDL DIAGNOSTIC TESTS

General Knowledge

1. Ⓐ Ⓑ Ⓒ Ⓓ   11. Ⓐ Ⓑ Ⓒ Ⓓ   21. Ⓐ Ⓑ Ⓒ Ⓓ   31. Ⓐ Ⓑ Ⓒ Ⓓ   41. Ⓐ Ⓑ

2. Ⓐ Ⓑ Ⓒ Ⓓ   12. Ⓐ Ⓑ Ⓒ Ⓓ   22. Ⓐ Ⓑ Ⓒ Ⓓ   32. Ⓐ Ⓑ Ⓒ Ⓓ   42. Ⓐ Ⓑ Ⓒ Ⓓ

3. Ⓐ Ⓑ Ⓒ Ⓓ   13. Ⓐ Ⓑ Ⓒ Ⓓ   23. Ⓐ Ⓑ   33. Ⓐ Ⓑ Ⓒ Ⓓ   43. Ⓐ Ⓑ Ⓒ Ⓓ

4. Ⓐ Ⓑ Ⓒ Ⓓ   14. Ⓐ Ⓑ Ⓒ Ⓓ   24. Ⓐ Ⓑ Ⓒ Ⓓ   34. Ⓐ Ⓑ   44. Ⓐ Ⓑ Ⓒ Ⓓ

5. Ⓐ Ⓑ   15. Ⓐ Ⓑ   25. Ⓐ Ⓑ   35. Ⓐ Ⓑ   45. Ⓐ Ⓑ Ⓒ Ⓓ

6. Ⓐ Ⓑ Ⓒ Ⓓ   16. Ⓐ Ⓑ Ⓒ Ⓓ   26. Ⓐ Ⓑ Ⓒ Ⓓ   36. Ⓐ Ⓑ Ⓒ Ⓓ   46. Ⓐ Ⓑ Ⓒ Ⓓ

7. Ⓐ Ⓑ   17. Ⓐ Ⓑ Ⓒ Ⓓ   27. Ⓐ Ⓑ   37. Ⓐ Ⓑ Ⓒ Ⓓ   47. Ⓐ Ⓑ Ⓒ Ⓓ

8. Ⓐ Ⓑ Ⓒ Ⓓ   18. Ⓐ Ⓑ Ⓒ Ⓓ   28. Ⓐ Ⓑ Ⓒ Ⓓ   38. Ⓐ Ⓑ Ⓒ Ⓓ   48. Ⓐ Ⓑ Ⓒ Ⓓ

9. Ⓐ Ⓑ Ⓒ Ⓓ   19. Ⓐ Ⓑ Ⓒ Ⓓ   29. Ⓐ Ⓑ Ⓒ Ⓓ   39. Ⓐ Ⓑ Ⓒ Ⓓ   49. Ⓐ Ⓑ Ⓒ Ⓓ

10. Ⓐ Ⓑ   20. Ⓐ Ⓑ Ⓒ Ⓓ   30. Ⓐ Ⓑ   40. Ⓐ Ⓑ Ⓒ Ⓓ   50. Ⓐ Ⓑ Ⓒ Ⓓ

Air Brakes

1. Ⓐ Ⓑ   6. Ⓐ Ⓑ Ⓒ Ⓓ   11. Ⓐ Ⓑ Ⓒ Ⓓ   16. Ⓐ Ⓑ   21. Ⓐ Ⓑ

2. Ⓐ Ⓑ Ⓒ Ⓓ   7. Ⓐ Ⓑ   12. Ⓐ Ⓑ   17. Ⓐ Ⓑ Ⓒ Ⓓ   22. Ⓐ Ⓑ Ⓒ Ⓓ

3. Ⓐ Ⓑ Ⓒ Ⓓ   8. Ⓐ Ⓑ Ⓒ Ⓓ   13. Ⓐ Ⓑ   18. Ⓐ Ⓑ   23. Ⓐ Ⓑ Ⓒ Ⓓ

4. Ⓐ Ⓑ Ⓒ Ⓓ   9. Ⓐ Ⓑ Ⓒ Ⓓ   14. Ⓐ Ⓑ Ⓒ Ⓓ   19. Ⓐ Ⓑ Ⓒ Ⓓ   24. Ⓐ Ⓑ

5. Ⓐ Ⓑ   10. Ⓐ Ⓑ Ⓒ Ⓓ   15. Ⓐ Ⓑ Ⓒ Ⓓ   20. Ⓐ Ⓑ Ⓒ Ⓓ   25. Ⓐ Ⓑ Ⓒ Ⓓ

Combination Vehicles

1. Ⓐ Ⓑ   5. Ⓐ Ⓑ Ⓒ Ⓓ   9. Ⓐ Ⓑ Ⓒ Ⓓ   13. Ⓐ Ⓑ Ⓒ Ⓓ   17. Ⓐ Ⓑ Ⓒ Ⓓ

2. Ⓐ Ⓑ Ⓒ Ⓓ   6. Ⓐ Ⓑ Ⓒ Ⓓ   10. Ⓐ Ⓑ Ⓒ Ⓓ   14. Ⓐ Ⓑ Ⓒ Ⓓ   18. Ⓐ Ⓑ Ⓒ Ⓓ

3. Ⓐ Ⓑ   7. Ⓐ Ⓑ Ⓒ Ⓓ   11. Ⓐ Ⓑ Ⓒ Ⓓ   15. Ⓐ Ⓑ Ⓒ Ⓓ   19. Ⓐ Ⓑ Ⓒ Ⓓ

4. Ⓐ Ⓑ   8. Ⓐ Ⓑ Ⓒ Ⓓ   12. Ⓐ Ⓑ Ⓒ Ⓓ   16. Ⓐ Ⓑ   20. Ⓐ Ⓑ

GENERAL KNOWLEDGE DIAGNOSTIC TEST

50 Questions – 90 Minutes

Directions: This test consists of a combination of true/false and multiple-choice questions. Only one answer is correct for each question.

1. The operator required to obtain a commercial driver's license is a

   A. farm equipment vehicle driver.

   B. military vehicle driver.

   C. firefighting vehicle driver.

   D. commercial grain hauler driver.

2. The sole responsibility of providing proper placards for shipment of hazardous materials belongs to

   A. the carrier.

   B. the driver.

   C. the shipper.

   D. the state regulators.

3. On the US interstate system, the maximum width for most commercial motor vehicles is

   A. 13 feet 6 inches.

   B. 14 feet 6 inches.

   C. 8 feet 6 inches.

   D. 9 feet 0 inches.

4. After beginning a trip, a driver must stop to check the cargo and its securing devices within the first

   A. 25 miles.

   B. 40 miles.

   C. 50 miles.

   D. 150 miles.

5. Blocking cargo is used to prevent cargo from moving by going from the upper part of the cargo to the floor or walls of the cargo compartment.

   A. True

   B. False

6. When a driver doubles the speed, it takes

   A. twice as much distance to stop the commercial vehicle.

   B. the driver little time to stop the vehicle.

   C. four times as much distance to stop the vehicle.

   D. three times as much distance to stop the vehicle.

7. For an alert driver, the average perception time is 1½ seconds.

   A. True

   B. False

8. While driving, the most important space around the commercial vehicle is

   A. the space behind it.

   B. the space to the right of it.

   C. the space to the left of it.

   D. the space ahead of it.

9. During mountain driving, the braking effect of the engine is greatest when it is near the regulated rpms and the transmission is in the/a

   A. top gear.

   B. neutral gear.

   C. low gear.

   D. drive gear.

10. A typical tractor-trailer unit takes at least 14 seconds to clear a double track from being stopped.

    A. True

    B. False

11. All of these are true for testing the service brake's stopping action during a vehicle inspection EXCEPT:

    A. Pushing the brake pedal firmly

    B. Any "pulling" to one side or another can imply brake problems

    C. The uncommon brake pedal "feeling" or delayed stopping action can mean danger

    D. Going about 15 miles per hour

12. When a commercial driver does not sleep enough and "owes" more sleep to himself/herself, it is known as

    A. "sleep exhaustion".

    B. "sleep death".

    C. "sleep debt".

    D. "sleep apnea".

13. The pressure gauge that should build from 50 to 90 psi within three minutes during the pre-trip inspection is

    A. temperature.

    B. air.

    C. oil.

    D. voltmeter.

14. A driver should not use water on a

    A. paper fire.

    B. wood fire.

    C. cloth fire.

    D. gasoline fire.

15. Since enough treading is extremely important during winter conditions, the front tires must have at least 2/32-inch tread depth.

    A. True

    B. False

16. All of these are general reasons for drivers to use signals EXCEPT:

    A. Slowing down

    B. Turning the vehicle

    C. Directing traffic

    D. Changing lanes

17. The penalty for a driver who operates a commercial vehicle with a suspended CDL is

    A. a license suspension for at least a year.

    B. a six-month license suspension.

    C. a $100 fine.

    D. a permanent suspension of the license.

18. The best course of action for a driver who is driving on a two-lane road and sees an oncoming motorist drift into his or her lane from the left will be to

    A. brake hard.

    B. steer to the right.

    C. steer to the left.

    D. steer straight.

19. All of these steps are to be taken at an accident scene EXCEPT:

    A. Calling 911

    B. Placing road flares on the ground

    C. Moving someone who is near a fire

    D. Moving the vehicle to the side of the road

20. Driving impairment occurs quickly because the liver can only process

    A. one-half a liter of alcohol per hour.

    B. one-third a pint of alcohol per hour.

    C. one-third an ounce of alcohol per hour.

    D. one-half an ounce of alcohol per hour.

21. A driver sees a moving vehicle that has a red triangle with an orange center on the rear and recognizes that it

    A. may be a slow-moving vehicle.

    B. is law enforcement personnel.

    C. has the right of way.

    D. has a student driver behind the wheel.

22. To get rid of water and oil inside the air tanks, manual air tanks must be drained

    A. monthly.

    B. weekly.

    C. bi-weekly.

    D. daily.

23. A ramp leading to an extended bed of loose soft material, sometimes also on an upgrade, that is used to slow down a runaway vehicle is a truck escape ramp.

    A. True

    B. False

24. The act of pulling forward while backing a trailer to reposition it is known as a

    A. pull-forward.

    B. pull-back.

    C. pull-down.

    D. pull-up.

25. When the road is slippery, retarders can cause the vehicle to skid.

    A. True

    B. False

26. If a driver is caught texting and operating a commercial motor vehicle, the driver's license will be disqualified after

    A. two or more convictions.

    B. one conviction.

    C. three or more convictions.

    D. sixty days.

27. During extremely hot weather, a driver should release some hot air out of the tires to allow the pressure to go back to normal.

    A. True

    B. False

28. During intense rain, the best way for a driver to drive through deep puddles is to

    A. quickly drive through the puddle in a high gear.

    B. slow down and place the transmission in neutral gear.

    C. reverse and avoid the deep puddles.

    D. slow down and place transmission in a low gear.

29. Antifreeze will help the engine during

    A. hot conditions.

    B. cold conditions.

    C. both hot and cold conditions.

    D. neither hot nor cold conditions.

30. If commercial drivers hold a Class A license, they cannot operate vehicles that are listed in Classes B and C even if they hold the appropriate endorsements.

    A. True

    B. False

31. The most important hand signal a driver and the backing helper should agree on is

    A. go.

    B. stop.

    C. pull up.

    D. right.

32. In comparison to empty trucks, fully loaded trucks are

    A. five times as likely to roll over in an accident.

    B. twice as likely to roll over in an accident.

    C. four times as likely to roll over in an accident.

    D. ten times as likely to roll over in an accident.

33. Tank vehicles are used to carry any liquid and are dangerous to drive because of a

    A. low center of gravity.

    B. flat center of gravity.

    C. wide center of gravity.

    D. high center of gravity.

34. If a straight vehicle with no trailer or articulation goes into a front-wheel skid, it will turn the direction of the steering wheel.

    A. True

    B. False

35. A CMV may exceed the speed limit if doing so will allow the vehicle to maintain the flow of traffic.

    A. True

    B. False

36. The combination vehicles that encounter the worst rearward amplification during a quick lane change are

    A. those trucks pulling a single trailer.

    B. those trucks pulling two trailers.

    C. those trucks pulling three trailers.

    D. all vehicles pulling any number of trailers encounter an equal amount of rearward amplification.

37. The federal standard for maximum weight on a tandem axle vehicle is

    A. 34,000 lbs.

    B. 22,500 lbs.

    C. 20,000 lbs.

    D. 80,000 lbs.

38. All of these are types of retarders EXCEPT:

    A. Hydraulic

    B. Electric

    C. Engine

    D. Robotic

39. If truck drivers are being tailgated, they should

    A. flash their taillights or brake lights.

    B. signal the tailgater to pass when safe to do so.

    C. increase the space with the vehicles in front of them.

    D. speed up.

40. The structures that protect drivers from freight moving into the cab in the event of a collision or an emergency stop are the

    A. front-end header boards.

    B. cargo stoppers.

    C. head braces.

    D. stabilizers.

41. Pumping the brake pedal three times, applying firm pressure to the pedal and holding for five seconds, and the pedal not moving when being used is an indicator of working hydraulic brakes.

    A. True
    B. False

42. A driver can recognize hazardous materials by looking for the container's

    A. color.
    B. shape.
    C. label.
    D. markings.

43. A good rule to follow while driving at night and avoiding roadway distractions is to

    A. maintain the speed slow enough to stop within the range of the headlights.
    B. look towards the bright lights of other cars.
    C. always use the high beams for clarity.
    D. always have the cab lights bright.

44. If a driver drinks three cups of coffee after consuming two beers with dinner, it is reasonable to assume he/she is alert to drive.

    A. True
    B. False

45. Hard steering is caused by

    A. too much weight on the steering axle.
    B. too little weight on the driving axle.
    C. the torque shaft.
    D. a high center of gravity.

46. If a driver is feeling fatigued, the best thing to do to remain alert is to

    A. stop and buy a cup of coffee.
    B. stop and go out for a quick walk.
    C. stop as soon as possible to sleep.
    D. plan on driving thirty minutes longer.

47. A placarded vehicle must display

    A. four identical placards.
    B. four distinguishable placards.
    C. two identical placards.
    D. two distinguishable placards.

48. Hazardous flammable gases, such as propane, are in class

    A. 8.
    B. 3.
    C. 2.
    D. 1.

49. If the air brake system is not properly checked or its components are not properly identified, the

    A. M restriction will be issued.
    B. E restriction will be issued.
    C. V restriction will be issued.
    D. L restriction will be issued.

50. If a commercial vehicle's antilock braking system is working improperly, the malfunction lamp will light up

    A. red.
    B. purple.
    C. yellow.
    D. white.

GENERAL KNOWLEDGE DIAGNOSTIC TEST ANSWER KEY AND EXPLANATIONS

1. D	11. D	21. A	31. B	41. A
2. C	12. C	22. D	32. D	42. C
3. C	13. B	23. A	33. D	43. A
4. C	14. D	24. D	34. B	44. B
5. B	15. B	25. A	35. B	45. A
6. C	16. C	26. A	36. C	46. C
7. B	17. A	27. B	37. A	47. A
8. D	18. B	28. D	38. D	48. C
9. C	19. B	29. C	39. C	49. D
10. B	20. C	30. B	40. A	50. C

1. **The correct answer is D.** Commercial grain haulers are required to obtain a commercial driver's license. According to the Federal Motor Carrier Safety Administration, farm equipment vehicle drivers (choice A), military vehicle drivers (choice B), and firefighting vehicle drivers (choice C), are not subject to the federal and state requirements of the commercial driver's license.

2. **The correct answer is C.** According to regulations, shippers are solely responsible for supplying the proper placards. The carrier (choice A) and the driver (choice B) are responsible for making sure the shipment is in complete compliance with the required regulations mandated by state regulators (choice D).

3. **The correct answer is C.** Although drivers must obey posted signs regarding weight, height, and width limits in all states, the maximum width for most vehicles traveling the US interstate system is 8 feet 6 inches. In most states, the maximum height limit is 13 feet 6 inches (choice A). In some states, like Idaho, the maximum height limit is 14 feet 6 inches (choice B). Some states, like Hawaii, have a maximum width limit of 9 feet 0 inches (choice D).

4. **The correct answer is C.** A driver is required to check the cargo within the first 50 miles. Since the driver is required to check the cargo within the first 50 miles, a check at the first 25 miles (choice

A) and 40 miles (choice B) are not mandatory. After the first stop, a driver is required to stop within 3 hours or 150 miles (choice D), whichever comes first.

5. **The correct answer is B.** Going from the upper part of the cargo to the floor or walls of the cargo compartment is bracing and prevents the cargo from moving. To keep cargo from sliding, blocking is used in the front, back or sides adjacent to the cargo.

6. **The correct answer is C.** The distance needed to stop a vehicle depends on its speed and weight in addition to factors like energy, heat, and friction. If speed is doubled, the stopping power needs to be increased four times to stop in the same distance.

7. **The correct answer is B.** Although certain mental and physical conditions can affect perception distance, the average perception time for an alert driver is 1¾ seconds.

8. **The correct answer is D.** The area a driver is driving into is the most important space because the commercial vehicle needs time to make sudden stops. Since most commercial vehicle accidents occur with vehicles in front of them, the space behind the vehicle (choice A), the space to the right of the vehicle (choice B), and the space to the left of the vehicle (choice C) are not the most important spaces around them.

9. **The correct answer is C.** When mountain driving a commercial vehicle, the steeper the grade, the longer the grade, and/or the heavier the load, the more a driver will have to use the lower gears to climb or go down hills and mountains. Since gravity causes the vehicle to slow down on an uphill, it is safest to get to a lower gear from the top gear (choice A). Since gravity will cause the speed of a commercial vehicle to increase while descending long and steep downgrades, using a neutral gear (choice B) or the drive gear (choice D) will only allow the vehicle to increase its speed.

10. **The correct answer is B.** It actually takes a typical tractor trailer unit at least 14 seconds to clear a single track, but it takes more than 15 seconds to clear a double track from being stopped.

11. **The correct answer is D.** During a vehicle inspection, a driver should go about 5 mph when testing the service brake's stopping action.

12. **The correct answer is C.** The difference between the amount of sleep a person gets and what they should have is known as sleep debt. Sleep exhaustion (choice A) occurs as a result of not getting enough sleep. Sleep death (choice B) is unexpected death during sleep. Sleep apnea (choice D) occurs when breathing repeatedly stops and starts during sleep.

13. **The correct answer is B.** During the pre-trip inspection, the air pressure should build from 50 to 90 psi within 3 minutes. The temperature (choice A) and oil (choice C) pressures should rise gradually to normal operating ranges. The voltmeter (choice D) should show 13 or 14 volts once completely charged.

14. **The correct answer is D.** Since water will spread the flames in a gasoline fire, it should not be used. Water is effective for paper (choice A), wood (choice B), and cloth (choice C) fires.

15. **The correct answer is B.** The front tires must have at least 4/32-inch tread depth while the other tires must have at least 2/32-inch tread depth.

16. **The correct answer is C.** Drivers use signals for a variety of reasons, but directing traffic is not one of them. Slowing down (choice A) the vehicle, turning the vehicle (choice B), and changing lanes (choice D) are general reasons why truckers use signals.

17. **The correct answer is A.** A driver with a suspended CDL who is convicted of operating a commercial vehicle will receive a license suspension for at least a year. A first offense for an out-of-service-order can receive a six-month license suspension (choice B). A driver's failure to release all traffic violations and CDL suspensions to the state and their employer can receive a fine of at least $100 (choice C). Violations to any convictions already given for major offenses can result in a permanent suspension of the commercial driver's license (choice D).

18. **The correct answer is B.** Steering to the right to avoid an accident is the best course of action for a driver who is driving on a two-lane road and sees an oncoming motorist drift into his or her lane from the left. Depending on speed and other factors, braking hard (choice A) can cause a commercial vehicle's wheels to lock and skid. Steering to the left (choice C) and steering straight (choice D) would almost guarantee an accident.

19. **The correct answer is B.** Placing road flares on the ground near an accident scene can cause any leaking flammable liquids to ignite. Calling 911 (choice A), moving someone who is near a fire (choice C), and moving the vehicle to the side of the road (choice D) are steps to be taken at an accident scene.

20. **The correct answer is C.** Since the liver can only handle one-third an ounce of alcohol per hour and this is substantially less than the alcohol in a typical drink, driving impairment can occur quickly. Consuming one-half a liter of alcohol per hour (choice A), one-third a pint of alcohol per hour (choice B), one-half an ounce of alcohol per hour (choice D) is significantly more than the liver can process effectively and will impair driving.

21. **The correct answer is A.** Slow-moving vehicles, such as road maintenance vehicles, display a red triangle with an orange center on the rear. Law

enforcement personnel (choice B) typically display sounds and lights on their vehicles to indicate their presence. Although a moving vehicle that has a red triangle with an orange center on the rear MAY have the right of way (choice C), it is not always the case. A student driver behind the wheel (choice D) will have a clear student driver decal or sign affixed to the commercial vehicle.

22. **The correct answer is D.** In order to get rid of water and oil from inside the air tanks, manual air tanks must be drained daily by the driver via the drain valve. Therefore, attempting to drain the manual air tanks monthly (choice A), weekly (choice B) and bi-weekly (choice C) can cause damage to the air brake system.

23. **The correct answer is A.** A truck escape ramp provides rolling resistance with an extended bed of loose soft material to slow down the vehicle.

24. **The correct answer is D.** Performing a pull-up while backing a trailer to reposition it and getting out to look should be a part of the backing check-list. The term pull-forward (choice A) is known as the act of pulling the truck forward for any reason, not just while backing the truck. The terms pull-back (choice B), and pull-down (choice C) are not commonly used in the trucking industry.

25. **The correct answer is A.** Since retarders are mechanisms that help slow down a vehicle and lessen the need for braking, using a retarder when the road is slippery may cause wheels to skid because they have poor traction.

26. **The correct answer is A.** According to federal law, if a driver is caught texting and operating a commercial motor vehicle, the driver's license will be disqualified after two or more convictions. After one conviction (choice B), a civil penalty is imposed. After three or more convictions (choice C), longer disqualification intervals and increased civil penalties are imposed. A sixty-day (choice D) commercial license disqualification occurs after the second offense.

27. **The correct answer is B.** Air should not be released out of hot tires because the pressure will be low when they cool.

28. **The correct answer is D.** It is best to slow down and place the transmission in a low gear when a driver must drive through deep puddles in intense rain. Quickly driving through the puddle in a high gear (choice A) is dangerous and can cause problems with the brakes or a hydroplane. Slowing down and placing the transmission in neutral gear (choice B) can make the vehicle "float" through the puddle. Reversing and avoiding the deep puddles (choice C) is never recommended because of the inability for a driver to see other drivers in the blind spots.

29. **The correct answer is C.** Since antifreeze helps the engine during hot and cold conditions, checking the engine cooling system to be sure it has enough water and antifreeze is important. Therefore, checking the engine cooling system exclusively during hot conditions (choice A), cold conditions (choice B), or neither hot nor cold conditions (choice D) are not effective ways to maintain a vehicle in extreme weather conditions.

30. **The correct answer is B.** If drivers hold a Class A license and have the correct endorsements, they may also operate vehicles listed in Classes B and C.

31. **The correct answer is B.** A backing helper and the driver should always agree on a stop hand signal. Therefore, the go (choice A), pull up (choice C), and right (choice D) hand signals are not the most important gestures that a driver and backing helper should agree on.

32. **The correct answer is D.** Since the center of gravity moves higher up in fully loaded trucks, they are ten times as likely to roll over in an accident than empty trucks.

33. **The correct answer is D.** Since tank vehicles carry any liquid and liquids are prone to move around in the tank, tanks will have a high center of gravity.

34. **The correct answer is B.** The straight vehicle will continue to go straight ahead in a front wheel skid even if the steering wheel is turned.

35. **The correct answer is B.** As the CDL manual suggests, driving at the speed of other vehicles will likely prevent collision; however, following the

flow of traffic should only occur at legal and safe speeds at a safe distance.

36. **The correct answer is C.** Combination vehicles pulling three trailers will encounter 3.5 times the rearward amplification during a quick lane change and cause a crack-the-whip effect because they are usually heavier and longer. For this reason, trucks pulling a single trailer (choice A) or trucks pulling two trailers (choice B) will encounter less rearward amplification because of the number of trailers they are pulling. Therefore, not all vehicles pulling any number of trailers encounter the same level of rearward amplification (choice D).

37. **The correct answer is A.** The federal standard for maximum weight on a tandem axle vehicle is 34,000 lbs. The federal standard for maximum weight on a single axle weight is 20,000 lbs. (choice C). The federal standard for maximum weight on a gross vehicle weight is 80,000 lbs. (choice D). Some states, like Hawaii, allow up to 22,500 lbs. (choice B) on a single axle vehicle.

38. **The correct answer is D.** Robotic is not a type of retarder. However, hydraulic (choice A), electric (choice B), and engine (choice C) are each a type of retarder.

39. **The correct answer is C.** If drivers are being tailgated and do not have enough space ahead of them, the vehicles in front of the drivers can come to a sudden stop and trigger an accident. It is recommended to avoid flashing the taillights or brake lights (choice A) to try to communicate with the tailgater or signal the tailgater to pass when safe to do so (choice B) because drivers can lose their focus on driving, triggering an accident. Speeding up (choice D) closes the most important area of space that drivers have in this situation, the area in front of them.

40. **The correct answer is A.** In the event of a collision or emergency stop, the front-end header boards, also known as "headache racks," are structures used to protect drivers from freight that may try to enter the cab if it shifts forward. Cargo stoppers (choice B) are structures welded to the deck of a naval vessel to prevent cargo from moving. Head

braces (choice C) are a type of orthodontic appliance. Stabilizers (choice D) absorb some of the movement in the vehicle's suspension.

41. **The correct answer is A.** Pumping the brake pedal three times, applying firm pressure to the pedal and holding it for five seconds, and then the pedal not moving is an indicator of working hydraulic brakes. If the pedal moves, there may be leaks or other problems.

42. **The correct answer is C.** Drivers can recognize hazardous materials by looking for the container's shipping label because it will have all the information needed to confirm the contents of the container. Although the color (choice A), shape (choice B), and markings (choice D) can assist drivers in identifying certain contents of a container, the shipper's label has all the required information needed to confirm the contents of the container.

43. **The correct answer is A.** Maintaining the speed slow enough to stop within the range of the headlights is a good rule to follow while driving at night and helps to avoid roadway distractions. Looking towards the bright lights of other cars (choice B) can cause blindness for a short period of time and be distracting. Always using the high beams (choice C) can be distracting for other drivers and can create distractions that would impact reaction abilities. Always having the cab lights bright (choice D) is distracting because it can make it more difficult to see the area outside.

44. **The correct answer is B.** Coffee does not make a driver sober, therefore, a driver will not be sufficiently alert to drive after consuming two beers and three cups of coffee–only time will.

45. **The correct answer is A.** Too much weight on the steering axle can cause hard steering. Too little weight on the driving axle (choice B) can cause poor traction. The torque shaft (choice C) in the power steering unit gives maximum steering assistance when needed but does not cause hard steering. A high center of gravity (choice D) can cause a commercial vehicle to tip over.

46. **The correct answer is C.** If a driver is feeling fatigued, stopping as soon as possible to sleep is the only cure for it. Stopping to buy a cup of coffee (choice A) or stopping to go out for a quick walk (choice B) will only help for a limited time. It can be dangerous for the driver and other motorists if the plan is to drive thirty minutes longer (choice D) after experiencing fatigue.

47. **The correct answer is A.** The required four identical placards are placed on the front, rear, and both sides of the vehicle. Since there must be four identical placards on the vehicle, four distinguishable placards (choice B), two identical placards (choice C), and two distinguishable placards (choice D) are incorrect.

48. **The correct answer is C.** Flammable gases, like propane, are in class 2. Hazardous corrosives, such as battery fluid, are in a class 8 (choice A). Hazardous flammable liquids, such as gasoline, are in class 3 (choice B). Explosives are class 1 hazardous materials (choice D).

49. **The correct answer is D.** A CDL will have an L restriction if the following occurs: the driver fails the written air brakes test or the driver fails to complete the physical skills test in a vehicle with a full air brake system. The M restriction will be issued (choice A) if a driver has a Class A CDL but acquires a passenger or school bus endorsement in a Class B vehicle. The E restriction will be issued (choice B) to drivers prohibiting them from operating a vehicle with a manual transmission. The V restriction will be issued (choice C) to a driver who has a medical variance.

50. **The correct answer is C.** The yellow or amber-colored malfunction lamp of commercial vehicles will light up if the antilock braking system is working improperly. A red (choice A) light warns a driver of possible engine problems. A purple (choice B) light is typically used as a clearance light on commercial vehicles. A white (choice D) light is used to indicate to other drivers that the vehicle is reversing.

NOTES

AIR BRAKES DIAGNOSTIC TEST
25 Questions – 60 Minutes

> **Directions:** This test consists of a combination of true/false and multiple-choice questions. Only one answer is correct for each question.

1. Air brakes are four different braking systems: service brakes, radial brakes, parking brake, and emergency brakes.

   A. True

   B. False

2. The control that blocks the compressor from pumping air when the "cut-out" level reaches around 125 psi is the

   A. governor.

   B. wig wag.

   C. alcohol evaporator.

   D. safety relief valve.

3. The part NOT associated with the drum brake is the

   A. slack adjuster.

   B. axle.

   C. return spring.

   D. power screw.

4. If the spring brakes are on, the driver should NOT engage the

   A. dual parking control valve.

   B. modulating control valve.

   C. brake pedal.

   D. limiting valve.

5. A driver can tell that a vehicle is equipped with antilock brakes if it is manufactured after 1998.

   A. True

   B. False

6. If a vehicle has dual parking control valves, a driver can use pressure from a separate tank to

   A. balance out the service brake system when the driver is parked.

   B. remain parked twice as long without utilizing service air pressure.

   C. employ more brake pressure if the central tank is becoming low.

   D. release the spring parking/emergency brakes in order to go a short distance.

7. If there is a leak in the air brake lines, the air pressure decreases, deactivating the brakes at the wheels and bringing the vehicle to a safe stop.

   A. True

   B. False

8. On older vehicles, the parking brakes may be regulated by a

   A. knob.

   B. switch.

   C. button.

   D. lever.

9. As the slack adjuster unit rotates,

   A. the push rod travel is at a maximum.

   B. the camshaft locks in place, preventing brake operation.

   C. the camshaft turns and applies the brakes.

   D. the s-cam seizes and results in brake failure..

10. It would be unsafe to drive a vehicle that has brake drums or discs with cracks that are longer than

   A. one-fourth of the width of the friction area.

   B. one-third of the width of the friction area.

   C. one-half of the width of the friction area.

   D. one-eighth of the width of the friction area.

11. A truck with minimum-size air tanks and a well-functioning dual air brake system should have the air pressure build from 85 to 100 psi within

   A. 60 seconds.

   B. 20 seconds.

   C. 30 seconds.

   D. 45 seconds.

12. Fanning the brakes on a long downhill will consume air from the air tank(s), resulting in the increase of brake air pressure.

   A. True

   B. False

13. The front wheel brakes are effective under all conditions.

   A. True

   B. False

14. When testing to see if the service brakes work, the driver should

   A. wait for low air pressure, release the parking brake, move the vehicle forward 5 mph, and apply the foot brake.

   B. wait for normal air pressure, release the parking brake, move the vehicle forward 10 mph, and apply the foot brake.

   C. wait for normal air pressure, push in the parking brake, move the vehicle forward 5 mph, and apply the foot brake.

   D. wait for normal air pressure, release the parking brake, move the vehicle forward 5 mph and apply the foot brake.

15. The air brake lag effect adds

   A. 2 seconds to the total stopping distance formula.

   B. 1 second to the total stopping distance formula.

   C. ½ a second to the total stopping distance formula.

   D. ¼ of a second to the total stopping distance formula.

16. To inspect the air brake system of the vehicle, the driver should perform the basic five-step inspection procedure.

   A. True

   B. False

17. When a driver's "safe" speed is 45 mph and is traveling 60 mph on a downgrade in the correct lower gear, application of the brakes should continue until he/she has slowed down to

   A. 35 mph.

   B. 45 mph.

   C. 40 mph.

   D. 30 mph.

18. The use of brakes on a steep downgrade is only a supplement to the braking effect of the engine.

    A. True

    B. False

19. When the vehicle is parked and the parking brakes are not being used, then the driver

    A. uses the emergency brakes.

    B. should use the parking brake.

    C. should use the wheel chocks.

    D. should leave the truck in gear when parked.

20. A fully loaded tractor-trailer weighing 80,000 lbs. traveling under the best conditions at 65 mph will take

    A. 316 feet to stop.

    B. 525 feet to stop.

    C. 700 feet to stop.

    D. 250 feet to stop.

21. To dry out wet brakes, the driver should drain the storage tank.

    A. True

    B. False

22. Checking the manual slack adjusters on the s-cam brakes is done during

    A. Step 2–Engine Compartment Checks.

    B. Step 7– Final Air Brake Check.

    C. Step 5–Walk-around Inspection.

    D. None of the steps

23. Although red is used to identify the emergency lines, the service lines are identified with

    A. yellow.

    B. green.

    C. blue.

    D. black.

24. Air brake lag is the time it takes for the brakes to operate once the driver presses on the brake pedal.

    A. True

    B. False

25. The shut-off valves which must be closed are located

    A. at the back of the last trailer.

    B. on the first trailer.

    C. in the middle trailer.

    D. in the back of the cab.

AIR BRAKES DIAGNOSTIC TEST ANSWER KEY AND EXPLANATIONS

1. B	6. D	11. D	16. B	21. B
2. A	7. B	12. B	17. C	22. C
3. D	8. D	13. A	18. A	23. C
4. C	9. C	14. D	19. C	24. A
5. A	10. C	15. C	20. B	25. A

1. **The correct answer is B.** There are three different air braking systems: service brakes, parking brake, and emergency brakes.

2. **The correct answer is A.** The governor control blocks the compressor from pumping air when the "cut-out" level reaches around 125 psi. The wig wag device (choice B) releases a mechanical arm into the driver's view when the pressure in the system declines below 60 psi. The alcohol evaporator (choice C) deposits alcohol into the air system. The safety relief valve (choice D) safeguards the tank and the remainder of the system from too much pressure but does not cut out the air being pumped.

3. **The correct answer is D.** The power screw is part of a disc brake, not a drum brake. The slack adjuster (choice A), axle (choice B), and the return spring (choice C) are parts of the drum brake.

4. **The correct answer is C.** The driver should not engage the brake pedal because the spring brakes can be damaged by collective forces of the springs and air pressure. The dual parking control valve (choice A) means that the driver can use pressure from a separate tank to free the spring brakes in order to move a short distance. The modulating control valve (choice B) is a dashboard control handle that can be used to apply the spring brakes steadily. The limiting valve (choice D) is found in older trucks and decreases the "normal" air pressure to the front brakes by half.

5. **The correct answer is A.** After March 1st, 1998, all commercial vehicles were required to be equipped with antilock braking systems.

6. **The correct answer is D.** Releasing the spring emergency/parking brakes to go a short distance is done when the driver uses pressure from a separate tank if the vehicle has dual control valves. Balancing out the service brake system when the driver is parked (choice A), remaining parked twice as long without utilizing service air pressure (choice B), and employing more brake pressure if the central tank is becoming low (choice C) are not ways in which a driver can use pressure from a separate tank when the vehicle has dual parking control valves.

7. **The correct answer is B.** If there is a leak in the air brake lines, the air pressure decreases and actually engages the brakes at the wheels, bringing the vehicle to a safe stop.

8. **The correct answer is D.** On older vehicles, the parking brakes may be regulated by a lever. On newer vehicles, the parking brakes are controlled by a control knob (choice A). None of the vehicles use switches (choice B) or buttons (choice C) to control the parking brakes.

9. **The correct answer is C.** As the slack adjuster unit rotates (as caused by air entering the brake chamber and moving the push rod out), this rotates the camshaft, thus engaging the s-cam and forcing the brake shoe lining against the brake drum. If the slack adjuster is properly adjusted, the push rod travel should be at a minimum (choice A). As the slack adjuster turns, so should the camshaft (choice B). And the s-cam should rotate along with the camshaft to engage the brake shoes (choice D).

10. **The correct answer is C.** It is not safe to drive any vehicle with brake drums or discs with cracks that

are longer than one half of the width of the friction area. Therefore, driving with brake drums or discs with cracks that are longer than one-fourth of the width of the friction area (choice A), one-third of the width of the friction area (choice B), or one-eighth of the width of the friction area (choice D) are acceptable, but need to be inspected frequently for additional wear and tear.

11. **The correct answer is D.** A well-functioning dual air brake system with minimum-size air tanks should have the air pressure build from 85 to 100 psi within 45 seconds. Therefore, 60 seconds (choice A) is too lengthy of a time while 20 seconds (choice B) and 30 seconds (choice C) are not great enough time periods.

12. **The correct answer is B.** Fanning the brakes on a long downhill will consume air from the air tank(s), resulting in the loss of brake air pressure.

13. **The correct answer is A.** Tests have shown that even on ice, front wheel skids from braking are not likely.

14. **The correct answer is D.** To test if the service brakes are working properly, the driver should wait for normal air pressure, release the parking brake, move the vehicle forward 5 mph, and apply the foot brake.

15. **The correct answer is C.** The air brake lag effect adds half a second to the total stopping distance formula.

16. **The correct answer is B.** The driver should perform the basic seven-step inspection procedure to inspect the air brake system of the vehicle.

17. **The correct answer is C.** When a driver is traveling on a downgrade, brakes should be applied until he/she is traveling at 5 mph below the "safe" speed. Therefore, applying the brakes until 35 mph (choice A), 45 mph (choice B), and 30 mph (choice D) are incorrect.

18. **The correct answer is A.** The use of brakes on a long downgrade is only a supplement to the braking effect of the engine.

19. **The correct answer is C.** Since there may be times when the parking brakes are very hot or wet during freezing conditions, using wheel chocks is the best option while the parking brakes cool or dry. There would be no reason to use the emergency brakes (choice A) because the vehicle is already parked. Using the parking brake (choice B) prevents the car from rolling, but in this situation, they are not being used. Leaving the truck in gear when parked (choice D) has the potential to allow the truck to jump forward.

20. **The correct answer is B.** Remembering that Perception Distance + Reaction Distance + Brake Lag Distance + Braking Distance = Total Stopping Distance, it will take a fully loaded tractor-trailer weighing 80,000 lbs., traveling under the best conditions at 65 mph, 525 feet to stop, about the length of two football fields. A passenger car weighing 4,000 lbs., traveling under the best conditions at 65 mph would take 316 feet to stop (choice A), about the length of a football field. Considering all the factors given, the tractor-trailer will not take 700 feet to stop (choice C). Considering all the factors given, the tractor-trailer will not be able to stop in 250 feet (choice D).

21. **The correct answer is B.** The driver should not drain the storage tank but use the brakes while driving in a low gear so that the heat generated will dry them out.

22. **The correct answer is C.** Step 5–Walk-Around Inspection is the part of the seven-step inspection procedure where the manual slack adjusters on the s-cam brakes are examined.

23. **The correct answer is C.** To keep from mixing up the lines, service lines are identified with blue. Therefore, yellow (choice A), green (choice B), and black (choice D) are incorrect code colors for the service lines.

24. **The correct answer is A.** Brake lag is the time necessary for the brakes to operate after the brake pedal is pushed.

25. **The correct answer is A.** Since all shut-off valves must be in the open position to allow airflow, the ones located at the back of the last trailer are the only ones to be closed to keep air in the system. The shut-off valves on the first trailer (choice B), or in the middle trailer (choice C) must remain open. There are no shut-off valves in the back of the cab (choice D).

NOTES

COMBINATION VEHICLES DIAGNOSTIC TEST

20 Questions – 60 Minutes

> **Directions:** This test consists of a combination of true/false and multiple-choice questions. Only one answer is correct for each question.

1. Quick lane changes can cause the trailer to flip over without the tractor also flipping.

    A. True

    B. False

2. How many seconds of stopping time per 10 feet of vehicle length is needed when a combination vehicle is driving over 40 miles per hour?

    A. 4 seconds per 10 feet

    B. 1 second per 10 feet plus an additional second

    C. 1 second per 10 feet

    D. 2 seconds per 10 feet plus an additional second

3. Bobtail tractors take longer to stop than a combination vehicle at the maximum gross weight.

    A. True

    B. False

4. A 65 foot conventional double tractor-trailer has a rearward amplification of 2.5.

    A. True

    B. False

5. Trailer skids often occur after

    A. braking strongly.

    B. switching lanes quickly.

    C. excessive speed on a turn.

    D. quick acceleration.

6. When turning, which set of wheels goes off-track the most?

    A. Front wheels on the tractor

    B. Back wheels on the tractor

    C. Front wheels on the trailer

    D. Back wheels on the trailer

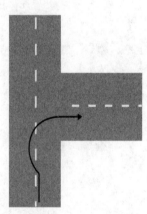

7. The above image illustrates what type of turn?

    A. Button Hole

    B. Jug Handle

    C. Jackknife

    D. Off-track

8. If you must back up on a curve, choose the

    A. driver's side as it's the easiest to control.

    B. passenger's side as it's the easiest to control.

    C. driver's side due to increased visibility.

    D. passenger's side due to increased visibility.

9. The Johnson bar refers to

   A. the trailer hand valve.

   B. emergency brake.

   C. parking brake.

   D. interlock system.

10. Where are the shut-off valves located?

    A. At the front of each trailer

    B. In the cabin of the tractor

    C. At the back of each trailer

    D. At the front of the tractor

11. If a trailer has no spring brakes, what added safety measures should be used when it is parked?

    A. The emergency brakes

    B. Chocks

    C. The parking brake

    D. The tractor protection valve

12. Which of the following is true about the antilock braking system (ABS)?

    A. It increases braking capacity.

    B. It decreases stopping distance required.

    C. It helps avoid locked up wheels.

    D. It replaces regular service brakes.

13. The purpose of glad hands is to

    A. connect the trailer body to the tractor.

    B. connect trailer brake lights.

    C. secure the Johnson bar.

    D. connect service and emergency air lines from tractor to trailer.

14. What is the first step when coupling a tractor-semitrailer?

    A. Inspect the fifth wheel

    B. Inspect the area around the vehicle and put in wheel chocks

    C. Position the tractor

    D. Check trailer height

15. What is the correct height for a trailer prior to coupling?

    A. Slightly above the tractor

    B. Flush with the tractor

    C. Slightly below the tractor

    D. Below the tractor

16. When uncoupling, pull the tractor partially clear of the trailer before inspecting the trailer supports.

    A. True

    B. False

17. When inspecting the coupling system, make sure there is

    A. enough space between the upper and lower fifth wheel.

    B. enough grease on the fifth wheel plate.

    C. locking around the head of the kingpin.

    D. an engaged release arm in the upright position.

18. What is the recommended pressure range for air brakes by most manufacturers?

    A. 100-120 psi

    B. 20-45 psi

    C. 45-60 psi

    D. 80-85 psi

19. A pintle hook, drawbar, and gooseneck are all examples of

    A. hitches.

    B. brake systems.

    C. safety latches on a coupling.

    D. shut-off valves.

20. It is acceptable to switch gears when crossing railroad tracks as long as the traffic light is green.

    A. True

    B. False

COMBINATION VEHICLES DIAGNOSTIC TEST ANSWER KEY AND EXPLANATIONS

1. A	**5.** A	**9.** A	**13.** D	**17.** B
2. B	**6.** D	**10.** C	**14.** A	**18.** A
3. A	**7.** B	**11.** B	**15.** C	**19.** A
4. B	**8.** C	**12.** C	**16.** A	**20.** B

1. **The correct answer is A.** Quick lane changes can cause a crack-the-whip effect, which occurs when the movement from the front tractor remains steady, but the following trailers move at a much quicker speed due to excessive side speed from the lane change. The trailer will move too quickly, sliding out from behind the tractor and/or flipping over.

2. **The correct answer is B.** A combination vehicle needs 1 second per 10 feet of vehicle length, plus an additional 1 second, for stopping distance during speeds above 40 miles per hour. When driving less than 40 miles per hour, the required stopping distance drops to 1 second per 10 feet of length (choice C). 4 seconds (choice A) and 2 seconds plus an additional 1 second (choice D) per 10 feet of length are both unnecessary and excessive.

3. **The correct answer is A.** Although the assumption is that heavier vehicles require longer distances to stop, this is not true with tractor trucks. A bobtail tractor is one that is empty, without a trailer hitched on. It has decreased traction because the weight is all centered towards the front of the vehicle, which then increases the stopping distance needed. A fully loaded combination vehicle with the maximum gross weight is evenly distributed across all regions of the vehicle, with solid weight pushing the vehicle down onto the ground, providing excellent traction.

4. **The correct answer is B.** A double tractor-trailer of this length has a rearward amplification of only 2.0 as the added trailer doubles the likelihood of a rollover.

5. **The correct answer is A.** Trailer skids often occur after braking strongly, as this can lead to the brakes locking, which in turn causes the wheels to lock up and skid. Switching lanes quickly (choice B), excessive speed on a turn (choice C), and quick acceleration (choice D) cannot in and of themselves cause a trailer skid, although braking strongly because of these choices can.

6. **The correct answer is D.** The back wheels on the trailer go off-track the most when turning as the back of the trailer moves in the opposite direction of the turn before self-correcting towards the end. The front and back wheels on the tractor (choices A and B) and the front wheels on the trailer (choice C) all off-track less when compared to the back wheels of the trailer.

7. **The correct answer is B.** The above illustration shows a jug handle turn. This type of turn occurs when a combination vehicle steers widely early in a turn, which is not best practice. A button hole turn (choice A) is not a type of turn but a button hook is. A jackknife (choice C) is not a turn, but rather occurs when the trailer gets ahead of the tractor. Off-track (choice D) is not a turn but refers to the wheels during the turn.

8. **The correct answer is C.** If you must back up on a curve, choose the driver's side as it provides increased visibility. The driver's side is not necessarily easier to control (choice A), and the passenger side is absolutely the last option as it is the hardest to control (choice B) and provides the least visibility (choice D).

9. **The correct answer is A.** The Johnson bar is another term for the trailer hand valve. The Johnson bar does not refer to the emergency brake (choice B), the parking brake (choice C), or the interlock system (choice D).

10. **The correct answer is C.** The shut-off valves are located at the back of each trailer. They all remain open except for the last trailer, which needs to be closed, thus keeping the air in the entire service line from the tractor through all of the trailers. It is not located at the front of each trailer (choice A), in the cabin of the tractor (choice B), or at the front of the tractor (choice D).

11. **The correct answer is B.** Chocks, also called wheel chocks, go behind and in front of wheels to add extra protection for rigs, especially if there are no spring brakes. Not every combination vehicle will have a parking brake (choice C) because spring brakes are the parking brake. Emergency brakes (choice A) are not as mechanically reliable as physical wheel chocks and can fail. The tractor protection valve (choice D) refers to the valve that keeps air in the tractor line should the rest of the service brake system fail or become disconnected.

12. **The correct answer is C.** The ABS system helps to avoid locked up wheels by modulating the pressure applied to avoid the strong braking that leads to locks. It does not increase braking capacity (choice A), decrease stopping distance required (choice B), or replace the regular service brakes (choice D).

13. **The correct answer is D.** The purpose of glad hands is to connect the service and emergency air lines (which connect the brakes) from the tractor to each trailer. They do not connect the trailer body to the tractor (choice A), connect the trailer brake lights (choice B), or secure the Johnson bar (choice C).

14. **The correct answer is A.** The first step when coupling a tractor-semitrailer is to inspect the fifth wheel. Inspecting the area around the vehicle and putting in the wheel chocks (choice B) is the second step. Positioning the tractor (choice C) is the third step, and checking the trailer height (choice D) is the sixth step.

15. **The correct answer is C.** The trailer should be slightly below the tractor prior to coupling as the coupling process will raise it up slightly. If the trailer is flush with the tractor (choice B) or slightly above the tractor (choice A), it will be too high after coupling and can damage the coupling. If the trailer is far below the tractor (choice D), it can damage the trailer hose after coupling.

16. **The correct answer is A.** Pulling the tractor partially clear, but not fully clear, of the trailer before inspecting the trailer supports allows the trailer to have a safety net should the trailer supports give out. This will prevent the trailer from dropping to the ground and possibly injuring someone if the trailer supports are not properly in place.

17. **The correct answer is B.** When inspecting the coupling system, make sure there is enough grease on the fifth wheel plate. There should never be space between the upper and lower fifth wheel (choice A). The locking should occur around the shank of the kingpin, not the head (choice C). The release arm (choice D) should be lowered and disengaged.

18. **The correct answer is A.** Most manufacturers put the recommended pressure range for air brakes between 100-120 psi. Many vehicles will provide a warning when the pressure reaches 80-85 psi (choice D). Pressure that drops below 45-60 psi (choice C) results in improper air in the lines and a warning being given, and pressure of 20-45 psi (choice B) will enable the emergency system to kick in, causing the trailer protection valve and parking brake to pop out.

19. **The correct answer is A.** A pintle hook, drawbar, and gooseneck are examples of hitches used to couple trailers to tractors. Brake systems (choice B) are divided into service, emergency, and parking. Safety latches on a coupling (choice C) and shut-off valves (choice D) do not have specialized labels.

20. **The correct answer is B.** It is never advised to shift gears when crossing railroad tracks as the combination vehicle is at a higher risk of getting stuck when shifting. Shifting before crossing or immediately after completing the crossing is best practice to avoid getting stuck.

SCORE SHEET

Use the following table to calculate your scoring percentage. Remember that a passing score is 80% for each subject.

CDL SCORE SHEET		
Subject	**# Correct ÷ # of Questions**	**× 100 = _____ %**
General Knowledge	_____ ÷ 50 = _____	× 100 = _____ %
Air Brakes	_____ ÷ 25 = _____	× 100 = _____ %
Combination Vehicles	_____ ÷ 20 = _____	× 100 = _____ %

Study Reference Guide

STUDY REFERENCE GUIDE		
Subject	**Chapter**	**Page**
General Knowledge	Chapter 3	42
Air Brakes	Chapter 4	74
Combination Vehicles	Chapter 5	94

NOTES

CHAPTER

General Knowledge

GENERAL KNOWLEDGE

OVERVIEW

Exam Format

CDL Requirements

Inspections

Safe Driving

Safely Transporting Cargo

Summing It Up

Practice Test

The general knowledge test is required for anyone applying for a commercial driver's license (CDL). This test covers what you need to know about operating a vehicle that requires a CDL, including questions about vehicle inspection, safe driving, and transporting cargo. Commercial vehicles require special licensing and endorsements due to their size, special operation, and cargo. This chapter will prepare you for the basics of driving a commercial vehicle for Class A, B, and C. However, you should also refer to your state's CDL manual and contact your motor vehicle department or division for greater detail.

 NOTE

At the end of Chapter 3, you will find a General Knowledge Practice Test that will test your knowledge of the information contained in this chapter and better prepare you for the CDL general knowledge test.

EXAM FORMAT

The general knowledge test is a written test that consists of 50 multiple-choice questions. To pass the exam, you must answer at least 40 questions correctly (80%). If you don't pass the exam the first time, your local department of motor vehicles may allow you to take it several times before a new fee is applied. Check with your local DMV to find out specific policies for testing and re-testing.

Scheduling

Scheduling the exam is state-specific, so it's important to check with your local department of motor vehicles to find out when you can schedule the exam. You must pass the general knowledge test to receive your commercial learner's permit (CLP); some DMVs require that you hold your CLP for 14 days before being allowed to complete your skills test, which includes the vehicle inspection, test of basic vehicle control, and the on-road test. Check with your local DMV for more information on scheduling both components.

CDL REQUIREMENTS

There are different license classes depending on the type and weight of the commercial vehicle. The total weight of a rig and its cargo should be known under the following definitions:

- Gross Vehicle Weight (GVW) is the true weight of a vehicle including its load.
- Gross Vehicle Weight Rating (GVWR) is the maximum weight rating for a vehicle, including its load, that is given by the manufacturer.
- Gross Combination Weight (GCW) is the same thing as GVW but for a combination vehicle (a vehicle with a trailer).
- Gross Combination Weight Rating (GCWR) is the same thing as GVWR, but for a combination vehicle (a vehicle with a trailer).

The vehicle classes that require a CDL are defined as follows:

- **Class A:** combination vehicles with a GCWR of 26,001 or more pounds
- **Class B:** heavy straight vehicles with a GVWR of 26,001 or more pounds
- **Class C:** small vehicles with a GVWR of less than 26,001 pounds that fall into one of the following subcategories:
  - Used to carry 16 or more passengers, including the driver (van, buses, etc.)
  - Used to transport hazardous materials in quantities requiring placarding under the Hazardous Materials Regulations (49 CFR Part 172, Subpart F)
  - Carrying material listed as a select agent or toxin in 42 CFR part 73

There are also state-specific requirements for obtaining a CDL, so check your state's CDL manual for more information about requirements.

 NOTE

A few states have different minimum age requirements. Hawaii requires drivers to be at least 21. New York requires drivers to be 21 for a class A license. Check with your local DMV for state-specific information.

Eligibility

There are state-specific requirements for eligibility, so check your state's CDL manual for specifics. Generally, the following criteria are used to determine eligibility:

- **Age:** The CDL requires test takers to be at least 18. However, if transport includes crossing state lines, the driver must be 21.

- **Commercial Learner's Permit (CLP):** A CLP is required prior to receiving the CDL. A driver is awarded a CLP after passing the general knowledge test and any other relevant exams for the class of vehicle they intend to drive. In most states, a driver must hold the CLP for at least 14 days before they can take the physical skills exam. Check with your DMV for state-specific requirements.

- **DOT Medical Card:** A DOT physical is required for all CDL exam takers and must be renewed every two years (unless otherwise specified) even after the CDL is obtained. The physical covers everything from physical fitness to medications to underlying health conditions (such as high blood pressure, sleep apnea, and mental health).

- **Proof of Residency:** The driver must provide proof of residency for their state. A CDL does not transfer between states, thus if the driver moves, they will need to retake the exam in the new state per state regulations.

Disqualification

Violations in both commercial and private vehicles can lead to a suspension or revocation of a driver's CDL. These rules vary by state, but the following are universal grounds for disqualification:

- Alcohol/Substance use while driving
- Certain driving related felonies
- Driving without a license
- Driving when commercial vehicle has "Out-of-Service" orders
- Railroad crossing violations
- Transporting hazardous materials without endorsement or in a dangerous fashion
- Leaving the scene of an accident

Endorsements and Restrictions

Endorsements allow drivers to operate certain types of vehicles. To gain an endorsement, the driver must pass an additional test about that type of vehicle. Restrictions prohibit the driver from certain types of vehicle operation. The vehicle used during the skills test may lead to certain restriction codes being present on the CDL. For the skills test, be sure to use the same type of vehicle that you plan to operate with your CDL to avoid potential restrictions.

 NOTE

If you plan on only driving intrastate, the DOT medical card may not be required. Check with your local DMV.

The following table provides is a summary of possible endorsement and restriction codes and their meanings. There may be questions on the general knowledge test covering these codes.

ENDORSEMENT CODES	
T	Double and triple trailers—allows Class A drivers to pull double and triple trailers.
P	Passenger vehicles—allows drivers of all classes to drive vehicles designed to carry 16 or more people (including the driver)
S	School buses—allows drivers to drive a school bus
N	Tanker vehicles—allows drivers to haul a tank of liquid or gaseous materials of an individual capacity of 119 gallons or aggregate capacity of 1,000 gallons
H	Hazardous material vehicles—allows drivers of any vehicle class to haul hazardous material as designated by 49 U.S.C. 5103 and that requires placarding under 49 CFR part 172, or is listed as a toxin under 42 CFR Part 73
X	Hazardous material and tank, combined—allows drivers to transport hazardous material in tanker vehicles

RESTRICTION CODES	
E	No operation of manual transmission vehicles
K	Intrastate only, no operation of a commercial vehicle crossing state lines
L	No operation of a vehicle partially equipped with air brakes
M	No operation of a Class A passenger vehicle, only Classes B and C
N	No operation of class A or B passenger vehicles, only Class C

O	No operation of a tractor-trailer connected by a fifth wheel
P	Only a restriction if placed on a CLP, which means no operation unless the passengers are instructors, test examiners, other trainees, or federal/state auditors or inspectors
X	CLP only: no cargo in tank vehicle and tank must be purged; restricts "N" endorsement
V	Medical variance code: restrictions related to DOT medical certification, such as high blood pressure or diabetes
Z	No operation of a vehicle that is fully equipped with air brakes

INSPECTIONS

Pre- and post-trip inspections allow drivers to assess both the inside and the outside of the vehicle, verifying that everything is in working order and is safe for operation. A large truck crash causation study by the Federal Motor Carrier Safety Administration found vehicle issues were the critical reason for 10% of crashes. Driver performance accounted for another 9% of crashes with brake problems being an associated factor in incidents. Regular and thorough vehicle inspections form a key component of safe commercial driving. It is important to note that inspections should be completed at every major stop, including, but not limited to, when loading cargo and after overnight sleep.

While the skills test includes a physical inspection of a vehicle, the general knowledge test includes questions about vehicle inspection. To prepare you for these questions, this section includes the following:

- Seven-Point Pre-Trip Inspection List
- CDL Vehicle Inspection Memory Aid

The following list provides a sequence of steps for your pre-trip inspection. See your state CDL manual for greater detail.

SEVEN-POINT PRE-TRIP INSPECTION LIST

1

GENERAL INSPECTION

Focus: Review the previous after-trip report and assess the general condition of the vehicle.

2

ENGINE (OFF)

Focus: Perform a visual inspection of under-hood components and fluid levels while the engine is off.

3

CAB

Focus: Perform an interior inspection, including gauges, buttons, emergency kit, etc., while the engine is on.

4

LIGHTS

Focus: Inspect headlights, parking lamps, emergency lights, etc. while the engine is off.

5

WALKAROUND

Focus: Walk the exterior of the vehicle to inspect tires, air brakes, suspension, axles, cargo safety, etc.

6

TURN SIGNALS/PAPERWORK

Focus: Check all turn signals, stop lights, and the trip paperwork (manifests, permits, etc.).

7

ENGINE (ON)

Focus: Assess vehicle functions while in motion, including hydraulics, stopping, braking, etc.

The following image provides a visual inspection memory aid for you to use when practicing. When taking the skills test or general knowledge test, you cannot bring a checklist or memory aid with you. You must memorize inspection points prior to the exam. For a more detailed list, check your state-specific CDL manual as requirements may vary by state.

CDL Vehicle Inspection Memory Aid

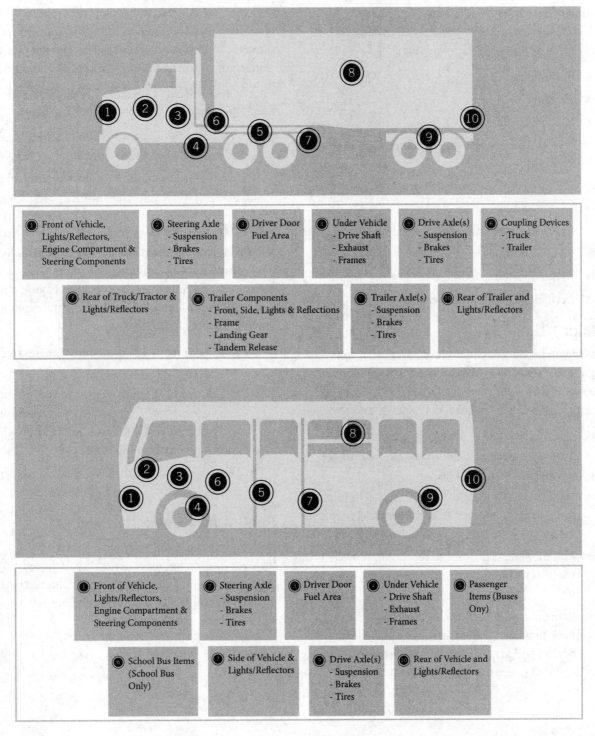

SAFE DRIVING

Commercial vehicles are much larger and heavier than other vehicles, and thus they require greater skill to drive and specific safety practices. It's for these reasons that a driver needs a CDL and the appropriate endorsements to drive certain vehicles. Whether driving a commercial straight truck or a trailered vehicle, it is always important to follow general safe driving practices as well as those for the following:

- Backing Up
- Shifting
- Sight While Driving
- Spatial Awareness (including Braking and Parking)
- Signaling and Communications
- Turning and Steering
- Railroad Crossings and Drawbridges
- Road Conditions
- Driver-Related Conditions
- Accidents and Emergencies

Backing Up

Backing up in a large vehicle presents a host of challenges and should be avoided when possible. Look for opportunities for pull-through parking. Otherwise, if backing up cannot be avoided, drive slowly and remember the following key points:

- Turn the wheel the opposite direction of where you need the trailer to go.
- If the trailer starts to drift out of place, or in a direction you don't want, turn the wheel in the direction of the drift to correct it.
- Pull the vehicle forward to reposition if needed. Use this technique sparingly during the skills test.
- Remember GOAL: Get Out And Look. Even the most practiced, experienced, and skilled truck drivers will get out of their vehicle to look around and make sure they are backing in correctly.

Shifting

When driving a manual transmission vehicle, a driver needs to know when (and when not) to shift gears. Optimal shifting times can depend on the vehicle you're driving and the driving situation. You should always familiarize yourself with the vehicle's manual. However, the engine's revolutions per minute (RPM) combined with the vehicle's miles per hour (MPH) often indicate when to switch gears. The following are important general points to remember when shifting:

- Downshift before a curve and before going downhill.
- Ascending a hill causes a loss in momentum, so downshift when this occurs.
- Shifting gears should be used before relying on braking when going downhill.

Sight While Driving

While driving, you should always keep your sight and focus ahead of you by looking in front of your vehicle, being aware of your surroundings, and paying attention to what is approaching. Here are some strategies to help you remain vigilant when driving:

- Keep your focus 12–15 seconds or a quarter of a mile in front of you.
- Regularly check your mirrors, including the rearview mirror. This can help you see hazards and catch sight of a rollover or jackknife when entering a curve or braking.
- Dim high beams within 500 feet of oncoming traffic.

Spatial Awareness

Spatial awareness related to commercial driving includes knowledge about general spatial needs of the larger vehicle, including height and width restrictions. Spatial awareness also includes following and stopping distance, braking, and parking.

General Spatial Needs

Many areas have height or width restrictions, especially tunnels, bridges, and parking areas. To safely navigate roadways, a driver should note the height and width of a commercial vehicle during the pre-trip inspection.

- The standard acceptable width of a commercial vehicle is 8 feet 6 inches. However, different states have intrastate restrictions (such as Hawaii which allows 9 feet of width), so check with your state CDL manual.

- The maximum vehicle height is generally 13 feet 6 inches. However, 14 feet is sometimes permitted on certain roads at a state level, so check with your state CDL manual for additional information.

Following and Stopping Distances

Commercial vehicles are much larger and heavier than standard personal vehicles, and thus they take more time to move or stop. It is up to you to pay attention to your surroundings and calculate both following and stopping distances.

Following distance is the amount of space needed between your commercial vehicle and the vehicle in front of it. You can assess appropriate following

distance by selecting a position on the road the car ahead has passed and counting how long it takes you to reach the same point. At minimum, your following distance should match the following calculations:

- At speeds of 40 mph OR LESS, add 1 second per 10 feet of your vehicle's length.

  o Example: A 40-foot combination vehicle will need 4 seconds of following distance when traveling at a speed of 35 mph.

- At speeds of OVER 40 mph, add 1 second for every 10 feet of your vehicle's length plus 1 extra second.

  o Example: A 40-foot combination vehicle will need 5 seconds of following distance when traveling at a speed of 50 mph (4 seconds for 40 feet PLUS 1 extra second = 5 seconds).

Stopping distance is the amount of space needed to stop and includes perception distance, reaction distance, and braking distance. The formula is as follows:

- Perception Distance + Reaction Distance + Braking Distance = Stopping Distance

  o Example: A combination vehicle traveling at a speed of 45 mph will need 319 feet of stopping distance: 117 ft. (perception distance) + 50 ft. (reaction distance) + 152 ft. (braking distance).

 NOTE ------------------------------

Normal stopping is affected by wet or slippery conditions, going downhill, or driving with an empty trailer. In these situations, it will take longer to stop your vehicle, and you must adjust the distance and time you will need to stop.

Braking

With the increased size and weight of commercial vehicles, greater breaking power and distance are required for safe driving and stopping. Stopping a commercial vehicle is often aided by an antilock braking system (ABS), which automatically fluctuates the braking power to keep the wheels from locking up. ABS does not, however, increase the braking power of the service brakes on a vehicle. On larger commercial vehicles, the service brakes are often air brakes because they can provide the stable and significant braking power needed by the vehicle's size.

See the following for some additional considerations for braking when driving a commercial vehicle:

- **Skids:** When braking hard enough that the wheels lock up, the locked wheels can go into a skid. Skids occur due to the locked wheels not rolling freely and losing traction as they slide across the road. This can lead to a loss of vehicle control and possibly a trailer jackknife. To correct a skid, continue to drive on course and remove your foot from the brake, allowing the wheels to roll freely and regain traction. Accelerating, steering, and further braking cannot correct the skid, and, in some cases, such decisions can make the skid even worse.

- **Wet Conditions:** When driving in wet conditions lightly brake sooner than you would in normal conditions. The light pressure being applied to the brakes will create enough friction to help warm and dry the brakes off before you begin to apply normal braking pressure, which will decrease the likelihood of the brakes slipping.

- **Brake Fading:** Brakes may also slip due to brake fading, which occurs when the braking system becomes too hot. The driver must then repeatedly apply the brakes harder and harder to achieve the same stopping abilities as brakes at a normal temperature.

- **Retarders:** Some vehicles are equipped with retarders, which will help slow the vehicle without using the brakes. There are four basic types: exhaust, engine, hydraulic, and electric retarders (all of which are controlled by the driver as needed). Retarders apply their braking power to the drive wheels whenever the accelerator pedal is released. Retarders should never be on when driving on wet, icy, or snowy roads and/or when the wheels have poor traction. Having them on in any of these conditions can cause the wheels to skid.

Retarders should never be on when driving on wet, icy, or snowy roads and/or when the wheels have poor traction.

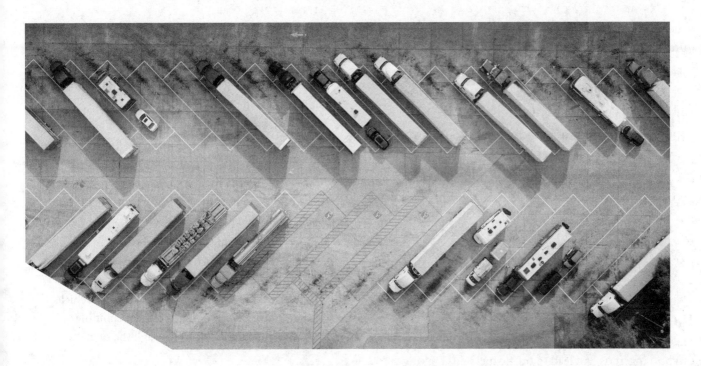

Parking

When parking a commercial vehicle, the parking brake should always be used, or, if the vehicle lacks spring breaks, chock the wheels (placing blocks behind and in front of each set of wheels). The parking brake manually engages the spring brakes (also called the emergency brakes). However, if unable to park on a level surface, having the wheel chocks in place adds an extra layer of safety should the parking brake fail.

Remember, when parking, always attempt to park in an area where you can pull through to avoid backing up. This will require planning and surveying the area as necessary. If this is not possible, mentally map out how you will back in and/or turn around if required. Make use of a spotter on the ground if pull through parking is not an option.

Signaling and Communications

Signaling and communications alert other drivers on the road of your intentions and your location. There are many symbols and labels that communicate information to other drivers that are often put on commercial vehicles. For example, placards are placed on a truck to state what type of hazardous material is being carried. An *Oversized Load* sign indicates a vehicle's load may take up

more of the road than a normal vehicle. Red triangles with orange centers indicate a slow-moving vehicle. Other labels often found on commercial vehicles include signs that state "This vehicle makes wide turns" or "This vehicle stops at railroad crossings." Signage can also communicate at what distance other vehicles should follow the commercial vehicle.

Beyond explicit signage, you'll also make use of vehicle signals, such as turn signals and hazards, to let drivers know where you're headed or that there are unsafe road conditions ahead. The following are best practices related to signaling:

- When you are preparing to make a turn, use the turn signal well in advance. This will let the other drivers around you know your intentions so they can adjust their speed and position to allow for the turn.

- Flash your brake lights by lightly tapping the brake pedal to alert drivers behind you of hazards ahead as your vehicle size can prohibit them from seeing in front of you.

- If you need to stop on the side of the road for any reason, put out your triangle reflectors within 10 minutes of stopping.

When stopping on different types of roads, there are different ways to place the signals:

- If stopped on a one-way or divided highway, the signals should be placed at 10, 100, and 200 feet toward oncoming traffic.

- Stopping on a two-lane road or undivided highway requires signals at 10 and 100 feet in front of and behind the vehicle for both sides of oncoming traffic to see.

- Stopping beyond or behind a hill, curve, or other obstruction requires signals to be placed in the direction of the obstruction to a view distance of 100 to 500 feet from the stopped commercial motor vehicle.

Turning

Making turns too quickly, too hard, and too narrowly can be dangerous and lead to traffic incidents. Taking a turn or curve too quickly can lead to a loss of vehicle control or rollover. Posted speeds on turns and curves are meant for smaller vehicles in perfect conditions, so always go slower than what is posted. And when in doubt, slow down. See the following for advice on specific methods of turning:

- A jug handle turn is when the driver turns wide at the beginning of the turn, thus thrusting the nose of the vehicle into the other lane before completing the turn. This can send mixed signals to the other drivers that you are switching lanes and not turning. They may try to pass you on the inside, creating the possibility of a collision.

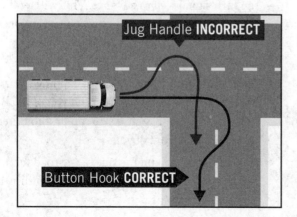

- A button hook turn is when the driver turns wide through the turn. This allows the truck to go straight forward and then turn widely into the other lane mid-turn, which decreases the possibility of inside passing by smaller cars.

- Left turns should always be made in the outermost turning lane (furthest from the median) if the intersection has two or more turning lanes. Using the inner turn lane can cause the vehicle to drift into the outermost lane, thus cutting off or colliding with a passing vehicle.

- When making right turns, keep the back of the trailer near the curb. An opening between the trailer and the curb could confuse a driver behind you, and they may try to drive between the vehicle and the curb. This can result in them colliding with the trailer as it cuts in through the turn.

Steering

Steering should be as smooth and precise as possible when driving. Erratic and inconsistent steering can lead to a loss of vehicle control, especially at higher speeds. If ever a tire loses pressure or fails completely and the vehicle is pulling to one side, firmly hold the wheel at the three and nine o'clock positions to prevent the steering wheel from twisting out of grip.

Railroad Crossings and Drawbridges

Generally, a commercial vehicle should stop at all railroad crossings and drawbridges. At such crossings, commercial drivers should take the following precautions:

- Commercial vehicles should stop within 15–50 feet of a railroad crossing.

  o Railroad traffic is often controlled by an active crossing sign, which is a sign that has traffic control installed on it. It can take a tractor-trailer 14 seconds to cross a single track from a complete stop and 15 seconds or more to cross a double track. Never shift gears while going over railroad tracks.

- Commercial vehicles carrying passengers or hazardous materials should stop at least 50 feet from the start of a drawbridge.

There are situations in which stopping at a railroad or drawbridge is not required, but in these situations, speed should be reduced and surroundings should be observed. These situations include the following:

- A green traffic light
- Railroads that follow the middle of the road
- Streetcar crossing areas
- An individual directing traffic (such as a police officer or flagger, or a control officer/attendant for a drawbridge)
- A non-functioning or abandoned railroad or bridge

Road Conditions

Road conditions can significantly affect how you drive—both the precautions you take and how you react. Road conditions can vary by weather as well as terrain. The following section provides an overview of common road conditions you may encounter and how to navigate them.

Wet/Slippery Conditions

Wet or slippery conditions—caused by rain, snow, and ice—decrease the traction of the vehicle. To reduce the risk of sliding, check that tires for winter conditions have a minimum tread depth of 4/32-inch at the front of the vehicle and 2/32-inch in back; decrease traveling speed by 1/3. Further, when reducing speed, do so by lightly braking, then gradually increase pressure to achieve full braking. Gradual braking will allow the brakes to dry off and avoid locking.

Standing water on roadways can cause hydroplaning, which is when a layer of water causes the tire to separate from the road surface. Hydroplaning will result in a loss of steering or braking control. Let off the accelerator to correct. If this does not help, push in the clutch to let the wheels roll more freely. Avoid braking as it could result in greater loss of traction.

Extreme Heat

Heat above 85 degrees Fahrenheit can cause the tar on the roads to melt and become sticky, impacting vehicle handling. Additionally, extreme heat can lead to tire damage, which will increase the likelihood of a blowout. Stop every 2 hours or 100 miles, whichever comes first, to check your tires for damage.

Decreased Visibility

With low visibility, such as during foggy conditions, it is best to decrease your speed by at least 1/3 or more, depending on how far you can see. In addition, turn on the low beam lights. High beams in fog will actually lead to decreased visibility as the fog will reflect light, creating a glare and increasing driving risk for you and others. Decreased visibility due to darkness (such as night driving, in tunnels, etc.) can be improved with low beams, but they only provide a visibility range of 250 feet, whereas high beams provide a range of 350 to 500 feet.

High Elevations

Mountainous areas and places with steep grades represent dangerous obstacles for CMV drivers. Prior to entering the downgrade, shift into a lower gear. Downshifting after the vehicle has picked up speed will have less of an effect. Additionally, relying on your brakes too much will lead to overheating, warping, or failure. The best practice is to slow down and downshift early on, then use the brakes intermittently to maintain a safe speed. For example, if your safe speed is 40 mph, downshift and then briefly brake as needed to a speed of 35 mph, repeating the process as necessary.

Driver-Related Conditions

In addition to road conditions, it is equally important to pay attention to driver conditions. These include both the conditions of other drivers on the road as well as your condition while driving, including road rage, distractions, impairment, and fatigue.

Road Rage

Never engage with an aggressive driver by antagonizing them or by trying to pass or prevent merging. Drive defensively, not aggressively. The best way to deal with an aggressive driver is to give them space and ignore them. Anything other than ignoring them could lead to escalation. In serious circumstances, report aggressive drivers to authorities.

The road rage of other drivers poses a serious risk; however, you also need to be aware of your own emotional state when driving. If you feel yourself becoming overly

aggressive when driving, it is best to pull over and take a break. Such feelings while driving can be a sign of other issues: fatigue, hunger, or anxiety—none of which will help you drive better.

Distracted Driving

Distracted driving includes both physical and mental distractions. Anything from using a phone or GPS device, listening to music, eating, drinking, or smoking—even talking to a passenger—directs your attention away from the road to something else. A safe driver eliminates all in-vehicle distractions prior to driving. Plan your route before driving, including loading your needed directions if applicable. Remember, all mobile phone use must be 100% hands free as regulations do not allow for any usage once the vehicle is in motion. Additionally, a safe driver must also be able to avoid external distractions created by other drivers. Learn to look for the behavior patterns of distracted drivers (inconsistent speed, lane drifting, etc.) and pass carefully.

Impaired Driving

A driver should never operate a commercial vehicle under the influence of alcohol. The repercussions for doing so can result in a suspension or complete revocation of the CDL. The allowable limit when operating a commercial vehicle is a Blood Alcohol Content (BAC) of 0.04%, which for the average person is 1–2 drinks at most.

The use of illegal drugs in any amount is expressly prohibited. However, prescription medications can also impair driving. If you are prescribed medications that expressly impair driving or have such side effects, take them after driving and during your downtime to avoid any impairments.

Driver Fatigue

Fatigue can be just as dangerous as driving under the influence of alcohol or drugs. Even if you don't fall asleep at the wheel, fatigue can reduce your reaction time, which can lead to overcorrections and swerving. Such conditions dramatically increase the likelihood of incidents and jeopardize not only your health and safety but also that of other drivers. Remember the following about driver fatigue:

- **Warning Signs of Fatigue:** Zoning out, struggling to keep your head up, missing an exit, not remembering the past few exits, excessive or prolonged blinking, vehicle drifting, anxiety and irritability, and yawning

- **Risk Factors for Fatigue:** Getting 6 or less hours of sleep (triples the risk), dealing with insomnia, changing time zones (including flying), driving alone, taking certain medications, working multiple jobs, working 60 or more hours a week, driving too far without proper rest

  o Federally, drivers are only allowed to drive 11 hours daily (or 10 hours when carrying passengers) with a 30-minute break required for an 8-hour period and with 10 consecutive hours off duty between driving stints; these figures sometimes vary by state.

Accidents and Emergencies

Although it is impossible to prepare for every type of accident or emergency, there are important areas to focus on should you find yourself and your vehicle in any of the following situations.

Accidents

If you are involved in an accident and are not hurt, remember the following basic steps:

- **Protect the Area:** Pull over to the side of the road if possible. Put on your flashers and set out reflective triangles.

- **Notify the Authorities:** Call the police. Call your carrier and notify the insurance company.

- **Care for the Injured:** Never move someone unless passing traffic or a fire threatens their safety. Apply direct pressure on areas of heavy bleeding. Keep the injured warm.

Four Common Causes of Fires

FUEL	CARGO	TIRES	ELECTRICAL
Are you smoking while fueling? Do you follow safe protocols when fueling? Are the fueling connections tight?	Is the cargo properly ventilated? Are there any leaks of flammable cargo?	Are the tires properly inflated?	Are there any loose or damaged wires?

Fires

Problems with fuel, cargo, tires, and electrical equipment are common causes of fires. A commercial driver needs to consider whether their behaviors and operation of equipment may be increasing the risk of fires (refer to the preceding figure).

Some fires can be prevented, but addressing the causes safely requires vigilance. In case of a fire, you should pull off the road immediately. Keep the fire contained. Do not open the door where the fire is located (hood, trailer, etc.). This adds oxygen and can strengthen the fire. Extinguish the fire if possible. Know the rules for which extinguisher works on which type of fire and fuel type. See your state CDL manual for more detailed information.

SAFELY TRANSPORTING CARGO

Cargo should always be treated in the most secure and safe manner when transporting in a commercial vehicle. Factors like the cargo's security, weight distribution, and total amount can impact the best methods for safely securing it. This section will cover the following considerations when transporting cargo:

- Placarding
- Shipping Papers
- Hazardous Materials
- Carrying Cargo
- Securing Cargo
- Types of Cargo

Placarding

When transporting hazardous materials (HazMat), placards are used to communicate hazards, support appropriate emergency response, and meet federal regulations as described in 49 CFR 172 and 42 CFR 73. The shipper will provide proper placards, but the driver is responsible for placarding and labeling a vehicle transporting HazMat in any amount that requires placards. This must include four identical placards: one on the front of the vehicle, one on the back of the vehicle, and one on each side of the vehicle. However, placard quantity and placement can vary by material quantity and type. Placarding requirements should always be verified before transporting any HazMat that requires placarding. If placards are missing, the material cannot be transported.

Shipping Papers

Shippers are responsible for properly labeling and plac-arding packages and shipments, and it is the job of the carrier and shipper to ensure this is done properly. The shipper will also fill out and provide the driver with the appropriate shipping papers. These must be kept in the pouch of the driver's door, within reach on the dash-board while driving, or on the driver's seat if out of the vehicle. Important information about shipping papers is as follows:

- If ever there is a fire or other emergency that causes the driver to need to leave the vehicle, then the driver must take the shipping papers and keep them on their person. The shipping papers will allow the driver and others to know what the cargo is, the dangers it poses, and whom to call in an emergency.

- Never fight a HazMat fire, only minor truck fires. Emergency response for HazMat requires very special training due to the volatility of the materials being transported.

HAZARDOUS MATERIALS CLASS			
Class	Division	Name of Class or Division	Examples
1	1.1	Mass Explosion	Dynamite
	1.2	Projection Hazard	Flares
	1.3	Fire Hazard	Display Fireworks
	1.4	Minor Explosion	Ammunition
	1.5	Very Insensitive	Blasting Agents
	1.6	Extremely Insensitive	Explosive Devices
2	2.1	Flammable Gases	Propane
	2.2	Non-Flammable Gases	Helium
	2.3	Poisonous/Toxic Gases	Fluorine, Compressed
3	-	Flammable Liquids	Gasoline
4	4.1	Flammable Solids	Ammonium Picrate, Wetted
	4.2	Spontaneously Combustible	White Phosphorus
	4.3	Dangerous When Wet	Sodium
5	5.1	Oxidizers	Ammonium Nitrate
	5.2	Organic Peroxides	Methyl Ethyl Ketone Peroxide
6	6.1	Poison (Toxic Material)	Potassium Cyanide
	6.2	Infectious Substances	Anthrax Virus
7	-	Radioactive	Uranium
8	-	Corrosives	Battery Fluid
9	-	Miscellaneous Hazardous Materials	Polychlorinated Biphenyls (PCB)
None	-	ORM-D (Other Regulated Material-Domestic)	Food Flavorings, Medicines

TIP

HazMat is briefly covered on the general knowledge test. If you plan on getting the HazMat endorsement, study Chapter 8 for more in-depth information.

Hazardous Materials

Hazardous Materials (HazMat) are grouped into classes and divisions. There are nine classes with up to six divisions within a class. The table on the preceding page provides the delineation of common HazMat and the class and division under which they are classified.

Carrying Cargo

While drivers do not have the responsibility of creating placards and shipping papers, they are responsible for the cargo. The following four responsibilities all fall directly to the driver:

1. Inspecting the cargo
2. Recognizing overloads and poorly balanced weight
3. Ensuring the cargo is secured and does not obstruct the view of the driver
4. Ensuring the cargo does not restrict access to the emergency equipment

Securing Cargo

Cargo must be properly secured to prevent it from moving or shifting, which can lead to damage or even loss of control during transit. Shifting weight can pull a vehicle in the direction of the shift and can make a vehicle swerve, skid, or even roll over. Some cargo will need to be properly strapped down while others can be packed or braced together with no room for them to move. The following are ways to secure cargo:

- **Blocking and Bracing:** This can be done to the front, back, or sides of a load in order to keep it in place. When blocking or bracing, always place

the weight in the middle of the trailer so that its weight is evenly distributed. Grouping it too far to one side (whether front, back, or either side) can increase the chances of a rollover or cause damage to the trailer.

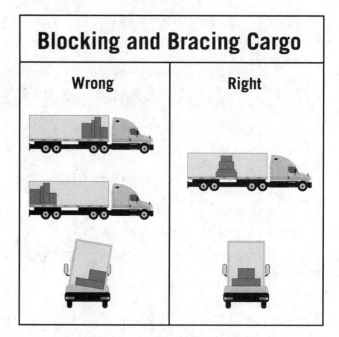

- **Tie-downs:** These are typically used on flatbeds or similar cargo areas that have no side walls. However, they can be used on the inside of a closed cargo area to keep cargo in place and prevent shifting. There are specific types and strength ratings for tie-downs, and a tie-down should never be used if it is not the correct type or strength for the application. The load limit of a securement system, under federal regulation,

Tie-Down Spacing

should be at least one-half times the weight of the load that it is securing. When using tie-downs there should be at least one tie-down per every ten feet of the cargo. Even if the cargo is very small and under ten feet in total, there should still be at least 2 tie-downs on the cargo.

- **Header Boards:** These are commonly called headache racks or front-end header boards and are used to protect the driver from the cargo in case there is a crash or other emergency that can shift the cargo forward. Always make sure the front-end structure is in good shape because it should block any movement forward that the cargo may take.

- **Covering Cargo:** Cargo coverings are used to protect exposed cargo from weather and protect people from cargo spills. Spill safety is a common requirement in many states, so be sure of the local laws where you will be traveling. While driving, it is a good idea to occasionally check the covers through your mirrors. This will allow you to notice any loose or flapping sections of the cover that can potentially rip off and disturb the rest of the cover in the wind.

- **Sealed or Contained Cargo:** Generally used when a portion of the transport is done by rail or ship and the beginning or end done by truck. Sealed cargo cannot be inspected on the inside. However, you can ensure that you are not exceeding any weight limits with your load. You can also make sure the cargo is properly secured as many containers have their own special securing systems.

Types of Cargo

There are some types of cargo that are commonly transported with a truck that need special attention or treatment. The following are examples of some that you may encounter:

- **Dry Bulk Cargo:** This cargo comes in a tank and has a higher center of gravity than most loads. Driving slowly and cautiously is essential when transporting this cargo, especially around curves and sharp turns.

- **Refrigerated Cargo:** This cargo is temperature sensitive and transported in a refrigerated trailer. Monitor and make sure that the refrigeration inside the trailer is at an acceptable temperature for the cargo you are transporting.

- **Hanging Meat:** This cargo is hung within a refrigerated trailer and has a high center of gravity. Make sure that the refrigeration is always at an acceptable temperature for the cargo and drive cautiously around curves and sharp turns.

- **Livestock Cargo:** Livestock can move around the trailer while in transport as well as lean in turns. Drive cautiously around curves and turns and be prepared to manage livestock movement when you see any concerning portions of the road approaching. If there is not enough livestock to fill the trailer, then you can use a false bulkhead (or temporary wall) to keep the livestock packed together. Even if livestock is properly packed, be wary of their movement and leaning.

- **Oversized Cargo:** This is any cargo that is over-length, over-width, or overweight. This type of cargo requires special permits to transport, is usually restricted to certain times it can be transported, and sometimes requires police or pilot vehicle escort. Equipment such as warning signs that say, "oversized load" or "wide load," flashing lights, and flags should be used during transport. Because it is oversized, take special care when driving so that the cargo does not contact vehicles or road structures. Slow and cautious driving should be used, especially if you are approaching a section of unfamiliar road.

SUMMING IT UP

- Commercial vehicles require special licensing and endorsements due to their size, special operation, and cargo.

- The general knowledge test is a written test that consists of 50 multiple-choice questions. To pass the exam, you must get at least 40 questions correct (80%).

- Requirements, eligibility, and disqualifications can vary by state. Check with your local department of motor vehicles for more details regarding paperwork, medical exams, and test scheduling.

- Endorsements allow drivers to operate certain types of vehicles. Restrictions prohibit the driver from certain types of vehicle operation. Questions covering endorsement codes and restriction codes may appear on the general knowledge test.

- The pre-trip inspection allows the driver to completely inspect both the inside and the outside of the vehicle, verifying that everything is in working order and safe for operation.

- Commercial vehicles are much larger and heavier than other vehicles, so they take more skill to drive and have specific safety practices.

  - Avoid backing up whenever possible. Look for pull through parking when available.

  - To know when to switch gears, you need to familiarize yourself with the vehicle's manual. The engine's RPM combined with the vehicle's MPH indicate when to switch gears.

  - Keep your focus 12–15 seconds or quarter of a mile in front of you. Regularly check your mirrors, including the rearview mirror.

  - Calculate following and stopping distances to ensure enough space between you and other drivers.

  - Know how to properly brake, especially during skids and in wet conditions. Know when to use retarders.

  - When parking a commercial vehicle, the parking brake should always be used, and the wheels should be chocked (which go behind and in front of each set of wheels).

- Use proper procedures to communicate your movements and intentions to other drivers, including turn signals, brake lights, and hazards.

- Posted speeds on turns and curves are meant for smaller vehicles in optimal conditions, so drive slower than posted speeds.

- Steering should be as smooth and precise as possible when driving. Erratic and inconsistent steering can cause a driver to lose control of a vehicle, especially at higher speeds.

- When stopping is required, commercial vehicles should stop within 15–50 feet of a railroad crossing and 50 feet of a drawbridge.

- Pay attention to road conditions and adjust how you drive to accommodate for wet roads, extreme heat, decreased visibility, and high elevations.

- Consider and adjust for human-related driving conditions, such as road rage, distracted or impaired driving, and fatigue.

- If you are involved in an accident, protect the area, notify the authorities, and care for the injured.

- In case of a fire, pull off the road immediately, keep the fire contained, and extinguish the fire if possible.

- Cargo should always be treated in the most secure and safe manner when transporting in a commercial vehicle. Factors like the cargo's security, weight distribution, and total amount can impact the best methods for safely securing it.

- Ultimately, the carrier is responsible for proper placarding and labeling of the vehicle transporting any hazardous materials. For most cargo, this must include four identical placards: one on the front of the vehicle, one on the back of the vehicle, and one on each side of the vehicle.

- Shipping papers must be kept in the pouch of the driver's door, within reach on the dashboard while driving, or on the driver's seat if out of the vehicle.

- Cargo must be properly secured to prevent it from moving or shifting, which can lead to damage or even loss of control during transit. Shifting weight can pull a vehicle in the direction of the shift and can make a vehicle swerve, skid, or even roll over.

GENERAL KNOWLEDGE PRACTICE TEST

50 Questions—90 Minutes

> **Directions:** Read each question below and choose the correct answer from the four choices provided. Only one choice is correct, so choose carefully.

1. A vehicle that transports 25 passengers and has a GCWR of over 26,001 pounds requires which type of CDL?

   A. Class A

   B. Class B

   C. Class C

   D. Class B or C

2. What is the correct formula for calculating stopping distance?

   A. Perception Distance + Reaction Distance = Stopping Distance

   B. Reaction Distance + Braking Distance = Stopping Distance

   C. Perception Distance + Braking Distance = Stopping Distance

   D. Perception Distance + Reaction Distance + Braking Distance = Stopping Distance

3. A T endorsement allows the driver to operate a double or triple trailer.

   A. True

   B. False

4. The engine should be on when completing the fluid checks under the hood during the pre-trip inspection.

   A. True

   B. False

5. A pre-trip inspection should be completed

   A. at the beginning of a new trip.

   B. after any major stops such as unloading cargo.

   C. whenever a new driver takes over.

   D. All of the above.

6. The oil pressure gauge should be inspected during which part of the pre-trip inspection?

   A. Step 1: Overview

   B. Step 2: Engine (off)

   C. Step 3: Cab

   D. Step 5: Walkaround

7. Which of the following is NOT the responsibility of the driver?

   A. Securing the cargo

   B. Recognizing poorly balanced weight

   C. Creating the shipping papers

   D. Ensuring the load does not obstruct the driver view

8. Which of the following is the maximum weight rating for a vehicle, including its load, that is given by the manufacturer?

   A. GVW

   B. GVWR

   C. GCWR

   D. GCW

9. All of the following are true about parking a commercial vehicle EXCEPT:

    A. The parking brake should always be used.

    B. The wheels should always use chocks.

    C. A driver should attempt to pull through for parking whenever possible.

    D. A driver should avoid parking in safe havens.

10. What is the following distance needed for a tractor-trailer that is 60 feet in length traveling at 55 mph?

    A. 5 seconds

    B. 6 seconds

    C. 7 seconds

    D. 12 seconds

11. By how much should a driver reduce their speed under wet and/or slippery conditions?

    A. 1/3

    B. 1/2

    C. 2/3

    D. 3/4

12. Driver fatigue and alcohol intoxication affect a driver in similar ways.

    A. True

    B. False

13. Commercial vehicles should stop at least _____ feet before a railroad crossing.

    A. 10

    B. 15

    C. 25

    D. 50

14. Which condition puts a person at the greatest risk for driver fatigue?

    A. Getting 6–7 hours of nightly sleep

    B. Working 50 hours a week

    C. Working 3 jobs

    D. Remaining in the same time zone

15. How long can a driver operate a passenger transport vehicle during a 24-hour period?

    A. 8 hours

    B. 10 hours

    C. 11 hours

    D. 14 hours

16. When driving in wet or slippery conditions, the front tires should have a minimum tire tread of

    A. 2/32-inch.

    B. 3/32-inch.

    C. 4/32-inch.

    D. 6/32-inch.

17. What is the legal blood alcohol content (BAC) limit for a person operating a commercial vehicle?

    A. 0.02%

    B. 0.04%

    C. 0.06%

    D. 0.08%

18. Sealed cargo coming from a ship-based transport service should always be checked for

    A. proper content.

    B. leaks.

    C. verified weight.

    D. smells.

19. Tie downs should be placed every 5 feet of cargo.

    A. True

    B. False

20. There are _____ classes of hazardous materials.

    A. 6

    B. 8

    C. 9

    D. 10

21. When backing up with a trailer, always turn the wheel _____ to ensure the trailer goes the necessary direction.

    A. the opposite direction of the trailer

    B. to the right of the trailer

    C. to the left of the trailer

    D. the direction of the trailer

22. How far ahead should vision be focused while driving?

    A. 12–15 seconds or ¼ mile ahead

    B. 15–18 seconds or ⅓ mile ahead

    C. 18–21 seconds or ½ mile ahead

    D. 22–25 seconds or ⅔ mile ahead

23. Reflective triangles must be put out within how many minutes of pulling over onto the side of the road?

    A. 30 minutes

    B. 10 minutes

    C. 5 minutes

    D. 2 minutes

24. At least 2 tie-downs should be used for every load, even if it is under 10 feet in length.

    A. True

    B. False

25. To get out of a skid, a driver should

    A. accelerate lightly.

    B. brake lightly.

    C. steer the opposite direction.

    D. remove foot from brake.

26. A Class B license allows a person to operate both a Class B and Class C vehicle.

    A. True

    B. False

27. When driving in excessively hot weather, the tires should be inspected every

    A. 4 hours or 200 miles.

    B. 2 hours or 120 miles.

    C. 2 hours or 100 miles.

    D. 1 hour or 60 miles.

28. When should the post-trip report be reviewed during the pre-trip inspection?

    A. Step 1: Overview

    B. Step 7: Engine (on)

    C. Step 3: Cab

    D. Step 5: Walkaround

29. What is the maximum vehicle width in inches allowed in most states?

    A. 96

    B. 102

    C. 108

    D. 114

30. What is the maximum vehicle height allowed in most states?

   A. 12 feet 6 inches

   B. 13 feet

   C. 13 feet 6 inches

   D. 14 feet

31. If a fire is detected inside a trailer, the driver should open the trailer and put out the fire.

   A. True

   B. False

32. Which of the following is NOT a sign of driver fatigue?

   A. Excessive blinking

   B. Yawning

   C. Feeling hot

   D. Drifting lanes

33. When stopped on a one-way road or divided highway, where should the signals be placed in relation to the oncoming traffic?

   A. 5, 10, and 20 feet

   B. 10, 20, and 50 feet

   C. 10, 100, and 200 feet

   D. 100, 150, and 200 feet

34. How should a driver alert others to hazards ahead that may be blocked from view due to vehicle size?

   A. Stop and pull over

   B. Flash brake lights

   C. Change lanes

   D. Slam on the brakes

35. All of the following are true about turning in a commercial vehicle EXCEPT:

   A. Left turns should always be made in the outer-most lane, farthest from the median.

   B. Right turns should be made in a jug handle fashion.

   C. Steering should be as smooth as possible.

   D. Always take turns slowly, going slower than the posted speed.

36. When driving in low visibility conditions, it is best to decrease speed by at least

   A. 1/5

   B. 1/4

   C. 1/3

   D. 1/2

37. All of the following are proper procedures following an accident where the driver is unharmed EXCEPT:

   A. Ensure safety of cargo

   B. Protect the area

   C. Notify the authorities

   D. Care for the injured

38. Which of these is the correct term for the true weight of a vehicle including its load?

   A. Gross Vehicle Weight Rating (GWVR)

   B. Gross Combination Weight (GCW)

   C. Gross Combination Weight Rating (GCWR)

   D. Gross Vehicle Weight (GVW)

39. How many identical placards should be placed on a vehicle transporting any hazardous materials?

    A. 3

    B. 4

    C. 5

    D. 6

40. Which of the following is NOT the driver's responsibility in relation to cargo?

    A. Inspecting the cargo

    B. Recognizing overloads and poorly balanced weight

    C. Creating placards

    D. Ensuring the cargo is secure and does not obstruct the driver's view

41. What is another name for header boards that protect the driver in case cargo is thrown forward in an accident?

    A. Headache racks

    B. Header walls

    C. Cargo boards

    D. Cargo racks

42. What type of cargo is hung in a refrigerated trailer and has a high center of gravity?

    A. Dry bulk cargo

    B. Refrigerated cargo

    C. Livestock cargo

    D. Hanging meat

43. Which of these is NOT true regarding oversized cargo?

    A. Oversized cargo requires special permits to transport.

    B. Oversized cargo sometimes requires police or pilot vehicle escort.

    C. Oversized cargo can be transported at any time.

    D. Equipment such as warning signs, flashing lights, and flags should be used during transport.

44. What is the correct procedure when transporting livestock that does not fill the trailer?

    A. Request a smaller trailer

    B. Insert a false bulkhead or temporary wall

    C. Drive slower to account for livestock movement

    D. Tie down livestock to prevent movement

45. When should retarders be on?

    A. In wet conditions

    B. In icy conditions

    C. When wheels have poor traction

    D. None of the above

46. If a tire ever loses pressure or fails completely and the vehicle begins pulling to one side, the driver should hold the wheel at nine o'clock and three o'clock to prevent the wheel from twisting out of grip.

    A. True

    B. False

47. All of the following are conditions where a driver may simply reduce speed and observe the surroundings near a railroad crossing or drawbridge EXCEPT:

   A. When an individual is directing traffic

   B. When the driver is transporting hazardous materials

   C. When there is a green traffic light

   D. When the railroad or bridge is either not functioning or abandoned

48. In the case of a fire or emergency, a driver should leave the vehicle as quickly as possible, leaving behind the shipping papers in the truck, if necessary.

   A. True

   B. False

49. Which of the following is NOT a class 1 hazardous material?

   A. Dynamite

   B. Flares

   C. Gasoline

   D. Display fireworks

50. What is NOT true of covered cargo?

   A. Cargo is often covered to protect it from weather.

   B. Covered cargo helps protect people from spills.

   C. Covers should be checked periodically while driving via the mirrors.

   D. Cargo is generally covered if another portion of transport was done by rail or ship.

ANSWER KEY AND EXPLANATIONS

1. A	11. A	21. A	31. B	41. A
2. D	12. A	22. A	32. C	42. D
3. A	13. B	23. B	33. C	43. C
4. B	14. C	24. A	34. B	44. B
5. D	15. B	25. D	35. B	45. D
6. C	16. C	26. A	36. C	46. A
7. C	17. B	27. C	37. A	47. B
8. B	18. C	28. A	38. D	48. B
9. D	19. B	29. B	39. B	49. C
10. C	20. C	30. C	40. C	50. D

1. **The correct answer is A.** Any vehicle with a GCWR over 26,001 pounds requires a Class A CDL, regardless of whether it is transporting passengers. A Class B and a Class C CDL do not allow a driver to operate a vehicle of this type and weight.

2. **The correct answer is D.** Stopping distance, or the amount of space needed to bring a vehicle to a stop, is the sum of three factors: perception distance, reaction distance, and braking distance.

3. **The correct answer is A.** The T endorsement code indicates that a driver can operate both double and triple trailers.

4. **The correct answer is B.** The engine should be off during this portion of the inspection. This allows you to test the fluids while the engine is cool, per the requirements of the CDL inspection regulations.

5. **The correct answer is D.** A pre-trip inspection should be completed at the beginning of a new trip, after any major stops, and whenever a new driver takes over. This should never be skipped, even if the stop or the driver change off occurs shortly after the last pre-trip inspection.

6. **The correct answer is C.** The oil pressure gauge is located inside the cab; thus, it will be inspected during Step 3: Cab. The overview (choice A) does not involve cab inspections. The engine (off)

(choice B) is under the hood and the oil pressure gauge is not there. The walkaround (choice D) is also exterior.

7. **The correct answer is C.** Creating the shipping papers does not fall to the driver but rather the shipper and the carrier. It is the responsibility of the driver to secure the cargo (choice A), recognize poorly balanced weight (choice B), and ensure there are no obstructions of the driver's view (choice D).

8. **The correct answer is B.** GVWR stands for Gross Vehicle Weight Rating, which is the maximum weight rating for a vehicle, including its load, as given by the manufacturer. GVW (choice A) stands for Gross Vehicle Weight. GCWR (choice C) stands for Gross Combination Weight Rating. GCW (choice D) stands for Gross Combination Weight.

9. **The correct answer is D.** Choices A, B, and C are all true regarding parking a commercial vehicle. As opposed to being avoided, designated safe havens are optimal places to park a commercial vehicle.

10. **The correct answer is C.** The formula to calculate following distance is 1 second for every 10 feet of vehicle length plus one extra second if the speed is over 40 mph. This equates to 6 seconds plus 1 more, thus requiring 7 seconds.

3

11. **The correct answer is A.** When driving in wet and/or slippery conditions, such as a snow or rain, the speed should be reduced by one-third.

12. **The correct answer is A.** Driver fatigue can and does affect a driver similarly to alcohol intoxication and should be rectified with rest and sleep.

13. **The correct answer is B.** Commercial vehicles should stop at least 15 feet before a railroad crossing. 10 feet (choice A) is too close. 25 feet (choice C) is acceptable, but the vehicle could stop closer. 50 feet (choice D) is the maximum distance to stop before a railroad crossing.

14. **The correct answer is C.** A person with multiple jobs is at the greatest risk for driver fatigue. A person with 6–7 hours a night of sleep (choice A), that works 50 hours a week (choice B), or remains in the same time zone (choice D) is not at greater risk for driver fatigue.

15. **The correct answer is B.** When operating a passenger transport vehicle, a driver may only drive 10 hours in a 24-hour period before they must rest for at least 10 hours. After 8 hours (choice A), all drivers must take a 30-minute break. If there are no passengers, the time is increased to 11 hours (choice C). They can work (but not all under driving time) for 14 hours a day (choice D). This includes wait times, loading, and unloading.

16. **The correct answer is C.** In wet or slippery conditions, the front tire tread should be a minimum of 4/32-inches. 2/32-inch (choice A) is the minimum tread for the rear tires. 3/32-inch (choice B) and 6/32-inch (choice D) are not depths used for specific weather conditions.

17. **The correct answer is B.** 0.04% BAC is the legal limit for someone operating a commercial vehicle. 0.02% (choice A) is the BAC after one drink for most adults. 0.06% (choice C) is the BAC for most adults after 3 drinks. 0.08% (choice D) is the legal BAC limit in most states for drivers operating private vehicles.

18. **The correct answer is C.** Sealed cargo coming from a ship-based transport service should always be checked for verified weight. Sealed cargo does not always allow for the driver to check for leaks (choice B) or proper content (choice A). Depending on what is being transported, it may or may not have a smell (choice D).

19. **The correct answer is B.** Tie downs do not need to be placed that closely together, but should be spaced out every 10 feet, unless the cargo is under 10 feet in which case 2 tie downs are required, regardless of length.

20. **The correct answer is C.** There are 9 classes of hazardous materials.

21. **The correct answer is A.** Always turning the wheel the opposite direction of the trailer will ensure it moves the necessary direction. If you turn the wheel the same direction (choice D) it will go the wrong way. Although the correct way may be to the right (choice B) or left (choice C) this is not always the case depending on where it needs to go.

22. **The correct answer is A.** Vision should be focused 12–15 seconds or ¼ mile ahead.

23. **The correct answer is B.** Reflective triangles must be put out within 10 minutes of pulling over onto the side of the road. Thirty minutes (choice A) is too long and may not give those passing by enough notice of the presence of a commercial vehicle on the side of the road. While they can be placed earlier at 2 minutes (choice D) and 5 minutes (choice C), this is not required by law.

24. **The correct answer is A.** At least 2 tie-downs must be used at all times, even if the load is shorter. This provides back up should the original tie-down break.

25. **The correct answer is D.** To get out of a skid, a driver should remove their foot from the brake and allow the wheels to roll freely. Accelerating (choice A), braking (choice B), and steering (choice C) can all aggravate a skid.

26. **The correct answer is A.** A Class B license does permit the driver to operate both Class B and Class C vehicles but does not allow them to operate a Class A vehicle.

27. **The correct answer is C.** When driving in excessively hot weather, the tires should be inspected every 2 hours or 100 miles, whichever comes first. Every 4 hours (choice A) is too infrequent and can increase the likelihood of a blowout. Every 2 hours or 120 miles (choice B) is not quite frequent enough from a mileage perspective. Every hour (choice D) is more frequent than necessary.

28. **The correct answer is A.** The post-trip report should always be reviewed during the first step of the pre-trip inspection. This alerts the driver to any problems that arose during the last trip so they can verify they have been rectified during their own inspection. Step 7 (choice B) is too late as the vehicle is in motion. Step 3 (choice C) focuses on the inside of the cab and is not the time to review the report. Step 5 (choice D) involves walking around the vehicle, which should occur after the post-trip report has been reviewed.

29. **The correct answer is B.** The maximum vehicle width allowed in most states is 102 inches, or 8 feet 6 inches. 96 inches (choice A) is not the maximum width. 108 inches (choice C) is allowed on certain roads in specific states. 114 inches (choice D) is too wide on all roads.

30. **The correct answer is C.** The maximum vehicle height allowed in most states is 13 feet 6 inches. 12 feet 6 inches (choice A) and 13 feet (choice B) are both below the maximum height. 14 feet (choice D) is above the legal limit.

31. **The correct answer is B.** The driver should not open the trailer as this will add oxygen to the fire. Knowing what is in the trailer can help a driver determine if opening it is warranted and can help with selecting and using the correct fire extinguisher.

32. **The correct answer is C.** Feeling hot is not a sign of driver fatigue. Excessive blinking (choice A), yawning (choice B), and drifting lanes (choice D) are all signs of driver fatigue.

33. **The correct answer is C.** On a one-way or divided highway, the signals should be placed at 10, 100, and 200 feet toward the oncoming traffic. Choices A and B are too small and do not provide enough

forewarning to other drivers. Choice D includes unnecessarily long distances.

34. **The correct answer is B.** The best way to alert other drivers of hazards ahead is by lightly tapping on the brake pedal and flashing the brake lights. Pulling over (choice A), changing lanes (choice B), and slamming on the brakes (choice D) are not effective ways of communicating with other drivers about an upcoming hazard.

35. **The correct answer is B.** Rather than completing a right turn using the jug handle method, complete a right turn using the button hook method to avoid confusing nearby drivers. Choices A, C, and D are all true regarding turning in a commercial vehicle.

36. **The correct answer is C.** It is best practice to reduce speed by at least ⅓ in low visibility conditions, perhaps slower, depending on how far ahead you can see. Decreasing speed by one-fifth (choice A) or one-fourth (choice B) will likely not allow you enough space to brake. Decreasing speed by half (choice D) may be reasonable given how far ahead you are able to see, but it is not always necessary.

37. **The correct answer is A.** Following an accident, it is not necessary to ensure safety of cargo. However, protecting the area (choice B), notifying the authorities (choice C), and caring for the injured (choice D) are all necessary steps.

38. **The correct answer is D.** Gross Vehicle Weight, or GVW, is the term for the true weight of a vehicle including its load. Gross Vehicle Weight Rating, or GWVR (choice A), is the term for the maximum weight rating for a vehicle, including its load. GCW (choice B) and GCWR (choice C) are terms specifically related to combination vehicles.

39. **The correct answer is B.** A vehicle transporting hazardous material must have four identical placards: one on the front, one on the back, and one on each side. Choice A is an insufficient number, and choices C and D are higher numbers than necessary.

40. The correct answer is C. Creating placards and properly placing them on packages is the responsibility of the shipper, not the driver. Inspecting the cargo (choice A), recognizing overloads and poorly balanced weight (choice B), and ensuring the cargo is secure (choice D) are all responsibilities of the driver.

41. The correct answer is A. Headache racks, or header boards, protect the driver from cargo being thrown forward in an accident.

42. The correct answer is D. Dry bulk cargo (choice A) and livestock cargo (choice C) are not transported in refrigerated trailers. Refrigerated cargo (choice B) does not necessarily have a high center of gravity, so the only correct answer is choice D, hanging meat.

43. The correct answer is C. Oversized cargo is often restricted to certain times that it can be transported. Choices A, B, and D are all true regarding oversized cargo.

44. The correct answer is B. The best practice when moving livestock that does not completely fill the trailer is to insert a false bulkhead or temporary wall to keep the livestock packed together. While driving slowly to account for livestock movement (choice C) is common procedure, it is not specific to a partially full trailer.

45. The correct answer is D. Retarders should never be used when driving in wet conditions (choice A), icy conditions (choice B), or when the wheels have poor traction (choice C). Having the retarders on in any of these conditions could cause the wheels to skid.

46. The correct answer is A. The optimal hand positions on the wheel to prevent it from twisting out of grip are the nine o'clock and three o'clock positions.

47. The correct answer is B. A driver may simply reduce speed and observe the surroundings near a railroad or drawbridge when an individual is directing traffic (choice A), there is a green traffic light (choice C), or the railroad or bridge is not functioning or abandoned (choice D). However, vehicles carrying hazardous materials should always stop at least 50 feet from the start of a drawbridge.

48. The correct answer is B. In the case of an emergency or a fire, the driver should always take the shipping papers with them because the shipping papers contain information about what the cargo is, its dangers, and whom to contact during an emergency.

49. The correct answer is C. Dynamite (choice A), flares (choice B), and display fireworks (choice D) are all class 1 hazardous materials. Gasoline is a class 3 hazardous material.

50. The correct answer is D. Sealed or contained cargo is cargo that is partially transported via rail or ship. All other answer choices are true of covered cargo specifically.

CHAPTER

Air Brakes

AIR BRAKES

OVERVIEW

Exam Format

Requirements and Restrictions

Air Brake Components

Operation

Inspection and Safety

Summing It Up

Practice Test

Every driver that intends to use their commercial driver's license to drive a vehicle with air brakes must take the air brakes written test. The exam is commonly taken by drivers applying for a Class A or Class B license. Although there is no endorsement for using air brakes, failing or not completing the air brakes written test or taking the physical skills test in a vehicle without air brakes will place a restriction on your CDL. The following chapter provides details about the exam as well as a summary of air brake use and operation.

 NOTE

At the end of Chapter 4, you will find an Air Brakes Practice Test that will test your knowledge of the information contained in this chapter and better prepare you for the CDL air brakes test.

ALERT -

Questions from this section may also be included in the following endorsement exams: combination trailers, double and triple trailers, HazMat, and passenger transport.

EXAM FORMAT

The air brakes test is a written test that consists of 25 multiple-choice questions. To pass the exam, you must get at least 20 questions correct (80%). Topics covered include the following: operation and maintenance of air brake systems, air brake system components, different kinds of braking systems, driving conditions and brake usage, antilock brakes, and more.

Scheduling

It is common for drivers applying for their Class A or Class B license to take the air brakes written test as air brakes are common in such vehicle groups. As such, when scheduling or taking your written tests, you'll likely take the general knowledge, combination (for Class A), and air brakes tests at the same time. Taking the tests at the same time may reduce some testing fees and hasten the licensing process. Check with your local department of motor vehicles for more information on scheduling the exams.

REQUIREMENTS AND RESTRICTIONS

When applying for a commercial learner's permit and taking the requisite tests, you may be required to take the air brakes test. However, unless you plan to drive a vehicle equipped with full air brakes, it is not necessary to do so. The air brakes test is commonly required for Class A licenses and many, but not all, Class A vehicles are equipped with air brakes. Additionally, the same rules for CDL eligibility apply to this test, but state-specific requirements may vary. Check with your local DMV to assure that you are both eligible to take the test and required to do so for your intended use of the CDL.

This test allows a licensed CDL driver to operate a vehicle with air brakes. However, if a person fails the written test or is unable to take the skills test in a vehicle with air brakes, a restriction goes on the driver's CDL. Below is a summary of possible restriction codes related to air brakes:

RESTRICTION CODES	
L	If the air brakes test is not passed OR air brake system components not correctly identified OR air brake system check not completed OR the skills test is not taken in a vehicle with a full air brake system, drivers are not authorized to operate a vehicle with air brakes.
Z	Skills test taken with an air over hydraulic brake system. Drivers are not authorized to operate a CMV equipped with full air brakes.

To avoid a restriction, you then have four objectives:

1. Pass the air brakes written exam
2. Correctly identify all air brake system components
3. Perform an air brake system check
4. Pass the basic vehicle control and on-road skills test in a vehicle with a full air brakes system

AIR BRAKE COMPONENTS

It is important to have a basic understanding of the main components of air brakes as both the pre-trip inspection and safe operation of the air brakes system while driving rely on this knowledge. This section covers important components of an air brake system with attention to the following:

- Overview of the Commercial Truck Braking System
- Components of an Air Brake System
- Brakes at the Wheel Level
- Dual Air Brake System
- Inside the Cab

Overview of the Commercial Truck Braking System

The air brake system is three brake systems combined to ensure safety when operating a commercial vehicle. They are as follows:

SERVICE BRAKES
(ALSO CALLED THE AIR BRAKES)

These are the brakes that are engaged when the driver presses the brake pedal (also called the foot valve or treadle valve). They operate using air pressure.

PARKING BRAKE (LOCATED INSIDE THE CAB)

This is a button or lever that operates the emergency (spring) brakes when the air pressure is released and the vehicle is not in motion.

EMERGENCY BRAKES
(ALSO CALLED SPRING BRAKES)

These brakes are springs that are held back by the air pressure built up by the air brakes. When the air pressure drops too low (usually 20–40 psi) the springs are automatically released, causing the brakes to engage.

Components of an Air Brake System

Air brakes are a complex system. Understanding how the system operates is essential to safe operation. The following image provides an illustration of an air brake system along with descriptions of key components.

1. **Air Compressor:** This component is used to pump air into the reservoir tanks. It gains its power to pump by being connected to the engine through gears or a v-belt system. Some air compressors have their own oil supply, and the oil level should be checked regularly.

2. **Air Compressor Governor (not pictured):** This component regulates when the air compressor will begin or stop pumping air into the reservoirs. The governor's "cut-out" (stop pumping) limit is around 125 psi, and the "cut-in" (begin pumping) is when pressure falls below 100 psi.

3. **Air Storage Tanks/Reservoirs:** These components are the storage reservoirs for the compressed air that comes from the air compressor.

4. **Low Air Pressure Warning:** This component is found in the cab of the vehicle and alerts the driver when there is low pressure in the air braking system. Warnings will begin when psi drops to a range below 60 psi, and the parking brake and tractor protection valves will fail and pop between 45 and 20 psi. The warning system will lock up the brakes when the parking brake and tractor protection valves pop out.

5. **Safety Valve:** This component is located on the first air tank that receives air from the compressor. Its main function is to protect the air tank and the rest of the system from becoming overpressurized. The standard pressure that opens the valve and releases air is 150 psi.

6. **Supply Pressure Gauge:** This component directly reports the amount of pressure in the air tanks.

7. **Application Pressure Gauge (not pictured):** This component directly reports the amount of air pressure being applied to the air brakes. They are not found on all vehicles, but if you have one then it will aid you in knowing if your brakes are

Air Brake System Components and Location

(single circuit system)

1. Air Compressor
2. Air Compressor Governor
3. Air Storage Tanks/Reservoirs
4. Low Air Pressure Warning
5. Safety Valve
6. Supply Pressure Gauge
7. Application Pressure Gauge (not pictured)
8. Tractor Protection Valve
9. Spring Brakes
10. Air Tank Drains
11. Alcohol Evaporator (not pictured)
12. Foundation Brakes
13. Brake Pedal (Foot Valve)
14. Dual Parking Control Valve (not pictured)

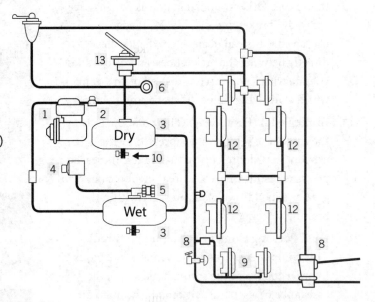

operating correctly. If you need to increase pressure to keep the same speed, then something may be wrong with your braking system.

8. **Tractor Protection Valve:** This component provides air supply and will close automatically if the supply drops when driving. The trailer protection valve will also automatically close when the parking brake is engaged.

9. **Spring Brakes:** This component is also known as an emergency brake or parking brake. Air pressure holds back powerful springs in these air braking vehicles, and if the driver engages the spring brakes or there is a leak in the air brake system, then the springs will put on the brakes as the air is no longer holding them back. Spring brakes generally fully come on when the air pressure decreases to a range of 20–45 psi. If the pressure is low, a low pressure warning light will turn on (around 60 psi) and the system will buzz, indicating that the vehicle needs to be brought to a safe stop while the driver still has control of the brakes.

10. **Air Tank Drains:** These components are used to drain the water and oil that occur within an air-compressed system. It is important that these liquids be drained because they can cause damage to the air brake system. There are two kinds of draining valves: manual drains and automatic drains, and both need to be used to drain the tanks daily. Manual drains are quarter turned to drain the tank.

11. **Alcohol Evaporator (not pictured):** This component is used to introduce alcohol into the air brake system to try to prevent ice buildup. Alcohol levels should be checked daily, especially in cold weather. However, the use of an alcohol evaporator does not negate the need to drain air tanks daily. If present, the alcohol evaporator is found between the compressor and supply air tank.

12. **Foundation Brakes:** This component is located on each wheel and is commonly of the s-cam drum brake variety. Engaging the s-cam drum brakes allows air to fill the brake chambers and push the rod out, which moves the slack adjuster and turns

the brake camshaft. This then turns the s-cam and forces the brake shoes apart and into the inside of the brake drum, causing friction to slow the wheels. Other foundation brakes you may see are wedge brakes and disc brakes. Wedge brakes use a wedge instead of an s-cam that pushes directly between the brake shoes, and disc brakes operate with a power screw instead of an s-cam, which clamps the caliper liners around the rotor.

13. **Brake Pedal (Foot Valve):** This component is in the cab of the vehicle and is pressed by the driver's foot in order to engage the brakes. Increased pressure results in greater breaking force but also greater expenditure of air pressure within the braking system.

14. **Dual Parking Control Valve (not pictured):** This component is found on vehicles like buses in order to release the spring brakes with the assistance of a separate air tank if the main air pressure is low, allowing you to move in an emergency. Engaging the valve (whether push-pull or spring loaded to stay out) will cause air to rush in and release the spring brakes.

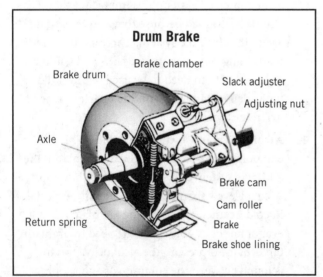

Drum Brake

Brake chamber
Brake drum
Slack adjuster
Adjusting nut
Axle
Brake cam
Cam roller
Return spring
Brake
Brake shoe lining

Source: California Commercial Driver Handbook, Figure 5.2

Brakes at the Wheel Level

At the wheel level, there are several key components in a drum brake that function as part of an air brakes system:

BRAKE CHAMBER

When the brake pedal is pushed, air enters the brake chamber.

SLACK ADJUSTER

The air pressure from the brake chamber moves the slack adjuster. Although most brake systems since 1994 have automatic slack adjusters, if necessary, a driver can reduce the slack manually if it becomes to loose.

CAMSHAFT

As the slack adjuster moves, it turns the camshaft.

BRAKE CAM (S-CAM)

The brake cam, which can be in an S shape, is responsible for pushing the brake shoes away from each other and up against the inside of the brake drum.

BRAKE SHOES AND LININGS

As the s-cam turns, the brake shoes separate and create friction with the inside of the brake drum, thus decreasing speed. As the brake pedal is released and air leaves the brake chamber, the s-cam returns to its original position, allowing the return spring to pull the brake shoes away from the drum.

Dual Air Brake System

Many newer vehicles will utilize a dual brake system in which two individual systems are run by the same universal brake controls. Oftentimes these dual systems are split between the axles of the vehicle. They are divided into subsections that operate the front and the back, which greatly reduces the likelihood of total brake failure as both systems or the air compressor would have to fail.

Inside the Cab

There are several components related to the air brakes system that are located inside the cab, including the following:

STOP LIGHT SWITCH

This component is an electrical switch that turns on the brake lights when the air brakes are engaged in order to notify those behind the vehicle that it is braking.

SUPPLY PRESSURE GAUGES

This component is found in the cab of the truck and directly reports the pressure within the air tank. Dual air brake systems will either have two gauges for each half of the system or two needles within one gauge.

LOW AIR PRESSURE WARNING DEVICES

Depending on the age of the vehicle, different devices will be used to signal low air pressure within the air brakes system, including modern lighting systems and, in older vehicles, drop arm "wig-wags" that fall into a driver's field of view.

OPERATION

Air brakes are used on heavy vehicles because hydraulic brakes do not offer the same amount of stopping power for a vehicle of immense size and weight. Air brakes work by building up air pressure to engage the brakes in the drum or discs. Understanding how air brakes operate is essential to proper use. This section will cover some main components of air brake operation:

- How Air Brakes Work
- Types of Braking
- Antilock Braking Systems (ABS)
- Stopping Distance

How Air Brakes Work

The following is a simple breakdown of how air brakes work:

 By pressing the brake pedal, the brake chambers are pressurized, thus actuating the braking mechanism. When released, this air pressure leaves the system. The air compressor governor monitors air pressure and activates the air compressor to generate more, thus filling the reservoirs and replacing any air lost in the emergency or service lines. Every time the brake pedal is pressed, this process repeats. This process happens quickly, and the goal is to have the pressure build from 85 psi to 100 psi within 45 seconds.

 The optimal pressure is between 100 and 125 psi. The air compressor will continue to push air into the lines until this range is reached (when the air compressor governor will indicate cut-out). Even if the driver continues to pump the brakes, the governor will max out at 135 psi in most commercial vehicles.

 The air pressure is then constantly monitored by the pressure gauge, ensuring the pressure always stays above 60 psi. Should it drop below this, the Low Air Warning system will begin signaling. If the pressure drops dangerously low (between 20–40 psi), the emergency (spring) brakes will automatically engage. In a vehicle with a dual parking control valve, the operator would be able to move the vehicle for emergency situations.

Types of Braking

Various types of braking operation exist and can be utilized to fit the demands of a situation. Let's examine two different methods: controlled braking and stab braking.

Controlled braking is braking as hard as possible without locking the wheels up. Throughout controlled braking you should only make very small steering adjustments, and if a large adjustment must be made then release the brakes. It is also important to release the brake right before coming to a complete stop to allow the suspension to settle over the chassis before reengaging the brakes and coming to a full stop. This is called a defensive stop and will decrease the jerking often caused by long braking.

Stab braking is applying the brakes hard enough to lock the wheels, releasing the brakes to let the wheels roll free, and braking hard again. It can take a second or so for the wheels to start rolling again, so make sure they are rolling before braking or else the vehicle will not gain a straightened correction. This type of braking is often used when there is a need for quick stopping, such as a drop in pressure, a possible collision, or steep downgrades.

Antilock Braking System (ABS)

An antilock braking system (ABS) allows for better control when braking on hazardous surfaces such as slippery roads. ABS does not brake a vehicle faster or increase braking power and should never be used as an excuse to drive dangerously. ABS utilizes components such as Electronic Control Units (ECUs) and speed sensors for the wheels to assist in braking so that the wheels do not lock up. If ABS is not working properly, the brakes or air braking system will still function the same on the vehicle, but you will not have assistance on hazardous surfaces.

When first starting a vehicle, you will notice an ABS light in the dash illuminated for a moment. If the light remains on, then the ABS is not functioning properly and needs attention. If the light is blinking in a pattern, take note of that pattern. Blinking patterns can be identified by mechanics to pinpoint the problem.

A trailer can also have its own ABS. The dashboard light equivalent for trailers come in the form of a yellow light/lamp on the left side of the trailer either in the front or (most commonly) back. This light should operate the same as the dashboard light of the vehicle. However, if the trailer is older the light may continue to be on until the trailer reaches a speed of around 5 mph.

Stopping Distance

A driver's stopping distance is the time it takes a driver to recognize the need to stop and to physically stop the vehicle from moving. Stopping distance can be impacted by driver awareness, road conditions, and successful operation of brakes. Drivers should be able to calculate their stopping distance in any driving situation to avoid collision and to successfully operate their motor vehicle. This section will cover the following:

- Understanding the Stopping Distance Formula
- Brake Lag

 NOTE -

When driving in wet conditions, lightly brake sooner than you would in normal conditions. The light pressure being applied to the brakes will create enough friction to help warm and dry the brakes before you begin to apply normal braking pressure, which will decrease the likelihood of the brakes slipping.

Understanding the Stopping Distance Formula

The following is the stopping distance formula:

Perception Distance + Reaction Distance + Braking Distance = Total Stopping Distance

This formula is used to determine the stopping distance needed at different speeds. Let's look at each part to better understand the total stopping distance.

- **Perception Distance:** This is distance traveled during the time a driver's eyes see a hazard until the brain recognizes it.

- **Reaction Distance:** The distance traveled during the time it takes a driver's foot to react after the brain recognizes the hazard. Driver reaction times vary significantly, but the following figures approximate it at about 0.75-1 second.

- **Braking Distance:** This is the distance traveled from the time the brake is engaged to the time it takes to come to a complete stop. Braking distance increases directly with increased speed. Increasing speed from 20 mph to 40 mph would increase braking distance by a factor of four.

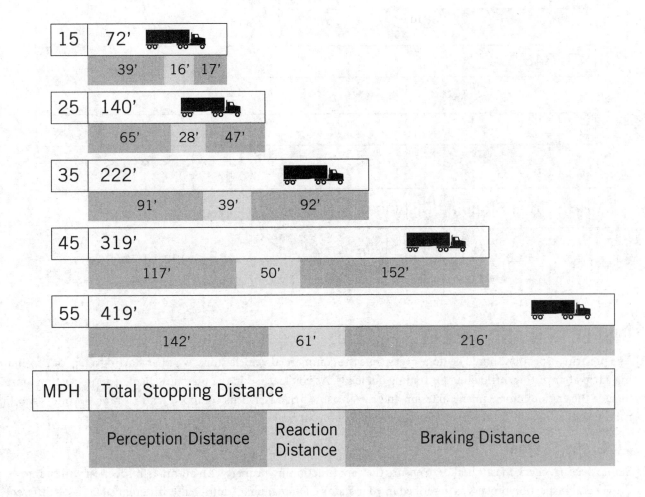

Brake Lag

In addition to stopping distance, you should also be aware of brake lag. Vehicles with air brakes suffer a delay from when the brake pedal is depressed to when the brakes engage. Brake lag ranges from 0.4 seconds to 1 second. At a speed of 55 mph, if estimated as 0.4 seconds, brake lag accounts for approximately 32 feet in additional stopping distance.

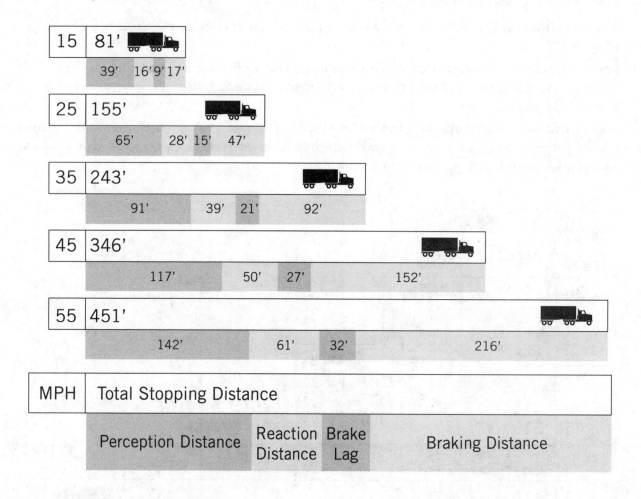

MPH	Total Stopping Distance			
15	81'	39'	16' 9' 17'	
25	155'	65'	28' 15'	47'
35	243'	91'	39' 21'	92'
45	346'	117'	50' 27'	152'
55	451'	142'	61' 32'	216'
		Perception Distance	Reaction Distance / Brake Lag	Braking Distance

INSPECTION AND SAFETY

The pre-trip inspection should be done every time the commercial vehicle stops, whether starting a trip or continuing a trip after resting, offloading, or trading out loads. As you learned in the previous chapter, an inspection must include the engine compartment, exterior, and cab areas. When a vehicle is equipped with air brakes, your inspection routine will change to incorporate specific elements of the air brakes system.

Air Brake System

Before driving, check the air brakes to ensure they are functioning properly. An air brake inspection will fit into the general inspection process as described in your state's CDL manual. Additionally, different states have different requirements for checking and maintaining air brakes, so read your state CDL manual for further details on each point. Otherwise, here are some general points of inspection for air brake systems:

- Secure wheel chocks and build wheel air pressure to 100 psi.
- Examine air tanks.
- Manually drain the air tanks on a daily basis or, if needed, again when inspecting. This applies to older vehicles without automatic drain valves, though automatic valves should still drain daily and receive inspection.
- Examine the foundational brake components, including shoe/drum contact and shoe condition, contamination, and thickness.
- Check the brake chambers, ensuring that the size matches on both sides and the pushrod is attached at the same hole on both sides.
- Inspect air lines and tubing, ensuring they are connected at all necessary points. Pay special attention to hanging lines or tubing.
- Check the air compressor. If it has a belt (older units), ensure it has proper tension.
- Examine the air compressor governor.

Vehicle Cab

The focus of the inspection once inside the vehicle is on the operation of the brakes. This can be divided into the following areas:

- Governor (minimum and maximum pressure)
- Low Air Warning (visible and audible)
- Automatic Engagement of Emergency Brakes
- Build Up (Compressor)
- Air Leakage Rate

A comprehensive inspection can be completed by starting with the first part and working through all five areas. A driver must ensure the brake safety and hit every inspection requirement during the physical skills test. The following is an overview of the air brake operation inspection process. Refer to your CDL manual for how these steps fit into a general vehicle inspection.

- Before starting, make sure the wheel chocks are in place, the engine is running, and the parking brake is released.

- Test Governor: Pump down to 85–90 psi, throttle up, and then verify that the governor cuts-in and the needle shows the pressure rising.
- Low Air Warning: Pump down until low air warning system sounds (usually 60 psi). This can be an audible alarm and a button releasing or a wig-wag colored paddle in older vehicles.
- Emergency Brakes Engage: Continue to pump down to 20–40 psi; the emergency brakes (spring brakes) should engage automatically.
- Air Pressure Build up (Compressor): Now that the pressure is low, the brakes should build from 50–90psi at a high idle (1,000–1,200 rpm) in 3 minutes. As it rises above 60 psi, the Low Air Warning should also turn off.
- Air Leakage Rate (Air Loss): After the three minutes, allow the system to build to maximum pressure (usually 125 psi). If the system has an air dryer, do not rely on it purging for an indication that the system is at maximum pressure. Check the gauge for the pressure level as well as a stationary needle. Parking brakes are off. Make a full brake application for the full minute. A loss of 3 psi shows a possible leak. If you have a combination vehicle with one trailer, the allowable loss is 3 psi. In the cab, check the governor (minimum and maximum pressure), low air warning (visible and audible), automatic engagement of emergency brakes, build up (compressor), and air leakage rate.

SUMMING IT UP

- Drivers applying for their commercial driver's license who plan to drive vehicles equipped with air brakes must air brakes test and drive a vehicle equipped with air brakes during the physical skills test. Although there is no endorsement for using air brakes, not passing the air brakes test will place a restriction on your license.

- The air brakes test is a written test that consists of 25 multiple-choice questions. To pass the exam, you must get at least 20 questions correct (80%).

- It is important to have a basic understanding of the main components of air brakes as both pre-trip inspections and safe operation while driving rely on this knowledge.

- An air brake system is three brake systems combined to ensure safety when operating a commercial vehicle: service brakes (air brakes), parking brakes, and emergency brakes (spring brakes).

- Air brakes are a mechanically complex system. Understanding how the system operates is essential to safe operation. Be able to identify and express understanding of the following components: air compressor, air compressor governor, air storage tanks/reservoirs, low air pressure warning, safety valve, supply pressure gauge, application pressure gauge, tractor protection valve, spring brakes, air tank drains, alcohol evaporator, foundation brakes, brake pedal (foot valve), and dual parking control valve.

- At the wheel level, it is important to know the appearance and function of the brake chamber, slack adjuster, camshaft, s-cam, and brake shoes.

- Many newer vehicles will utilize a dual air brake system, which each have their own individual systems but are run by the same universal brake controls.

- Inside the cab, it is important to know the location and function of the stop light switch, supply pressure gauges, and Low Air Warning system.

- Air brakes work by building up air pressure to engage the brakes in the drum or discs. Understanding how air brakes operate is essential to proper use.

  o The goal is to have the pressure build from 85 psi (pounds per square inch) to 100 psi within 45 seconds. The optimal psi is between 100 and 125 psi. These values may vary by manufacturer.

  o Should the pressure drop below 60 psi, the Low Air Warning system will begin signaling. If the pressure drops between 20–40 psi, the emergency brakes will automatically engage.

- Controlled braking is braking as hard as possible without locking the wheels up. Stab braking is applying the brakes hard enough to lock the wheels, releasing the brakes to let the wheels roll free, and braking hard again.

- An antilock braking system (ABS) allows for better control when braking on hazardous surfaces such as slippery roads.

- A driver's stopping distance is the time it takes a driver to recognize the need to stop and to physically stop the vehicle from moving. To calculate stopping distance, use this formula:

  o Perception Distance + Reaction Distance + Braking Distance = Total Stopping Distance

- Brake lag is the delay from when the brake pedal is pressed to when air brakes engage. Brake lag can be from 0.4 to 1 second.

- Before driving, check the air brakes to make sure they are functioning properly.

- Check the foundational brake components, brake chambers, air lines and tubing, air tanks, air compressor, and air compressor governor and verify that they are secure, undamaged, and not leaking.

AIR BRAKES PRACTICE TEST

25 Questions—60 Minutes

> **Directions:** This test consists of a combination of true/false and multiple-choice questions. Only one answer is correct for each question.

1. All of the following elements are part of the air brake system EXCEPT:

   A. Service brakes

   B. Parking brake

   C. Emergency brakes

   D. Automatic brakes

2. The parking brake is located inside the cab.

   A. True

   B. False

3. Which of the following is NOT true of stab braking?

   A. It is often used when there is a need for quick stopping, such as a steep downgrade.

   B. It entails applying the brakes hard enough to lock the wheels, releasing the brakes, and then braking hard again.

   C. It is important to release the brake right before coming to a complete stop.

   D. The wheels must be rolling before braking again in order to get a straightened correction.

4. Which component tells the air compressor to send air into the lines?

   A. Application pressure gauge

   B. Air compressor governor

   C. Foot valve

   D. Safety valve

5. What should be corrected if the brakes are not calibrated correctly?

   A. S-cam brake

   B. Air compressor

   C. Slack adjuster

   D. Brake drum

6. Another term for the foot valve is the brake pedal.

   A. True

   B. False

7. Where does the air go after being released by the air compressor?

   A. The air compressor governor

   B. The service lines

   C. The air storage tank

   D. The air tank drain

8. The Low Warning System triggers when the air pressure is

   A. between 20 and 40 psi.

   B. at or below 60 psi.

   C. between 80 and 100 psi.

   D. over 135 psi.

9. Stab braking is when the driver presses firmly to engage the brakes without locking them.

   A. True

   B. False

10. Stopping distance is the same as braking distance.

    A. True

    B. False

11. The braking distance of a CMV traveling at 55 miles per hour is

    A. 451 feet.

    B. 419 feet.

    C. 216 feet.

    D. 32 feet.

12. The brake lag for a CMV going 55 mph is

    A. 27 feet.

    B. 32 feet.

    C. 61 feet.

    D. 142 feet.

13. All commercial trucks have belt-driven air compressors.

    A. True

    B. False

14. To check that the emergency brakes engage, the air pressure must be

    A. 85–100 psi.

    B. 25–40 psi.

    C. 60 psi.

    D. over 125 psi.

15. If the air pressure drops 3 psi in a minute in a single vehicle, it has failed the air leak rate test.

    A. True

    B. False

16. The brake pedal is also known as the foot valve and the compressor valve.

    A. True

    B. False

17. For a vehicle with s-cam brakes, a slack adjuster uses

    A. the space between the rear wheels to adjust the brakes.

    B. the adjusting nut under the cab to adjust the springs.

    C. the power screw to clamp the disc or rotor.

    D. the adjusting nut on the rear side of the brake drum to adjust the brakes.

18. All vehicles that have automatic slack adjusters have been built since

    A. 1992.

    B. 1994.

    C. 1998.

    D. 2001.

19. If using the controlled braking method, a driver should keep steering wheel actions very small.

    A. True

    B. False

20. The low-pressure gauge will signal when the air pressure is at

    A. 150 psi.

    B. 125 psi.

    C. 100 psi.

    D. 60 psi.

21. Although the hydraulic brakes for cars and light/medium trucks work instantly, it takes trucks with air brakes a bit more time, one third of a second or more, for air to move through the lines to the brakes.

    A. True

    B. False

22. The need for increased air pressure can be caused by all of these EXCEPT:

    A. Brakes that are not properly adjusted

    B. Air that is escaping

    C. Front wheel braking

    D. Mechanical matters

23. With a manual air tank, the oil and water are ejected by turning the drain valve a half turn.

    A. True

    B. False

24. The right way to slow down a vehicle on long downgrades is to

    A. hold the brakes firmly.

    B. use exhaust braking.

    C. use controlled braking.

    D. use a low gear while driving slowly.

25. Automatic slack adjusters should not be manually adjusted.

    A. True

    B. False

ANSWER KEY AND EXPLANATIONS

1. D	6. A	11. C	16. B	21. B
2. A	7. C	12. B	17. D	22. C
3. C	8. B	13. B	18. B	23. B
4. B	9. B	14. B	19. A	24. D
5. C	10. B	15. A	20. D	25. A

1. **The correct answer is D.** The air brake system is composed of the service brakes, the parking brake, and the emergency brake. Automatic brakes are not inherently part of the system.

2. **The correct answer is A.** The parking brake is always located inside the cab. It is a button or lever that operates the emergency brakes.

3. **The correct answer is C.** Releasing the brake right before coming to a complete stop is an important part of controlled braking, not stab braking. The statements in choices A, B, and D are all true of stab braking.

4. **The correct answer is B.** The air compressor governor tells the air compressor to send air whenever the psi falls around or below 100. The application pressure gauge (choice A) reports the amount of pressure being applied to the brakes. The foot valve (choice C) is another term for the brake pedal. The safety valve (choice D) is on the first air tank and protects the system from being over-pressured.

5. **The correct answer is C.** The slack adjuster on older vehicles can be manually adjusted if the brakes are not calibrated correctly. The s-cam brake (choice A) cannot be adjusted for proper calibration. The brake drum (choice D) is also not part of the brake calibration process. The air compressor (choice B) is not part of the brake construction.

6. **The correct answer is A.** The foot valve is another term for the brake pedal.

7. **The correct answer is C.** The air storage tank, also called the reservoir, receives the air being pumped out by the air compressor. The air compressor governor (choice A) signals the need for more air. The service lines (choice B) receive the air from the reservoir. The air tank drain (choice D) catches the moisture generated while driving.

8. **The correct answer is B.** The Low Warning System triggers when the air pressure is at or below 60 psi. When the pressure is between 20 and 40 psi (choice A), the emergency brakes are engaged. Between 80 and 100 psi (choice C) is the acceptable rate when driving. Over 135 psi (choice D) is unlikely as the maximum pressure usually caps at this point.

9. **The correct answer is B.** Stab braking is when the driver presses firmly enough to lock the brakes, then releases until the wheels start moving again, repeating as needed to stop completely in an emergency.

10. **The correct answer is B.** Stopping distance is the combination of perception distance + reaction distance + braking distance.

11. **The correct answer is C.** The braking distance of a CMV traveling at 55 miles per hour is 216 feet. 451 feet (choice A) is the total stopping distance including the brake lag. The total stopping distance without brake lag is 419 feet (choice B). 32 feet (choice D) is the brake lag for the same vehicle.

12. **The correct answer is A.** The brake lag for a CMV going 55 mph is 32 feet. 27 feet (choice A) is the brake lag at a speed of 45 mph. 61 feet (choice C) is the reaction distance at 55 mph. 142 feet (choice D) is the perception distance at the same speed.

13. **The correct answer is B.** Newer commercial vehicles do not have belt-driven air compressors, but they will commonly have gear-driven air compressors.

14. **The correct answer is B.** The emergency brakes should engage when the air pressure is between 25–40 psi. 85–100 psi (choice A) is normal operating levels. 60 psi (choice C) initiates a low warning system. Over 125 psi (choice D) is usually improbable as this is the upper range that the air compressor governor will allow.

15. **The correct answer is A.** For a single vehicle, the air leak rate must not be equal to or higher than 3 psi.

16. **The correct answer is B.** The brake pedal is also known as the foot valve and the treadle valve.

17. **The correct answer is D.** The slack adjuster uses an adjusting nut on the rear side of the brake drum to adjust the brakes. Therefore, it does not use the space between the rear wheels to adjust the brakes (choice A), nor the adjusting nut under the cab to adjust the springs (choice B). Disc brakes, not s-cam brakes, have a power screw to clamp the disc or rotor between the brake lining pads of a caliper (choice C).

18. **The correct answer is B.** All vehicles that have been built since 1994 have automatic slack adjusters. Consequently, the automatic slack adjusters were not built in 1992 (choice A) nor in 2001 (choice D). A driver can tell that a vehicle is equipped with antilock brakes if it is manufactured after 1998 (choice C).

19. **The correct answer is A.** Since the controlled braking method requires drivers to apply the brakes as firmly as possible without locking the wheels, the driver should then keep the steering wheel actions very small.

20. **The correct answer is D.** No matter if the vehicle has a single or dual air brake system, if any air pressure gauge reads below 60 psi, the warning device will signal the low air pressure, even if the second system is fully charged. The safety valve is usually set to reduce air pressure at 150 psi (choice A). The air compressor should stop pumping at about 125 psi (choice B). The air compressor should start pumping at about 100 psi (choice C).

21. **The correct answer is B.** Although the hydraulic brakes for cars and light/medium trucks work instantly, it takes trucks with air brakes a bit more time, one half second or more, for air to move through the lines to the brakes.

22. **The correct answer is C.** Since front wheel braking is effective under all conditions, it does not have a need for increased pressure. However, the need for increased pressure can be caused by brakes that are not properly adjusted (choice A), air that is escaping (choice B), and mechanical matters (choice D).

23. **The correct answer is B.** The drain valve should be quarter turned when a manual air tank is ejecting the oil and water.

24. **The correct answer is D.** Since brakes can overheat on long downgrades, using a low gear while driving slowly is the right way to slow down the vehicle. Holding the brakes firmly (choice A) is done to test the service brakes and in normal use, not on long downgrades. Using exhaust braking (choice B) would hold the compression in the engine, thus stopping the vehicle, while engine braking releases the compressed air through an exhaust valve and slows the vehicle. Using controlled braking allows the driver to apply the brakes as hard as possible without locking the wheels (choice C), but it does allow the brakes to heat up with no way of cooling down.

25. **The correct answer is A.** Manually adjusting an automatic slack adjuster is dangerous and will not always solve the problem.

NOTES

CHAPTER

Combination Vehicles

COMBINATION VEHICLES

OVERVIEW

Exam Format

Endorsement Requirements

Inspections

Safety

Coupling and Uncoupling

Summing It Up

Practice Test

Combination vehicles are a varying group of trucks that all consist of a vehicle, which can be referred to as a truck or tractor, and a trailer. Any tractor that does not have a trailer attached to it is commonly called a bobtail. Due to the lack of a trailer, bobtails are not subjected to the same considerations associated with pulling a trailer.

 NOTE

At the end of Chapter 5, you will find a Combination Vehicles Practice Test that will test your knowledge of the information contained in this chapter and better prepare you for the CDL combination vehicles endorsement exam.

5

ALERT -

Make sure to study the General Knowledge, Air Brakes, and Double and Triple Trailers chapters as questions covering these topics will appear on the combination vehicles endorsement exam.

As the combination vehicles endorsement exam covers topics that involve a driver hauling a load using a combination of two or more vehicles and trailers, you'll be expected to demonstrate knowledge of operation of the following:

- Tractor-trailer combination
- Straight truck pulling a trailer
- Tractor with two or more trailers

EXAM FORMAT

The combination vehicles endorsement test is a written test that consists of 20 multiple-choice questions with a required pass rate of 16 correct questions (80%).

Scheduling

This exam is required for drivers applying for the CDL Class A license, so it does not require a separate scheduled time from the general knowledge test. Check with your local department of motor vehicles for more information on scheduling the exams.

ENDORSEMENT REQUIREMENTS

This endorsement requires test takers to be at least 18 years old (21 in Hawaii and New York). However, if transport includes crossing state lines, the driver must be 21. Check your local department of motor vehicles for further state-specific rules.

This endorsement allows a CDL driver to operate a vehicle with a combination of truck/tractor and trailers. Most Class A vehicles qualify as combination vehicles.

In addition, some Class B and Class C vehicles are also included if they are carrying an additional trailer behind the straight truck.

There is only one specific restriction code attached to the combination vehicle endorsement:

RESTRICTION CODES	
O	Skills test in Class A vehicles with a pintle hook or other non-fifth wheel connection. This prohibits the driver from driving a Class A vehicle with a fifth wheel connection.

To avoid an unwanted restriction code, you should complete your skills test in the vehicle that you intend to be driving when using your CDL. This may require planning with your CDL program or the company you intend to work with and a qualified driver who will accompany you to and from the skills test location.

INSPECTIONS

Inspections play a critical role in the proper operation of commercial vehicles. All commercial vehicles must be inspected before and after driving. Combination vehicles require additional inspection points because of the coupling that occurs between the truck and the trailer.

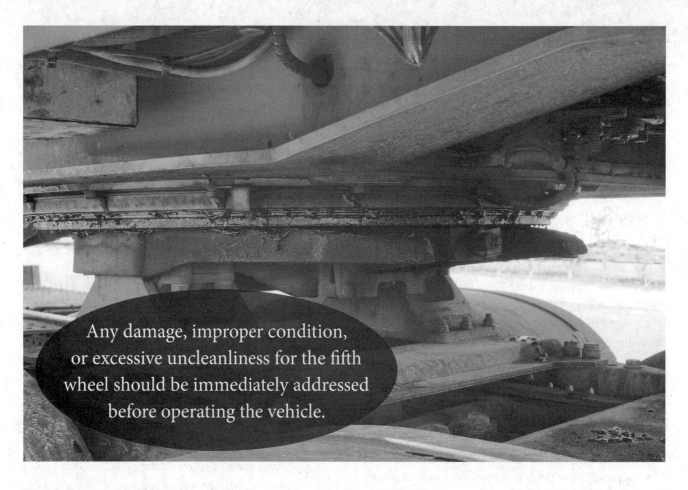

Any damage, improper condition, or excessive uncleanliness for the fifth wheel should be immediately addressed before operating the vehicle.

Coupling Systems

The coupling system between a truck and trailer, or trailer and trailer, must be properly maintained. Any damage, improper condition, or excessive uncleanliness for the fifth wheel should be immediately addressed before operating the vehicle. These conditions can cause the systems to falter or fail, which can cause loss of control or damage. Look for the following when inspecting the couplings:

- There is no visible space between the apron plate (upper fifth wheel) and lower fifth wheel skid plate.

- Lockjaws are firmly around the shank, not the kingpin head.

- The hose couplers (more commonly referred to as glad hands) properly attach the service and emergency lines from the tractor to the trailer, and they are in working order.

- The release arm is correctly in place, and the safety latch/lock is active.

- All air and electrical lines are properly mounted, connected, and free of damage. Air lines show no signs of leaks. Service line couplers are not always color coded, but if they are, they are blue. Emergency lines are red.

- The sliding fifth wheel is undamaged and properly greased.

- The fifth wheel has enough distance between it and the landing gear to avoid contact with the tractor when turning the vehicle.

- All lock pins are accounted for and locked into place.

- The shut-off valve at the back of the trailer is closed. If you are pulling more than one trailer, the shut-off valves of the trailers in front of the farthest back trailer are open with the farthest back trailer's valves closed.

Landing Gear

The landing gear should be fully raised, free of damage, and clean before driving. The crank handle should be secured in its proper storage position. If the landing gear is power operated, check for and address any air or hydraulic leaks.

Lights

There are several lights that are specifically added to trailers aside from the braking, turning, and reversing indicators that are on all vehicles. These special lights should always be in working order. When illuminated, they signify the following:

- A green light on the trailer means that all systems are working correctly.
- A red light on the trailer means that there is a problem with the coupling between the tractor and trailer.
- A yellow light on the trailer means that there is a problem with the antilock braking system (ABS).
- Orange lights are used to mark the edges of the trailer to help other drivers see it better at night.

Brakes

Air brakes are the main types of brakes that are used on combination vehicles. Air lines that run from the truck to the trailer(s) allow for the brakes to have pressure applied much faster than would be possible without them. If you are driving a combination vehicle, you must pass the air brakes endorsement as well; otherwise, the air brakes restriction will limit your vehicle class.

It is common and best practice to use wheel chocks when parking a combination vehicle with air brakes because not all trailers will have a parking brake (spring brakes) present. Never assume that a trailer has spring brakes, and always chock the wheels if you are unsure. Air brake checks specifically for combination vehicles include, but are not limited to, the following:

- Making sure the air is flowing to all trailers
- Testing that the trailer protection valve is working
- Testing that the trailer emergency brakes are working
- Testing that the trailer service brakes are working

SAFETY

Driving a combination vehicle takes more skill and knowledge than a standard straight truck because they are longer and heavier while also using multiple connections. Combination vehicles are at a higher risk of rollovers. On top of this, due to their size, combination vehicles can easily collide with other vehicles, buildings, and objects if proper vehicle awareness is not upheld. The following topics about safety are discussed in this section:

- Rollovers
- Steering
- Rearward Amplification
- Braking
- Trailer Skids
- Antilock Braking System (ABS)
- Following and Stopping Rates
- Railroad Crossings
- Turning Wide
- Backing Up

 NOTE

For more detailed information regarding inspections and checks, refer to the chapters on General Knowledge and Air Brakes or your state's CDL manual.

Rollovers

Rollovers are extremely dangerous accidents that result in the truck flipping onto its side, top, or even completely rolling over. They account for more than half of all truck driver deaths. Rollover prevention is a key concern for drivers. Consider the following rollover factors:

- Cargo shifts that change the center of gravity of a vehicle
- A higher center of gravity
- Increased speed in curves

To prevent rollovers, remember the following guidelines:

- Keep the center of gravity of your truck and trailer as low as possible by shifting the distribution of cargo
  - Stack cargo in the center of the trailer
  - Distribute the load at a low level before stacking

- Secure cargo to prevent shifting during transport
- Take curves slowly, well below the posted speeds
  - Keep in mind the distribution and height of your cargo when entering curves

Steering

The weight and length of the combination of truck and trailer makes steering more difficult. Steering too quickly or sharply can have a ripple effect for the trailers behind the tractor. Sudden steering can cause the weight of the cargo to shift rapidly, known as the *crack-the-whip* effect, leading to a rollover or trailer skid. This can affect the entire combination vehicle or just one or more trailers. The likelihood of this occurring increases based on the length of the vehicle.

Rearward Amplification

Rearward amplification refers to the compacted risk a vehicle has towards the crack-the-whip effect based on its overall length, number of pivot points and axles, and the length of the last trailer in the combination. To compensate for rearward amplification, the driver must pay attention to the total length of their combination vehicle and the number of axles in the combination. While longer vehicles tend to have greater rearward amplification, a driver must also keep in mind the length of the last trailer in the combination; shorter last trailers have a greater impact on the amount of rearward amplification (e.g. the California truck full trailer).

The following image shows the different combination types and the influence these combinations have on reward amplification. The numbers indicate how likely the last trailer is to roll over. For example, a rearward amplification of 1.5 means the trailer is 1.5 times more likely to roll over than the tractor it is connected to. A rearward amplification of 3.0 means the last trailer is 3 times more likely to roll over.

To limit the incidence of the crack-the-whip effect, avoid fast lane changes and quick turns. Always look ahead on the road and be prepared for any turns or lane changes that you see you will have to make. If visibility is low or conditions are slippery, slow the vehicle and let your turns and lane changes be even slower and more careful than normal.

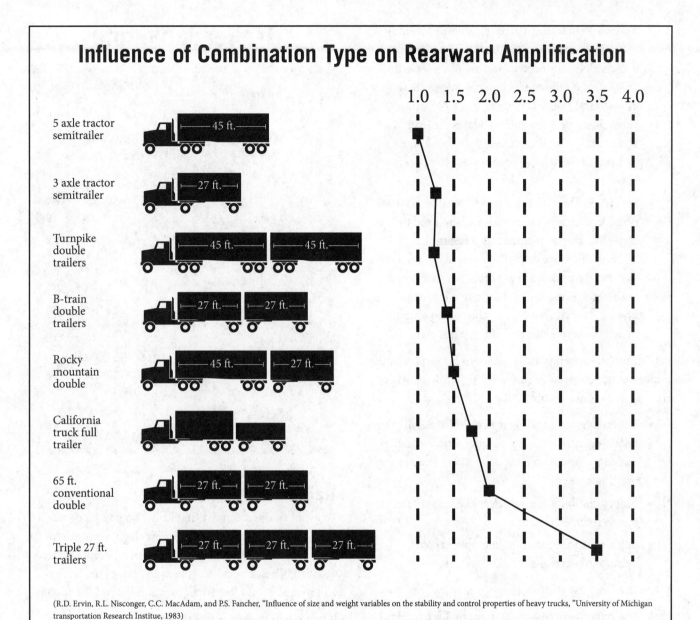

Influence of Combination Type on Rearward Amplification

5 axle tractor semitrailer — 45 ft.

3 axle tractor semitrailer — 27 ft.

Turnpike double trailers — 45 ft. | 45 ft.

B-train double trailers — 27 ft. | 27 ft.

Rocky mountain double — 45 ft. | 27 ft.

California truck full trailer

65 ft. conventional double — 27 ft. | 27 ft.

Triple 27 ft. trailers — 27 ft. | 27 ft. | 27 ft.

1.0 1.5 2.0 2.5 3.0 3.5 4.0

(R.D. Ervin, R.L. Nisconger, C.C. MacAdam, and P.S. Fancher, "Influence of size and weight variables on the stability and control properties of heavy trucks, "University of Michigan transportation Research Institue, 1983)

Braking

There are many components to the brakes in a combination vehicle, and they all have their own purposes. Using these components in an improper fashion can lead to accidents. Here is a list of common brake components you can find on your vehicle:

- **Parking Brake:** Used to lock the spring brakes on the vehicle when parked to keep the vehicle from moving. This is a yellow diamond knob on the vehicle's dashboard. Not all trailers, especially older ones, have spring brakes where the parking brake will not affect the trailer. In turn, never assume that it does, and always chock the wheels if unsure.

- **Trailer Hand Valve:** Also called the trolley valve or Johnson Bar, it is used to test the brakes on the trailer. This should never be used when driving or to replace the parking brake or service brakes. If it is used in place of the service brakes, it can cause the trailer to skid.

- **Tractor Protection Valve:** This keeps air in the brake system in case the trailer becomes detached, disconnected, or develops a leak. It is controlled by the red, octagonal trailer air supply knob found in the cab of the truck. When this valve closes or pops out, it releases air from the trailer and locks the brakes. This should not be used while driving or to replace the parking brake.

- **Service Brakes:** These are controlled by the foot pedal in the cab of the truck and are used to come to a stop while driving. The brake lights on the vehicle are directly connected to turn on when these brakes are engaged. Because service brakes need constant pressure to engage the brakes, they cannot replace the parking brake, which is operated by springs and not air.

In addition to knowing the function of important brake components, you need to consider the following when braking in a combination vehicle:

- Bobtails (tractors without a trailer attached) can take longer to brake than combination vehicles due to the lower amount of friction present in the braking system.

- Empty combination vehicles take longer to brake due to reduced traction.

- Skids are more common in empty vehicles because of decreased trailer traction.

When braking, use the following guidelines:

- Use only the necessary amount of force to brake and/or come to a stop while still being in control.

- As you brake, keep an eye on your truck and trailer and release the brakes if you need to gain traction back to correct a skid.

- Apply constant but even pressure as you brake.

Trailer Jackknife

Line of Travel

Trailer Wheels Locked-Up and Sliding

Trailer Skids

To avoid skids, you must first know how to recognize a skid. When you apply your brakes, check your mirrors. Your mirrors will reveal whether the trailer has entered a skid. This will be noticeable as the tail of the trailer will move beyond its proper location behind the tractor.

If you begin to skid, release the brakes. During a skid, using the brakes further will keep the wheels locked and continue the trailer skid. Releasing the brakes will enable you to force traction back to the trailer wheels. Do not use the trailer hand brake and do not try to steer or swerve with the trailer. Once the wheels have regained their traction, they will fall in line back behind the truck and will straighten themselves out. If the skid does not respond to correction and the trailer is significantly displaced from behind the tractor, it is likely that a trailer jackknife will ensue.

Antilock Braking System (ABS)

Antilock braking systems (ABS) are a current standard on trailers and converter dollies made after March 1, 1998. Many of the trailers and dollies made before this date have had ABS added to them along with the yellow ABS lights/lamps that are on the front or back left corners of the trailers. However, not all older vehicles with ABS added will have the indicator light. Important things to remember about ABS are as follows:

- ABS will not increase your stopping distance or braking power.
- ABS is meant to keep your wheels from locking, hence the "antilock" in its name.
- If the ABS is faulty, you can still drive as it does not affect your normal braking system.
- If the ABS is faulty, you need to have it looked at during your next stop.

Following and Stopping Rates

When trying to stop a combination vehicle, you must keep active awareness of adequate following and stopping rates. The values for the size and speed of your vehicle will inform the amount of space you should place between you and the vehicle in front of you. Use the following figures to calculate appropriate distances:

- If the vehicle is traveling at a speed of less than 40 mph, the calculation is 1 second per 10 feet of vehicle length.
- If the vehicle is traveling at a speed greater than 40 mph, the calculation is 1 second per 10 feet of vehicle length plus 1 extra second.
  - Example: If you are driving a 60-foot vehicle at a speed of 50 mph, it will take 7 seconds to stop—6 seconds based on the vehicle length plus one extra second. When driving in less than perfect conditions, especially wet or slippery ones, this stopping time can increase; begin braking sooner to compensate.

Railroad Crossings

Railroad crossings can pose a problem for combination vehicles if the vehicle has low underneath clearance (e.g., moving vans, livestock trailers, etc.). Drive carefully over crossings, and, if you are unsure of being able to cross them, try to find another route to avoid becoming stuck.

If you become stuck on a railroad crossing, immediately exit the vehicle and move away from the tracks. Seek out signal stations or signs with emergency notification numbers. Call 911 or any other appropriate emergency number and give them the location of the crossing using any available DOT numbers.

Turning Wide

Combination vehicles do not turn in the same manner as a standard straight vehicle because of *off-tracking*. Off-tracking refers to how the rear wheels on the trailer(s) do not follow the same line as the front wheels of the truck.

Because the rear wheels do not follow the line of the front tires, taking sharp turns too narrowly will cause the rear wheels to cut in early around the turn. This

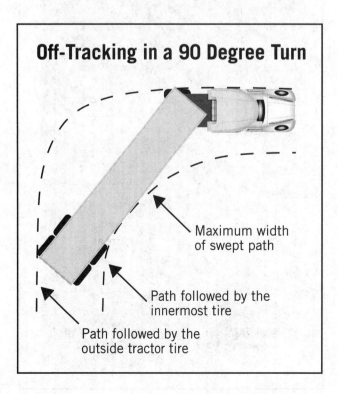

Off-Tracking in a 90 Degree Turn

Maximum width of swept path

Path followed by the innermost tire

Path followed by the outside tractor tire

means that if you are turning a street corner and do not turn wide enough, the back of the trailer can run up onto the corner of the street and hit the sidewalk or a structure near the road. If there is more than one trailer, the rear wheels of the farthest back trailer will off-track more than those closer to the tractor.

Backing Up

Backing up a trailer can be tricky as a trailer moves differently from a car or straight truck. The trailer will move in the opposite direction of the steering wheel when reversed. To avoid difficult maneuvers, when possible, try to position your vehicle so that you can back up in a straight line. If not possible, position your combination vehicle so that you can back up in a curved path towards the driver's side as this will increase your field of view. If possible, work with a spotter on the ground while backing up so that they can guide your positioning.

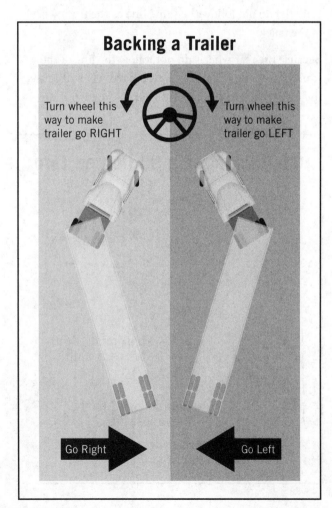

Backing a Trailer

Turn wheel this way to make trailer go RIGHT

Turn wheel this way to make trailer go LEFT

Go Right

Go Left

Those guidelines can help you prepare to back up, but be sure to use the following procedure whenever backing up a trailer:

- Look at your path.
- Check clearance near the vehicle and along the path.
- Use your mirrors on both sides of the vehicle.
- Reverse slowly.
- Correct any drifts immediately by turning the steering wheel in the directions of the drift.
- Pull forward to readjust as needed.

COUPLING AND UNCOUPLING

Combination vehicles come in many different variations, and the same level of variation applies to the ways in which these vehicles and their trailers are coupled and uncoupled. It is essential to have the knowledge of how to properly couple and uncouple combination vehicles to avoid dangerous driving situations. This section will cover the basic steps of coupling and uncoupling and some of the common coupling styles:

- Fifth Wheel Couplings
- Pintle Hook Couplings
- Drawbar Couplings
- Gooseneck Couplings

Fifth Wheel Couplings

The most common style for all Class A vehicles (including common on-the-road tractor-trailer combination vehicles) is the fifth-wheel connection. A fifth wheel is a U-shaped hitch that interacts with the kingpin of a trailer, offering greater stability and control for the load.

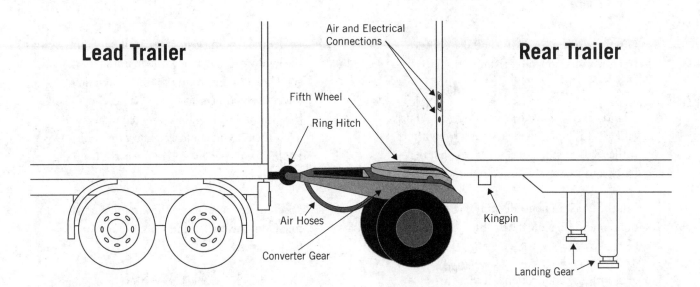

Lead Trailer

Air and Electrical
Connections

Fifth Wheel

Ring Hitch

Rear Trailer

Air Hoses

Converter Gear

Kingpin

Landing Gear

Coupling Semitrailers

01 Check the fifth wheel by looking for any damage, missing parts, dirt, or improper positioning. Check that the mounting components between the truck and trailer are secure with no damage to framing. Ensure the fifth wheel plate is in good shape, properly lubricated, and in the correct positioning to be coupled. Ensure the wheel is tilted down toward rear of truck, jaws are open, and the safety unlocking handle is properly set to automatic lock. If this is a sliding fifth wheel, make sure it is properly locked. Check the condition of the trailer kingpin.

02 Make sure cargo is locked down and unable to move and that there are no hazards in the area. Properly chock the wheels and engage the spring brakes (if applicable).

03 Utilizing your outside mirrors, position the truck in front of and parallel to the trailer. Do not back up to the trailer at an angle, as this can cause damage by pushing the trailer or breaking the landing gear.

04 Slowly back up to the trailer until you are just barely touching it. Do not hit the trailer or go fully underneath it.

05 Engage the parking brake and put the transmission in neutral.

06 The trailer should be low enough that it is slightly raised by backing the truck under it. Raise or lower the trailer to the correct height if needed.

07 Check the seals of the emergency air line and service air line and connect them. Ensure the connections are not leaking and are positioned so that they will not be damaged while traveling.

08 Engage the air supply knob in the cab of the truck or set the tractor protection valve from emergency to normal. Let the air pressure stabilize to normal. Ensure the brake system does not have crossed lines. Turn the engine off so that you can hear the brakes. Engage and disengage the trailer brakes to listen to them. When engaged, you should hear them moving, and when disengaged, you should hear air escaping. Observe the pressure gauge for the air braking system to verify no major air losses. Once you verify that there are no problems, you can turn the truck back on and ensure air pressure returns to (or is already at) normal.

09 Disengage the air supply knob or set the tractor protection valve from normal to emergency.

10 Slightly raise the trailer's landing gear. Slowly and carefully pull the truck forward with the trailer brakes still locked to check that the truck and trailer are locked together.

11 Put the truck in neutral, apply the parking brakes, and turn off the engine.

12 Verify everything is locked and there are no gaps or loose connections. If there are any problems with the coupling, do not drive the truck until addressed.

13 Connect the electrical cord from the truck to the trailer.

14 Raise the front landing gear.

15 Remove the wheel chocks on the trailer.

Uncoupling Semitrailers

01 Position the semitrailer on a flat, clear area that can support the weight of the vehicle. Be sure that the truck and trailer are parallel.

02 Release some pressure from the locking jaws. Turn off the air supply to the trailer to lock its brakes. Slowly back up the truck to release some pressure from the locking jaws. Engage the truck's parking brake to keep the pressure off the jaws.

03 Chock the wheels of the trailer.

04 Lower the landing gear. If the trailer is empty, the landing gear can be lowered until it has a solid hold on the ground. If the trailer is loaded, lower the landing gear until it has a solid hold on the ground, then set the crank to low and give it a few turns to lift some weight off the trailer. Do not lift the trailer enough to remove it from the fifth wheel.

05 Disconnect and remove the air and electrical line from the trailer and store them properly back on the truck.

06 Unlock the fifth wheel. Raise the release handle lock and set it to be open. Make sure you and others do not stand close to the trailer wheels.

07 Pull the truck partially out from under the trailer, leaving enough under to catch the trailer in case the supports fail.

08 Secure the truck by setting the parking brake and putting the transmission in neutral again.

09 Ensure that the trailer supports are not showing any signs of damage or failure and that the ground is solid enough to support the trailer.

10 Remove the truck fully out from under the trailer.

Pintle Hook Couplings

Pintle hooks are a common type of coupling hitch that are used in heavy duty towing applications. They are a hinged hook on the back of a truck or trailer that clamps around a circular connection point on the front of a trailer or dolly. The following images portray a pintle hook in open and closed positions and list its various components.

Being able to properly utilize a pintle hook will be extremely important when coupling and uncoupling a combination vehicle. Inability to do so could result in

Open

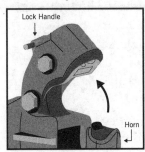

Unlocked

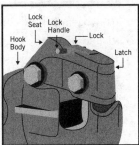

Locked

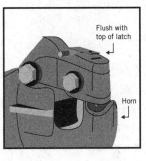

Locked

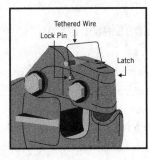

serious accidents, injury, and even death. When a pintle hook fails due to damage or incorrect usage, the trailer will disconnect from the truck. Do not drive with a damaged or improperly prepared pintle hook.

Coupling a Pintle Hook

01 Inspect the pintle hook by looking for damage, dirt, and any improper securing of components.

02 Unlock the lock pin and open the latch. Remove the tethered wire lock pin and open the lock, then open the hook away from the horn.

03 Lower the ring hitch eye over the horn of the pintle and lower it into place.

04 Lock the pintle hook. Push the hook down and close the lock latch until it is flush with the top, then insert the tethered wire lock pin.

Uncoupling a Pintle Hook

01 Park on a clear, level surface that can support the weight of the trailer.

02 Disconnect air and electrical lines and any other connections from the trailer and properly store them on the truck.

03 Unlock the coupler.

04 Double check the ground to make sure that it can support the trailer.

05 Rotate the jack handle and transfer the weight of the trailer from the tongue to the jack.

06 Raise the coupler so that it is above the towing vehicle's hitch.

07 Drive forward and remove the vehicle from under the trailer.

Drawbar Couplings

The third most common style of coupling used for heavy duty towing is a drawbar. Drawbars, in a sense, create a solid connection between the truck and trailer by tightening down on the connection point of the trailer.

You should be able to identify the following components of a drawbar coupling:

- Safety lock screw
- Adjustment screw
- Safety cover bar
- Drawbar coupling ball
- Ball cup drawbar eye
- Bellows protection cover
- Counter nut
- Self-locking nut
- Guard disk
- Grease nipple

As is the case with pintle hooks, being able to properly use a drawbar is extremely important. Do not drive a damaged or improperly set up drawbar.

Coupling a Drawbar

01 Remove the safety lock screw and rotate the safety cover bar outwards. Be sure to recover and keep the self-locking nut.

02 Slowly reverse the truck so that the ball cup drawbar eye is above the drawbar coupling ball.

03 Lower the drawbar until the drawbar eye completely covers the coupling ball.

04 Rotate the safety cover bar inwards. Once the cover bar is rotated all the way inwards, place the lock screw in and fit it with the self-locking nut.

05 Adjust the adjustment screw so that there is 0.3–0.5 mm of vertical clearance between the guard disk and ball cup. Once adjusted, lock in place with the counter nut. If the safety cover bar does not sit in a perfectly lodged position, do not drive the vehicle as travel is forbidden in this condition.

06 Anchor the edge of the bellows protection cover directly to the exposed part of the coupling ball.

07 Lubricate the inside of the drawbar eye cup by applying lubricant through the grease nipple.

Uncoupling a Drawbar

01 Engage the trailer brake.

02 Remove the bellows protection cover, loosen the adjustment screw and counter nut, and remove the lock screw and self-locking nut.

03 Rotate the cover bar outwards and lift the trailer drawbar until the coupling ball is completely visible. Once the drawbar is lifted, slowly drive the truck out from under the trailer. Rotate the cover bar inwards again once the truck is clear until it closes into its housing.

04 Place the lock screw back into place and tighten the self-locking nut on it.

Gooseneck Couplings

Goosenecks are another common way of coupling a tractor and trailer and are called such due to the craning features of their design. This allows them to reach over into the bed of a truck or reach the coupling point of a tractor if the trailer is very low to the ground. Never drive a damaged or improperly coupled gooseneck.

Coupling a Gooseneck

01 Open the latch and lubricate the gooseneck ball.

02 Position the coupler and latch the clamp.

03 Attach safety chains.

04 Connect trailer light wiring.

05 Lower and stow the trailer jacks away.

Uncoupling a Gooseneck

01 Remove safety pin and safety clip.

02 Rotate the handle and raise the trailer off the gooseneck ball.

03 Install the safety pin and safety clip.

SUMMING IT UP

- Every person that applies for the CDL Class A will take the combination vehicles endorsement test.

- The combination vehicles endorsement test is a written test that consists of 20 multiple-choice questions with a required pass rate of 16 correct questions (80%).

- This endorsement allows CDL holders to drive vehicles with truck/tractor and trailers in a variety of configurations. Most Class A vehicles fall under the combination vehicles endorsement. In addition, some Class B and Class C vehicles are also included if they are carrying an additional trailer behind the straight truck.

- Combination vehicles are a varying group of trucks that all consist of a vehicle, which can be referred to as a truck or tractor, pulling a trailer. This can be a straight truck with a trailer or a tractor-trailer with one, two, or three trailers.

- All commercial vehicles must be inspected before and after driving. Combination vehicles require additional inspection points because of the coupling that occurs between the tractor/truck and the trailer.

- Any damage, improper condition, or excessive uncleanliness in coupling systems should be immediately addressed before operating the vehicle. These conditions can cause the systems to falter or fail, which can cause the vehicle to lose control or become damaged.

- The landing gear should be fully raised, free of damage, and clean before driving. The crank handle should be in its proper place and secured. If the landing gear is power operated, there should be no air or hydraulic leaks.

- All lights should be in working order before driving the vehicle.

- Air lines that run from the truck to the trailer(s) allow for the air brakes to have pressure applied much faster than would be possible without them.

- It is common and best practice to use wheel chocks when parking a combination vehicle with air brakes because not all trailers will have a parking brake (spring brakes) present.

- The term *rollover* describes when a vehicle flips onto its side or top or completely rolls over. These incidents account for more than half of all truck driver deaths. The best ways to combat the risk of rollovers is to keep the center of gravity of your truck and trailer as low as possible, secure cargo, and take turns slowly.

- Steering too quickly or sharply can have a ripple effect for the trailers behind the tractor. This is called the crack-the-whip effect, which causes the weight of the cargo to shift rapidly, leading to a rollover or trailer skid.

- Rearward amplification refers to the compacted risk a vehicle has towards a crack-the-whip effect based on its length. To calculate the rearward amplification, the driver must first know the total length of their combination vehicle. The longer the length, the higher the risk.

- There are many components to the brakes in a combination vehicle, and they all have their own purposes.

  ○ Parking brakes are used to lock the spring brakes on the vehicle when parked to keep the vehicle from moving.

  ○ Trailer hand valves, also called trolley valves or Johnson bars, are used to test the brakes on the trailer.

  ○ Tractor protection valves keep air in the brake system in case the trailer becomes detached, disconnected, or develops a leak.

  ○ Service brakes are controlled by the foot pedal in the cab of the truck and are used to come to a stop while driving.

- If you are skidding, stop using the brakes. Using the brakes further will continue to keep the wheels locked and the trailer skidding. Releasing the brakes will enable you to give traction back to the trailer wheels.

- The antilock braking system (ABS) will not increase your stopping distance or braking power and is meant to keep your wheels from locking. If the ABS is faulty, you can still drive as it does not affect your normal braking system, but you need to have it looked at during your next stop.

- When driving a combination vehicle, it is important to know the amount of time needed to stop. Be able to calculate the number of seconds that you should place between you and the vehicle in front of you to ensure proper distance is achieved based on the speed you are traveling and the length of your vehicle.

- If you do ever become stuck on a railroad crossing, immediately exit the vehicle, and stay away from the tracks. Look around you and see if there are any signal stations or signs with emergency notification numbers. Call 911 or any other appropriate emergency number and give them the location of the crossing by referencing its DOT number, if available, or identifiable landmarks.

- Combination vehicles do not turn the same way as a standard straight vehicle because the rear wheels on the trailer(s) do not follow the same line as the front wheels of the truck.

- When backing up a trailer, turn the wheel in the opposite direction of the desired direction for the trailer. If possible, always try to position your vehicle to back up in a straight line.

- The most common coupling style for all Class A vehicles (including common on-the-road tractor-trailer combination vehicles) is the fifth-wheel connection.

- Pintle hooks are a common type of coupling hitch that are used in heavy duty towing applications. They are a hinged hook on the back of a truck or trailer that clamps around a circular connection point on the front of a trailer or dolly.

- Drawbars create a solid connection between the truck and trailer by tightening down on the connection point of the trailer.

- Gooseneck couplings have a craning feature for their design that allows them to reach over into the bed of a truck or reach the coupling point of a tractor if the trailer is very low to the ground.

NOTES

COMBINATION VEHICLES PRACTICE TEST

20 Questions—60 Minutes

> **Directions:** This test consists of a combination of true/false and multiple-choice questions. Only one answer is correct for each question.

1. The last trailer in a series should have its shut-off valve closed.

   A. True

   B. False

2. What amount of space is acceptable between the upper and lower fifth wheel?

   A. ¼ inch

   B. ½ inch

   C. 1 inch

   D. None

3. Orange is used as safety lighting on the outside of some trailers.

   A. True

   B. False

4. When backing up a trailer, always turn the wheel the same direction as you wish the trailer to move.

   A. True

   B. False

5. A Johnson bar is another term for the

   A. trailer hand valve.

   B. trailer protection valve.

   C. parking brake.

   D. foot valve.

6. Which of the following is the safest way to get out of a skid?

   A. Accelerate lightly

   B. Brake lightly

   C. Remove foot from the brakes

   D. Steer in the opposite direction as the skid

7. The most common type of coupling used on a Class A combination vehicle is a

   A. fifth wheel.

   B. pintle hook.

   C. drawbar.

   D. It depends on the load.

8. The kingpin fits into the

   A. drawbar.

   B. pintle hook.

   C. fifth wheel.

   D. It is present on all couplings.

9. There should be 0.3–0.5mm of vertical clearance between the ball disc and the guard cup on a drawbar coupling.

   A. True

   B. False

10. More than half of all truck driver deaths are rollover related.

    A. True

    B. False

11. If a combination vehicle gets stuck on railroad tracks, the driver should

    A. downshift and try again.

    B. reverse and try to rock off the rails.

    C. get out of the vehicle immediately.

    D. accelerate and try again.

12. To reduce rollover risk, always keep the cargo in the front half of the trailer.

    A. True

    B. False

13. What is the last step when coupling a trailer?

    A. Raising the landing gear

    B. Checking trailer height

    C. Removing wheel chocks

    D. Lowering the landing gear

14. Test the trailer service brakes using the

    A. service brakes.

    B. emergency brakes.

    C. trailer hand valve.

    D. parking brake.

15. Hose couplers are also called

    A. glad hands.

    B. button hooks.

    C. jug handles.

    D. Johnson bars.

16. When the steering wheel is turned to the right, the trailer will turn to the right.

    A. True

    B. False

17. If a combination vehicle turns too tightly around a corner, the back inner wheels may

    A. lock up.

    B. not clear the curb.

    C. get stuck on the curb.

    D. swing wide into the next lane.

18. A bobtail tractor is a tractor with 2 semitrailers connected to it.

    A. True

    B. False

19. Combination vehicles should follow behind other vehicles at a rate of 1 second, plus an additional second to the total time for every 10 feet of length at speeds above 40 miles per hour.

    A. True

    B. False

20. All of the following are necessary steps during brake inspection on combination vehicles EXCEPT:

    A. Testing the trailer spring brakes

    B. Testing that the trailer protection valve is working

    C. Testing that the trailer emergency brakes are working

    D. Making sure that air is flowing to all trailers

ANSWER KEY AND EXPLANATIONS

1. A	5. A	9. A	13. C	17. B
2. D	6. C	10. A	14. C	18. B
3. A	7. A	11. C	15. A	19. A
4. B	8. C	12. B	16. B	20. A

1. **The correct answer is A.** When there are a series of trailers, the last trailer should have its shut-off valve closed. This is to stop the air from flowing out. Every other trailer should have the shut-off valve open so air can flow through the entire system.

2. **The correct answer is D.** There should be no space between the upper and lower fifth wheel. If there is any space, including ¼ inch (choice A), ½ inch (choice B), or 1 inch (choice C), there is something wrong with the connection, and it should be further inspected.

3. **The correct answer is A.** Orange is used as safety lighting on the exterior of some combination vehicles.

4. **The correct answer is B.** When backing up a trailer, always turn the wheel in the opposite direction as you wish the trailer to move. This is because the trailer will respond in the opposite direction as the steering wheel.

5. **The correct answer is A.** The Johnson bar refers to the trailer hand valve, which is used to test the trailer brakes during inspection. It does not refer to the trailer protection valve (choice B), the parking brake (choice C), or the foot valve (choice D).

6. **The correct answer is C.** Removing your foot from the brakes is the safest way to get out of a skid as it allows the wheels to regain traction. Accelerating lightly (choice A), braking lightly (choice B), and steering in the opposite direction of the skid (choice D) can all make things worse.

7. **The correct answer is A.** The most common type of coupling used on a Class A combination vehicle is a fifth wheel. This is because the fifth wheel holds the most weight. A pintle hook (choice B)

and a drawbar (choice C) are more commonly used with lighter loads. Although load weight can affect the type of coupling (choice D), the fifth wheel remains the most common type in use for Class A vehicles.

8. **The correct answer is C.** The kingpin fits into the fifth wheel. It is not present on a drawbar (choice A) or a pintle hook (choice B), thus it is not present on all couplings (choice D).

9. **The correct answer is A.** The vertical clearance should be between 0.3 and 0.5mm.

10. **The correct answer is A.** More than half of all truck driver deaths are due to trucks rolling over. The height of combination trucks creates a higher center of gravity, thus dramatically increasing the likelihood of rollovers. Couple this with good tire traction, excessive speed, possible weight shifts of the cargo, damaged roads, and severe weather and the likelihood of rollovers increases exponentially.

11. **The correct answer is C.** Anytime a combination vehicle gets stuck on railroad tracks, the driver should get out immediately and call for help. Any type of shifting while on the tracks (choices A and B) are always discouraged as they promote getting stuck rather than rectifying it. Accelerating (choice D) can be dangerous and decreases the notification to potential trains that may encounter your stuck vehicle, thus increasing the likelihood of a potentially fatal crash. Always leave the vehicle and make the proper calls to warn others and get assistance.

12. **The correct answer is B.** To reduce rollover risk, always keep the cargo evenly distributed and as low to the ground as possible, as an increased

height of cargo is the number one risk for rollovers.

13. **The correct answer is C.** Removing the wheel chocks should be the last step as it ensures that you have performed all the safety checks and are ready to move the vehicle. Raising the gear (choice A) is the second to last step. Checking the trailer height (choice B) is the sixth step. Lowering the landing gear (choice D) is not applicable when coupling as the landing gear is already lowered on a stationary trailer.

14. **The correct answer is C.** The trailer hand valve is specifically designed to test the trailer service brakes. It cannot be used when the truck is in motion. The service brakes (choice A) are used when the vehicle is in motion but not for testing. The emergency brakes (choice B) and the parking brake (choice D) are not used to test service brakes as they are separate lines.

15. **The correct answer is A.** Hose couplers are more often referred to as glad hands, which is the connection of the air lines between the tractor and the trailer. Button hooks (choice B) and jug handles (choice C) are types of turns. Johnson bars (choice D) are another name for tractor handle valves.

16. **The correct answer is B.** When the steering wheel is turned to the right, the trailer will turn left as the trailer always goes the opposite direction as the wheel initially.

17. **The correct answer is B.** If a combination vehicle turns too tightly around a corner, the back inner wheels may not clear the curb. As they may not clear the curb, they cannot get stuck on the curb (choice C). The tight turn does not cause wheels to lock up (choice A), nor would it cause the wheels to swing wide into the next lane (choice D).

18. **The correct answer is B.** A bobtail tractor refers to a tractor that does not have any trailers connected to it.

19. **The correct answer is A.** When speeds exceed 40 miles per hour, the following distance is 1 second for every 10 feet of vehicle length, plus an additional second to the total time.

20. **The correct answer is A.** Testing that the trailer protection valve is working (choice B), that the trailer emergency brakes are working (choice C), and that air is flowing to all trailers (choice D) are all necessary parts of brake inspections on combination vehicles. Rather than testing the trailer spring brakes, the last essential step is testing the trailer service brakes.

NOTES

CHAPTER

Double and Triple Trailers

DOUBLE AND TRIPLE TRAILERS

OVERVIEW

Exam Format

Endorsement Requirements

Inspections

Safety

Coupling and Uncoupling

Summing It Up

Practice Test

Drivers that possess a Class A commercial driver's license (CDL) are eligible to test for the double and triple trailer endorsement. This endorsement allows drivers to transport combination vehicles that have two or three trailers. Although double trailers are allowed in all 50 states, triples are only allowed in 13. This chapter provides a summary of the information present in the CDL manual, along with a review of information from the Combination Vehicles chapter and helpful tips to prepare you for this exam.

NOTE

At the end of Chapter 6, you will find a Double and Triple Trailers Practice Test that will test your knowledge of the information contained in this chapter and better prepare you for the CDL double and triple trailers endorsement exam.

ALERT

Make sure to also study the General Knowledge, Air Brakes, and Combination Vehicles chapters as questions from these topics will appear on the double and triple trailers endorsement exam.

EXAM FORMAT

This endorsement requires only a written test. The written test consists of 20 multiple-choice and true/false questions with a required pass rate of 16 correct questions (80%).

Scheduling

This is state-specific, but overall, the written test can be scheduled at the same time as the CDL exam. Check with your local department of motor vehicles for more information on scheduling both components.

ENDORSEMENT REQUIREMENTS

A double and triple trailers endorsement allows a driver to transport longer combination vehicles (LCVs). This endorsement is only needed if the combination vehicle has two or more trailers. Triple trailers are restricted in most states but are permitted in the following 13 states:

- Arizona
- Colorado
- Idaho
- Indiana
- Kansas
- Montana
- Nebraska
- Nevada
- North Dakota
- Oklahoma
- Oregon
- South Dakota
- Utah

This endorsement requires test takers to be at least 18. However, if transport includes crossing state lines, the driver must be 21.

Codes

The following table provides is a summary of possible codes and their meanings. There is no restriction code directly related to this endorsement. Pay attention to the difference between Endorsement Codes and Restriction Codes as there may be questions on the exam.

ENDORSMENT CODES	
T	Allows a driver to operate a combination vehicle with two or three trailers
RESTRICTION CODES	
V	Medical variance code: restrictions related to DOT medical certification, such as high blood pressure or diabetes

INSPECTIONS

All commercial vehicles must be given a standard inspection before and after being driven. Combination double and triple vehicles require additional inspection points because of the coupling that occurs between the trailers.

Coupling Systems

The coupling system between a truck and trailer, or trailer and trailer, is extremely important to maintain. Any damage, improper condition, or excessive uncleanliness should be immediately addressed before operating the vehicle. These conditions can cause the systems to falter or fail, which can lead to loss of control or damage to the vehicle. Look for the following when inspecting the couplings:

- There should be no visible space between the apron plate (upper fifth wheel) and lower fifth wheel skid plate.
- Lockjaws are firmly around the shank, not the kingpin head.
- The hose couplers (more commonly referred to as glad hands) should be properly attaching the service and emergency lines from the tractor to the trailer and to any additional trailers, and they should be in working order.
- The release arm is correctly in place, and the safety latch/lock is active.
- Inspect the air and electrical lines running to all the trailers. All lines should be properly mounted and connected, free of damage, and air lines should show no signs of leaks. Service line couplers are not always color coded, but if they are, they should be blue. Emergency lines should be red.
- Inspect all sliding fifth wheels for damage at each connection (tractor/trailer and trailer/trailer), and make sure they are properly greased.
- Make sure all lock pins are accounted for and locked into place.
- Ensure the fifth wheel is properly placed behind the tractor or trailer so it does not pivot too far forward.
- Ensure the shut-off valve at the back of the trailer is closed. If you are pulling more than one trailer, the shut-off valves of the trailers in front of the farthest back trailer should be open with the farthest back's valve being closed.

Any damage, improper condition, or excessive uncleanliness should be immediately addressed before operating the vehicle.

Landing Gear

The landing gear should be fully raised, free of damage, and clean before driving. The crank handle should be in its proper place and secured. If the landing gear is power operated, there should be no air or hydraulic leaks. Verify this for every trailer.

Lights

There are a few different lights that are specifically added to trailers aside from the braking, turning, and reversing indicators that are on all vehicles. These special lights should always be in working order. If illuminated while driving, they may indicate malfunctions:

- A green light on the trailer means that all systems are working correctly.
- A red light on the trailer means that there is a problem with the coupling between the tractor and trailer.
- A yellow light on the trailer means that there is a problem with the antilock braking system (ABS).
- Orange lights are used to mark the edges of the trailer to help other drivers see it better at night.

Brakes

Combination vehicles use air brakes as their primary form of braking. This is because the air lines that run from the truck to the trailer(s) allow for the brakes to have pressure applied much faster than would be possible without them. However, when parking a combination vehicle with air brakes, it is common and best practice to use wheel chocks as not all trailers will have a parking brake (spring brakes) present. Never assume that a trailer has spring brakes, and always chock the wheels if unsure. Air brake checks specifically for combination vehicles include, but are not limited to, the following:

- Making sure the air is flowing to all trailers
- Testing that the trailer protection valve is working
- Testing that the trailer emergency brakes are working
- Testing that the trailer service brakes are working

For more detailed information regarding inspections and checks, refer to your state's CDL manual, the General Knowledge chapter, and the Air Brakes chapter.

SAFETY

Most states do not allow triple trailers because of the increased risk of rollovers and accidents that are present with combination vehicles of this length. It is your duty as a driver to ensure that you are not only knowledgeable in handling rigs of this size but also that you feel confident once it is in motion. Pay special attention to the following topics.

Steering

The weight and length of the combination of truck and trailer makes steering more difficult. Turning too quickly or sharply can have a ripple effect for the trailers behind the tractor. This is called the *crack-the-whip* effect. This causes the weight of the cargo to shift rapidly, thus leading to a rollover or trailer skid. This can affect the entire combination vehicle or just one or more trailers. The likelihood of this occurring increases based on the length of the vehicle.

Rearward Amplification

Rearward Amplification refers to the compacted risk a vehicle has towards a crack-the-whip effect based on its length. To calculate the rearward amplification, the driver must first know the total length of their combination vehicle. The greater the length, the higher the risk. The following image shows the risk of rearward amplification for different combination types. The number provided on the image indicates how likely the last trailer will roll over. For example, a rearward amplification of 1.5 means the trailer is 1.5 times more likely to roll over than the tractor it is connected to. A rearward amplification of 3.0 means the last trailer is 3 times more likely to roll over. Rearward amplification is at its highest with double and triple trailers configurations.

The most common time for a crack-the-whip effect to happen is during fast lane changes and quick turning. Always look ahead on the road and be prepared for any turns or lane changes that you will have to make. If visibility is low or road conditions are wet or icy, slow the vehicle and make turns and lane changes slowly and carefully.

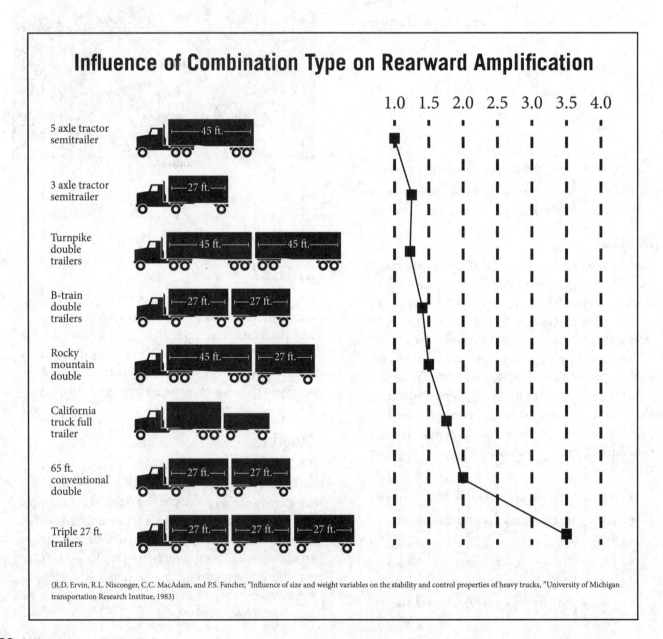

Influence of Combination Type on Rearward Amplification

(R.D. Ervin, R.L. Nisconger, C.C. MacAdam, and P.S. Fancher, "Influence of size and weight variables on the stability and control properties of heavy trucks, "University of Michigan transportation Research Institue, 1983)

Staging

Staging is the process of organizing your trailers prior to coupling. When dealing with multiple trailers, remember the following:

- The heaviest trailer should always go FIRST, directly behind the tractor.
- The lightest trailer should always go LAST, at the farthest spot from the tractor.
  - This is due to rollover rates and rearward amplification. Should the trailer roll over, the heavier ones are more likely to remain upright given their position.
- Loads can adjust the height of each trailer, with lighter loads resulting in taller trailers. If the load is uncertain, check the height of the trailers and organize them with the lowest trailer FIRST and the highest trailer LAST.

Parking

Parking a long combination vehicle (LCV, another name for a double or triple trailer) requires a pull-through option. The best option is a straight line as backing up in any fashion with a rig of this length combined with at least two hitches is extremely difficult. Follow these tips when parking.

- Plan ahead and survey the area well in advance. If heading into a fueling station, select one that is set up for long combination vehicles so pull-through parking is readily available.
- Call ahead to the receiving location and ask about parking options for double and triple trailers.
- Park with a helper guiding you on the ground if available.
- Opt for street-side parking if there is no safe pull-through option. Transporting goods by hand or with smaller vehicle in smaller loads may be a safer option.

Pup Trailers and Dollies

Pup trailers are trailers that range in length from 26 to 29 feet. They can be used in a single configuration but are also common in combination configurations. They can provide a greater load capacity than a box trailer for one truck when in double and triple rigs.

Converter dollies are used to connect one trailer to another for double and triple combination vehicles. They are usually connected with a ring hitch on their front to the pintle hook on the back of a trailer. The fifth wheel on their back is connected to the front of another trailer's kingpin. They can have either one or two axles depending on the model.

Components of a Converter Dolly and Trailer Coupling System

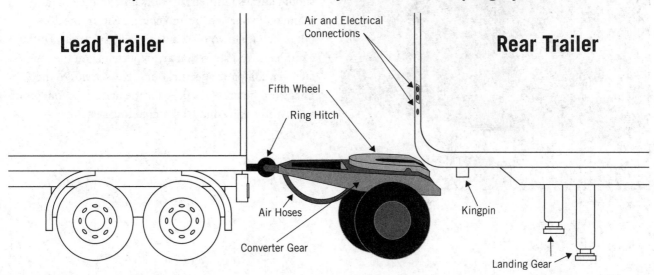

The following are important points regarding converter dollies:

- Dollies built on or after March 1, 1998 are required to have an antilock braking system (ABS). Just like for trailers, a skid can occur for a dolly, and without ABS, they will be more prone to skids. There will be a yellow light on the driver's side of the dolly if it has ABS, and if the light is on, then there is a problem with the ABS.

- If the dolly has a shut-off valve, it should always be open if a trailer is connected to the back of it.

- The air tank drain valve should be closed on the dolly for the same reason that it should be for trailers—so that the air in the tank does not leak out and keeps proper pressure throughout the system.
  - Make sure that you know the difference between the tank drain valve and the shut-off valve.

COUPLING AND UNCOUPLING

The converter dolly and trailer will have the same fifth wheel connection between each other as covered earlier, so this section will briefly cover the coupling and uncoupling of a converter dolly, not the basics of generic coupling/uncoupling.

It is important to know that coupling systems can vary greatly between manufacturers and vehicle types. You should always familiarize yourself with the operations manual of your vehicle and equipment. If this does not match up to your own vehicle, be sure to learn the equipment and steps that are expected from the manufacturer/company specifications. Please refer to the image on the previous page for the basic components of a converter dolly and trailer coupling system.

Coupling

Use the following steps to guide the coupling process:

01 Release the dolly brakes and position the converter dolly in front of the secondary trailer (or tertiary, whichever you are currently coupling) so that it is lined up in a straight line with the kingpin.

02 Back the first trailer into place and connect to the dolly's ring hitch with the pintle hook on the back of the trailer.

03 When connecting the rear trailer, you must make sure the brakes are engaged and the wheels are chocked.

04 If the rear trailer does not have spring brakes, then you should connect the emergency line, charge the air tank, and disconnect the emergency line so that the emergency brakes will set in place of the nonexistent spring brakes.

05 Make sure that the trailer's height is correct and back the dolly underneath.

06 Slightly raise the landing gear so it is not damaged if the trailer moves and test the connection by pulling against the pin of the rear trailer.

07 Inspect the coupling between the fifth wheel and kingpin and connect all the necessary safety chains, air hoses, and light cords.

08 Engage the dolly brakes.

09 Turn off the service and emergency valves of the rear trailer and open the same valves on the trailers in front of it.

10 Raise the landing gear and test the airlines to make sure all the brakes are receiving the air and pressure that they need.

11 If you are connecting a third trailer, repeat this process.

Uncoupling

For uncoupling, use the following steps:

01 Remove the rear trailer first. NEVER uncouple a dolly from the trailer in front of it if a trailer is still coupled to the back of the dolly.

02 Park the whole rig on a stable area in a straight line and apply the parking brakes and chock the wheels of the rear trailer.

03 Lower the landing gear of the rear trailer just enough to decrease the weight put on the dolly.

04 Shut off the valves on the trailer in front of the rear trailer, then disconnect all the air and electrical lines from the rear trailer and dolly and secure them.

05 Release connection between the dolly's fifth wheel and the trailer's kingpin, leave the rear trailer chocked in place, release the brakes on the other trailer and dolly, and pull the dolly out from under the rear trailer.

06 Now that the dolly is uncoupled from the rear trailer, it needs to be uncoupled from the front trailer. Lower the dolly landing brake, remove the safety chains, apply the spring brakes, and chock the wheels.

07 Release the pintle hook connection of the dolly to the front trailer and pull the trailer clear of the dolly. NEVER disconnect the dolly from the front trailer while still under the rear trailer. The dolly's tow bar can fly up if this is done. Not only will it be very difficult to recouple, but it also has a chance of causing serious injury.

08 If your rig is a triple trailer, repeat this process.

SUMMING IT UP

- The double and triple trailers endorsement allows drivers to transport combination vehicles that have two or three trailers. Although double trailers are allowed in all 50 states, triples are only allowed in 13.

- This endorsement requires only a written test. The written test consists of 20 questions with a required pass rate of 16 correct questions (80%).

- Combination double and triple vehicles require additional inspection points because of the coupling that occurs between the trailers.

- Rearward amplification refers to the compacted risk a vehicle has towards a crack-the-whip effect as created by its length.

  ○ To calculate the rearward amplification, the driver must first know the total length of their combination vehicle. The longer the length, the higher the risk.

- Parking a longer combination vehicle (LCV, another name for a double or triple trailer) requires a pull-through option. The best option is a straight line as backing up in any fashion with a rig of such length, combined with at least two hitches, is extremely difficult.

- Pup trailers range in length from 26 to 29 feet. They can be used in a single configuration but are also common in combination configurations.

- Converter dollies are used to connect one trailer to another for double and triple combination vehicles. They are usually connected with a ring hitch on their front to the pintle hook on the back of a trailer.

NOTES

DOUBLE AND TRIPLE TRAILERS PRACTICE TEST

20 Questions—60 Minutes

> **Directions:** This test consists of a combination of true/false and multiple-choice questions. Only one answer is correct for each question.

1. The coupling type on a converter dolly for the rear trailer that it connects to is

    A. a pintle hook.

    B. a ring hitch.

    C. a fifth wheel.

    D. a drawbar.

2. Why are pup trailers often used in double and triple rigs?

    A. They are larger than box trailers.

    B. They can have a higher load capacity than a box trailer for one truck.

    C. They are the only acceptable trailer for double and triple rigs.

    D. Pup trailers are not used in double and triple rigs.

3. When coupling two trailers together with a converter dolly, you should connect the dolly to the first trailer, then align it with the second trailer.

    A. True

    B. False

4. When uncoupling the converter dolly from the trailer in front of it, the safety chains, air hose, and light cords should be disconnected before the dolly's landing gear is lowered.

    A. True

    B. False

5. Which valve must be closed on the converter dolly in a double or triple rig?

    A. Air tank drain valve

    B. Trailer shut-off valves ahead of the last rear valve

    C. Hitch valve

    D. Trailer air supply valve

6. What is best practice when merging onto the highway with a double rig?

    A. Look ahead and manage speed to make sure that you will be able to merge

    B. Always merge at a speed that is below the limit

    C. Get up to highway speeds and let other drivers make room for you

    D. Do not merge as double rigs cannot go on the highway

7. The service brakes of double and triple rigs are commonly

    A. spring brakes.

    B. hydraulic brakes.

    C. electrical brakes.

    D. air brakes.

8. Double and triple rigs, due to their many hinging points between trailers, do not need to swing wide around corners and other non-curving turns.

    A. True

    B. False

9. What is the variable, aside from construction and size, that can affect the height of the separate trailers in double and triple rigs?

   A. The coupling between trailers

   B. The firmness of the road

   C. The weight of each trailer's load

   D. The aerodynamics from driving

10. What does it mean when driving a double or triple trailer and a red light on the trailer turns on that is not from the brake lights?

   A. There is a problem with the coupling between the trailer and tractor/dolly.

   B. There is a problem with the antilock braking system.

   C. There is a problem with the air pressure system.

   D. There are no red lights other than the brake lights.

11. How many states allow triple trailers?

   A. 50

   B. 48

   C. 37

   D. 13

12. Another name for the upper fifth wheel is the

   A. pintle hook.

   B. drawbar.

   C. gooseneck.

   D. apron plate.

13. Service brake lines are usually blue.

   A. True

   B. False

14. Glad hands is another name for hose couplers.

   A. True

   B. False

15. A pup trailer is usually

   A. 23–25 feet in length.

   B. 25–27 feet in length.

   C. 26–29 feet in length.

   D. 22–24 feet in length.

16. It is best practice to uncouple the first trailer from the tractor and work your way backwards.

   A. True

   B. False

17. A converter dolly made after March 1, 1998 will be equipped with

   A. antilock brakes.

   B. spring brakes.

   C. double axles.

   D. a shut-off valve.

18. When uncoupling a double trailer, the driver should not pull the tractor forward until both trailers and the converter dolly are uncoupled.

   A. True

   B. False

19. Where on the kingpin should the lockjaws close?

   A. The shank

   B. The head

   C. The neck

   D. The base

20. What is the easiest way to verify that a converter dolly has an antilock braking system?

   A. Ask your supervisor

   B. Check the owner's manual

   C. Locate the yellow lamp on the left side

   D. Look under the belly of the dolly

ANSWER KEY AND EXPLANATIONS

1. C	5. A	9. C	13. A	17. A
2. B	6. A	10. A	14. A	18. B
3. B	7. D	11. D	15. C	19. A
4. B	8. B	12. D	16. B	20. C

1. **The correct answer is C.** A fifth wheel is the coupling type that is on the back of a converter dolly and connects to the rear trailer. A pintle hook (choice A) is found at the back of a trailer and connects to the ring hitch (choice B) that is on the front of the dolly. A drawbar (choice D) is a coupling type that is not commonly a part of a converter dolly.

2. **The correct answer is B.** Pup trailers are used in double and triple rigs because they can have a higher load capacity than a box trailer can for one truck. Pup trailers are not always bigger than box trailers (choice A) because a semi-trailer is a very large box trailer. They are not the only acceptable trailer to use for doubles and triples (choice C), but they are definitely used in those rigs (choice D).

3. **The correct answer is B.** The converter dolly should be aligned with the second (rear) trailer first in order to ensure that it will couple correctly. Once it is aligned then the first trailer can be backed up to the converter dolly and connected before connecting the rear trailer.

4. **The correct answer is B.** Lowering the landing gear is the first step in uncoupling the trailer in front of the converter dolly, and then the safety chains, air hose, and light cords can be disconnected.

5. **The correct answer is A.** The air tank drain valve must always be closed on the converter dolly air tank because, if it is not, the air tank will constantly be draining, and proper pressure will not be kept in the air system. The trailer shut-off valve (choice B) and trailer air supply valve (choice D) should be open (or in case of the air supply, on)

in order to allow air to move through the system. The only exception that will always apply is that the shut-off valve at the rear of the farthest back trailer should be closed to keep air in. The hitch valve (choice C) is not a valve that you will find on a vehicle.

6. **The correct answer is A.** Looking ahead and managing your speed to be able to safely merge is the best way to merge onto a highway. Merging at a speed below the limit (choice B) is not always necessary. At times, this behavior can be dangerous if you are not looking ahead to match the flow of traffic. Getting to highways speeds and letting other drivers move for you (choice C) is not a safe choice because you do not know how aware other drivers are of your approach, and there is no guarantee that they will move for you. Double rigs are allowed on highways (choice D), but be sure to look at local regulations to make sure that there are no sections of the highway that prohibit them.

7. **The correct answer is D.** Air brakes are the most common service brakes for double and triple rigs because of their power and consistency for the size and weight of these rigs. Although hydraulic and electrical brakes (choices B and C) could be used on a double or triple rig, they are not as optimal a choice as air brakes. Spring brakes (choice A) are used as parking brakes, not service brakes.

8. **The correct answer is B.** Double and triple rigs must swing wide around turns because, just like other combination vehicles, the back wheels of the trailers will off-track and could hit curbs or structures near the corner.

6

9. **The correct answer is C.** The weight of each trailer's load can directly affect the height comparison between the trailers, with the lightest being the tallest. The coupling between the trailers (choice A) should not directly affect the height because the trailers should be level with each other when coupled. The firmness of the road (choice B) and the aerodynamics from driving (choice D) should not affect the trailer height, especially in a way that the height difference will be a concern.

10. **The correct answer is A.** If a red light on the trailer or dolly turns on, then there is a problem with the coupling between the trailer and tractor/dolly. There is a red light on the trailer aside from the brake lights that signifies a coupling problem (choice D). The antilock braking system warning light (choice B) is a yellow lamp on the left side of the trailer or dolly. If there is a problem with the air pressure system (choice C), then there are alarms and gauges in the cab of the vehicle to warn you.

11. **The correct answer is D.** Only 13 states (Arizona, Colorado, Idaho, Indiana, Kansas, Montana, Nebraska, Nevada, North Dakota, Oklahoma, Oregon, South Dakota, and Utah) allow triple trailers.

12. **The correct answer is D.** The upper fifth wheel is also referred to as the apron plate. A pintle hook (choice A), drawbar (choice B), and gooseneck (choice C) all refer to different types of hitches.

13. **The correct answer is A.** Service brake lines aren't always color coded, but when they are, they are blue.

14. **The correct answer is A.** Glad hands is the more common name for hose couplers.

15. **The correct answer is C.** A pup trailer, which is shorter than a typical trailer, is usually 26–29 feet in length. Although some variations may include 22–27 feet these lengths are not common.

16. **The correct answer is B.** Due to safety and weight distribution, you should always start with the last trailer and work your way up to the front of the rig.

17. **The correct answer is A.** All dollies made after March 1, 1998 must have antilock brakes. This date does not ensure the presence of spring brakes (choice B), double axles (choice C), or a shut-off valve (choice D).

18. **The correct answer is B.** The driver should pull the vehicle forward slowly after uncoupling the second trailer from the dolly to allow the dolly to come out from underneath the trailer.

19. **The correct answer is A.** The lockjaws should close on the shank, or middle of the kingpin. If it is around the head (choice B) or the base (choice D) the trailer could become uncoupled. There is no neck (choice C) on a kingpin.

20. **The correct answer is C.** The easiest way to verify that a converter dolly has ABS is to locate the yellow lamp on the left side of the dolly. While asking a supervisor (choice A), checking the owner's manual (choice B), and looking under the belly of the dolly (choice D) are all options, they are not necessarily accurate or easy.

CHAPTER

Tanker Vehicles

TANKER VEHICLES

OVERVIEW

Exam Format

Endorsement Requirements

Inspections

Safety

Summing It Up

Practice Test

Drivers that already possess a commercial driver's license (CDL) are eligible to test for the tanker endorsement (N). This endorsement allows drivers to transport liquids and gaseous materials in tanks. The tanker endorsement can be combined with the HazMat endorsement to add the X endorsement code to a CDL. This chapter covers information present in the CDL manual about the tanker endorsement, along with helpful tips to prepare you for this exam.

 NOTE

At the end of Chapter 7, you will find a Tanker Vehicles Practice Test that will test your knowledge of the information contained in this chapter and better prepare you for the CDL tanker endorsement exam.

ALERT

Make sure to also study the Air Brakes, Combination Vehicles, and HazMat chapters as questions are pulled from these areas for the tanker endorsement exam.

EXAM FORMAT

This endorsement requires a written test. The written test consists of 20 questions with a required pass rate of 16 correct questions (80%).

Scheduling

Scheduling the exam is state specific. Check with your local department of motor vehicles for more information on scheduling both the written and skills tests.

ENDORSEMENT REQUIREMENTS

A Tanker Endorsement is only needed if the cargo meets the following criteria:

- The cargo includes individual containers of liquid or gases that are larger than 119 gallons.

- The containers are loaded. Empty containers do not require this endorsement.

- The total combined volume in the filled containers exceeds 1,000 gallons.

This endorsement requires test takers to be at least 18 years old (21 in HI and NY). However, if transport includes crossing state lines, the driver must be 21. This endorsement allows a licensed CDL driver to transport large volumes of liquids and gases (excluding hazardous materials).

The following is a summary of possible codes and their meanings. Pay attention to the difference between Endorsement Codes and Restriction Codes as there may be questions about them on the exam.

ENDORSMENT CODES	
N	Allows driver to transport tanks but not hazardous material per guidelines.
X	Allows the driver to transport hazardous material in tanks as required.
RESTRICTION CODES	
X	Commercial Learner's Permit Only: No cargo in tank vehicle and tank must be purged; restricts "N" endorsement.
V	Medical variance code: restrictions related to DOT medical certification, such as high blood pressure or diabetes.

INSPECTIONS

A driver with a CDL should always complete all general inspection requirements on every commercial vehicle before and after driving. When in doubt, refer to the General Knowledge chapter of this book as well as your state-specific CDL manual. Further, a driver must be familiar with a vehicle's operations manual to understand points of inspection as related to emergency equipment. This section covers how to inspect tanker vehicles, including the following:

- Leaks
- Special Purpose Equipment

Leaks

Tanker inspections follow all the main vehicle inspection points listed in the General Knowledge chapter. Additionally, you'll be checking for leaks on tanker vehicles during the pre- and post-travel inspections. Traveling with a leaking tanker is illegal, and you can be cited as well as prevented from further traveling until repairs are made. Any spills are the responsibility of the driver, which may require HazMat clean up and costs. In order to properly check for leaks, be sure to inspect the areas outlined in the following chart.

PROPER CHECKING FOR TANKER LEAKS		
Common Locations on Tanker	Leak Areas	What to Look For
1	Dents	Look for dents on either the inside or outside of the tank.
2	Cracks	Look for cracks on the inside or outside of the tank and on valves, covers, or gaskets.
3	Valves	Valves include discharge, intake, and cut-off valves. Look for dents, cracks, or poor/missing seals. They should be fully closed before driving.
Varies	Hoses	This includes all hoses that are used to load the cargo as well as any hoses present inside or outside the tank.
Varies	Hoses	Look for dents, cracks, or poor seals.
4	Covers	This includes manhole covers. Dents, cracks, missing, or stripped seals can all contribute to leaks. Manhole covers should be fully closed before driving.
Varies	Gaskets	Dents, cracks, missing or stripped seals can all contribute to leaks.

 ALERT -

Knowingly transporting hazardous materials in a leaking tank can result in a maximum fine of $75,000. Check for leaks before and after every trip.

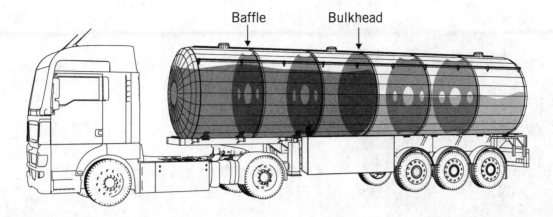

Baffle   Bulkhead

Special Purpose Equipment

Your tanker may or may not have the following equipment. Refer to the vehicle manual and your tanker company to make sure you have everything required. If your vehicle has any or all of the following equipment, make sure the equipment is in good condition and working properly:

- Built-in fire extinguisher
- Emergency shut-off systems
- Grounding and bonding cables
- Vapor recovery kits
- Personal Protective Equipment (PPE)

SAFETY

Driving a tanker is different than driving a standard semi-trailer combination as the liquid component adds another layer of safety concerns. The following are important considerations when transporting liquid or gaseous cargo in a tank:

- Surges
- Bulkheads
- Unbaffled and Baffled Tanks
- Loading and Unloading the Tank
- Rules for Safely Driving a Tanker

Surges

Surges occur when a partially filled tank experiences a sudden shift in the liquid. This most likely occurs from front to back but can also occur from side to side. Accelerating too quickly can cause the surge from front to back.

Sudden braking can result in a surge from back to front. Surges can lead to loss of vehicle control even if brakes are engaged. To limit surges and their impact, practice slow and steady braking and acceleration, be mindful of tank volume, and make appropriately wide turns.

Bulkheads

Bulkheads are used to separate a larger tank into multiple smaller compartments. By separating the liquid volume, the liquid is better distributed and less likely to have front-to-back surges. Side-to-side surges are still possible, so caution when turning is very important. Additionally, because of the separate compartments within the tank, special attention needs to be paid to the distribution of the liquids when loading and unloading. Weight should be distributed evenly across the tank to avoid creating an imbalance at the front or rear of the vehicle.

Unbaffled and Baffled Tanks

Unbaffled tanks (also known as smooth bore tanks) possess no bulkheads. They could be considered a traditional tank, simply a large cavity with smooth walls and no internal divisions. Generally, unbaffled tanks are used to transport materials that, for sanitary reasons, are not allowed to have bulkheads. One example is milk because of the sanitation requirements and the added difficulty of cleaning separate bulkheads. Unbaffled tanks are more dangerous to haul because they are prone to surges, even when proper driving precautions are followed.

Baffled tanks are tanks that have bulkheads with holes inside the bulkhead walls that allow liquid to flow between different segments of the tank. This helps to

Liquids expand when heated, and different liquids will have different rates of expansion.

prevent powerful surges because the liquid will not have the same amount of open space to move throughout the tank as it would in a smooth bore space. The baffling disperses the power of the surge as the liquid travels through each baffle. However, it does not eliminate the risk.

Loading and Unloading the Tank

When loading a tank, a driver must be aware of the necessary outage. Outage refers to how much expansion will occur when the temperature of the transported liquid increases. Liquids expand when heated, and different liquids will have different rates of expansion. Because of this, a driver must know the particular outage for their cargo, which is based on the liquid's weight. Keep in mind, not all liquids weigh the same. Always know the outage of a bulk liquid you are transporting. Remember the following when calculating how much to fill the tank:

- The amount that the liquid will expand (outage)
- The weight of the liquid loaded
- The legal weights that a tanker can carry

Unloading procedures will differ by vehicle and the transported liquid. Use the vehicle operations manual and follow relevant cargo procedures related to sanitation, electrical grounding, and more.

Rules for Safely Driving a Tanker

Due to the nature of the cargo, the way in which a driver approaches common driving tasks must be adjusted to maintain safety. The following are areas to focus on to help maximize safe practices when operating a tanker.

Higher Center of Gravity

The center of gravity is higher on a tanker vehicle compared to a lighter passenger type vehicle such as a car or SUV. In addition, the center of gravity shifts because of the liquid cargo. This means that taking a turn too quickly will result in the higher weight pulling in one direction and the weight shifting in that same direction. The result of the larger weight shift provides a greater chance of rollover compared to a standard truck when turning.

Smooth Driving

Because of shifting cargo volumes, drive tanker vehicles as smoothly as possible. Sudden jerks in the wheel during acceleration and when braking will shift the weight of the liquid around and can cause you to lose control of the vehicle.

Braking

Use consistent pressure when braking. Even when you have come to a stop, do not ease off the brakes in case of a surge, leading to vehicle rocking or lurching. Additionally, begin braking further in advance than you would in most vehicles, and increase the following distance that you would normally use to account for changes to vehicle handling caused by surging.

If you must stop quickly for an emergency, such as avoiding a crash, use controlled or stab braking while avoiding sharp and sudden steering. Controlled braking is engaging the brakes hard but not hard enough to lock the wheels. Stab braking requires you to engage the brakes hard enough to lock the wheels, then as soon as they are locked, release the brakes until the wheels roll freely again.

Always be aware of how much distance will be needed to stop the vehicle and double that distance when the road conditions are wet. Also remember that it could take longer for an empty tanker to stop compared to a full one due to the reduced friction in the braking and suspension system.

Curves

When driving a tanker vehicle, slow down for curves to below posted speeds and begin to accelerate when partially through the curve. The posted speed for a curve is meant for small cars, not trucks. There have been numerous rollovers caused by tanker vehicles traveling at posted speeds.

Skids

To avoid skids, which can lead to jackknifing the tanker, do not oversteer, over accelerate, or over brake. Tank trailers can jackknife if either your driver wheels or trailer wheels skid. The only way to recover from jackknifing is to get the vehicle to gain back wheel traction by releasing the brakes. Never brake to get out of a skid.

SUMMING IT UP

- Drivers that already possess a commercial driver's license (CDL) are eligible to test for the tanker endorsement.

- This endorsement allows drivers to transport liquids and gases in tanks.

- This endorsement requires a written test. The written test consists of 20 questions with a required pass rate of 16 correct questions (80%).

- Traveling with a leaking tanker is illegal, and you can be cited as well as prevented from further traveling until repairs are made.

- Make sure all special purpose equipment is in good condition and working properly according to the vehicle's operation manual.

- Surges occur when a partially filled tank experiences a sudden shift in the liquid.

- Bulkheads are used to separate a larger tank into multiple smaller tanks on the inside.

- Unbaffled tanks are the traditional single tank with no divisions. They are often called smooth bore tanks because there are no bulkheads on the inside.

- Baffled tanks are tanks that have bulkheads with holes inside the bulkhead walls that allow liquid to flow between compartments.

- Remember the following when calculating how much to fill the tank:

  - The amount that the liquid will expand (outage)

  - The weight of the liquid loaded

  - The legal weights that a tanker can carry

- The center of gravity is higher on a tank compared to a lighter passenger type vehicle such as a car or SUV.

- Drive as smoothly as possible. Sudden jerks in the wheel during acceleration and when braking will shift the weight of the liquid around and can cause you to lose control of the vehicle.

- Use consistent pressure on the brakes. If you must stop quickly for an emergency, such as avoiding a crash, use controlled or stab braking while avoiding sharp and sudden steering.

- Slow down for curves in the road and apply a little acceleration through the curve.

- To avoid skids, which can lead to jackknifing the tanker, do not oversteer, over accelerate, or over brake.

NOTES

TANKER VEHICLES PRACTICE TEST

20 Questions—60 Minutes

> **Directions:** This test consists of a combination of true/false and multiple-choice questions. Only one answer is correct for each question.

1. A tanker endorsement is required for all transport of tanks, whether full or empty.

   A. True

   B. False

2. The total combined amount of liquid must be over _____ gallons to require a tanker endorsement.

   A. 119 gallons

   B. 120 gallons

   C. 999 gallons

   D. 1,000 gallons

3. Which letter represents both an endorsement code and a restriction code related to transporting tanks?

   A. X

   B. V

   C. N

   D. P

4. Dents can be located on

   A. the inside of the tank.

   B. the outside of the tank.

   C. both the inside and the outside of the tank.

   D. on the bottom of the tank.

5. The carrier, not the driver, is always responsible for cleanup that occurs due to a known leaking tank.

   A. True

   B. False

6. The maximum fine for a first-time offense regarding a leaky tank with hazardous materials is

   A. $5,000.

   B. $55,000.

   C. $75,000.

   D. $100,000.

7. All liquids have roughly the same weight.

   A. True

   B. False

8. Stab braking is when the driver

   A. pushes lightly on the brakes and then backs off and repeats.

   B. slams on the brakes firmly and does not back off.

   C. pushes slowly but firmly on the brakes.

   D. pushes firmly, allows the wheels to lock, then backs off and repeats.

9. Baffled tanks

   A. have nothing inside them and are also called smooth-bore tanks.

   B. are primarily used to transport food items, such as milk.

   C. are divided by bulkheads with holes to slow liquid flow and reduce surges.

   D. are no longer used in long distance driving.

10. Which of the following is an example of a type of cargo that requires a tank endorsement?

    A. Milk

    B. Hogs

    C. Steel Bars

    D. Apples

11. A liquid surge can be decreased by using baffled tanks.

    A. True

    B. False

12. A smooth-bore tank is often used to transport

    A. flammable liquids.

    B. liquid food products.

    C. liquids with lower viscosity.

    D. gases.

13. A manhole cover is usually located on

    A. the top of the tank.

    B. the front of the tank.

    C. the back of the tank.

    D. both sides of the tank.

14. When unloading liquids from a bulkhead tank, which of the following is important to pay attention to?

    A. Weight distribution on bulkheads

    B. Total outage

    C. Surges

    D. Risk of rollover

15. The three factors to consider when calculating how much a tank can hold are the expansion of the liquid, the legal weight limits, and the weight of the liquid.

    A. True

    B. False

16. Before driving, manhole covers should always be

    A. partially open to prevent pressure from building.

    B. in the closed position.

    C. opened and reclosed again.

    D. padlocked.

17. Baffled tanks help to reduce

    A. side-to-side surges.

    B. front-to-back surges.

    C. outage.

    D. rollover.

18. Which of the following should you do when driving a tanker around a curve?

    A. Brake slightly midturn

    B. Accelerate slightly midturn

    C. Accelerate slightly before the turn

    D. Downshift midturn

19. Some tanks are divided into smaller compartments called

    A. bulkheads.

    B. baffled tanks.

    C. possum bellies.

    D. surges.

20. All of the following are part of every tanker vehicle inspection EXCEPT:

    A. Intake valves

    B. Pipes

    C. Hoses

    D. Vapor recovery kits

ANSWER KEY AND EXPLANATIONS

1. B	**5.** B	**9.** C	**13.** A	**17.** B
2. D	**6.** C	**10.** A	**14.** A	**18.** B
3. A	**7.** B	**11.** A	**15.** A	**19.** A
4. C	**8.** D	**12.** B	**16.** B	**20.** D

1. **The correct answer is B.** A tanker endorsement is only required for tanks that are in use. An empty tank does not need this endorsement.

2. **The correct answer is D.** The total combined amount of liquid must be over 1,000 gallons to require a tanker endorsement. If a single container exceeds 119 gallons (choice A), meaning it is 120 gallons (choice B) or more, the endorsement is required. If it is 999 gallons combined (choice C) but in smaller units below 120 gallons, the endorsement is not required.

3. **The correct answer is A.** The code X is a combination endorsement code that combines both the tanker and HazMat endorsements into one. It is also used as a restriction code for a person with a CLP (permit only) and restricts them to dry tanks only. V (choice B) relates to medical restrictions. N (choice C) is the tanker endorsement code. P (choice D) is the passenger endorsement code.

4. **The correct answer is C.** Dents can be located on both the inside and the outside of the tank. The inside only (choice A), outside only (choice B), and bottom only (choice D) all leave out crucial areas for inspection.

5. **The correct answer is B.** The driver is usually responsible for cleanup that is due to a known leak in the tank. The carrier may offer to assist or cover part of the cost, but that is based on company policy.

6. **The correct answer is C.** The maximum fine for a first-time offense regarding a leaky tank with hazardous materials is $75,000. The maximum civilian penalty was once $55,000 (choice B). $5,000 (choice A) is the rate for a first-time offense

for nonhazardous materials. $100,000 (choice D) can occur after the first offense.

7. **The correct answer is B.** All liquids do not have the same weight. Certain acids and metals are much heavier than others, such as water. Always know the weight of the liquids being transported.

8. **The correct answer is D.** Stab braking is when the driver pushes firmly enough to lock the wheels, backs off to gain traction, and then repeats. Pressing lightly on the brakes (choice A) will not slow the truck down. Slamming on the brakes and not backing off (choice B) may cause a skid. Pushing slowly but firmly (choice C) is called controlled braking.

9. **The correct answer is C.** Baffled tanks are divided by bulkheads with holes that allow the liquid to freely flow to slow or reduce surges. They are not called smooth-bore tanks (choice A) and are not used to transport food items, such as milk (choice B), two things that are true of unbaffled tanks. Baffled tanks are used heavily in long distance driving (choice D).

10. **The correct answer is A.** Any liquid or gas of a sufficient quantity, including milk, requires a tank endorsement. Hogs (choice B), steel bars (choice C), and apples (choice D) can all be transported without the tank endorsement.

11. **The correct answer is A.** Baffled tanks have bulkheads with holes in them to allow the liquid to flow through, thus decreasing the volume of liquid in any one location. This in turn reduces, but does not eliminate, liquid surges.

12. **The correct answer is B.** A smooth-bore tank, also called an unbaffled tank, is often used to transport

liquid food products, such as milk, because baffled tanks are more difficult to sanitize in order to meet food safety standards. Flammable liquids (choice A), liquids with lower viscosity (choice C), and gases (choice D) do not have the same restrictions and, therefore, can be transported in baffled tanks.

13. **The correct answer is A.** A manhole cover is usually located on the top of the tank. They are not located on the front (choice B), back (choice C), or both sides (choice D) of the tank.

14. **The correct answer is A.** Bulkheads are used to divide tanks, and thus the transported liquid, into separate compartments. Because of this, it is important to unload the liquids with weight distribution in mind. If too much is left on the front or back axles, it can cause damage or affect vehicle control. Total outage (choice B) is only a risk when loading, not unloading. Surges (choice C) and risk of rollover (choice D) are both concerns when the vehicle is in motion.

15. **The correct answer is A.** A driver must consider the weight of the liquid, the expansion of the liquid, and the legal weight limits when calculating how much they can transport.

16. **The correct answer is B.** The manhole covers should always be in the closed position before driving. They should never be partially open (choice A) as that allows for leaks when driving.

They do not need to be opened and reclosed again (choice C), and they are not usually padlocked (choice D).

17. **The correct answer is B.** Baffled tanks divide up the liquid using bulkheads with holes that reduce front-to-back surges. They do not reduce side-to-side surges (choice A) or rollovers (choice D). Outage (choice C) is not reduced using baffled tanks but rather by the expansion space needed as determined by the liquid and temperatures.

18. **The correct answer is B.** Accelerating slightly midturn increases the traction of the vehicle. Braking slightly midturn (choice A) can decrease the traction. Accelerating before the turn (choice C) can lead to a rollover. Downshifting midturn (choice D) can also be dangerous.

19. **The correct answer is A.** Some tanks are divided into smaller compartments by bulkheads. Baffled tanks (choice B) have bulkheads inside them that have holes to restrict and direct liquid movement. Possum bellies (choice C) are a type of livestock trailer. Surges (choice D) are a result of liquid moving quickly from one side of the tank to the other.

20. **The correct answer is D.** Vapor recovery kits fall under the category of special purpose equipment, which is not present on every tanker. Intake valves (choice A), pipes (choice B), and hoses (choice C) are all part of every tank inspection.

CHAPTER

Hazardous Materials

HAZARDOUS MATERIALS

OVERVIEW

Exam Format

Endorsement Requirements

Safety

Vehicle Operation

Summing It Up

Practice Test

Hazardous materials (also called HazMat or HM) are any kind of cargo that poses a risk to health, safety, and property when being transported. There are many regulations from federal, state, and company sources that help to keep the transportation of hazardous materials as safe as possible. It is important to obtain a copy of the regulations for any state or local area that you may travel to or through while transporting hazardous materials. Additionally, some areas may require you to possess an additional permit to transport certain materials, such as explosives or large quantities of one material.

 NOTE

At the end of Chapter 8, you will find a Hazardous Materials Practice Test that will test your knowledge of the information contained in this chapter and better prepare you for the CDL hazardous materials endorsement test.

Regulations are constantly changing on all levels to keep everything as up-to-date and safe as possible, so be sure to refer to your state CDL manual and regulations as contained in title 49 of the Code of Federal Regulations, parts 171–180.

EXAM FORMAT

This endorsement requires a written test that is one of the most difficult among endorsement tests. It is 30 questions long and requires 24 correct responses to pass (80%).

Scheduling

Scheduling is state-specific, so check with your local department of motor vehicles for information on scheduling the test. However, prior to scheduling a test with your DMV, you'll need to complete an application and background check with the Transportation Security Administration (TSA) at a local application center. Processing time for your application can vary, but acceptance has been reported to take as long as two months.

ENDORSEMENT REQUIREMENTS

Any transportation of a hazardous material that is defined by the Hazardous Materials Regulations (HMR) in 49 CFR 383.5 of the Code of Federal Regulations requires a HazMat endorsement. If the hazardous materials are transported in bulk tanks, a tank vehicle endorsement is also required (see Chapter 7). Drivers must be 21-year-old to transport hazardous materials both intrastate and interstate. Drivers seeking this endorsement for any class of vehicle must pass a background check with the TSA, which reviews criminal, immigration, and FBI records. Failure to pass the background check will result in denial of the endorsement. Further information on the Hazardous Materials Endorsement Threat Assessment Program can be found here: **universalenroll.dhs.gov/programs/hme.**

Certain restrictions can inhibit a driver from being able to drive certain vehicles. The following is a summary of possible codes and their meanings.

ENDORSEMENT CODES	
H	Code received when HazMat transportation is approved for said CDL driver.
X	Code received when HazMat transportation in a tank vehicle is approved for said CDL driver.

RESTRICTION CODES	
V	Medical variance code: Restrictions related to DOT medical certification, such as high blood pressure or diabetes.

SAFETY

Due to their dangerous nature, the containment rules for hazardous materials have been put in place to protect you (the driver), those around you, and the environment. These rules set a standard for how the shippers must package the materials and how the drivers must load, transport, and unload them.

Communicating Risks

Regulations for communications require shippers to properly label and package the hazardous materials, provide shipping paperwork, and give access to emergency response information. This allows the shipper, carrier, driver, and anyone near the packaged materials to know what they are and what their hazard risk is.

Shippers

Shippers are responsible for using the HazMat regulations to do the following:

- Determine the following for the material:
  - Identification number
  - Proper shipping name
  - Hazard class
  - Packing group
  - Correct packaging
  - Necessary labels and markings
  - Necessary placards
- Properly label, mark, and/or placard packages and shipments
- Fill out the shipping papers to reflect the proper shipping description of the material
- Approve on the shipping papers that the shipment has been identified and prepared according to regulations with a hand signature
- Provide the necessary emergency contact information
- Keep a copy of the shipping papers (or an electronic image of them) for a period of 2 years after the primary carrier accepts the materials

Carriers

Carriers are responsible for using the HazMat regulations to do the following:

- Ensure that the shipment makes it from the shipper to the destination in a safe manner
- Ensure labeling of the packages and shipments are correct
- Ensure the shipping papers are filled out correctly by the shipper
- Refuse any shipments that are improperly handled or damaged
- Keep a copy of the shipping papers (or an electronic image of them) for a period of 1 year if they are not the originators of the shipment

Drivers

Drivers are responsible for using HazMat regulations to do the following:

- Identify hazardous materials and what type they are
- Safely load and unload the materials
- Ensure the proper labeling of the vehicle with the needed warnings and placards
- Safely transport the materials and follow special rules of transporting the material
- Refuse any packages that are leaking or damaged
- Refuse any improperly labeled packages or shipments
- Refuse any improperly filled out shipping papers
- Properly report and respond to accidents and emergencies

Identifying and Marking Rules

Much of the communication for HazMat is done through proper labeling. There are many kinds of divisions and classes that different materials fall under, and this is done to properly communicate what the hazards are of the materials being carried. You should know all different types of materials, their classes, and divisions before taking the HazMat test.

The Hazardous Materials Regulations (HMR) are found in parts 171–180 of title 49 in the Code of Federal Regulations (CFR). The reference for this is 49 CFR 171–180 and is used by shippers, carriers, and drivers. Within this, there are three main lists used by shippers, carriers, and drivers to identify hazardous materials. They are as follows:

1. 49 CFR 172.101, the Hazardous Material Table
2. Appendix A to Section 172.101, the List of Hazardous Materials and Reportable Quantities
3. Appendix B to Section 172.101, the List of Marine Pollutants

HAZARDOUS MATERIALS CLASS

Class	Division	Name of Class or Division	Examples
1	1.1	Mass Explosion	Dynamite
	1.2	Projection Hazard	Flares
	1.3	Fire Hazard	Display Fireworks
	1.4	Minor Explosion	Ammunition
	1.5	Very Insensitive	Blasting Agents
	1.6	Extremely Insensitive	Explosive Devices
2	2.1	Flammable Gases	Propane
	2.2	Non-Flammable Gases	Helium
	2.3	Poisonous/Toxic Gases	Fluorine, Compressed
3	-	Flammable Liquids	Gasoline
4	4.1	Flammable Solids	Ammonium Picrate, Wetted
	4.2	Spontaneously Combustible	White Phosphorus
	4.3	Dangerous When Wet	Sodium
5	5.1	Oxidizers	Ammonium Nitrate
	5.2	Organic Peroxides	Methyl Ethyl Ketone Peroxide
6	6.1	Poison (Toxic Material)	Potassium Cyanide
	6.2	Infectious Substances	Anthrax Virus
7	-	Radioactive	Uranium
8	-	Corrosives	Battery Fluid
9	-	Miscellaneous Hazardous Materials	Polychlorinated Biphenyls (PCB)
None	-	ORM-D (Other Regulated Material-Domestic)	Food Flavorings, Medicines

Refer to your state CDL Manual and 49 CFR 171–180 for more information on the definitions and characteristics of the different class hazardous materials, how to transport them, and how to react to emergencies.

The following visual can be used to help you remember the different classes. It also illustrates the placards associated within each class. You can find color versions of the placards in the Pipeline and Hazardous Materials Safety Administration's DOT Chart 15: Hazardous Materials Markings, Labeling and Placarding Guide.

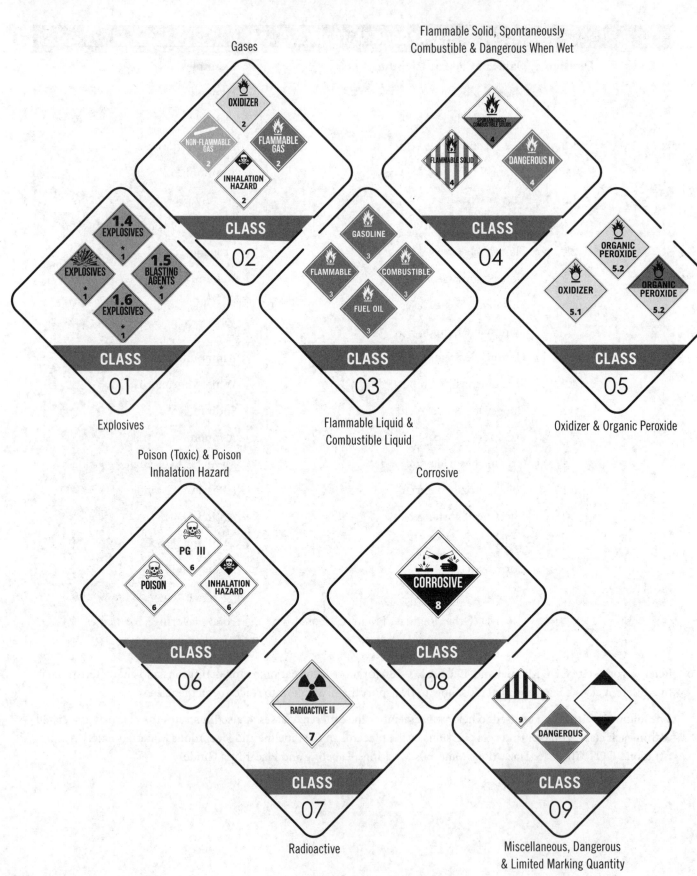

Gases

Flammable Solid, Spontaneously
Combustible & Dangerous When Wet

CLASS
02

CLASS
04

CLASS
01

CLASS
03

CLASS
05

Explosives

Flammable Liquid &
Combustible Liquid

Oxidizer & Organic Peroxide

Poison (Toxic) & Poison
Inhalation Hazard

Corrosive

CLASS
06

CLASS
08

CLASS
07

CLASS
09

Radioactive

Miscellaneous, Dangerous
& Limited Marking Quantity

Hazardous Materials Table, 49 CFR 172.101

The Hazardous Materials Table is used by shippers to correctly identify hazardous materials and how they are to be labeled, packed, shipped, etc. You can see an excerpt in the following table:

49 CFR 172.101 HAZARDOUS MATERIALS TABLE									
Symbols	Hazardous Materials Description & Proper Shipping Names	Hazard Class or Division	Identification Numbers	PG	Label Codes	Special Provisions (172.102)	Packaging (173.***)		
							Exceptions	Non-Bulk	Bulk
(1)	(2)	(3)	(4)	(5)	(6)	(7)	(8A)	(8B)	(8C)
A	Acetaldehyde	9	UN1841	III	9	IB8, IP3, IP7, T1, TP33	155	204	240

Column 1: Symbols for Shipping Related Codes

This column uses symbols to explain when and if Hazardous Material Regulations are required during different shipping modes (air, land, water, etc.). There are six symbols that can be put into column 1:

1. +: This indicates the material poses a risk to humans even if it does not meet the hazard class definition.

2. A: The material defined in Column 2, unless a hazardous substance or waste, is only subject to HMR when it is meant to be transported by air. Air pollutants are not generally recognized by shippers, carriers, and drivers.

3. W: The material defined in Column 2, unless a hazardous substance/waste or marine pollutant, is only subject to HMR when it is meant to be transported by water.

4. D: The proper shipping name is accurate for the material if it is meant to be transported domestically. However, the shipping name may not be proper for transporting internationally.

5. I: The proper shipping name is accurate for transporting internationally, but another name may be used for transporting domestically.

6. G: The material defined in Column 2 is the generic shipping name and must be accompanied by a proper technical name.

Column 2: Description and Proper Shipping Name

This column holds the proper shipping and definition/description of a regulated material. Please note the following for column 2:

- Entries for materials are in alphabetical order.
- All proper shipping names are in regular type.
- If a name is in italics, it means that it is not the proper shipping name.

Column 3: Hazard Class and Division

There are nine classes and up to six divisions within several classes. Be aware of the following for column 3:

- At times, the word *forbidden* may be written.
- Materials labeled "Forbidden" are never to be transported.

Column 4: Identification Number

This column lists each identification number for every material on the table. You'll see the following:

- Identification numbers will always be preceded by UN, NA, or ID.

  - UN is associated with proper shipping names recognized by the United Nations.

  - NA is associated with the proper shipping names used in the US and when shipping to and from Canada.

  - ID is associated with proper shipping names recognized by the International Civil Aviation Organization (IACO).

- This number must be on the shipping paper, packaging, cargo tanks, and other bulk packaging.

Column 5: Packing Group

This column holds the packing group for the material, and this is depicted in Roman numerals.

Column 6: Required Hazard Warning Labels

This column holds the hazard warning label(s) the shipper must put on the packages of that material.

Column 7: Additional and/or Special Provisions

This column lists the additional and/or special provisions that must be given to the material.

- If an entry is in this column for a material, the federal HMR must be referred to for the specific information on that material.

- If ever the numbers 1–6 are in this column, then that material is a poison inhalation hazard (PIH), which have special requirements for shipping papers, markings, and placards.

Column 8: Packing Requirements

This column is split into three parts holding the section numbers that pertain to the packaging requirements for that material. This includes the following:

- Exceptions
- Non-Bulk
- Bulk

Reportable Spills

Appendix A of 49 CFR 172.101, *List of Hazardous Substances and Reportable Quantities*, covers substances that the DOT and EPA will want to know about if spills reach a certain amount. If any of the listed materials are transported at a reportable quantity (RQ) or greater in a singular package, then the shipper must display the letters *RQ* on the package(s). The letters *RQ* can be displayed before or after the basic description. Any spills of these materials that occur in a reportable quantity must be reported by you or your employer.

Appendix B of 49 CFR 172.101, *List of Marine Pollutants*, lists chemicals and materials that are toxic to marine life. Regarding highway transportation, the List of Marine Pollutants only applies to chemicals in a container that has a capacity of 119 gallons or more without a placard or label from the HMR. These bulk packages of marine pollutants must display the marking of a white triangle with a fish and an *X* through the

APPENDIX A TO 49 CFR 172.101 LIST OF HAZARDOUS SUBSTANCES AND REPORTABLE QUANTITIES	
Hazardous Substances	Reportable Quanity (RQ) Pounds (Kilograms)
Phenyl mercaptan	100 (45.4)
Phenylmercury acetate	100 (45.4)
Phenylthiourea	100 (45.4)
Phorate	10 (4.54)
Phosgene	10 (4.54)
Phosphine	100 (45.4)
Phosphoric acid	5,000 (2,270)
Phosphoric acid, diethyl 4-nitrophenyl ester	100 (45.4)
Phosphoric acid, lead (2+) Salt (2:3) salt	10 (4.54)

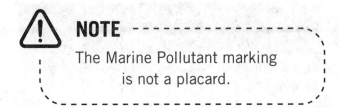

NOTE

The Marine Pollutant marking is not a placard.

fish. The marking must also be on the vehicle and the shipping papers must have a notation saying *Marine Pollutant* near the material description.

Shipping Papers

Shipping papers (also called shipping orders, bills of lading, and manifests) play a vital role in communicating the type of material and how it should be handled. Proper shipping papers should be obtained before transport because they can identify and communicate what the materials are to emergency response personnel if the driver is unable to clearly communicate. Shipping papers should always be kept in the following three locations:

1. The pouch on the driver's door
2. In clear view and within reach when driving with a seat belt on
3. In the driver's seat if the driver is out of the vehicle

Shipping papers, if listing hazardous as well as non-hazardous packages, must indicate the hazardous packages so that they will be more easily identified. This can include marking the HM column with an *X,* or *RQ* can be used to replace the *X* if it is a Reportable Quantity HazMat. Non-hazardous materials cannot have any hazard class or identification number attached to them. Shipping papers must contain the identification and information of a material that is worked out on the Hazardous Materials Table, and they should also include the following information:

- Total quantity and unit of measure of the material(s)

- RQ for any Reportable Quantity materials and the proper name of the substance if it is not in the shipping name
- Any material with "G" in the HazMat Table must have its technical name listed
- A list of emergency response phone numbers
- The name or contact number and phone number of the emergency response information (ERI) provider or the person registered with the ERI
- Emergency information either in the shipping papers, a separate document, or the Emergency Response Guidebook (ERG) that, at minimum, contains the following:
  - Basic description and technical name
  - Immediate health hazards
  - Risks of fire or explosions
  - Immediate actions to take in an accident or incident
  - Immediate methods for dealing with fires
  - Initial reactions to be taken to deal with spills or leaks (without there being a fire)
  - First aid measures
- Total quantity and type of packages displayed either before or after the basic description
- If the materials are hazardous waste, the word *waste* before the proper shipping name

Other Important Communication Rules

Use the following guidelines to facilitate your communications:

- HazMat placards should always be 250mm (9.84 inches square) in size, diamond shaped, and 3 inches away from any other markings or labels. There will be 4 placards on each load or vehicle: one for each side. Placards must never use slogans such as *Drive safely.* They are meant to simply and effectively warn of the hazards on board.
- If the shipper provides additional signage, place the signage as required by the shipper.

- Shipping labels should have a 24/7 emergency number to call in case of an accident. This will usually be an 800 number of some kind that will have professionals ready to assist with the material being transported.

- Drivers transporting hazardous waste must sign a Uniform Hazardous Waste Manifest by hand and carry it with them. Shippers will also sign the manifest, and it should be treated like shipping papers for the hazardous waste.

- It is important to know the difference between placards and labels.

  ○ Labels are used on packaging or overpacks.

  ○ Placards are used on outer containers and vehicles.

- If a material is marked or referred to as forbidden, then it cannot be transported by truck.

When Do You Use a Placard?

The general rule is that 1,001 pounds or more of hazardous materials need to be placarded. The Placard Table 2 shows hazardous materials that require placarding under this general rule. However, if it is on the "any amount" table (Placard Table 1), then it must be placarded no matter how much or little is being transported.

Memorize these *any amount* materials so that you are always able to recognize them in the future.

PLACARD TABLE 1 ANY AMOUNT	
If your vehicle contains any amount of...	Placard as...
1.1 Mass Explosives	Explosives 1.1
1.2 Project Hazards	Explosives 1.2
1.3 Mass Fire Hazards	Explosives 1.3
2.3 Poisonous/Toxic Gases	Poison Gas
4.3 Dangerous When Wet	Dangerous When Wet
5.2 (Organic Peroxide, Type B, liquid or solid, Temperature controlled)	Organic Peroxide
6.1 (Inhalation hazard zone A & B only)	Poison/toxic inhalation
7 (Radioactive Yellow III label only)	Radioactive

Emergencies

Emergencies can arise in several different ways when traveling on the road, especially when carrying HazMats. This includes accidents, cargo being damaged or spilled, and even cargo catching fire or exploding. To ensure safety during these emergencies and to protect you, regulations have been put in place.

The National Response Center (NRC) is your main contact for 24-hour toll-free assistance in responding to emergencies involving chemical hazards. They also aid police and firefighters in these situations and can be reached at (800) 424-8802. However, your employer may also rely on the services of organizations such as CHEMTREC. CHEMTREC offers an emergency call center staffed by emergency service specialists, stating that they "establish communication between shippers, carriers, emergency response and medical personnel, chemical experts, and law enforcement agencies during incidents involving hazardous materials." CHEMTREC coordinates with the NRC but also offers additional services to shippers and carriers.

Catagory of Material (Hazard class or division number and additional description, as appropriate)	Placard Name
1.4 Minor Explosion	Explosives 1.4
1.5 Very Insensitive	Explosives 1.5
1.6 Extremely Insensitive	Explosives 1.6
2.1 Flammable Gases	Flammable Gas
2.2 Non-Flammable Gases	Non-Flammable Gas
3 Flammable Liquids	Flammable
Combustible Liquid	Combustible*
4.1 Flammable Solids	Flammable Solid
4.2 Spontaneously Combustible	Spontaneously Combustible
5.1 Oxidizers	Oxidizer
5.2 (other than organic peroxide, Type B, liquid or solid, Temperature Controlled)	Organic Peroxide
6.1 (other than inhalation hazard zone A or B)	Poison
6.2 Infectious Substances	(None)
8 Corrosives	Corrosive
9 Miscellaneous Hazardous Materials	Class 9**
ORM-D	(None)

PLACARD TABLE 2 — 1,001 POUNDS OR MORE

* FLAMMABLE may be used in place of a COMBUSTIBLE on a cargo tank or portable tank.

** Class 0 Placard is not required for domestic transportation.

You or your employer must contact the NRC if any of the following occurs due to hazardous materials:

- Someone is killed
- Someone is injured and needs hospitalization
- Estimated damage to property is over $50,000
- Evacuation of the public is required for more than an hour
- One or more major traffic arteries or locations closes for more than an hour
- Breakage, spilling, fire, or suspected radioactive contamination takes place
- Breakage, spilling, fire, or suspected contamination of an infectious substance takes place
- Marine pollutant quantity greater than 119 gallons or 882 pounds is released. If a scenario such as this continues to threaten life at the scene of an accident/incident it can be reported, but this is left to the decision of the carrier.

Best practices when transporting hazardous materials to maintain safety include the following:

- Ensure the team driver is in good health and able to make the trip.
- Ensure others who will be working on or around the vehicle know of the hazardous cargo.
- Only attempt to contain a leak in your HazMat cargo if you know you can do so in a safe manner. If it cannot be done safely, the leak and situation could escalate into a greater emergency.
- If you believe that an emergency is occurring, call for help.
  - It is better to contact emergency response professionals for a false alarm than to not call anyone and have the situation continue and escalate.
- Follow all protocols and rules for transporting and dealing with hazardous materials.
- DO NOT drive the vehicle if there is a leak. This not only can make the leak worse but will also spread the material across a wider area.

If an emergency arises, such as an accident, you should follow the protocols of your company. The following checklist contains some important universal protocols to remember.

CHECKLIST

- ☐ Check that the driver or driving partner is okay (if someone else is present in the vehicle). Make sure that they are not injured or affected in any way.

- ☐ Grab the shipping papers and emergency response information and keep them with you. Leaving these papers in the truck will not allow you to access them immediately when needed, and it is not always guaranteed that you will be able to return to the cab of the vehicle to retrieve them.

- ☐ Warn everyone in the vicinity of the hazard danger. Vacate the area and remove anyone else around from the danger, letting them know what the material is and what its hazards are.

- ☐ Keep yourself and others far away and upwind of the situation. This will keep everyone out of the reach of the materials if the wind were to stir them up and blow some of them away.

- ☐ Call for help. Do not go to get help yourself, send someone else if possible. If not, reference the emergency response information and call the appropriate numbers.

- ☐ Follow the instructions and protocols for an emergency given to you by your company.

If a fire starts, or you believe one has started:

- DO NOT open the doors of the trailer. Doing so can feed the fire by supplying more air into the compartment, leading to an increase in the fire's size.

- Unless the fire is a very small truck fire with a nonhazardous source, DO NOT try to fight the fire by yourself. HazMat fires require special training and equipment to be properly fought.

- Extinguishers can be used for small trailer fires but not HazMat fires; to combat a HazMat fire, you will need to use a 10 B:C fire extinguisher must be used.

RESPONDING TO EMERGENCIES WITH SPECIFIC HAZARDS

Hazard Class	Response
Class 1 HazMat (Explosives)	• Warn everyone around of the danger. • Keep everyone far away from the vehicle. • Do not allow any smoking or fires nearby. • If there is a fire involved, warn every one of the danger of an explosion. • If safe to do so, remove all explosives from the vehicle and place them at least 200 feet away from the vehicle. Once this is done the vehicle can be moved if it is able and is safe to do so.
Class 2 HazMat (Gases)	• Warn anyone around of the danger. • Only allow those involved in dealing with the hazard and wreckage to get close. • Do not allow smoking near the scene. • Shippers must be notified if Class 2 materials are involved in an accident. • Do not transfer Class 2 materials from one tank to another on public roads unless fueling heavy machinery used on that road.
Class 3 HazMat (Flammable and Combustible Liquids)	• Warn everyone around of the danger. • Have them stand far away. • Do not allow anyone to smoke nearby. • Do not transfer Class 3 HazMat from one vehicle to another unless it is an emergency.
Class 4 HazMat (Flammable Solids, Spontaneously Combustible, Dangerous When Wet)	• Warn others of the danger. • Have them stand far away. • If the material packages are smoldering, but not on fire, do not open them. • Remove the packages from the vehicle if it is safe to do so. • Remove unbroken packages if it will decrease the fire hazard.
Class 5 HazMat (Oxidizers)	• Contact emergency personnel. • Warn others in the area of the danger. • Have them stand away from the packages. • Turn off the vehicle's ignition if safely accessible. • Prevent smoking or any fires in the vicinity. • Remove combustible materials from the area if you can avoid exposure to the oxidizers.
Class 6 HazMat (Poisons)	• Division 6.1 and 6.3 can sometimes be flammable, and if you believe they are, then taking the same precautions as you would with Classes 2 and 3 is best practice. • Keep everyone far away and upwind. • If a vehicle is ever involved in a leak or spill from a Class 6 HazMat, then it should be checked thoroughly for any residual poison before being used again. • If a Division 6.2 package is damaged before transporting, it should not be accepted. • If it is damaged during transport, then you should immediately notify your supervisor.

RESPONDING TO EMERGENCIES WITH SPECIFIC HAZARDS

Class 7 HazMat (Radioactive)	• If a class 7 package is damaged or leaking, immediately notify your supervisor. • Do not touch or inhale the material. • Do not use the vehicle until it is properly cleaned and surveyed with a meter.
Class 8 HazMat (Corrosive)	• If there is a spill or leak, be careful of not creating more damage to the package when handling it. • If parts of the vehicle are exposed to the spill, thoroughly wash it with water. • Before reloading the vehicle, make sure it is properly washed.

SEGREGATION TABLE FOR HAZARDOUS MATERIALS

Class or division		Notes	1.1 & 1.2	1.3	1.4	1.5	1.6	2.1	2.2
Explosives	1.5 and 1.2	A	*	*	*	*	*	X	X
Explosives	1.3		*	*	*	*	*	X	
Explosives	1.4		*	*	*	*	*	O	
Very insensitive explosives	1.5	A	*	*	*	*	*	X	
Extremely insensitive explosives	1.6		*	*	*	*	*		
Flammable gases	2.1		X	X	O	X			
Non-toxic, non-flammable gases	2.2		X			X			
Poisonous gas Zone A	2.3		X	X	O	X		X	
Poisonous gas Zone B	2.3		X	X	O	X		O	
Flammable liquids	3		X	X	O	X			
Flammable solids	4.1		X	X	O	X			
Spontaneously combustible materials	4.2		X	X		X			
Dangerous when wet materials	4.3		X	X		X			
Oxidizers	5.1	A	X	X		X			
Organic peroxides	5.2		X	X		X			
Poisonous liquids PG I Zone A	6.1		X	X	O	X		O	
Radioactive materials	7		X			X		O	
Corrosive liquids	8		X	X	O	X			

VEHICLE OPERATION
Loading and Unloading

One of the top rules for loading and unloading hazardous materials is to not use any methods or tools that may damage the packaging of the materials. Damaging the packaging can lead to exposure and spilling of the hazardous material.

Always engage the parking brakes and chock the wheels when loading or unloading a vehicle/trailer.

When loading hazardous materials, it is important to make sure that there is no opportunity for the packages to move freely. You as a driver are responsible for double checking that everything is filled out, labeled, and packed correctly before you begin loading to transport.

When dealing with HazMat there are certain types of materials that should not be transported together. Refer to the following Segregation Table for Hazardous Materials (also available in 49 CFR 177.848):

2.3 Gas Zone A	2.3 Gas Zone B	3	4.1	4.2	4.3	5.1	5.2	6.1 Liquids PG I Zone A	7	8 Liquids Only
X	X	X	X	X	X	X	X	X	X	X
X	X	X		X	X	X	X	X		X
O	O	O		O				O		O
X	X	X	X	X	X	X	X	X	X	X
X	O							O	O	
		X	X	X	X	X	X			X
		O	O	O	O	O	O			O
X	O					O		X		
X	O							X		O
X	O							X		X
X	O							X		O
X	O	O	O					X		O
X	O							X		O
		X	X	X	X	X	X			X
X	O			O	X	O	O	O	X	

Paragraph (e) of 49 CFR 177.848 provides the following instructions for use of the Segregation Table for Hazardous Materials:

01 The absence of any hazard class or division or a blank space in the table indicates that no restrictions apply.

02 The letter "X" in the table indicates that these materials may not be loaded, transported, or stored together in the same transport vehicle or storage facility during the course of transportation.

03 The letter "O" in the table indicates that these materials may not be loaded, transported, or stored together in the same transport vehicle or storage facility during the course of transportation unless separated in a manner that, in the event of leakage from packages under conditions normally incident to transportation, commingling of hazardous materials would not occur. Notwithstanding the methods of separation employed, Class 8 (corrosive) liquids may not be loaded above or adjacent to Class 4 (flammable) or Class 5 (oxidizing) materials; except that shippers may load truckload shipments of such materials together when it is known that the mixture of contents would not cause a fire or a dangerous evolution of heat or gas.

04 The "*" in the table indicates that segregation among different Class 1 (explosive) materials is governed by the compatibility table in paragraph (f) of 49 CFR 177.848.

05 The note "A" in the second column of the table means that, notwithstanding the requirements of the letter "X", ammonium nitrate (UN1942) and ammonium nitrate fertilizer may be loaded or stored with Division 1.1 (explosive) or Division 1.5 materials, unless otherwise prohibited by § 177.835(c).

06 When the § 172.101 table or § 172.402 of 49 CFR Chapter 1 Subchapter C requires a package to bear a subsidiary hazard label, segregation appropriate to the subsidiary hazard must be applied when that segregation is more restrictive than that required by the primary hazard. However, hazardous materials of the same class may be stowed together without regard to segregation required for any secondary hazard if the materials are not capable of reacting dangerously with each other and causing combustion or dangerous evolution of heat, evolution of flammable, poisonous, or asphyxiant gases, or formation of corrosive or unstable materials.

Beyond the proper separation of materials, keep in mind the following additional rules when loading/unloading HazMat:

- Never move a HazMat container/package that is leaking, damaged, or shows wet/oily stains.
- Do not store hazardous materials in (or near if it can be avoided) the cab of the truck in the sleeping area of the cab.
- Never load a HazMat near a heat source. This includes never using a cargo heater when transporting, loading, or unloading class 1, 3, or division 2.1 HazMat.
- Never smoke around class 1, 3, 4, or 5 HazMat or around division 2.1.

Compressed gas (Class 2) contained in bottles should be stored vertically in secure boxes or racks.

- As a safety precaution, it is best to never smoke around any HazMat so that a level of comfort or habit is not formed by smoking near them.

- HazMat class 1, 4, and 5 should always be transported in an enclosed cargo area. However, this does not have to be done if packaging or a tarp/cover that is water and fire resistant is fitted over them. Class 4 and 5 materials react to water, heat, and air, and they are capable of spontaneous reactions.

- Division 1.1, 1.2, and 1.3 explosives should be handled with the engine of the truck shut off, on top of there being no heat sources around and the floor of the trailer being equipped with non-metallic or non-ferrous metal.

  - Vehicles transporting explosives should also not be stopped on public roadways unless it is an emergency. If this is the case, put out electric red lights, red reflectors, and red flags. Do not use flares or fuses.

- Compressed gas (Class 2) contained in bottles should be stored vertically in secure boxes or racks. An alternative would be storing them horizontally, but they will need to be thoroughly strapped down to keep them from rolling/moving.

  - Relief valves are designed for bottles that are secured.

- Load breakable packages of Class 8 materials one by one if loading them by hand, and never load nitric acid above any other products.

Bulk Loading and Unloading

To be considered a bulk packaging, the materials will be put into a single container that has 119 gallons or more of a substance. When bulk loading, you need to:

- Be alert and aware of your surroundings.

- Always have a clear view of the cargo tank.

- Know what the materials being loaded in the tank are and what hazards they have.

- Know the proper procedures you must take if there is an emergency.

- Make sure you have the necessary authorizations and equipment to move and transport the tank.

- Close all manholes and valves to prevent leaks, even if it is just a small amount of loaded material. Moving the cargo tank with any amount of material loaded when the valves or manholes are open is illegal.

- Only run the engine when loading flammable liquids or compressed gas if it is needed to run a pump. If it is not needed to run a pump, leave the engine off.

- Make sure the tank is properly grounded before opening the filling hole, and make sure that it continues to stay grounded until after the filling hole is closed.

- Keep liquid discharge valves closed unless loading or unloading.

- Unhook all hoses before moving the tank after it has been loaded or unloaded.

When stopping at a railroad crossing, you should stop between 15–50 feet of the tracks, look both ways, and listen for any approaching trains.

Railroads

Like with many commercial vehicles, railroad tracks must not be crossed without stopping first, and you should never shift gears while going over the tracks. When stopping at a railroad crossing, you should stop between 15–50 feet of the tracks, look both ways, and listen for any approaching trains. If a train passes by on the tracks, wait and look/listen for another train because the first train may have hidden a second train as it passed you. Important factors that dictate whether you should stop before a railroad crossing include:

- The load is placarded
- If you are carrying any amount of chlorine
- If you are transporting loaded or empty HazMat cargo tanks

See the General Knowledge chapter for detailed information regarding railroad crossings.

Fueling and Fire Hazards

When fueling your vehicle while carrying HazMat, you should turn off the engine, and you (or a partner if present) must remain at the nozzle to regulate the flow of the fuel. Improper fueling could lead to an ignition that would only be increasingly more harmful due to the hazardous cargo. Additionally, never smoke or carry a cigarette, cigar, or pipe *within 25 feet* of a vehicle transporting class 1, 3, 4, 5, or division 2.1 or 4.2 hazardous materials.

- Never use flares, fuses, or other burning signals while operating a vehicle that carries class 3 materials or those in division 2.1, 1.1, 1.2, or 1.3 even if the vehicle/tank is unloaded.
- When combatting fires, there must be a 10 B:C or higher rated fire extinguisher in the power unit of a placarded vehicle.
- Placarded vehicles are able to drive near open flames if they can do so WITHOUT STOPPING.

Driving and Parking

The following is a collection of rules for driving and parking with hazardous materials. Not all rules will be covered here as regulations can change and vary by area. Be sure to review your state's CDL manual and any local regulations of places you will travel through on top of this list to guarantee you are aware of them all.

Division 1.1, 1.2, and 1.3 Explosives

- NEVER park your vehicle within 5 feet of the section of road that is being traveled on when carrying these explosive materials.

- NEVER park within 300 feet of bridges, tunnels, buildings, places of gathering, or open fires unless preforming a necessary task such as fueling.

- DO NOT uncouple a trailer carrying these explosive materials and leave it on a public street.

- NEVER park on private property unless the owner is aware of you and the danger of the cargo.

- Parking should be done for as short of an amount of time as possible.

- Safe havens are designated areas given by local authorities where vehicles can be left without needing to be watched.

- If your vehicle is parked outside of a safe haven, you must watch it the entire time. However, if the vehicle is on the shipper, carrier, or consignee's property, then someone else other than the driver can watch the vehicle.

Placarded Vehicles Carrying Materials OTHER than 1.1, 1.2, and 1.3 Explosives

- Parking within 5 feet of the section of road that is traveled on is permitted.

- Parking should be done for as short of an amount of time as possible.

- NEVER park within 300 feet of an open fire.

- Vehicles must always be watched when parked in a public area or on a road shoulder.

- DO NOT uncouple a trailer carrying HazMat and leave it on a public street.

- Know what material you are transporting and how to deal with an emergency.

- If parked and attending the vehicle, remain inside or do not be more than 100 feet away and out of clear eyesight.

- When parking, make sure that movement will not be hindered, and you will be able to move the vehicle if it must be moved suddenly.

Vehicles Carrying Chlorine

- If any amount of chlorine is being transported, vehicles MUST be stopped 15–50 feet before a railroad crossing.

- Approved gas masks MUST be in the vehicle if chlorine is being transported in cargo tanks.

- Emergency kits MUST be in the vehicle in order to contain and fix leaks in the dome cover plates of the cargo tank.

SUMMING IT UP

- While transporting hazardous materials, it is important that drivers obtain a copy of the regulations for any state or local area that may be traveled to or through.

- Some areas may require you to possess an additional permit to transport certain materials, such as explosives or large quantities of one material.

- This endorsement requires a written test that is one of the most difficult among endorsement tests. It is 30 questions long and requires 24 correct responses to pass (80%).

- Any transportation of a hazardous material that is defined by the Hazardous Materials Regulations (HMR) in 49 CFR 383.5 of the Code of Federal Regulations requires a HazMat endorsement.

- Drivers must be 21 years old to transport hazardous materials both intrastate and interstate. Drivers seeking this endorsement for any class of vehicle must pass a background check with the Transportation Security Administration, which reviews criminal, immigration, and FBI records. Failure to pass the background check will result in denial of the endorsement.

- HazMat regulations for communications affect shippers, carriers, and drivers. Know the requirements and responsibilities each have for shipping hazardous materials.

- You should know all different types of materials, their classes, and divisions before taking the HazMat test.

- Familiarize yourself with the Hazardous Materials Table, which is used by shippers to correctly identify hazardous materials and how they are to be labeled, packed, shipped, etc.

- Appendix A of 49 CFR 172.101, *List of Hazardous Substances and Reportable Quantities*, covers substances that the DOT and EPA will want to know about if spills reach a certain amount. If any of the listed materials are transported at a reportable quantity (RQ) or greater in a singular package, then the shipper must display the letters *RQ* on the package(s).

- Proper shipping papers should be obtained before transport. Shipping papers should be kept in the pouch on the driver's door, in clear view and within reach when driving with a seat belt on, or in the driver's seat if the driver is out of the vehicle.

- Shipping papers, if listing hazardous as well as non-hazardous packages, must indicate the hazardous packages so that they will be more easily identified.

- The general rule is that when carrying 1,001 pounds or more of hazardous materials, you need to be placarded. Placard Table 2 lists these materials. Memorize Placard Table 1 for "any amount" so you can always recognize them in the future.

- Other important communication rules regarding transporting hazardous materials include the following: display additional shipper signage as required, ensure shipping labels have a 24/7 emergency number to call in case of an accident, sign a Uniform Hazardous Waste Manifest by hand and carry it with you, know the difference between labels and placards, do not transport any material marked or referred to as *forbidden*.

- Emergencies can arise when traveling on the road, including accidents, cargo being damaged or spilled, and even cargo catching fire or exploding. The National Response Center (NRC) is your main contact for 24-hour toll-free assistance in responding to emergencies involving chemical hazards.

- One of the top rules for loading and unloading hazardous materials is to not use any methods or tools that may damage the packaging of the materials.

- Always engage the parking brakes and chock the wheels when loading or unloading a vehicle/trailer.

- When dealing with HazMat there are certain types of materials that should not be transported together. Reference 49 CFR 177.848 for a list of these, as well as instructions.

- To be considered a bulk packaging, the materials will be put into a single container that has 119 gallons or more of a substance.

- Familiarize yourself with safety best practices for bulk loading, such as being alert, always having a view of the cargo tank, knowing which materials are being loaded, making sure the tank Is properly grounded before opening the filling hole, etc.

- Railroad tracks must not be crossed without first stopping, and you should never shift gears while going over the tracks. Important factors that dictate whether you should stop before a railroad crossing include the following: if the load is placarded, if you are carrying any amount of chlorine, or if you are transporting loaded or empty HazMat cargo tanks.

- When fueling your vehicle while carrying HazMat, you should turn off the engine, and you (or a partner if present) must remain at the nozzle to regulate the flow of the fuel.

HAZARDOUS MATERIALS PRACTICE TEST

30 Questions—60 Minutes

Directions: This test consists of a combination of true/false and multiple-choice questions. Only one answer is correct for each question.

1. The endorsement codes that can apply to hazardous materials are

   A. H and M.

   B. M and N.

   C. H and X.

   D. N and X.

2. All of the following are responsibilities of the driver and carrier EXCEPT:

   A. Refuse any improperly labeled packages

   B. Refuse any damaged containers

   C. Properly label packages

   D. Ensure the shipping papers have been fully and correctly filled out

3. Which of the following is NOT one of the 6 symbols found in Column 1 of the Hazardous Materials Table?

   A. J

   B. A

   C. +

   D. G

4. Gasoline falls under what class of hazardous materials?

   A. 1

   B. 3

   C. 6

   D. 8

5. Vehicles carrying 1.1, 1.2, or 1.3 explosives should NOT:

   A. Park near buildings

   B. Avoid parking near open flames

   C. Avoid parking on private property unless the owner is aware of it

   D. Park in a safe haven

6. When bulk loading a vehicle with hazardous materials you should NOT:

   A. Close all manholes and valves

   B. Ground the vehicle before loading/unloading and until it is fully done

   C. Run the engine if a pump is needed

   D. Move the vehicle before unhooking all the hoses

7. Nitric acid should never be stored

   A. below other materials.

   B. on either side of other materials.

   C. above other materials.

   D. if it exceeds a specific weight.

8. During transportation, the products that can present a risk to health, safety, and property are known as

   A. cargo transport.

   B. material endorsement.

   C. hazardous materials.

   D. safety protocols.

9. HazMat placards are round in shape.

   A. True

   B. False

10. It is important for drivers to inspect their vehicles before and during each trip because law enforcement officers will always stop them to check for shipping papers, vehicle placards, HazMat endorsement on the driver license, and their knowledge of HazMat.

    A. True

    B. False

11. The eight HazMat classes signify the risks associated with each of them.

    A. True

    B. False

12. All of these are considered the correct way to refer to shipping papers EXCEPT:

    A. Shipping orders

    B. Bills of lading

    C. Shipping placards

    D. Manifests

13. When drivers are fueling their placarded vehicle, they must always be

    A. within five feet of the pump with a fire extinguisher.

    B. by the pump's emergency power shut-off.

    C. at the front, driver-side corner of the vehicle.

    D. at the nozzle, managing the fuel flow.

14. The use of the "Drive Safely" slogan is allowed when placarding a HazMat truck.

    A. True

    B. False

15. What is the appropriate symbol on the Hazardous Materials Table for a material that is subjected to HazMat regulations only when proposed or planned for transport by air (unless it is a hazardous substance or hazardous waste)?

    A. "W"

    B. "A"

    C. "+"

    D. "D"

16. If it can pass safely without stopping, a placarded vehicle can drive near open flames.

    A. True

    B. False

17. Column 1 of the Hazardous Materials Table can list one of the

    A. four different symbols affecting the shipping method(s).

    B. five different symbols affecting the shipping method(s).

    C. six different symbols affecting the shipping method(s).

    D. eight different symbols affecting the shipping method(s).

18. Flammable and combustible liquids are a Class

    A. 8 material.

    B. 6 material.

    C. 4 material.

    D. 3 material.

19. Marine Pollutant bulk packages are required to show a

    A. red triangle with a fish and an "X" through the fish as a Marine Pollutant marking.

    B. black triangle with a turtle and an "X" through the turtle as a Marine Pollutant marking.

    C. yellow triangle with a fish and an "M" through the fish as a Marine Pollutant marking.

    D. white triangle with a fish and an "X" through the fish as a Marine Pollutant marking.

20. Spills exceeding the RQ (Reportable Quantity) must be reported to the

    A. HHS and TSA.

    B. DMV and TSA.

    C. DOT and EPA.

    D. DOT and DMV.

21. Since some hazardous materials cannot be loaded together with other hazardous materials, restricted combinations are listed in the Hazardous Waste Manifest.

    A. True

    B. False

22. Drivers should never transport a package labeled poison if they are hauling

    A. porous products.

    B. food products.

    C. fuel.

    D. fireworks.

23. A tank endorsement is required if drivers are transporting liquid or gaseous hazardous materials in a cargo tank of any volume.

    A. True

    B. False

24. The identification markings of a product on a tank are required to be

    A. white 3.9" numbers on red panels.

    B. orange 3.9" numbers on black panels.

    C. green 3.9" numbers on orange panels.

    D. black 3.9" numbers on orange panels.

25. The Class 9 Miscellaneous placard does not have to be displayed on a vehicle hauling Class 9 in a domestic transportation, but drivers may display them if they wish.

    A. True

    B. False

26. After the material is accepted by the primary carrier, shippers are required to keep a copy of shipping papers, or an electronic image, of hazardous waste for a period of

    A. 3 years.

    B. 2 years.

    C. 1 year.

    D. 6 months.

27. A Class 7 radioactive material package with a transport index of 0.9 and a maximum surface radiation level of 70 millirems per hour would require a

    A. Yellow II label.

    B. White I label.

    C. Yellow III label.

    D. Yellow I label.

28. A copy of Federal Motor Carrier Safety Regulations (FMCSR), Part 401 must be given to each driver transporting Division 1.1, 1.2, or 1.3 explosives by the carrier.

    A. True
    B. False

29. A driver should never continue driving with hazardous materials leaking from the vehicle to find a phone, truck stop, or assistance.

    A. True
    B. False

30. Oxidizers are a Class

    A. 2 hazardous material.
    B. 3 hazardous material.
    C. 5 hazardous material.
    D. 7 hazardous material.

ANSWER KEY AND EXPLANATIONS

1. C	6. D	11. B	16. A	21. B	26. A
2. C	7. C	12. C	17. C	22. B	27. C
3. A	8. C	13. D	18. D	23. B	28. B
4. B	9. B	14. B	19. D	24. D	29. A
5. A	10. B	15. B	20. C	25. A	30. C

1. **The correct answer is C.** Endorsement code H allows a driver to transport hazardous materials, and endorsement code X allows a driver to transport hazardous materials in a tank vehicle. Code M (choices A and B) is a restriction code that does not allow a driver to operate a class A vehicle. Code N (choices B and D) is an endorsement code that allows a driver to transport non-hazardous materials in a tank vehicle and is also a restriction code that does not allow a driver to operate class A or B vehicles.

2. **The correct answer is C.** Properly labeling packages is the responsibility of the shipper. Refusing any improperly labeled (choice A) or damaged (choice B) packages and ensuring the shipping papers have been properly filled out (choice D) are responsibilities of the driver and carrier.

3. **The correct answer is A.** J is not one of the 6 symbols found in Column 1 of the Hazardous Materials Table. A (choice B) refers to shipping restrictions by air. + (choice C) identifies hazardous materials that pose a risk to humans. G (choice D) refers to the generic shipping name.

4. **The correct answer is B.** Gasoline falls under Class 3, flammable and combustible liquids. Class 1 (choice A) refers to explosives. Class 6 (choice C) refers to poisons. Class 8 (choice D) refers to corrosives.

5. **The correct answer is A.** Vehicles carrying 1.1, 1.2, or 1.3 explosives should NOT park near buildings. They should, however, avoid parking near open flames (choice B) and private property unless

the owner is aware of it (choice C). They should also always seek to park in a safe haven (choice D).

6. **The correct answer is D.** All hoses must be unhooked before moving the vehicle. Closing all manhole covers and valves (choice A), grounding the vehicle before loading/unloading and waiting until it is fully done (choice B), and running the engine ONLY if a pump is needed (choice C) are all things you should do when bulk loading a vehicle with hazardous materials.

7. **The correct answer is C.** Nitric acid should never be stored above other Class 8 materials. Regardless of total weight (choice D) it should always be stored either below (choice A) or on either side (choice B) of another material.

8. **The correct answer is C.** The products that can present a risk to health, safety, and property during transportation are known as hazardous materials. It is not known as cargo transport (choice A), material endorsement (choice B), or safety protocols (choice D).

9. **The correct answer is B.** HazMat placards are not round; they are diamond shaped.

10. **The correct answer is B.** Many times, if drivers are pulled over, they will be checked for the shipping papers, the vehicle placards, the HazMat endorsement on the driver license, and their knowledge of HazMat's, but it is not always a fact that they will be stopped to check for these specifically.

11. **The correct answer is B.** The nine HazMat classes signify the risks associated with each of them.

12. **The correct answer is C.** Shipping placards are not referred to as shipping papers. However, shipping orders (choice A), bills of lading (choice B), manifests (choice D) are all considered correct ways to refer to shipping papers.

13. **The correct answer is D.** Drivers must always be at the nozzle, managing the fuel flow when fueling their placarded vehicle. They must not always be within five feet of the pump with a fire extinguisher (choice A), by the pump's emergency power shut-off (choice B), nor at the front, driver-side corner of the vehicle (choice C).

14. **The correct answer is B.** The use of the "Drive Safely" slogan is NOT allowed when placarding a HazMat truck.

15. **The correct answer is B.** The symbol "A" is used in column one of the Hazardous Materials Table for materials that are subjected to the HazMat regulations only when proposed or planned for transport by air, unless it is a hazardous substance or hazardous waste. The symbol "W" (choice A) is used in column one for hazardous materials that are subjected to the HazMat regulations only when proposed or planned for transport by water vessel, unless it is a hazardous substance or hazardous waste. The symbol "+" (choice C) displays the appropriate shipping name, hazard class, and packing group to use, even if the substance does not meet the hazard class description. The symbol "D" (choice D) in column one of the Hazardous Materials Table indicates that the proper shipping name is suitable for defining the materials for domestic hauling but may not be suitable for international transport.

16. **The correct answer is A.** A placarded vehicle cannot drive near an open fire unless it can pass safely without stopping.

17. **The correct answer is C.** Column 1 of the hazardous materials table list one of the six different symbols affecting the shipping method(s).

18. **The correct answer is D.** Flammable and combustible liquids are a Class 3 hazardous material. Corrosives are a Class 8 hazardous material (choice A). Toxic or infectious substances are a Class 6

hazardous material (choice B). Flammable solids are a Class 4 hazardous material (choice C).

19. **The correct answer is D.** A white triangle with a fish and an "X" through the fish as a marine pollutant marking is shown on marine pollutant bulk packages.

20. **The correct answer is C.** Reporting any spills exceeding the RQ (Reportable Quantity) must be done to the DOT and EPA.

21. **The correct answer is B.** Because some hazardous materials cannot be loaded together with other hazardous materials, the restricted combinations are listed in the Segregation and Separation Chart.

22. **The correct answer is B.** Since poisons can be transmitted in any form, drivers should never transport it if they are hauling food products. As long as they are in line with transportation regulations, drivers can still transport porous products (choice A), fuel (choice C), and fireworks (choice D).

23. **The correct answer is B.** Drivers who transport hazardous materials in a cargo tank in volumes that require placarding must have the tank endorsement; having both the tanker and HazMat endorsements will be presented as an X on the CDL.

24. **The correct answer is D.** The rules require black 3.9" numbers on orange panels to be the identified marking of a product on a tank.

25. **The correct answer is A.** Although drivers may display them if they wish, the Class 9 Miscellaneous placard is not required to be displayed on a vehicle hauling Class 9 in a domestic transportation.

26. **The correct answer is A.** A copy of hazardous waste shipping papers, or electronic images of them, are required to be kept by the shipper for a period of 3 years after the material is accepted by the primary carrier. A copy of the shipping papers for hazardous materials (not waste) are kept for a period of 2 years.

27. **The correct answer is C.** Since the proper label to attach to a package of Class 7 radioactive material

is based on the transport index and the maximum surface of the package, a package with a transport index of 0.9 and a maximum surface radiation level of 70 millirems per hour would require a Yellow III label. Based on the information given, a Yellow II label (choice A), a White I label (choice B), or a Yellow I label (choice D) are not the proper labels to affix to this package.

28. **The correct answer is B.** If drivers are transporting Division 1.1, 1.2, or 1.3 explosives, then the carrier must supply the driver with a copy of Federal Motor Carrier Safety Regulations (FMCSR), Part 397.

29. **The correct answer is A.** Drivers should never continue operating a truck with hazardous materials leaking from the vehicle to find a phone, truck stop, or assistance.

30. **The correct answer is C.** A Class 5 hazardous material is an oxidizer. A Class 2 hazardous material (choice A) is a flammable gas. A Class 3 hazardous material (choice B) is a flammable liquid. A Class 7 hazardous material (choice D) is a radioactive material.

NOTES

CHAPTER

**Passenger Vehicles
and School Buses**

PASSENGER VEHICLES AND

OVERVIEW

Exam Format

Endorsement Requirements

Inspections

Safety

School Buses

Summing It Up

Practice Tests

The passenger vehicle endorsement (P) allows a driver with a CDL to drive a vehicle designed to transport large groups of people (16 or more, including the driver). It is required for bus drivers (excluding school buses) and large van transportation. The school bus endorsement (S) allows a driver with a CDL to drive a school bus. Both the passenger vehicle and school bus endorsements require special knowledge tests as well as physical skills tests completed in the respective vehicles. The following sections summarize the information present in the CDL manual and provide helpful tips to prepare you for these exams, starting with the passenger vehicle endorsement.

EXAM FORMAT

The passenger vehicle endorsement requires both a written and skills test. The written test consists of 20 questions, with a required pass rate of 16 correct questions (80%). In addition, the skills test (also known as the driving test) must be taken in a passenger vehicle.

Scheduling

This is state-specific, but in general, the written test and the skills test cannot be scheduled on the same day. Check with your local department of motor vehicles for more information on scheduling both components.

ENDORSEMENT REQUIREMENTS

This endorsement applies to vehicles in any class (A, B, or C) and allows a CDL holder to transport passengers in a commercial vehicle. One noted exception is when a permitted only (CLP) driver is operating a CMV with an instructor, test administrator, federal/state auditors and inspectors, and/or other trainees.

Some states may require a Class C CDL and/or this endorsement for fewer than 16 passengers, but the federal guideline is that a P endorsement is required for all passenger vehicles designed to transport 16 or more people.

Many states allow for people 18 and up to obtain an intrastate (only within one state) CDL. Check your state CDL manual and with your local DMV to determine whether you meet the legal age requirement for the endorsement in your state. Be aware that it is not uncommon for employers to restrict driver age to 25 and older for the purpose of meeting insurance requirements.

As of February 7, 2022, before completing the physical skills test for the passenger vehicle endorsement, the driver must complete an entry-level driver training (ELDT) program given by a provider indicated in the FMCSA Training Provider Registry.

The circumstances under which you apply and test for your CDL will determine the restriction codes present on the license. The following is a summary of possible codes and their meanings.

ENDORSEMENT CODE	
P	Code received when passenger endorsement is approved.
RESTRICTION CODES	
E	Completing test with an automatic transmission vehicle, which results in restricting the operation of a manual transmission vehicle.
M	Completing the passenger endorsement in a Class B vehicle, restricting the driver from operating a Class A passenger vehicle.
N	Completing the passenger endorsement in a Class C vehicle, restricting the driver from operating a Class A or Class B passenger vehicle.
V	Medical variance code: restrictions related to DOT medical certification, such as high blood pressure or diabetes.

To avoid unwanted restrictions, arrange to take your physical skills test in the vehicle class and type you plan to drive commercially.

 TIP

All inspections, both interior and exterior, must occur PRE and POST travel, regardless of if any passengers have been transported. Inspections must occur any time a new driver takes over.

INSPECTIONS

A driver should complete all general inspection requirements on every commercial vehicle. When in doubt, refer back to the General Knowledge chapter as well as your state-specific CDL manual. Inspections should include examination of all vehicle systems as well as specific points of inspection for the exterior and interior as required by the type of vehicle you're driving.

Exterior Passenger Transport Inspection

Passenger transport inspections follow all the main vehicle inspection points listed in the General Knowledge chapter. However, passenger transport inspection also includes the following specialized exterior areas specific to the type of vehicle—bus, van, motorcoach, etc.

Interior Passenger Transport Inspection

The following graphic indicates key inspection points for the interior of a passenger transport.

 NOTE

The only emergency exits that can be opened in non-emergency situations are the hatches in the top of the vehicle to provide added ventilation. However, open hatches will increase the height of the vehicle and must be accounted for when driving.

Tires should be inspected every 2 hours or 100 miles (whichever comes first) when driving in excessively hot (greater than 85 degrees Fahrenheit) conditions.

EXTERIOR PASSENGER TRANSPORT INSPECTION

Sample on Map	Passenger Transport Specific Inspection Item	Common Locations
1	Emergency Exits	Located on windows, skylights, and doors
2	Luggage Compartments	Located on one or both sides of the bus
3	Equipment Hatches	Located on the side or the back
4	Wheelchair Ramp	Can be on the side or in the back
Varies	Signs of Damage or Vandalism	All Exterior—common for passenger vehicles because of valuables
5	Coupling Device (If applicable—such as an articulated or accordion bus)	Between the back of the bus/van and the trailer or second bus
Varies	Air Hoses (If applicable—such as when towing a trailer)	Between the back of the bus/van and the trailer or second bus

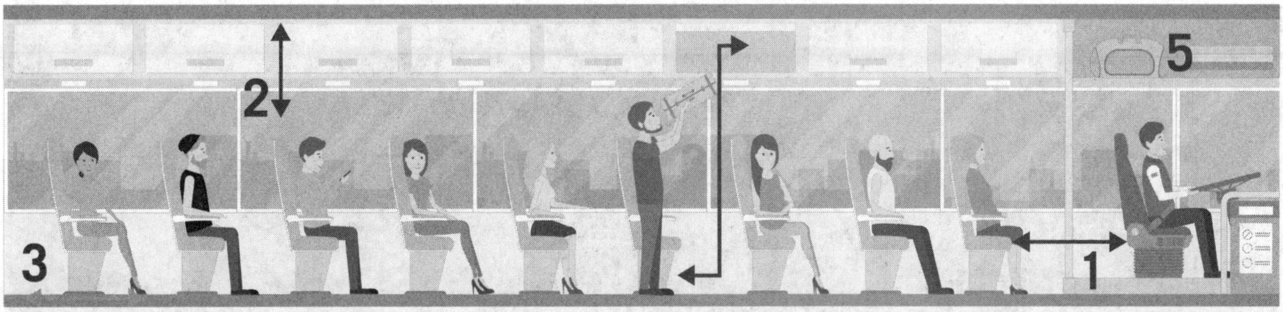

INTERIOR PASSENGER TRANSPORT INSPECTION		
Sample on Map	**Interior Inspection Item**	**What To Look For**
1	Seat and Seatbelts	Are they in working order? Does every seat have a seatbelt (if applicable)? Does the driver seat have a working seatbelt?
Varies	Handholds	Are the handholds properly mounted? Are they secure?
2	Windows/Emergency Exits	Are they in working order? Are the emergency exits correctly labeled? Can the emergency hatches on the roof open and close?
3	Aisle and Floor	Is the aisle free from debris and obstructions?
4	Luggage	Is luggage stored safely in the overhead compartment OR under the seat? Is it blocking the aisle?
5	Emergency Kit	Is it stocked and stored in its designated location? Does it contain either 3 reflective triangles OR 3 liquid flares? If needed, does it contain fuses (for buses without circuit breakers)?
Varies	Interlock System	Do the brakes engage when the passenger door is open? Do the brakes release when the passenger door closes?
Varies	PA System or Other Passenger Signaling System	Is the PA system in working order? Do all the speakers work? Does the signage work? Do the buttons and/or cords work? Does the lighting work?

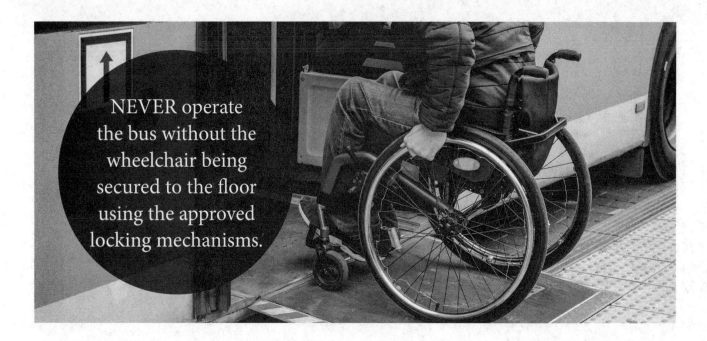

NEVER operate the bus without the wheelchair being secured to the floor using the approved locking mechanisms.

SAFETY

The safety of your passengers is paramount when driving a passenger transport. The following section covers passenger transport safety, route specific safety, and safe driving practices.

Passenger Transportation and Safety

There are specific areas to review for the endorsement exam. In an effort to streamline studying, the core components are highlighted here. If you as a learner would like more in-depth information, please refer to your state's CDL manual as regulations may vary from state to state.

Disruptive Passengers

Disruptive passengers may need to be removed from the vehicle. They should never be left on the side of the road in an area that is unsafe. This includes unlit or poorly lit spots at night. If a passenger must be discharged from the transport for being disruptive, try to discharge them at the next available stop. If this is not possible, then look for an area that is well lit and populated with other people. In addition, make sure to follow any company rules or procedures in doing so.

The Standee Line

The standee line is a two-inch thick line on the floor of the bus that designates where passengers can stand. They are never allowed to be in front of the standee line when the vehicle is in motion. If passengers must stand when in motion, make sure to announce the rules regarding the standee line.

Wheelchairs

Wheelchair loading, securing, and unloading is a crucial part of passenger transport. Remember the following:

- The wheelchair brakes should ALWAYS be engaged during loading and unloading.
- If present, locks on the lift itself must be utilized.
- Make sure to secure the wheelchair through BOTH wheels and the base using the locking mechanisms on the bus prior to driving.
- Wheelchair brakes should remain locked while the bus is in motion.
- Keep wheelchair seating open and available whenever possible so passengers using wheelchairs have access to the locks.
- NEVER operate the bus without the wheelchair being secured to the floor using the approved locking mechanisms.

Animals

It is standard for animals to be prohibited from public buses and vans unless they are service animals. Any person with a disability has the right to a service animal that is specifically trained to help them. Remember the following:

- It is okay to ask if the animal is for service, but it is illegal under federal law to request documented proof.

- As of 2011, under the ADA, only dogs are recognized as service animals. These rules can vary, however, between states and companies. If you are unsure of what animals fall under service animals in your region, confirm with your company and local DMV so you are aware.

- Common disabilities/conditions that passengers may have a service animal for can be, but are not limited to, the following:

    ○ Blindness or visual impairment

    ○ Deafness or hard of hearing

    ○ Seizure disorders

    ○ Physical limitations (requiring the use of braces, a wheelchair, etc.)

    ○ Post-Traumatic Stress Disorder or other major anxieties

    ○ A passenger with medications that the animal will help them to remember to take

- Passengers who are licensed/authorized to train service dogs for the blind or deaf are also able to bring the animal onto the bus.

- Service animals must be on a leash (or handhold) and must wear an issued service animal tag.

- Service animal tags are generally jackets worn by the animal that have bright colors and a label stating they are for service.

- Service animals should never be charged or given a security deposit for being transported. However, any damage done by the animal falls as liability to the responsible passenger.

- Unless otherwise required by circumstance and permitted by the passenger, do not touch or interact with a service animal.

Hazardous Materials

Hazardous materials (HazMat) are allowed onto transportation vehicles such as buses and vans depending on the amount and class of material. This section will not cover all transportation of hazardous materials with a CDL license, only the rules for carrying them on a passenger vehicle. For more in-depth information on HazMat transportation, refer to Chapter 8.

Sometimes passengers will unknowingly transport prohibited hazardous materials. However, as required by regulations, all hazardous materials should be labeled as hazardous and indicate the specific material contained therein. This should include the name of the material, an ID number for it, and the standard 4-inch diamond-shaped hazard label.

The following are allowed on buses/vans with proper labeling:

- Small-arms ammunition properly labeled "ORM-D"

- Emergency supplies and drugs for hospitals

- Small amounts of HazMat that cannot be shipped by any other means (see the following table).

The following is a list of HazMats and quantities that are NOT allowed to be on passenger transport vehicles:

- Gasoline (even in a gas can, as it is not properly labeled)
- Car batteries (even if carried on by a passenger)
- Division 2.3 poison gas
- Tear gas
- Irritating material (substances that can irritate and damage eyes, airways, and skin)
- Class 6 liquid poison
- Explosives in the passenger spaces (unless labeled small-arms ammunition)
- Radioactive material in passenger spaces
- Amounts greater than 100 pounds of Class 6 solid poison
- Amounts greater than 100 pounds of one class of HazMat
- Amounts greater than 500 pounds of allowed HazMat

HAZARDOUS MATERIALS CLASS

Class	Division	Name of Class or Division	Examples
1	1.1	Mass Explosion	Dynamite
	1.2	Projection Hazard	Flares
	1.3	Fire Hazard	Display Fireworks
	1.4	Minor Explosion	Ammunition
	1.5	Very Insensitive	Blasting Agents
	1.6	Extremely Insensitive	Explosive Devices
2	2.1	Flammable Gases	Propane
	2.2	Non-Flammable Gases	Helium
	2.3	Poisonous/Toxic Gases	Fluorine, Compressed
3	-	Flammable Liquids	Gasoline
4	4.1	Flammable Solids	Ammonium Picrate, Wetted
	4.2	Spontaneously Combustible	White Phosphorus
	4.3	Dangerous When Wet	Sodium
5	5.1	Oxidizers	Ammonium Nitrate
	5.2	Organic Peroxides	Methyl Ethyl Ketone Peroxide
6	6.1	Poison (Toxic Material)	Potassium Cyanide
	6.2	Infectious Substances	Anthrax Virus
7	-	Radioactive	Uranium
8	-	Corrosives	Battery Fluid
9	-	Miscellaneous Hazardous Materials	Polychlorinated Biphenyls (PCB)
None	-	ORM-D (Other Regulated Material-Domestic)	Food Flavorings, Medicines

Oxygen tanks are generally not allowed unless used for personal medical use. Tanks should be prescribed and in the possession of the passenger, and the container that it is in must be specifically designed for personal use.

Route Specific Safety

Here is a summary of important rules and practices to follow when on a route:

While Driving

- Ensure passengers are BEHIND the standee line.
- Check interior mirrors (passenger safety, no disruptions, etc.).
- DO NOT talk to passengers unless necessary.
- DO NOT engage in distracting events or activities that are happening on the bus.
- Rules regarding smoking, playing music out loud, loud talking, and moving about should all be given by your bussing company. Refer to them for all criteria that must be followed so that you can notify the passengers when necessary.

Stopping at Destinations

- When arriving at a destination, announce to the bus the following: location, reason for stop, departing time, and bus/van number.
- Always notify passengers to watch their step when getting on or off the bus.
- Learn your company's guidelines for helping passengers at stops.
- Utilize kneeling and fold/slide stairs at each stop if bus is equipped.
- Never fuel a bus with passengers on board, especially if the bus is in a closed building.
- Do not use the door interlock (which automatically applies the brake when the side door is open) in place of the parking brake. The interlock disengages when the passenger door closes.

- Before leaving a destination, make sure all passengers have a seat (or firm grip and placement in a standing zone) and that the doors are properly shut.
- Only allow passengers to board the vehicle when the departure time is approaching. Allowing them to board early increases the likelihood of theft.

Emergency and Evacuation

If an emergency occurs on board while driving, take the necessary precautions as indicated by your company in order to safely and effectively handle the situation. DO NOT allow your attention to be taken off the road. Even in an emergency, if you are still driving, you must do so without distraction and safely. If the emergency warrants the bus to be evacuated, you should do the following:

- Give the passengers an explanation of what is happening and how they will evacuate.
- Tell the passengers where and how they are to exit the bus in an orderly manner. This can be any door or any window that they can safely reach. Not all roof hatches will have an emergency manual open, or open all the way, and even if they do, the windows and doors should still be the primary points of exit.
- Tell the passengers where to gather after evacuating the bus fully and escaping the apparent danger.

However, if the danger is not directly on the bus and affecting the passengers, it is safer for the passengers to stay on the bus so they cannot wander or encounter hazards outside the bus.

If your bus needs to be towed and you have passengers on board, DO NOT allow them to stay on the bus as it is being towed. If there is no other option than to have passengers on board as the bus is being towed or pushed, then only move the bus the shortest distance possible to a safe location to allow the passengers to exit the vehicle.

SAFE DRIVING PRACTICES

Much of the following is meant to help you to avoid accidents when driving your passenger vehicle. Some rules may seem very familiar from day-to-day driving experience. Be aware of the following driving practices when on the road:

STEERING

When pulling away from a curb, keep in mind that the tail of the bus will swing opposite of the nose's direction. This means that steering left away from the curb will push the back end of the bus to the right, possibly into the curb.

MERGING

Do not assume that traffic will allow you to merge; it is best practice to merge when you have enough room to accelerate and accommodate the length of the bus.

CURVES

Avoid higher speeds on curves. Not only is this to keep the bus under control and safe, but it also will help keep the ride comfortable for yourself and the passengers. If a vehicle has good traction, high speeds in curves can lead to roll over with the increased grip leading to the creation of a pivot point. With poor traction, high speeds can lead to the vehicle sliding off the road.

WARNING SIGNS

Warning signs that provide suggested speeds for a section of road are not meant for passenger vehicles; they indicate speeds for smaller personal vehicles operated under optimal conditions. In general, CMVs should be driven through curves at reduced speeds. If ever in doubt of your ability to control the vehicle, slow down.

MIRRORS

Regularly scan mirrors when on the road. Awareness of your surroundings will improve your ability to drive safely. Surveying your mirrors may also allow you to identify a potential passenger approaching as you are preparing to leave a stop or station.

INTER-SECTIONS

The majority of accidents for transport vehicles, especially large ones like a bus, occur at intersections. This is because buses have more limited visibility, make wider turns, and have greater stopping distances than other vehicles.

9

Railroads and Drawbridges

All passenger transport vehicles should stop at railroad crossings and before drawbridges to ensure it is safe to cross. Not all railroads and drawbridges will have traffic lights or gates. When stopping at one of these locations be sure to both look and listen. Some intersections for railroads will not have good visibility, but a train can be heard before it is seen. Be sure to wait a moment after a train passes to make sure that there is not a second train hidden behind the first.

- For railroads, the vehicle should be stopped anywhere from 15–50 feet from the crossing.
- For drawbridges, the vehicle should be stopped at least 50 feet from the drawing point of the bridge.
- NEVER stop your vehicle on railroad tracks.
- If driving a manual vehicle, NEVER shift gears while going over tracks.

There are situations where stopping at a railroad or drawbridge is not required, but in these situations, speed should be reduced, and surroundings should be observed. These situations are as follows:

- If there is a green traffic light
- Railroads that follow the middle of the road (such as trolley tracks)
- Streetcar crossing areas
- Where an individual is directing traffic (such as a police officer or flagger, or control officer/attendant for a drawbridge)
- If the railroad or bridge is not functioning or abandoned

SCHOOL BUSES

Operating a school bus is similar to operating other passenger vehicles, but there are pressing safety concerns given that the passengers are all students, often children. As such, to ensure that drivers possess the necessary knowledge and skills to safely operate a school bus, there is a separate series of endorsement exams specifically for school buses, including both a written and physical skills exam. The written test has a combination of 20 multiple-choice and true/false questions (80% required for passing). Successfully passing the school bus endorsement exam and the school

NOTE

There is a practice test for the school bus endorsement at the end of this chapter after the Passenger Vehicle Practice Test.

bus skills test will result in an endorsement code of S being placed on your CDL. Due to the highly regulated nature of school bus driving, laws will vary from state to state, even district to district. Because of such variables, please refer to your state's CDL manual as well as materials and policies for the district in which you plan to drive.

The information that follows in this section and the ensuing practice questions can help you assess your preparedness for the exams, but know that your state's CDL manual and an approved driver-training program will provide the instruction necessary for safe and proper operation of a school bus.

Safety

The most important distinction between standard passenger vehicles and school buses is the additional safety practices. This section covers safety measures specific to school bus operation.

Danger Zones

Danger zones are the areas surrounding the school bus where students are at greatest risk due to poor visibility. The standard definition of a danger zone is the first 10 feet from the front, back, and sides of the bus. These zones may extend on the left and front sides of the bus when accounting for passing cars.

Mirrors

School buses use several different types of mirrors to allow maximum visibility of the area surrounding the bus. To operate a school bus safely, mirrors should be properly adjusted and consistently used to monitor the danger zones surrounding all sides of the school bus. This includes every time a new driver boards the bus or a new route is started, even if it's during the same day.

The four primary types of mirrors on a school bus are flat mirrors, convex mirrors, crossover mirrors, and the overhead inside rearview mirror.

FLAT MIRRORS

Flat mirrors are mounted on the windshield, either at the sides or on the front. They should be adjusted to ensure a visual distance of 4 buses (or 200 ft.) from the back of the bus.

CONVEX MIRRORS

Convex mirrors are located below the flat mirrors. They are used to give a wide-angle view of traffic, the left and ride sides of the bus, and of students that may be on either side of the bus.

CROSSOVER MIRRORS

Crossover mirrors provide a view of the danger zone in front of the bus, an area not visible when looking directly out of the windshield. They are mounted on both front corners of the bus.

OVERHEAD INSIDE REARVIEW MIRROR

The overhead inside rearview mirror should always be positioned for the driver to see all students, including the tops of the heads of the students located directly behind the driver's seat, and the window at the back of the bus in the top section of the mirror.

Loading and Unloading

Most student fatalities occur when they are loading and unloading from the bus. In fact, more students are killed during this procedure than during transport, regardless of where they sit. As a result, safety is of the utmost importance during loading and unloading.

Before beginning the loading or unloading process, you must first approach the stop. Approaching a school bus stop requires a series of operations that when executed create the safest environment for pedestrians and traffic. Always approach the stop at a slow speed; maintain awareness of all pedestrians, traffic, and objects; check all mirrors throughout the process; and use appropriate lights and indicators. When stopping, stop the vehicle at least 10 feet away from the students at the stop so that they must approach the bus; this can dramatically improve your ability to track student movements. Further, place the transmission in park and engage the parking brake for the vehicle. Turn on 8-way red lights and stop signals; ensure that all traffic in the area has stopped before signaling students to board. You can find more steps in your state CDL manual.

When loading at the bus stop, the key remains in the ignition and the parking brake is utilized. However, the ignition switch should be off on the school campus. Students must be accounted for at both locations, and they must load in single file at both locations. The key should only be removed at a bus stop if a student is unaccounted for and the driver is looking for them. The door of the school bus should always be closed before the driver pulls away from a stop.

Student Management

The most important part of operating a school bus is getting the students to and from school safely. Students may cause problems on the bus, intentionally or unintentionally, and they should be dealt with sensitively and quickly to alleviate any safety risks.

Handling serious problems on the bus should always be aligned with the school's disciplinary procedures. It is appropriate for the driver of a school bus to request that a student who is misbehaving move to a seat near the driver in order to alleviate the problem. If a serious problem is present on the bus, such as a student

tampering with anything on the bus, it should be dealt with after all uninvolved students are safely off the bus. Never let a student off the bus anywhere other than the school or their designated bus stop.

Antilock Braking Systems (ABS)

Not all school buses will be equipped with ABS, but most will. If a school bus has ABS, it will have a yellow ABS malfunction lamp on the instrument panel of the bus. This lamp will only turn on if the ABS is malfunctioning.

ABS aids the driver in avoiding wheel lockups and helps them to maintain control of the vehicle. While ABS can help the driver to stop more immediately, this is not always the case. When braking in a vehicle with ABS, the driver should brake as they normally would.

If the ABS braking system no longer works, skidding due to overbraking is more likely to occur. The bus is still able to stop, and the rate at which it stops may or may not be affected. However, all vehicle systems should be properly maintained. If an ABS malfunction is present, seeks maintenance as soon as possible.

Railroad Crossings

There are two different types of railroad crossings. Passive crossings do not include a traffic control device and are marked with a circular yellow sign. Determining whether or not to proceed is the responsibility of the driver. The driver should determine the safety of the crossing by making sure the tracks are not being used by a train and that there is space to proceed. Active crossings have an installed traffic control device that conducts traffic. They can be recognized by flashing red lights with bells, flashing red lights without bells, and flashing red lights with gates and bells.

A crossbuck sign indicates that there is a railway crossing and that the driver should yield to any oncoming trains. These signs may also have numbers on them indicating the number of tracks that the road crosses over. When there is no painted white line on the road, a bus must stop before the crossbuck sign, instead of at the painted line.

At a crossing, the driver should remain 15 feet away, but within 50 feet from the closest rail so that they have the clearest view of the railroad tracks.

In general, a school bus must stop at all railroad crossings before proceeding, even if a traffic light present is green. However, this may vary from state to state; in some states, a school bus is not required to stop when an "Exempt Crossing" sign is present or an emergency responder is directing traffic. Please check your state's CDL manual to confirm stopping procedures.

Strong Winds

High winds are an extreme weather pattern that may occur on their own or in conjunction with a severe storm or blizzard. Such strong winds can easily move a bus sideways or push a school bus off the road. Extreme high winds can even tip a bus over. The best practice during high winds is to grip the steering wheel to ensure control of the bus. It is never advised to pump the brakes or turn into the direction of the wind.

Backing a Bus

It is extremely dangerous to back a bus. A driver should only back a school bus when there is no other way to move it. Students should never be outside of the bus if it

A "safe place" during an emergency evacuation is at least 100 feet from the road.

needs to be backed. When backing is necessary, using a lookout is the best way to ensure safety.

Strobe Lights

Not all buses are equipped with strobe lights, but buses with strobe lights will have them roof mounted. Strobe lights are bright white and should be used when the driver's visibility is limited and they are unable to see clearly in front of, behind, or beside the bus. Whether minimally limited or completely obstructed, lack of visibility is a sign that the strobe lights should be used. Make sure to understand local regulations regarding the use of strobe lights.

Emergencies and Evacuations

Emergencies may occur while driving a school bus. The central decision that a driver must make during an emergency is whether to evacuate the bus. Generally, it is easier to maintain control over the situation and monitor the safety of the students by keeping them on the bus, so long as this does not increase the risk of harm in any way. Time permitting, drivers should contact dispatchers prior to deciding to evacuate the bus.

Mandatory evacuation of the school bus is necessary if there is a threat of fire or if the bus is on fire, if there is an immediate threat of a dangerous collision, or if a hazard spill is present. Additionally, the school bus should be evacuated if the bus is stalled on or next to a highway-rail crossing or if danger may be increased by a change in the position of the bus.

A "safe place" during an emergency evacuation is at least 100 feet from the road. The safe place should be facing oncoming traffic to increase visibility.

SUMMING IT UP

- The passenger vehicle endorsement allows drivers to transport large groups of people (usually 15 or more, but this number can vary from state to state). It is commonly required for bus drivers (excluding school buses) and large van transportation.

- The passenger vehicle endorsement requires BOTH a written and a skills test. The written test consists of 20 questions, with a required pass rate of 16 correct questions (80%). In addition, the skills test (also known as the driving test) must be taken in a passenger vehicle in the class of CDL for which a driver is applying.

- The driver of a passenger transport is responsible for completing the standard points of vehicle inspection; however, the driver must also complete exterior and interior passenger transport inspections, examining emergency exits, compartments, hatches, safety devices, and more.

- The safety of your passengers is paramount when driving a passenger transport. Disruptive passengers may need to be removed from the vehicle. They should never be left on the side of the road in an area that is unsafe.

- The standee line is a two-inch thick line on the floor of the bus that designates where passengers can stand. Passengers are never allowed to be in front of the standee line when the vehicle is in motion.

- It is standard for animals to be prohibited from public buses and vans UNLESS they are service animals. Any person with a disability has the right to a service animal that is specifically trained to help them.

- Hazardous materials are allowed onto transportation vehicles such as buses and vans, but only in certain quantities.

  - Some HazMat, such as gasoline and tear gas, are never allowed on passenger transportation vehicles.

- In the event of an emergency, if the danger is not directly on the bus and affecting the passengers, it is safer for the passengers to stay on the bus so they cannot wander or meet the danger outside the bus.

- All passenger transport vehicles should stop at railroad crossings and before drawbridges to ensure it is safe to cross.

- The S endorsement allows a CDL holder to drive school buses. To acquire the S endorsement, a driver must pass the school bus written test (20 questions) and physical skills test.

- School buses have additional safety practices in place to protect students.

  - Danger zones are the areas surrounding the school bus where students are more likely to get hit. The standard definition of a danger zone is the first 10 feet from the front, back, and sides of the bus.

  - The four primary types of mirrors on a school bus are flat mirrors, convex mirrors, crossover mirrors, and the overhead inside rearview mirror. These mirrors allow for maximum visibility of the area surrounding the bus.

  - If a school bus has ABS, it will have a yellow ABS malfunction lamp on the instrument panel of the bus. This lamp will only turn on if the ABS is malfunctioning.

  - A school bus must stop at all railroad crossings before proceeding, even if the traffic light is green. At a crossing, the driver should remain 15 feet away, but within 50 feet from the closest rail so that they have the clearest view of the railroad tracks. These stopping procedures may vary by state.

  - A driver should only back a school bus when there is no other way to move it. Students should never be outside of the bus if it needs to be backed. When backing is necessary, using a lookout is the best way to ensure safety.

  - Drivers operating school buses equipped with strobe lights should use them when visibility is limited and they are unable to see clearly in front of, behind, or beside the bus.

  - A "safe place" during an emergency evacuation is at least 100 feet from the road. In addition, the safe place needs to be facing oncoming traffic to increase visibility.

PASSENGER VEHICLES PRACTICE TEST

20 Questions—60 Minutes

Directions: This test consists of a combination of true/false and multiple-choice questions. Only one answer is correct for each question.

---

1. A passenger vehicle endorsement certifies the driver to operate all passenger vehicles, including a school bus.

   A. True

   B. False

2. Which of the following is prohibited on a bus?

   A. Medical oxygen

   B. Small arms ammunition

   C. Hairspray

   D. Car battery

3. When should a driver perform a vehicle inspection?

   A. Before every trip

   B. Before and after every trip

   C. Daily

   D. Weekly

4. Using excessive speed on curves may cause a bus with good traction to

   A. spin out.

   B. roll over.

   C. slide off the curve.

   D. hug the inside of the curve.

5. When is it permitted to stop on train tracks?

   A. When the traffic light is green

   B. After a train has passed

   C. When the crossing bar is raised up

   D. Never

6. The purpose of the standee line is to designate the area in which standing passengers must stay in front of when the bus is in motion.

   A. True

   B. False

7. A driver can ask for documentation verifying a passenger's need for a service dog.

   A. True

   B. False

8. To avoid restrictions on their license, drivers should

   A. study hard.

   B. take their skills test during daylight.

   C. take their skills test in a familiar vehicle.

   D. take their skills test in the same class of vehicle they plan to drive.

9. Which of the following is present on the interior portion of a vehicle inspection?

   A. Emergency exit handles

   B. Service brakes

   C. Windshield wipers

   D. Coupling devices

10. A disruptive passenger cannot be discharged in an unlit area at night.

A. True

B. False

11. Under federal law, all of the following require a driver of a commercial vehicle to obtain a passenger vehicle endorsement EXCEPT:

A. Driving an empty vehicle designed to carry 15 passengers

B. Driving a vehicle with 15 passengers

C. Driving a vehicle designed to carry 16 people, including the driver

D. Driving a 12-passenger vehicle

12. The proper storage for luggage is partially in the aisle under a seat, in the overhead storage area, and in the exterior luggage compartments.

A. True

B. False

13. All of the following are exterior inspection points EXCEPT:

A. Emergency exits

B. Interlock system

C. Roof hatches

D. Air hoses

14. The special inspection points for passenger vehicles are done in addition to the seven-step pre-trip inspection that all commercial vehicles undergo.

A. True

B. False

15. Class 6 liquid poisons are allowed on a passenger vehicle if the amount is less than 100 pounds, but Class 6 solid poisons are not.

A. True

B. False

16. Dogs are allowed on to passenger vehicles when the owner is training the animal to be a service dog.

A. True

B. False

17. Disruptive passengers cannot be discharged from the vehicle, and everyone must endure them.

A. True

B. False

18. Passengers are allowed to stay in the vehicle as it is being fueled if it is in an indoor environment.

A. True

B. False

19. The following are steps to take in an emergency when transporting passengers EXCEPT:

A. Explain the situation to the passengers

B. Keep passengers in the vehicle unless it is not possible to do so

C. Immediately stop and evacuate the vehicle no matter the emergency

D. Continue driving and focus on the road unless it is necessary to stop

20. The interlock system can replace the parking brakes on a bus.

A. True

B. False

PASSENGER VEHICLES ANSWER KEY AND EXPLANATIONS

1. B	5. D	9. A	13. B	17. B
2. D	6. B	10. A	14. A	18. B
3. B	7. B	11. D	15. B	19. C
4. B	8. D	12. B	16. A	20. B

1. **The correct answer is B.** There is a separate endorsement that enables drivers to operate a school bus.

2. **The correct answer is D.** A car battery cannot be transported on a bus as it is not properly labeled with the correct class of hazardous material and could contain prohibited and dangerous contents. Medical oxygen (choice A), small arms ammunition (choice B), and hairspray (choice C) are all hazardous materials that are permitted on a bus.

3. **The correct answer is B.** Vehicle inspections should be completed before and after every trip. This allows the driver to ensure that the vehicle is safe to operate before they begin driving. It also allows them to inspect the vehicle after driving to make notes of any new damage or repairs that are needed before the next time the vehicle is used. While it is required to inspect the vehicle before every trip (choice A), this choice does not include the required post inspection. Daily (choice C) and weekly inspections (choice D) may not be frequent enough depending on the usage of the vehicle, and this could decrease the safety of the vehicle.

4. **The correct answer is B.** A bus with good traction will grip the road and possibly roll over when using excessive speed on a curve. Spinning out (choice A) and sliding off the curve (choice C) are both related to poor traction combined with excessive speed. Hugging the inside of the curve (choice D) occurs at lower speeds, not excessive speeds.

5. **The correct answer is D.** It is never permitted to stop on train tracks, even if the traffic light is green (choice A), after a train has passed (choice B), and when the crossing bar is raised up (choice C).

6. **The correct answer is B.** The standee line designates the point which the standing passengers must stay behind when the bus is in motion.

7. **The correct answer is B.** It is illegal to ask for documentation verifying the status of a passenger's need for a service dog. A driver is allowed to ask if the dog is in fact a service dog, but they cannot ask for any proof for the passenger's disability.

8. **The correct answer is D.** It is important to take the skills portion of every endorsement test in the same class vehicle as the one you plan on driving. This will help you avoid restrictions on your license. Although it is important to study hard (choice A), this will not help you avoid restrictions on your license. Taking the skills test during daylight (choice B) and in a familiar vehicle (choice C) are best practices, but if the vehicle is a lower class than the one connected with your CDL, you will receive a restriction.

9. **The correct answer is A.** Emergency exit handles are present on both the interior and exterior of buses depending on the design of the bus. Service brakes (choice B), windshield wipers (choice C) and coupling devices (choice D) are all only present on the exterior of the bus.

10. **The correct answer is A.** It is the responsibility of the driver to find a well-lit area to discharge a disruptive passenger. This can be challenging as you are dealing with disruptive behavior, but the safety of all passengers must be in the forefront of your mind. An unlit area poses a danger to the passenger being discharged.

11. **The correct answer is D.** Driving a 12-passenger vehicle does not require the passenger vehicle endorsement. However, driving a vehicle that is carrying or designed to carry 16 or more people,

including the driver, requires a passenger vehicle endorsement.

12. **The correct answer is B.** Luggage should not be in the aisle, even partially. Luggage should also be fully and securely stored under a seat, in the overhead storage, or in the exterior luggage compartments.

13. **The correct answer is B.** The interlock system is inspected from the interior of the vehicle because its controls are located there. Emergency exits (choice A), roof hatches (choice C), and air hoses (choice D) are all inspection points that are located on the exterior of the vehicle.

14. **The correct answer is A.** The special inspection points for passenger vehicles are not enough to ensure that the vehicle is ready for a trip. They must be done on top of the seven-step pre-trip inspection that all commercial vehicles undergo.

15. **The correct answer is B.** Class 6 solid poisons are allowed on board if the amount is under 100 pounds, but liquid poisons are not.

16. **The correct answer is A.** An animal that is in training to be a service animal is allowed on public transportation.

17. **The correct answer is B.** If a passenger is disruptive, they can be discharged from the vehicle. However, they must be discharged in a safe and well-lit location with other people around, preferably at the next stop if possible.

18. **The correct answer is B.** Passengers are not allowed to be in a vehicle when it is being fueled, especially if the vehicle is being fueled indoors.

19. **The correct answer is C.** Immediately stopping and evacuating the vehicle is not a standard step during an emergency when transporting passengers. In fact, evacuating the vehicle can be dangerous in some cases. Explaining the situation to passengers (choice A), keeping passengers in the vehicle unless it is impossible to do so (choice B), and continuing to drive while focusing on the road (choice D) are all steps to take when an emergency arises.

20. **The correct answer is B.** The interlock system cannot replace the parking brakes because if the passenger door is closed, the brakes will disengage. Parking brakes do not disengage unless they are manually disengaged by the driver.

NOTES

SCHOOL BUSES PRACTICE TEST
20 Questions—60 Minutes

Directions: This test consists of a combination of true/false and multiple-choice questions. Only one answer is correct for each question.

---

1. The danger zones from the rear bumper and the left and right sides of the bus may extend

   A. 20 feet.

   B. 10 feet.

   C. 5 feet.

   D. only to where students are waiting at the designated school bus stop.

2. Repeated mirror adjustment and usage is unnecessary to operate a school bus safely after the initial daily inspection.

   A. True

   B. False

3. The flat mirrors of a school bus should be adjusted so that the driver can see each side of the bus, the back tires touching the ground, and a distance of 4 buses (or 200 feet) from the back of the bus.

   A. True

   B. False

4. All of the following are provided by the convex mirrors of a school bus EXCEPT:

   A. A wide-angled view of traffic at the sides of the bus

   B. A wide-angled view of students at the sides of the bus

   C. A wide-angled view of the danger zone at the front of the bus

   D. A wide-angled view of clearances at the sides of the bus

5. All of the following are true regarding crossover mirrors EXCEPT:

   A. Crossover mirrors are used to give a wide-angled view of traffic at the sides of the bus.

   B. Crossover mirrors are used to monitor the area from the front of the bus to the service door.

   C. When viewing a crossover mirror, the driver should be able to see the front tires of the left and right sides of the bus touching the ground.

   D. Crossover mirrors should be adjusted properly.

6. When approaching an official school bus stop, which of the following should the driver do?

   A. Approach the stop quickly and efficiently

   B. Turn on the left turn signal within 200–500 feet of the stop

   C. Check the flat mirrors to monitor blind spots

   D. Check all mirrors continuously

7. What is the primary difference between loading at a bus stop and loading at the school?

   A. Students must be accounted for at a bus stop only.

   B. The ignition switch should be off when loading at the school.

   C. The key should be removed when loading at a bus stop.

   D. The students must load single file at the school.

8. All of the following are involved in proper unloading procedures at school EXCEPT:

   A. The ignition switch should be turned off.

   B. The driver should supervise the unloading process according to specific state or local regulations.

   C. Once students are unloaded and accounted for at the school, it's unnecessary for the driver to perform a walkthrough of the bus.

   D. All mirrors should be checked to ensure that no students are returning to the bus.

9. All of the following are included in a post-trip walkthrough inspection of the school bus EXCEPT:

   A. Checking for opened doors and windows

   B. Checking for items that may have been left behind

   C. Ensuring that there are no hiding or sleeping students

   D. Reporting any special situations or issues the following business day

10. Which of the following does NOT require the mandatory evacuation of a school bus?

    A. Fire or threat of fire

    B. Threat of a dangerous collision

    C. Presence of a hazardous spill

    D. A missing student outside of the bus

11. A "safe place" during an emergency evacuation is at least 50 feet away from the road.

    A. True

    B. False

12. What is the proper protocol if a railroad crossing gate fails to raise after the train has passed?

    A. Call local police

    B. Call the utility company

    C. Press the automatic release lever on the gate

    D. Call the bus dispatcher

13. As a rule, how many feet should be added to the back of the bus when determining whether it can fit in a containment or storage area?

    A. 10 feet

    B. 15 feet

    C. 20 feet

    D. 25 feet

14. When handling serious problems on the bus, the driver should

    A. escort the problem student off the bus to ensure privacy when addressing issues.

    B. stop the bus immediately to ensure safety.

    C. remain sitting when addressing the issue to avoid intimidating students.

    D. remove the ignition key before addressing the situation.

15. An antilock braking system always reduces the stopping time of a school bus.

    A. True

    B. False

16. How is the braking affected when the ABS no longer works?

    A. The bus is unable to stop.

    B. The bus is not able to stop as quickly.

    C. Skidding due to overbraking is more likely to occur.

    D. There are no effects.

17. The strobe lights of a school bus should be used

    A. when the driver cannot see students inside the bus.

    B. only when visibility outside of the bus is greatly reduced.

    C. when the driver cannot see immediately behind the driver's seat.

    D. when visibility outside of the bus is reduced, even minimally.

18. What should a driver do during high winds?

    A. Grip the steering wheel

    B. Hold on to the steering wheel loosely

    C. Pump the brakes to slow down gradually

    D. Turn into the direction of the wind to avoid being blown sideways

19. When should a driver back a school bus?

    A. When the parking space is perpendicular to the bus

    B. When there is less than 10 feet clearance on either side of the bus

    C. When there is no other way to move the bus

    D. When students are safely unloaded

20. Antilock braking system (ABS) control may be lost if the malfunction lamp comes on while driving or if the lamp continues to stay on after checking the bulb.

    A. True

    B. False

SCHOOL BUSES ANSWER KEY AND EXPLANATIONS

1. B	5. A	9. D	13. B	17. D
2. B	6. D	10. D	14. D	18. A
3. A	7. B	11. B	15. B	19. C
4. C	8. C	12. D	16. C	20. A

1. **The correct answer is B.** The danger zone at the back of the bus extends 10 feet from the rear bumper and from the left and right sides of the bus. 20 feet (choice A) extends too far to be in the danger zone. 5 feet (choice C) is too short to include the entirety of the danger zone. Choice D is incorrect because there may be students, pedestrians, traffic, and/or other objects present in the area beyond the designated school bus stop.

2. **The correct answer is B.** To operate a school bus safely, mirrors should be adjusted properly and consistently used to monitor the danger zones surrounding all sides of the school bus. This includes every time a new driver boards the bus or a new route is started, even if it's during the same day.

3. **The correct answer is A.** The flat mirrors of the bus should be adjusted to ensure a distance of 4 buses (or 200 ft.) from the back of the bus.

4. **The correct answer is C.** Convex mirrors do not provide a view of the danger zone as that is the job of the crossover mirrors. The convex mirrors of a school bus are used to give a wide-angle view of traffic (choice A), the left and right sides of the bus (choice D), and of students that may be on either side of the bus (choice B).

5. **The correct answer is A.** Convex mirrors, not crossover mirrors, are used to give a wide-angle view of traffic at the left and right sides of the bus. Crossover mirrors should be adjusted properly (choice D) to ensure visibility of the front left and right tires touching the ground (choice C) and the area from the front of the bus to the service door (choice B).

6. **The correct answer is D.** When approaching an official school bus stop, the driver should continuously check all mirrors. Checking the flat mirrors is important (choice C) but not to monitor blind spots. Approaching a stop should be done carefully and at a speed that is slow in rate (choice A). The right turn signal indicator should always be activated within about 100 to 300 feet (or 3 to 5 seconds) of approaching the stop (choice B).

7. **The correct answer is B.** The biggest difference when loading at a bus stop versus loading at the school is that the ignition switch should be off on the school campus. When loading at the bus stop, the key remains in the ignition and the parking brake is utilized. Students must be accounted for (choice A) at both locations. The key should only be removed at a bus stop (choice C) if a student is unaccounted for and the driver is looking for them. Students must load single file (choice D) in both locations.

8. **The correct answer is C.** The driver should always perform a careful walkthrough of the bus after unloading students at the school to ensure there are no hidden or sleeping students or items left behind. The bus should be secured before instructing seated students to exit by turning off the ignition switch (choice A), supervising the unloading of students within the scope of required or recommended regulations (choice B), and checking all mirrors to ensure that no students are returning to the bus (choice D).

9. **The correct answer is D.** Any special situations or issues discovered during a post-trip inspection of the school bus should be reported right away to the school authorities or to the driver's supervisor.

In addition, as part of a walkthrough of the bus conducted post-trip, the driver should ensure that all windows and doors are secured properly (choice A), check for any items that may have been left behind by students (choice B), and confirm that there are no hiding or sleeping students on the school bus (choice C).

10. **The correct answer is D.** If a student disappears from sight as they are approaching the school bus, it is likely that they have dropped an object and are picking it up or returning to retrieve it. While dangerous, this situation does not require the mandatory evacuation of the bus. The student should be instructed to leave the object and to move out of the danger zones to safety. Mandatory evacuation of the school bus is necessary if there is a threat of fire or if the bus is on fire (choice A), if there is an immediate threat of a dangerous collision (choice B), or if a hazardous spill is present (choice C). In addition, the school bus should be evacuated if the bus is stalled on or next to a highway-rail crossing or if danger may be increased by a change in the position of the bus.

11. **The correct answer is B.** A "safe place" during an emergency evacuation is at least 100 feet from the road, not 50 feet. In addition, the safe place needs to be facing oncoming traffic to increase visibility.

12. **The correct answer is D.** When the crossing gate fails to raise after the train has passed, the driver must call the bus dispatcher and await further instructions. They should not call the police (choice A) or the utility company (choice B). There is no automatic release lever (choice C), and it would never be permissible to interfere with the railroad communication system.

13. **The correct answer is B.** As a rule, add 15 feet to the back of the bus when determining whether it can fit in a containment or storage area. 10 feet (choice A) may not be enough. 20 feet (choice C) and 25 feet (choice D) are extravagant and unnecessary for determining adequate length.

14. **The correct answer is D.** The driver should remove the key from the ignition before addressing the situation to ensure that the bus remains safe. The problem student should never be escorted off (choice A). The bus should only be stopped immediately if it is in a safe location (choice B). The driver should not remain seated when addressing the situation (choice D); the driver should stand up to focus on the students and ensure the bus does not move when speaking to the students.

15. **The correct answer is B.** ABS does not necessarily reduce braking time. Antilock brakes prevent wheel lock up and overbraking to help a driver maintain vehicle control.

16. **The correct answer is C.** If the ABS no longer works, skidding due to overbraking is more likely to occur. The bus is able to stop (choice A) and the rate at which it stops (choice B) may or may not be affected. However, there are benefits to ABS (choice D), so when it malfunctions, it is important to get it fixed as soon as possible.

17. **The correct answer is D.** Strobe lights should be used when the driver's visibility is limited and they are unable to see clearly in front of, behind, or beside the bus. Whether minimally limited or completely obstructed (choice B), lack of visibility is a sign that the strobe lights should be used. Choices A and C describe lack of visibility due to the blind spots of the overhead, inside rearview mirror of a school bus, and do not signify that strobe lights should be used.

18. **The correct answer is A.** The driver should grip the steering wheel to ensure control of the bus. Holding on to the steering wheel loosely (choice B) decreases control. Pumping the brakes (choice C) and turning into the direction of the wind (choice D) are not advisable during high winds.

19. **The correct answer is C.** A driver should only back a school bus when there is no other way to move it. It is very dangerous to back a bus. Even if the spacing is odd (choice A) or it is a tight space (choice B) it should not be attempted if unnecessary. Students should never be outside of the bus (choice D) if it needs to be backed.

20. **The correct answer is A.** The ABS malfunction lamp, located on the instrument panel of the bus is yellow in color and will turn on if the ABS is malfunctioning. Older ABS malfunction lamps may stay on until the driver has exceeded five miles per hour. One or more wheels may have lost ABS control if the malfunction lamp comes on while driving or if the lamp continues to stay on after the bulb-check.

NOTES

ADDITIONAL PRACTICE TESTS

| General Knowledge

| Air Brakes

| Combination Vehicles

| Double and Triple Trailers

| Tanker Vehicles

| Hazardous Materials

| Passenger Vehicles

| School Buses

ADDITIONAL PRACTICE TESTS

OVERVIEW

General Knowledge Practice Tests 1 & 2

Air Brakes Practice Tests 1 & 2

Combination Vehicles Practice Tests 1–3

Double and Triple Trailers Practice Tests 1–3

Tanker Vehicles Practice Tests 1–3

Hazardous Materials Practice Tests 1–3

Passenger Vehicles Practice Tests 1–3

School Buses Practice Tests 1 & 2

This section contains multiple practice tests for each of the eight CDL exams. Use these tests and answer explanations to practice and pinpoint any remaining weaknesses in your CDL knowledge. Set a timer for each exam's time limit, and once completed, score your answer sheet using the answer key and answer explanations available after each test. Using that information, revisit the relevant chapter in this book and your state's CDL manual.

GENERAL KNOWLEDGE PRACTICE TESTS ANSWER SHEET

Practice Test 1

1. Ⓐ Ⓑ	11. Ⓐ Ⓑ	21. Ⓐ Ⓑ	31. Ⓐ Ⓑ	41. Ⓐ Ⓑ Ⓒ Ⓓ
2. Ⓐ Ⓑ	12. Ⓐ Ⓑ Ⓒ Ⓓ	22. Ⓐ Ⓑ	32. Ⓐ Ⓑ Ⓒ Ⓓ	42. Ⓐ Ⓑ
3. Ⓐ Ⓑ Ⓒ Ⓓ	13. Ⓐ Ⓑ Ⓒ Ⓓ	23. Ⓐ Ⓑ Ⓒ Ⓓ	33. Ⓐ Ⓑ	43. Ⓐ Ⓑ
4. Ⓐ Ⓑ Ⓒ Ⓓ	14. Ⓐ Ⓑ Ⓒ Ⓓ	24. Ⓐ Ⓑ Ⓒ Ⓓ	34. Ⓐ Ⓑ Ⓒ Ⓓ	44. Ⓐ Ⓑ Ⓒ Ⓓ
5. Ⓐ Ⓑ Ⓒ Ⓓ	15. Ⓐ Ⓑ Ⓒ Ⓓ	25. Ⓐ Ⓑ Ⓒ Ⓓ	35. Ⓐ Ⓑ	45. Ⓐ Ⓑ
6. Ⓐ Ⓑ Ⓒ Ⓓ	16. Ⓐ Ⓑ	26. Ⓐ Ⓑ Ⓒ Ⓓ	36. Ⓐ Ⓑ	46. Ⓐ Ⓑ
7. Ⓐ Ⓑ	17. Ⓐ Ⓑ Ⓒ Ⓓ	27. Ⓐ Ⓑ Ⓒ Ⓓ	37. Ⓐ Ⓑ	47. Ⓐ Ⓑ Ⓒ Ⓓ
8. Ⓐ Ⓑ	18. Ⓐ Ⓑ Ⓒ Ⓓ	28. Ⓐ Ⓑ Ⓒ Ⓓ	38. Ⓐ Ⓑ Ⓒ Ⓓ	48. Ⓐ Ⓑ Ⓒ Ⓓ
9. Ⓐ Ⓑ Ⓒ Ⓓ	19. Ⓐ Ⓑ Ⓒ Ⓓ	29. Ⓐ Ⓑ Ⓒ Ⓓ	39. Ⓐ Ⓑ Ⓒ Ⓓ	49. Ⓐ Ⓑ Ⓒ Ⓓ
10. Ⓐ Ⓑ Ⓒ Ⓓ	20. Ⓐ Ⓑ Ⓒ Ⓓ	30. Ⓐ Ⓑ Ⓒ Ⓓ	40. Ⓐ Ⓑ Ⓒ Ⓓ	50. Ⓐ Ⓑ Ⓒ Ⓓ

Practice Test 2

1. Ⓐ Ⓑ Ⓒ Ⓓ	11. Ⓐ Ⓑ Ⓒ Ⓓ	21. Ⓐ Ⓑ Ⓒ Ⓓ	31. Ⓐ Ⓑ Ⓒ Ⓓ	41. Ⓐ Ⓑ Ⓒ Ⓓ
2. Ⓐ Ⓑ	12. Ⓐ Ⓑ	22. Ⓐ Ⓑ Ⓒ Ⓓ	32. Ⓐ Ⓑ Ⓒ Ⓓ	42. Ⓐ Ⓑ Ⓒ Ⓓ
3. Ⓐ Ⓑ Ⓒ Ⓓ	13. Ⓐ Ⓑ	23. Ⓐ Ⓑ Ⓒ Ⓓ	33. Ⓐ Ⓑ	43. Ⓐ Ⓑ Ⓒ Ⓓ
4. Ⓐ Ⓑ	14. Ⓐ Ⓑ	24. Ⓐ Ⓑ Ⓒ Ⓓ	34. Ⓐ Ⓑ Ⓒ Ⓓ	44. Ⓐ Ⓑ
5. Ⓐ Ⓑ Ⓒ Ⓓ	15. Ⓐ Ⓑ Ⓒ Ⓓ	25. Ⓐ Ⓑ Ⓒ Ⓓ	35. Ⓐ Ⓑ	45. Ⓐ Ⓑ Ⓒ Ⓓ
6. Ⓐ Ⓑ	16. Ⓐ Ⓑ	26. Ⓐ Ⓑ Ⓒ Ⓓ	36. Ⓐ Ⓑ Ⓒ Ⓓ	46. Ⓐ Ⓑ Ⓒ Ⓓ
7. Ⓐ Ⓑ Ⓒ Ⓓ	17. Ⓐ Ⓑ Ⓒ Ⓓ	27. Ⓐ Ⓑ Ⓒ Ⓓ	37. Ⓐ Ⓑ Ⓒ Ⓓ	47. Ⓐ Ⓑ Ⓒ Ⓓ
8. Ⓐ Ⓑ	18. Ⓐ Ⓑ	28. Ⓐ Ⓑ Ⓒ Ⓓ	38. Ⓐ Ⓑ Ⓒ Ⓓ	48. Ⓐ Ⓑ
9. Ⓐ Ⓑ	19. Ⓐ Ⓑ	29. Ⓐ Ⓑ	39. Ⓐ Ⓑ Ⓒ Ⓓ	49. Ⓐ Ⓑ Ⓒ Ⓓ
10. Ⓐ Ⓑ Ⓒ Ⓓ	20. Ⓐ Ⓑ	30. Ⓐ Ⓑ Ⓒ Ⓓ	40. Ⓐ Ⓑ Ⓒ Ⓓ	50. Ⓐ Ⓑ

ANSWER SHEET: PRACTICE TESTS

GENERAL KNOWLEDGE PRACTICE TEST 1

50 Questions - 90 Minutes

Directions: This test consists of a combination of true/false and multiple-choice questions. Only one answer is correct for each question.

---

1. Backing the vehicle towards the right is the preferred way to back a vehicle.

   A. True
   B. False

2. Air brake systems are four braking systems combined.

   A. True
   B. False

3. In any single offense a speed is deemed excessive at

   A. 20 mph or more over the posted speed limit.
   B. 10 mph or more over the posted speed limit.
   C. 5 mph or more over the posted speed limit.
   D. 15 mph or more over the posted speed limit.

4. A CDL driver will be criminally charged if operating a commercial vehicle with a blood alcohol concentration level of more than

   A. .01 percent.
   B. .02 percent.
   C. .03 percent.
   D. .04 percent.

5. On flatbed cargo, there should be at least

   A. one tie-down for each five feet of cargo.
   B. one tie-down for each ten feet of cargo.
   C. two tie-downs for each five feet of cargo.
   D. two tie-downs for each fifteen feet of cargo.

6. The total weight of a powered unit plus trailer(s) plus cargo is

   A. Gross Combination Weight Rating.
   B. Gross Combination Weight.
   C. Gross Vehicle Weight.
   D. Gross Vehicle Weight Rating.

7. Many large vehicles have convex mirrors that show a wider area than flat mirrors.

   A. True
   B. False

8. Fully loaded trucks take longer to stop than empty trucks.

   A. True
   B. False

9. The distance a driver's vehicle travels in standard conditions before the driver physically hits the brakes and responds to a danger seen ahead is considered a

   A. reaction distance.
   B. perception distance.
   C. braking distance.
   D. total stopping distance.

10. On a wet road, a driver should reduce their speed at minimum by about

    A. one-half.
    B. one-fourth.
    C. one-eighth.
    D. one-third.

11. Using engine speed (rpm) and road speed (mph) are two ways to know when to shift gears.

    A. True
    B. False

12. A crossing sign that regulates traffic at the railroad crossing and has traffic control devices installed is called a(n)

    A. no passing zone sign.
    B. passive crossing.
    C. advance warning sign.
    D. active crossing sign.

13. During night driving and with the low beams on, a driver can see at a maximum of about

    A. 500 feet ahead.
    B. 350 feet ahead.
    C. 250 feet ahead.
    D. 125 feet ahead.

14. During the pre-trip inspection, a driver will not check which of the following in the cab?

    A. Temperature
    B. Air pressure
    C. Coolant level
    D. Oil pressure

15. Drivers who must drive in fog need to do all the following EXCEPT:

    A. Turn on the high beams
    B. Follow all fog-related warning signs
    C. Be ready to stop in an emergency
    D. Enter slowly before a fog area

16. Retarders should be turned on whenever the road is wet, icy, or snow-covered to assist the drive wheels with traction.

    A. True
    B. False

17. If slack adjusters need adjusting, it is because they moved at least

    A. two inches.
    B. four inches.
    C. an inch.
    D. half an inch.

18. A commercial driver who is confronted by an aggressive motorist should

    A. stay in the motorist's lane.
    B. ignore the motorist.
    C. signal gestures to the motorist.
    D. increase the speed.

19. The most important reason why a driver must be alert to hazards is to

    A. avoid disciplinary actions by the employer.
    B. report accidents accurately to law enforcement and insurance companies.
    C. have time to avoid an emergency or plan an escape if the hazards become emergencies.
    D. remember to call law enforcement in a timely manner.

20. To correct a rear wheel (drive wheel) braking skid, a driver should

    A. apply more braking pressure to the brake pedal.
    B. release brakes and accelerate.
    C. apply more pressure to the brake pedal and counter-steer.
    D. release the brakes and counter-steer.

21. Authorities should be notified before you secure the scene of an accident.

    A. True
    B. False

22. A driver who has a legal prescription for medication may not be disqualified from driving a commercial motor vehicle.

    A. True
    B. False

23. When realizing a box is ahead in the right lane, a driver should

    A. brake hard and avoid hitting it.
    B. slow down and direct traffic around it.
    C. safely maneuver around it.
    D. push it off the road with the vehicle.

24. Multi-speed rear axles and auxiliary transmissions are used to provide

    A. extra room for hazardous materials.
    B. extra gears.
    C. better gas mileage.
    D. a smoother ride for the vehicle.

25. The system that helps the driver maintain control of the vehicle under heavy braking situations is known as the

    A. antilock braking system.
    B. air brake system.
    C. air spring system.
    D. air ride suspension system.

26. When drivers must change speed and/or direction to avoid hitting someone, they are considered to be

    A. in a panic.
    B. in a hurry.
    C. distracted.
    D. in a conflict.

27. A typical tractor-trailer truck will clear a single set of railroad tracks from a stop in

    A. 7 seconds.
    B. 10 seconds.
    C. 14 seconds.
    D. 20 seconds.

28. The B:C type fire extinguisher is meant to work on

    A. wood fires.
    B. cloth fires.
    C. paper fires.
    D. electrical fires and burning liquids.

29. Major commercial motor vehicle collisions due to fatigue and sleepiness most often occur between

    A. 6 a.m. and 12 p.m.
    B. 5 p.m. and 9 p.m.
    C. 11 a.m. and 1 p.m.
    D. 12 a.m. and 6 a.m.

30. Before starting downhill, it is very important to be in proper gear because

    A. the clutch is designed to be used on even surfaces.
    B. state laws require it.
    C. the driver will not be able to shift into a lower gear.
    D. it is difficult to shift gears once at the bottom of the hill.

31. Top-heavy vehicles cannot be blown around by serious windstorms.

    A. True
    B. False

32. To comply with most interstate requirements, the minimum distance from the ground for mud flaps is

    A. 4 inches.

    B. 10 inches.

    C. 8 inches.

    D. 6 inches.

33. It is safe to remove the radiator cap as long as the engine is not overheating.

    A. True

    B. False

34. While driving around curves and turns, if the rear wheels of a trailer move in a different direction than the front wheels do, it is called

    A. jackknifing.

    B. a pull-up.

    C. off-tracking.

    D. oversteering.

35. During fog, and other low-visibility conditions, drivers that see taillights or headlights in front of them are being warned of where the road is ahead of them.

    A. True

    B. False

36. Threshold braking, also called stab braking, should bring the vehicle to a quick and controlled stop, even in slippery conditions.

    A. True

    B. False

37. It is required knowledge for drivers to know basic chemistry when seeking HazMat endorsements.

    A. True

    B. False

38. After 10 consecutive hours off duty, a property-carrying driver may drive a maximum of

    A. 11 hours.

    B. 12 hours.

    C. 13 hours.

    D. 14 hours.

39. The vehicle class of a tractor with a single trailer is

    A. 1.

    B. 4.

    C. 7.

    D. 8.

40. The steering tires must have at least a

    A. 2/32-inch tread depth.

    B. 1/32-inch tread depth.

    C. 4/32-inch tread depth.

    D. 3/32-inch tread depth.

41. When hauling liquids, the needed room for the expanding liquid in the tank is called

    A. baffle.

    B. smooth bore.

    C. the bulkhead.

    D. the outage.

42. Steering arms should not have missing nuts, bolts, or cotter keys.

    A. True

    B. False

43. A vehicle's wheel bearings should be checked for color changes.

    A. True

    B. False

44. The primary principle in balancing cargo weight is to keep the load

 A. on the right side of the cargo area.

 B. balanced in the cargo area.

 C. balanced to the front.

 D. balanced to the rear.

45. Most heavy vehicles with automatic transmissions require double clutching to change gears.

 A. True

 B. False

46. The average perception time for an alert driver is ¾ seconds.

 A. True

 B. False

47. A trailer jackknife occurs when

 A. the rear tractor wheels lock up or spin.

 B. the trailer wheels lock and slide.

 C. the tractor wheels lock up.

 D. only the trailer wheels spin.

48. If the vehicle catches fire while driving, the first thing a driver should do is

 A. drive the vehicle off the road and to an open area.

 B. drive to the nearest gas station.

 C. immediately pull over near where others can assist.

 D. park the vehicle on the shoulder and spray the burning area with the fire extinguisher.

49. When a driver is out of the vehicle, it is important to keep the hazardous materials shipping papers

 A. with the driver.

 B. in a pouch on the driver's door.

 C. in clear view and within reach.

 D. inside the glove compartment.

50. After parking on the shoulder of the road, a driver must place the emergency warning devices within

 A. a reasonable amount of time.

 B. 15 minutes.

 C. 10 minutes.

 D. 5 minutes.

General Knowledge Practice Test 1 Answer Key and Explanations

1. B	11. A	21. B	31. B	41. D
2. B	12. D	22. B	32. D	42. B
3. D	13. C	23. C	33. B	43. B
4. D	14. C	24. B	34. C	44. B
5. B	15. A	25. A	35. B	45. B
6. B	16. B	26. D	36. A	46. B
7. A	17. C	27. C	37. B	47. B
8. B	18. B	28. D	38. A	48. A
9. A	19. C	29. D	39. D	49. B
10. D	20. D	30. C	40. C	50. C

1. **The correct answer is B.** Backing a vehicle towards the right limits the driver's visibility. Backing the vehicle towards the driver's side (left) allows the driver to look out the window and see the rear of the vehicle (choice A).

2. **The correct answer is B.** There are three combined braking systems. The service brake system applies and releases the brakes when a trucker uses the brake pedal during standard driving. The parking brake system applies and releases the parking brakes when a trucker uses the parking brake control. The emergency brake system uses parts of the service and parking brake systems to stop the vehicle in the event there is a brake system malfunction.

3. **The correct answer is D.** Any speed at 15 mph or more over the posted speed limit is considered excessive and is a serious traffic violation for any single offense. Since 15 mph at or over the posted speed limit is deemed excessive, 20 mph or more over the posted speed limit (choice A) would also be considered an excessive violation of speeding laws but does not represent the minimum. Conversely, 10 mph or more over the posted speed limit (choice B) and 5 mph or more over the posted speed limit (choice C) are not deemed excessive speeds but are still violations of speed limits.

4. **The correct answer is D.** CDL drivers will not be criminally charged unless there is a blood alcohol concentration level of at least .04 percent. CDL drivers who are operating commercial vehicles and are known to consume any amount of alcohol will be placed out of service for 24 hours but will not be criminally charged with .01 percent (choice A), .02 percent (choice B), and .03 percent (choice C) blood alcohol concentration levels.

5. **The correct answer is B.** There should be at least one tie-down for every ten feet of cargo. Therefore, one tie-down for each five feet of cargo (choice A), two tie-downs for each five feet of cargo (choice C), and two tie-downs for each fifteen feet of cargo (choice D) are incorrect options.

6. **The correct answer is B.** The Gross Combination Weight is the total weight of a powered unit plus trailer(s) and the cargo. The Gross Combination Weight Rating (choice A) is the maximum gross combination weight specified by the manufacturer for a specific combination of vehicles and its load. The Gross Vehicle Weight (choice C) is the total weight of a single vehicle plus its load. The Gross Vehicle Weight Rating (choice D) is the maximum specified by the manufacturer for a single vehicle and its load.

7. **The correct answer is A.** Convex mirrors do show a wider area, but everything does appear smaller and further away than it really is.

8. **The correct answer is B.** Since fully loaded trucks have more weight, causing better traction, an empty truck will take longer to stop.

9. **The correct answer is A.** Reaction distance is the distance a driver's vehicle travels in standard conditions before the driver physically hits the brakes and responds to a danger seen ahead. Perception distance (choice B) is the distance a driver's vehicle travels in standard conditions from the time a driver's eyes sees a danger until the brain understands it. The braking distance (choice C) is the distance the driver's vehicle will travel in standard conditions while the driver is braking. The total stopping distance (choice D) is the total minimum distance the driver's vehicle has traveled in standard conditions with all considered, including the perception, reaction, and braking distance until the driver can bring the vehicle to a complete stop.

10. **The correct answer is D.** Since wet roads can double stopping distances, it is best for a driver to reduce the speed of the commercial vehicle by about one-third. On packed snow, a driver should reduce speed by one-half (choice A) or more. Since it will take the vehicle longer to stop on a wet road, reducing speeds by one-fourth (choice B) or one-eighth (choice C) is not enough to avoid a possible skidding incident.

11. **The correct answer is A.** Learning the operating engine speed (rpm) range and learning what road speed (mph) each gear is good for are two ways to know when to shift gears.

12. **The correct answer is D.** Active crossing signs regulate the traffic at the railroad crossing using active devices such as flashing red lights, with or without bells, and flashing red lights with bells and gates. A no passing zone sign (choice A) has a white stop line painted on the road surface before the railroad tracks. A passive crossing (choice B) requires the driver to be aware of the crossing, but the decision to continue or stop at the crossing rests on the driver. An advance warning sign (choice C) informs the driver to slow down, look and listen for the train, and be ready to stop at the tracks if a train is approaching.

13. **The correct answer is C.** When using low beams, a driver is able to see about 250 feet ahead. A driver can see a maximum of 500 feet ahead (choice A) and a minimum of 350 feet ahead (choice B) when using high beams. Seeing at about 125 feet ahead (choice D) is not the maximum distance a driver can see ahead (choice D) during night driving.

14. **The correct answer is C.** Coolant levels are checked at the radiator during the pre-trip inspection, not in the cab. Temperature (choice A), air pressure (choice B), and oil pressure (choice D) are gauges that are checked in the cab during the pre-trip inspection.

15. **The correct answer is A.** Low beam headlights must be used during fog instead of the high beam headlights. In fog, the light from high beams often reflects off the fog, creating a glare that can obscure the driver's vision as well as that of fellow motorists. Following all fog-related warning signs (choice B), being ready to stop in an emergency (choice C) and entering slowly before a fog area (choice D) are necessary for drivers who must drive in fog.

16. **The correct answer is B.** Whenever the road is wet, icy, or snow covered, the drive wheels may have poor traction. Therefore, the retarders should be turned off to avoid skidding.

17. **The correct answer is C.** If a driver pulls on each slack adjuster that is within reach and it moves more than about an inch where the push rod attaches, it probably needs adjustment. Therefore, slack adjusters that move two inches (choice A) and four inches (choice B) require adjusting as they have exceeded the minimum of an inch. If slack adjusters move half an inch (choice D), adjustments do not need to be made.

18. **The correct answer is B.** Ignoring the motorist is the best way to deal with an aggressive driver. Staying in the motorist's lane (choice A), signaling gestures to the motorist (choice C), and increasing the speed (choice D) only challenge aggressive drivers.

19. **The correct answer is C.** Staying alert will allow drivers to have the time needed to avoid an emergency or plan an escape if the hazards become emergencies. Although keeping alert can help driver's avoid disciplinary actions by their employer (choice A), it is not the most important reason why a driver must be alert to hazards. Although drivers need to be alert in order to report hazardous incidents to law enforcement, they are not responsible for reporting it to the insurance companies (choice B). A driver is responsible for calling law enforcement in a timely manner after a hazard has occurred, regardless of whether or not a driver is alert (choice D).

20. **The correct answer is D.** Releasing the brakes and counter-steering will allow the rear wheels to catch up with the front wheels during a braking skid and keep the truck from turning too much. Applying more braking pressure to the brake pedal (choice A), applying more pressure to the brake pedal and counter-steering (choice C), and releasing the brakes and accelerating (choice B) can cause the rear wheels to continue skidding as they attempt to catch up with the front wheels.

21. **The correct answer is B.** Authorities should be notified after you secure the scene of an accident to avoid a secondary accident and assist with the flow of traffic.

22. **The correct answer is B.** A driver may be disqualified from driving a commercial motor vehicle if the legal medication prescriptions, such as pain killers, are shown to affect the driver's ability to operate the vehicle in a safe manner.

23. **The correct answer is C.** Safely maneuvering around the box is the best option to avoid an emergency on the road. Braking hard to avoid hitting it (choice A), slowing down and directing traffic around it (choice B), and pushing it off the road with the vehicle (choice D) are likely to increase the opportunities for an accident.

24. **The correct answer is B.** Since multi-speed rear axles and auxiliary transmissions are usually controlled by a selector knob on the gearshift lever, they are used to provide extra gears. Consequently, since multi-speed rear axles and auxiliary transmissions are used to provide extra gears, they do not provide extra room for hazardous materials (choice A). Matching axles, ratios, and loads are ways to better the vehicle's gas mileage (choice C). Shifting gears timely and accurately will make for a smoother vehicle ride (choice D).

25. **The correct answer is A.** The antilock braking system helps drivers maintain control of the vehicle under heavy braking situations. The air brake system (choice B) is a system of service brakes operated by air. The air spring system (choice C) is where the container and plunger are divided by pressurized air. The air ride suspension system (choice D) assists the weight of the load, plus the trailer on air-filled rubber bags.

26. **The correct answer is D.** Drivers in conflict come into situations where vehicles meet or there is a need for a lane change. This can occur at merges, in slow or stalled traffic in a lane, and in collision scenes. Drivers who are in a panic (choice A), in a hurry (choice B), or distracted (choice C) cause hazards for themselves and other drivers.

27. **The correct answer is C.** It takes approximately 14 seconds for a typical tractor-trailer truck to clear a single set of railroad tracks from a stop. Therefore, 7 seconds (choice A) or 10 seconds (choice B) is not sufficient time for a typical tractor-trailer truck to clear a single set of railroad tracks from a stop. Since it takes an average of 14 seconds for a typical tractor-trailer truck to clear a single set of railroad tracks, 20 seconds (choice D) is longer than expected.

28. **The correct answer is D.** Electrical fires and burning liquids are put out by a Class B:C fire extinguisher. Class A fire extinguishers work best to put out wood (choice A), cloth (choice B), and paper (choice C) fires.

29. **The correct answer is D.** Since most people are fatigued and sleepy between 12 a.m. and 6 a.m., major commercial motor vehicle collisions occur during this time. Since many people awake between 6 a.m. and 12 p.m. (choice A) are engaged in activities during 5 p.m. and 9 p.m. (choice B)

and 11 a.m. and 1 p.m. (choice C), vehicle collisions due to fatigue or sleepiness are less likely to happen during these times.

30. **The correct answer is C.** Since the driver will not be able to shift into a lower gear once starting downhill, it is important to be in the proper gear beforehand. To be in proper gear does not suggest that a clutch is designed to be exclusively used on even surfaces (choice A). Although state laws do not "require" the vehicle to be in proper gear before starting downhill, drivers are required to know proper gear placement before going downhill (choice B). Once at the bottom of the hill, it is not difficult for the driver to shift gears (choice D).

31. **The correct answer is B.** Top-heavy vehicles can be blown around by serious windstorms because they have a higher center of gravity that the wind can affect.

32. **The correct answer is D.** The most common distance for the mud flaps to be from the ground to satisfy interstate requirements is 6 inches. Some states do not allow mud flaps to be closer to the ground than 4 inches (choice A). And some states have a 10 inch (choice B) or an 8 inch (choice C) minimum distance requirement for mud flaps, but a standard 6-inch distance from the ground has been adopted by interstate motor carriers in order to keep uniform compliance with all states.

33. **The correct answer is B.** Although an engine is not overheating, the vehicle's radiator cap and circulating radiator fluid can still be hot if the vehicle has not had enough time to cool completely.

34. **The correct answer is C.** Off-tracking is an effect that drivers encounter because the rear wheels of a trailer move in a different direction than the front wheels do while negotiating curves and turns. Jackknifing (choice A) is when the truck and its cab folds or separates at its hinges in an accident. The act of pulling forward while backing a trailer to reposition it is a pull-up (choice B). Oversteering (choice D) is when the vehicle turns more sharply than the driver intends it to because the rear tires lose traction and swing outwards relative to the front of the vehicle.

35. **The correct answer is B.** Since foggy conditions make it difficult to perceive distance, taillights or headlights in front of drivers may not be a true indication of where the road is ahead.

36. **The correct answer is A.** In a vehicle not equipped with an antilock braking system, threshold braking will bring the vehicle to a quick and controlled stop as the driver brakes as hard as possible, allowing the wheels to begin to slip, and then releases the pressure on the pedal to release the wheel, being careful not to skid. This will eventually slow the vehicle down to the desired speed, even in slippery conditions.

37. **The correct answer is B.** Drivers are not required to know basic chemistry when seeking HazMat endorsements.

38. **The correct answer is A.** After 10 consecutive hours off duty, a driver may drive a maximum of 11 hours. A driver may drive 12 hours (choice B) and 13 hours (choice C) since they can extend the 11-hour maximum driving limit by up to 2 hours if they are faced with adverse driving conditions. After following the 10 consecutive off-duty hours, a driver may not drive beyond the 14th consecutive hour.

39. **The correct answer is D.** The vehicle class of a tractor with a single trailer is 8. Vehicle class 1 (choice A) is for small personal vehicles. Vehicle class 4 (choice B) is for medium sized trucks. Vehicle class 7 (choice C) is for a three axle, single unit vehicle.

40. **The correct answer is C.** The steering tires must have at least a 4/32-inch tread depth. All other tires must have at least a 2/32-inch tread depth (choice A). Since steering tires must have a 4/32-inch tread depth, steering tires with a 1/32-inch tread depth (choice B) will be cited and placed out of service. A driver who operates a vehicle with steering tires that have a tread depth of 3/32-inch will also be ticketed (choice D).

41. **The correct answer is D.** Liquids expand as they warm and the needed room for this expansion in the tank is called the outage. Baffled (choice A) tanks have bulkheads in them with holes that let

the liquid flow. A smooth bore—or unbaffled—tank (choice B) has nothing inside to slow down the flow of the liquids; as such, the back and forward surge is strong. Bulkheads (choice C) are liquid tanks that are divided into a number of smaller tanks.

42. **The correct answer is B.** Steering arms should not have mismatched, bent, or cracked lug nuts.

43. **The correct answer is B.** The wheel bearings should be checked for leaks.

44. **The correct answer is B.** The primary principle in balancing cargo weight is to keep the load balanced in the cargo area. Keeping the load on the right side of the cargo area (choice A), balanced to the front (choice C), or balanced to the rear (choice D) can render the vehicle unsafe to handle.

45. **The correct answer is B.** Most heavy vehicles with manual transmissions require double clutching to change gears.

46. **The correct answer is B.** The average perception time for an alert driver is 1.75 seconds while the average reaction time is 0.75 seconds.

47. **The correct answer is B.** When the trailer wheels lock and slide, the trailer will pitch out to the side of the tractor and, if uncorrected, will force the tractor to turn the opposite direction of movement, thus leading to jackknifing. A tractor jackknife occurs when the rear tractor wheels lock up or spin (choices A and C); in this situation, the trailer continues on its course, but the tractor pitches to turn in the direction opposite the direction of movement. Spinning trailer wheels will not lead to a jackknife (choice D).

48. **The correct answer is A.** Getting the vehicle off the road and to an open area away from anything that can cause additional hazards is the safest way a driver should deal with a vehicle fire. Driving to the nearest gas station (choice B), immediately pulling over near where others can assist (choice C), and parking the vehicle on the shoulder and spraying the burning area with the fire extinguisher (choice D) can create additional hazards in an already unsafe situation.

49. **The correct answer is B.** When out of the vehicle, drivers are required to keep the shipping papers in a pouch on the driver's side door or on the driver's seat. A driver should not take the shipping papers with them when they exit the vehicle (choice A). When in the vehicle, a driver must keep the shipping papers in clear view and within reach while driving (choice C). Shipping papers must be within the driver's reach and visible for any party entering the cab—whether a first responder or inspection authority (choice D)—not in the glove compartment.

50. **The correct answer is C.** A driver is required to place the emergency warning devices within 10 minutes of parking on the shoulder of the road. Therefore, a reasonable amount of time (choice A) is considered subjective, and 15 minutes (choice B) is considered too long in an emergency. Depending on the circumstances, it can take a bit of time to gather the warning devices, so 5 minutes (choice D) is incorrect.

GENERAL KNOWLEDGE PRACTICE TEST 2

50 Questions - 90 Minutes

Directions: This test consists of a combination of true/false and multiple-choice questions. Only one answer is correct for each question.

1. A driver who is found to have any trace of alcohol will be placed out of service for

   A. 12 hours.

   B. 24 hours.

   C. 36 hours.

   D. 48 hours.

2. Improper lane usage is considered a serious traffic violation.

   A. True

   B. False

3. At high speeds, a driver should look

   A. one mile ahead.

   B. a half mile ahead.

   C. a fourth mile ahead.

   D. one block ahead.

4. States only have maximums for gross vehicle weights and gross combination weights.

   A. True

   B. False

5. One way a brake fade occurs is when the

   A. brakes are experiencing normal wear and tear.

   B. braking system becomes too hot, forcing a driver to repeatedly apply the brakes harder and harder to achieve the same stopping capabilities.

   C. braking system is cooler than normal, forcing a driver to repeatedly apply the brakes harder and harder to achieve the same stopping power.

   D. brakes wear out sooner on one side than the other side.

6. All vehicles carrying hazardous material loads require placards.

   A. True

   B. False

7. "Texting for truckers" is known as

   A. using a headset.

   B. using a handheld mapping device.

   C. using a dispatching device.

   D. using an audio device.

8. If a front tire fails, it is best to hold the wheel at the twelve o'clock and six o'clock positions to prevent the twisting of the steering wheel out of the driver's hands.

   A. True

   B. False

9. Without regard for the safety or rights of others, aggressive driving is the action of operating a vehicle in a brash, selfish, or forceful manner.

    A. True

    B. False

10. The principle means of controlling speeds on long grades for all truck vehicle types is

    A. threshold braking.

    B. spring braking.

    C. engine braking.

    D. balanced braking.

11. The tendency for the vehicle to slide in a back and forth motion is known as

    A. bobtailing.

    B. hydroplaning.

    C. off-tracking.

    D. fishtailing.

12. When drivers take breaks, they should check tires, brakes, and the cargo.

    A. True

    B. False

13. When double-clutching and shifting, using the double clutch pedals will tell the driver when to shift.

    A. True

    B. False

14. Heavy vehicles can almost always turn more quickly than they can stop.

    A. True

    B. False

15. According to the Department of Transportation, medical certificates

    A. must be renewed annually.

    B. do not have to be renewed after the initial certification.

    C. must be renewed every two years.

    D. must be renewed every three years.

16. The baffles in a tank vehicle control the side-to-side movement surge.

    A. True

    B. False

17. When drivers use their high beams or multiple flashers, they are communicating that

    A. it is safe to merge in front of them.

    B. they need the other driver to stop.

    C. emergency personnel are close.

    D. it is not safe to merge in front of them.

18. If a driver has a blood alcohol level of .02, they may feel less alert, less self-focused, and less coordinated.

    A. True

    B. False

19. During mountain driving, winds are especially a problem coming out of tunnels rather than going into them.

    A. True

    B. False

20. It is preferable to stop along the side of the road if a driver comes into fog.

    A. True

    B. False

21. In case of a fire on a HazMat vehicle, a driver must always have on their person

    A. a fire extinguisher.

    B. their personal belongings.

    C. the shipping papers.

    D. the directions to the local fire station.

22. For rigs to manage safe space while going less than 40mph, a driver would need to calculate

    A. 1 second for each 10 feet of vehicle length.

    B. 2 seconds for each 10 feet of vehicle length.

    C. 1 second for each 5 feet of vehicle length.

    D. 2 seconds for each 5 feet of length.

23. During rain or snow, if the drive wheels begin to spin because of too much power, it is best to

    A. quickly apply your foot on the brakes.

    B. take your foot off the accelerator.

    C. use the hand valve.

    D. release the parking brake.

24. Place warning devices 10 feet, 100 feet, and 200 feet toward the approaching traffic if you must

    A. stop on a two-lane road carrying traffic in both directions.

    B. stop on a two-lane undivided highway.

    C. stop back beyond any hill, curve, or other obstruction.

    D. stop on or by a one-way or divided highway.

25. To keep all trucks from rolling back, release the parking brake only when you have

    A. applied enough engine power.

    B. applied enough pressure on the gas pedal.

    C. applied the trailer hand valve.

    D. applied the pressure safety valve.

26. In safe driving, "communicating" means

    A. the signaling of a driver's intentions to other motorists.

    B. staying in contact with dispatch to share a driver's location.

    C. blowing the horn so other motorists are aware of a driver's presence.

    D. utilizing hand gestures to let other motorists know to go around the vehicle.

27. The best way to see the sides and rear of the vehicle while driving is

    A. with a helper.

    B. with rear view cameras.

    C. by rolling down the windows.

    D. by using the mirrors.

28. All of these are mandatory emergency equipment EXCEPT:

    A. A tire changing kit

    B. Three red reflective triangles, six fuses, or three liquid burning flares

    C. A rated and properly charged fire extinguisher

    D. Spare electrical fuses

29. According to the Large Truck Crash Causation Study (LTCCS), it was reported that 8% of large-truck collisions happened when commercial motor vehicle (CMV) drivers were internally distracted.

    A. True

    B. False

30. The type of vehicles that are more likely to get trapped on a highway railroad crossing are

    A. double trailers.

    B. car carriers.

    C. meat trucks.

    D. freight company trucks.

31. All of these are special situations which require more than regular mirror checks EXCEPT:

    A. Lane changes
    B. Turns
    C. Tires
    D. Merges

32. To decrease road rage and minimize aggressive driving, a driver should perform all of the following EXCEPT:

    A. Being focused on the drive
    B. Acknowledging that there will be delays
    C. Playing loud and intense music
    D. Not driving slowly in the left lane

33. If the driver's license states that corrective lenses are mandatory but the driver is only going a short distance, it is legal to move a commercial vehicle without using corrective lenses.

    A. True
    B. False

34. Under usual circumstances, the best gear for a driver driving 45 mph is

    A. 9th gear.
    B. 10th gear.
    C. 7th gear.
    D. 8th gear.

35. A driver transporting chlorine in cargo tanks must have an authorized gas mask in the vehicle.

    A. True
    B. False

36. During a crash procedure, it is necessary for the driver to set out the reflective triangles by holding

    A. them along the right side of the body.
    B. them overhead while walking to the placement area.
    C. them between himself/herself and oncoming traffic.
    D. and waving them toward oncoming traffic.

37. The leading cause of commercial vehicle fires is

    A. spilled fuel.
    B. a driver smoking.
    C. improper use of flares.
    D. underinflated tires.

38. If a vehicle starts to hydroplane, the driver should immediately

    A. slam on the brakes.
    B. press down on the accelerator.
    C. pump the brakes.
    D. release the accelerator.

39. When the highway speed limit is 45mph but with heavy traffic becomes 30mph, a driver's safest speed is

    A. 45 mph.
    B. 20 mph.
    C. 40 mph.
    D. 30 mph.

40. Stab braking should not be used with a vehicle that has

    A. antilock brakes.
    B. spring brakes.
    C. air brakes.
    D. towing trailers.

41. High beam headlights are required to be dimmed when oncoming traffic is within

   A. 1,000 feet.
   B. 750 feet.
   C. 500 feet.
   D. 250 feet.

42. In hot weather, the driver needs to inspect the tires every

   A. 1 hour or 50 miles.
   B. 4 hours or 250 miles.
   C. 3 hours or 150 miles.
   D. 2 hours or 100 miles.

43. To drive a vehicle safely, a driver must be able to control its speed and

   A. acceleration.
   B. direction.
   C. steering.
   D. stopping.

44. During wintery roadway conditions, wet ice is much more slippery than ice that is not wet.

   A. True
   B. False

45. The best way to recover from a front wheel skid is to

   A. allow the vehicle to slow down without braking hard or turning.
   B. accelerate out of the skid.
   C. counter steer.
   D. even out the brake pressure by using the stopping brakes.

46. Most heavy vehicles with manual transmissions that require double clutching to change gears follow all these basic methods for shifting up EXCEPT:

   A. Release the accelerator, push in the clutch, shift to neutral
   B. Release the clutch and let the engine and gears slow to the rpm required for the next gear
   C. Push in the clutch and downshift to the low gear
   D. Release the clutch and press the accelerator at the same time

47. During a winter weather inspection, the system that should receive extra attention is the

   A. exhaust system.
   B. steering system.
   C. cargo compartment.
   D. electrical system.

48. The trailer hand valve is not used in driving because of the danger of making the trailer skid.

   A. True
   B. False

49. A driver should downshift before

   A. starting uphill and after exiting a curve.
   B. starting down a hill and exiting a curve.
   C. before entering a curve and starting down a hill.
   D. starting uphill and entering a curve.

50. Carrying liquids or gases in a leaking tank is a crime and the driver will be cited and prevented from driving further.

   A. True
   B. False

General Knowledge Practice Test 2 Answer Key and Explanations

1. B	11. D	21. C	31. C	41. C
2. A	12. A	22. A	32. C	42. D
3. C	13. B	23. B	33. B	43. B
4. B	14. A	24. D	34. A	44. A
5. B	15. C	25. A	35. A	45. A
6. B	16. B	26. A	36. C	46. C
7. C	17. D	27. D	37. D	47. A
8. B	18. B	28. A	38. D	48. A
9. A	19. A	29. B	39. D	49. C
10. C	20. B	30. B	40. A	50. A

1. **The correct answer is B.** As stated by the Federal Motor Carrier Safety Administration, CDL drivers who are operating commercial vehicles and are known to consume any amount of alcohol will be placed out of service for 24 hours. Therefore, 12 hours (choice A), 36 hours (choice C), and 48 hours (choice D) are incorrect options.

2. **The correct answer is A.** The Department of Transportation deems improper lane usage as a serious traffic violation because of the safety hazards it can impose on other drivers.

3. **The correct answer is C.** A good driver should always be shifting their attention back and forth, near and far, but when at high speeds, a driver should look ¼ mile ahead of the distance that he/she will travel. A driver looking 1 mile (choice A) and ½ mile (choice B) ahead of the distance that he/she will travel is not always possible. A driver looking one block ahead (choice D) is the equivalent of ¼ of a mile when driving at low speeds.

4. **The correct answer is B.** States also have maximums for axle weights.

5. **The correct answer is B.** One way a brake fade occurs is when there is excessive heat applied to the braking system, making it difficult for a commercial vehicle to stop. Although it is important to conduct routine brake system maintenance on commercial vehicles, a brake fade does not occur when brakes are experiencing normal wear and tear (choice A). Since a brake fade is caused by exceeding the heat capacity of the braking system, the braking system being cooler than normal does not force a driver to repeatedly apply the brakes harder and harder to achieve the same stopping power (choice C). Additionally, the brakes wearing out sooner on one side more than the other side does not cause brake fading (choice D) because it requires excessive heating.

6. **The correct answer is B.** Not all vehicles carrying hazardous material loads require placards, but it is important to have the placards if the vehicle does require it.

7. **The correct answer is C.** According to Federal Motor Carrier Safety Association, using a dispatching device is considered "texting for truckers." Using a headset (choice A), a handheld mapping device (choice B), and an audio device (choice D) are all distractions but are not considered "texting for truckers."

8. **The correct answer is B.** Holding the steering wheel firmly in the three o'clock and nine o'clock positions is the only way to prevent twisting of the steering wheel out of the driver's hands.

9. **The correct answer is A.** Without regard for the safety or rights of others, aggressive driving is the action of operating a vehicle in a brash, selfish, or forceful manner.

10. **The correct answer is C.** Since engine braking is an effective braking method that creates a massive amount of force, it can extend the life of friction brakes and helps drivers maintain better control of their vehicles, especially down long grades. Threshold braking (choice A) is primarily used in vehicles without antilock braking systems because it can bring the vehicle to a fairly quick and controlled stop, even in slippery conditions. Spring braking (choice B) is used when parking the vehicle. Balanced braking (choice D) is the use of the foot control valve in combination vehicles such as truck-tractors and semitrailers.

11. **The correct answer is D.** Fishtailing is when the vehicle slides in a back and forth motion. Bobtailing (choice A) is driving the truck tractor without its trailer attached. Hydroplaning (choice B) is when the water on the road prevents a vehicle's tire from gripping the road surface, causing the vehicle to "ski" across the water. Off-tracking (choice C) is when the rear wheels take a different, shorter direction than the front wheels while the vehicle is turning or cornering.

12. **The correct answer is A.** When drivers take breaks, they should check tires, brakes, and cargo to make sure they are all in proper shape to continue.

13. **The correct answer is B.** In fact, when double-clutching and shifting, using the sound of the engine will tell the driver when to shift.

14. **The correct answer is A.** In a traffic emergency, if a vehicle is in danger of colliding with another vehicle and the driver does not act, it is always good to remember that heavy vehicles can almost always turn more quickly than they can stop.

15. **The correct answer is C.** A driver must recertify for the medical certificate every two years. Since a driver must recertify every two years, a driver does not need to renew annually (choice A). It is against the law to not renew for the medical certificate after the initial certification (choice B). Renewing every three years (choice D) is a year over the recertification requirement.

16. **The correct answer is B.** The baffles in a tank vehicle control the forward and backward liquid surge.

17. **The correct answer is D.** Drivers will use their high beams or multiple flashers to communicate that it is not safe to merge in front of them. Therefore, drivers are NOT using their high beams or multiple flashers to communicate that it is safe to merge in front of them (choice A), that they need the other driver to stop (choice B), or that emergency personnel are close (choice C).

18. **The correct answer is B.** A blood alcohol level of .02 may make drivers feel less inhibited while a blood alcohol level of .04 may make drivers feel less alert, less self-focused, and less coordinated.

19. **The correct answer is A.** Winds are typically problematic when coming out of tunnels because the force of cross winds that is channeled in between smaller gaps of a tunnel is perpendicular to the road and can push a driver off track when exiting.

20. **The correct answer is B.** It is preferable for truckers to stop in a rest area unless there are no other options.

21. **The correct answer is C.** Since the shipping papers contain all the necessary hazmat information that a driver needs to know while transporting cargo, they should always have them in their possession during a vehicle fire. Although a fire extinguisher (choice A) is required on all HazMat vehicles, a driver is not required to have it on their person during the vehicle's fire. Drivers are not required to have their personal belongings (choice B) nor the directions to the local fire station (choice D) on them if the HazMat vehicle is on fire.

22. **The correct answer is A.** A good rule to use in order to determine how much safe space a driver should keep in front of them is to calculate 1 second for each 10 feet of vehicle length. This formula is standard accepted practice, therefore, 2 seconds for each 10 feet of vehicle length (choice B), 1 second for each 5 feet of vehicle length (choice C),

and 2 seconds for each 5 feet of length (choice D) are not accurate estimates.

23. **The correct answer is B.** Since spinning drive wheels indicate poor traction, taking pressure off the accelerator is the best way to manage them. Quickly applying pressure to the brakes (choice A) can cause the drive wheels to spin and slide more. The hand valve (choice C) is used only to test the trailer brakes. There would be no reason to release the parking brake (choice D) because it should not be engaged while a commercial vehicle is in the drive gear.

24. **The correct answer is D.** Stopping on or by a one-way or divided highway requires the driver to place warning devices 10 feet, 100 feet, and 200 feet toward the oncoming traffic. Stopping on a two-lane road carrying traffic in both directions (choice A) or stopping on a two-lane undivided highway (choice B) requires the driver to place warning devices within 10 feet of the front or rear corners to indicate the location of the vehicle and 100 feet behind and ahead of the vehicle, on the shoulder or in the lane the driver has stopped. Stopping back beyond any hill, curve, or other obstruction (choice C), the driver will need to place the warning signal in the direction of the obstruction to view a distance of 100 feet to 500 feet from the stopped commercial motor vehicle.

25. **The correct answer is A.** Employing the parking brake and then releasing it when enough engine power has been applied will prevent the truck from rolling back. The gas pedal should be given pressure (choice B) in order to get the engine power high enough, however, the power of the engine should be given the focus and not just the pressure on the pedal. The trailer hand valve (choice C) should only be applied to test the trailer brakes. The pressure safety valve (choice D) is used to quickly release gases from commercial motor vehicle equipment.

26. **The correct answer is A.** In safe driving, "communicating" is the signaling of a driver's intentions to other motorists. Staying in contact with dispatch to share a driver's location (choice B), blowing the horn so other motorists are aware of a driver's presence (choice C), and utilizing hand gestures to let other motorists know to go around the vehicle (choice D) are not methods of safe driving "communications."

27. **The correct answer is D.** Using the mirrors is the best way to know what is going on behind and to the sides of the vehicle. Consequently, using a helper (choice A), using rear view cameras (choice B), or rolling down windows (choice C) separately do not help with all the blind spots.

28. **The correct answer is A.** A tire changing kit is not mandatory emergency equipment. However, three red reflective triangles, six fuses, or three liquid burning flares (choice B), a rated and properly charged fire extinguisher (choice C), and spare electrical fuses (choice D) are required emergency equipment.

29. **The correct answer is B.** According to the Large Truck Crash Causation Study (LTCCS), it was reported that 8% of large-truck collisions happened when Commercial Motor Vehicle (CMV) drivers were externally distracted.

30. **The correct answer is B.** Since car carriers are incredibly low to the ground, they are more likely to get trapped at a highway railroad crossing. Although any vehicle can get trapped on a highway railroad crossing, double trailers (choice A), meat trucks (choice C), and freight company trucks (choice D) are less likely to get trapped on a highway railroad crossing then a car carrier.

31. **The correct answer is C.** Tire checks are a part of regular mirror checks and not considered to be a special situation that would require additional mirror checks. Special situations that require additional mirror checks are lane changes (choice A), turns (choice B), and merges (choice D).

32. **The correct answer is C.** Playing loud and intense music can intensify a driver's road rage and maximize aggressive driving habits. Being focused on the drive (choice A), acknowledging that there will be delays (choice B), and not driving slowly in the left lane (choice D) are ways to help drivers

decrease their road rage and minimize the aggressive driving habits.

33. **The correct answer is B.** It is illegal to move a commercial vehicle without corrective lenses if the driver's license says corrective lenses are mandatory.

34. **The correct answer is A.** Since the numbers on the speedometer can be added together to determine the best gear at a particular speed, a driver driving 45 mph will be driving in 9th gear (4+5 = 9) under usual circumstances. A driver who is driving 55 mph will be in 10th gear (choice B). A driver who is driving 25 mph will be in 7th gear (choice C). A driver who is driving 35 mph will be in 8th gear (choice D).

35. **The correct answer is A.** A driver transporting chlorine in cargo tanks must have an authorized gas mask in the vehicle along with an emergency kit to control leaks in the dome cover plate fittings on the cargo tank.

36. **The correct answer is C.** Since the driver has crashed, it is necessary for the driver to set out the reflective triangles and hold them between himself/herself and oncoming traffic while doing so. Holding them along the right side of the body (choice A), holding them overhead while walking to the placement area (choice B), or holding and waving them toward oncoming traffic (choice D) are not safe ways to set out the reflective triangles.

37. **The correct answer is D.** Since underinflated tires can easily reach high enough temperatures to start a fire, maintaining proper tire inflation is key. Although spilled fuel (choice A), a driver smoking (choice B), and improper use of flares (choice C) can cause commercial vehicle fires, the leading cause is underinflated tires.

38. **The correct answer is D.** A driver should immediately release the accelerator when the vehicle starts to hydroplane. Slamming on the brakes (choice A), pressing down on the accelerator (choice B), and pumping the brakes (choice C) can increase the loss of traction the vehicle is experiencing.

39. **The correct answer is D.** The safest speed to drive is the speed that is occurring during the heavy traffic. Driving at the highway speed of 45mph (choice A) is dangerous during heavy traffic. Going significantly below the speed limit at 20 mph (choice B) can cause more delays than necessary. Driving 40mph (choice C) is still faster than the flow of the heavy traffic and therefore not recommended.

40. **The correct answer is A.** Since stab braking is the applying and releasing of the brakes to prevent the locking of the wheels, skidding, and the inability to steer, stab braking should not be used with a vehicle that has antilock brakes. Stab braking can be used with vehicles that have spring brakes (choice B) and air brakes (choice C) and those that are towing trailers (choice D) if there are no antilock brakes on the vehicle.

41. **The correct answer is C.** Since glare from the headlights can be an issue for oncoming drivers, the high beams must be dimmed within 500 feet of the approaching vehicle. Therefore, if an oncoming driver is 1,000 feet (choice A) or 750 feet (choice B) away, the commercial vehicle driver is not required to dim the high beam headlights. The high beam headlights should already be dimmed if oncoming traffic is within 250 feet (choice D) because it can cause temporary vision impairments or accidents.

42. **The correct answer is D.** Driving in hot weather requires an inspection of the tires every two hours or every 100 miles. Therefore, examination of the vehicle's tires during hot weather at every hour or 50 miles (choice A), at every 4 hours or 250 miles (choice B), and at every 3 hours or 150 miles (choice C) are not the ideal inspection durations or distances.

43. **The correct answer is B.** Driving a vehicle safely requires a driver to control a vehicle's speed and direction. Now, operating a commercial vehicle safely necessitates skills in acceleration (choice A), steering (choice C) and stopping (choice D).

44. **The correct answer is A.** The increased slipperiness of wet ice is caused by the thin layer of liquid water and not directly by the solid ice itself.

45. **The correct answer is A.** The only way to slow a front wheel skid is to allow the vehicle to slow down without braking hard or turning. Accelerating (choice B), counter steering (choice C), and evening out the brake pressure by using the stopping brakes (choice D) will only foster additional skidding during a front wheel skid.

46. **The correct answer is C.** For most heavy vehicles with manual transmissions that require double clutching to change gears, it is necessary to push in the clutch and shift to the higher gear. The following are basic methods for shifting up in most heavy vehicles with manual transmissions that require double clutching to change gears: release the accelerator, push in the clutch, shift to neutral (choice A), release the clutch and let the engine and gears slow to the rpm required for the next gear (choice B), and release the clutch and press the accelerator at the same time (choice D).

47. **The correct answer is A.** Since the exhaust system can transfer carbon monoxide into the small cabin space of the vehicle, it should receive extra attention during a winter weather inspection. The steering system (choice B), the cargo compartment (choice C), and the electrical system (choice D) do not require as much extra attention during a winter weather inspection.

48. **The correct answer is A.** Since the trailer hand valve is not used in driving because of the danger of making the trailer skid, it is only used to test the trailer brakes.

49. **The correct answer is C.** It is necessary to downshift before entering a curve and starting down a hill because it allows the driver to use some power through the curve and have stability while turning. Starting uphill and after exiting a curve (choice A) would necessitate an upshift not a downshift. Although starting down a hill will necessitate a downshift, exiting a curve does not (choice B). Starting uphill and entering a curve (choice D) would require an upshift for starting the uphill and a downshift for entering the curve.

50. **The correct answer is A.** In addition to being cited and prevented from driving further, a driver may also be liable for the clean-up of any spill.

NOTES

AIR BRAKES PRACTICE TESTS ANSWER SHEET

Practice Test 1

1. Ⓐ Ⓑ Ⓒ Ⓓ
2. Ⓐ Ⓑ Ⓒ Ⓓ
3. Ⓐ Ⓑ Ⓒ Ⓓ
4. Ⓐ Ⓑ
5. Ⓐ Ⓑ

6. Ⓐ Ⓑ Ⓒ Ⓓ
7. Ⓐ Ⓑ Ⓒ Ⓓ
8. Ⓐ Ⓑ
9. Ⓐ Ⓑ Ⓒ Ⓓ
10. Ⓐ Ⓑ

11. Ⓐ Ⓑ
12. Ⓐ Ⓑ Ⓒ Ⓓ
13. Ⓐ Ⓑ Ⓒ Ⓓ
14. Ⓐ Ⓑ
15. Ⓐ Ⓑ Ⓒ Ⓓ

16. Ⓐ Ⓑ
17. Ⓐ Ⓑ Ⓒ Ⓓ
18. Ⓐ Ⓑ Ⓒ Ⓓ
19. Ⓐ Ⓑ
20. Ⓐ Ⓑ Ⓒ Ⓓ

21. Ⓐ Ⓑ Ⓒ Ⓓ
22. Ⓐ Ⓑ
23. Ⓐ Ⓑ Ⓒ Ⓓ
24. Ⓐ Ⓑ Ⓒ Ⓓ
25. Ⓐ Ⓑ

Practice Test 2

1. Ⓐ Ⓑ Ⓒ Ⓓ
2. Ⓐ Ⓑ
3. Ⓐ Ⓑ Ⓒ Ⓓ
4. Ⓐ Ⓑ Ⓒ Ⓓ
5. Ⓐ Ⓑ

6. Ⓐ Ⓑ
7. Ⓐ Ⓑ Ⓒ Ⓓ
8. Ⓐ Ⓑ Ⓒ Ⓓ
9. Ⓐ Ⓑ
10. Ⓐ Ⓑ Ⓒ Ⓓ

11. Ⓐ Ⓑ
12. Ⓐ Ⓑ Ⓒ Ⓓ
13. Ⓐ Ⓑ Ⓒ Ⓓ
14. Ⓐ Ⓑ Ⓒ Ⓓ
15. Ⓐ Ⓑ

16. Ⓐ Ⓑ
17. Ⓐ Ⓑ Ⓒ Ⓓ
18. Ⓐ Ⓑ Ⓒ Ⓓ
19. Ⓐ Ⓑ Ⓒ Ⓓ
20. Ⓐ Ⓑ

21. Ⓐ Ⓑ
22. Ⓐ Ⓑ Ⓒ Ⓓ
23. Ⓐ Ⓑ Ⓒ Ⓓ
24. Ⓐ Ⓑ
25. Ⓐ Ⓑ Ⓒ Ⓓ

AIR BRAKES PRACTICE TEST 1

25 Questions - 60 Minutes

Directions: This test consists of a combination of true/false and multiple-choice questions. Only one answer is correct for each question.

1. The service brake system of air brakes

   A. uses components of the service and parking brake systems to stop the vehicle.

   B. stops the vehicle during an emergency.

   C. applies and releases the parking brakes.

   D. applies and frees the brakes when the driver uses the brake pedal during normal driving.

2. The governor control will allow the compressor to start pumping again at

   A. 125 psi.

   B. 150 psi.

   C. 100 psi.

   D. 80-85 psi.

3. The most common type of foundation brake is the

   A. s-cam brake.

   B. wedge brake.

   C. disc brake.

   D. limiting valve.

4. Spring brakes are not going to engage completely until the psi drops to a 10 to 15 range.

   A. True

   B. False

5. The yellow malfunction lamps of the antilock braking system of a trailer will be on the right side of it.

   A. True

   B. False

6. The vehicles that must have low air pressure warning signals are

   A. those built after 2006.

   B. those built after 1998.

   C. all vehicles with air brakes operating at the current time.

   D. only 90% of the vehicles operating with air brakes and on the road.

7. Air braking requires more time than hydraulic braking because the air

   A. is compressible and takes more time to run through the lines than hydraulic fluid.

   B. tends to seep through the air brake tube fittings.

   C. brakes use various brake drums.

   D. brakes necessitate heavier return springs.

8. A safety relief valve is fitted in the back-up tank where the air compressor pumps the air.

   A. True

   B. False

9. A dashboard control handle that can be used to apply the spring brakes steadily is

   A. the modulating control valve.

   B. the limiting valve.

   C. a push-pull control knob.

   D. the wig wag.

10. A red warning light indicates a malfunction with the air brake system.

    A. True

    B. False

11. Both the primary and secondary air brake systems will supply air to the trailer.

    A. True

    B. False

12. The following are accurate statements about inspecting brake linings EXCEPT:

    A. Linings should not be loose.

    B. Linings should have some oil or grease around them.

    C. Linings should not be extremely thin.

    D. Linings should not be soaked with oil or grease.

13. Checking the manual slack adjusters on s-cam brakes should be done on

    A. an incline.

    B. a decline.

    C. level ground.

    D. vehicles with the wheels removed.

14. "Compounding" the brakes means that the service brake application is applied with the parking brake still employed.

    A. True

    B. False

15. Emergency control braking is when drivers

    A. brake hard, release the brakes when the wheels lock, and then reapply them when the wheels start moving.

    B. apply the brakes as hard as they can without locking the wheels.

    C. hold the braking by mechanical force.

    D. use components of the service and parking brake systems to stop the vehicle.

16. Foundation brakes are used at each of the front wheels.

    A. True

    B. False

17. On older vehicles, when a driver puts the control in the slippery position, the limiting valve drops the normal air pressure to the front brakes by

    A. half.

    B. a fourth.

    C. a third.

    D. three-fourths.

18. The mechanism which controls the air pressure that is applied to operate the brakes

    A. are the slack adjusters.

    B. is the brake pedal.

    C. is the limiting valve.

    D. are the linings.

19. Parking brakes should not be used if they are very hot or very wet in freezing temperatures.

    A. True

    B. False

20. Every combination vehicle has two air lines, the

    A. control line and the signal line.

    B. emergency line and the supply line.

    C. service line and the emergency line.

    D. front line and the back line.

21. On newer combination vehicles, the trailer air supply control is a

    A. red four-sided knob.

    B. yellow four-sided knob.

    C. yellow eight-sided knob.

    D. red eight-sided knob.

22. Perception Distance + Reaction Distance + Road Distance + Braking Distance = Total Stopping Distance

    A. True
    B. False

23. On dry pavement, the air brake lag distance at 55 mph adds about

    A. 32 feet to the stopping distance.
    B. 22 feet to the stopping distance.
    C. 10 feet to the stopping distance.
    D. 45 feet to the stopping distance.

24. When a driver's "safe" speed is 45 mph and they are traveling on a steep downgrade with the engine in the correct low gear, application of the brakes should not occur until they have reached

    A. 60 mph.
    B. 55 mph.
    C. 30 mph.
    D. 45 mph.

25. The brake linings' chemical change that reduces friction and causes the expansion of the brake drums is commonly known as overheated brakes.

    A. True
    B. False

Air Brakes Practice Test 1 Answer Key and Explanations

1. D	6. C	11. A	16. B	21. D
2. C	7. A	12. B	17. A	22. B
3. A	8. B	13. C	18. B	23. A
4. B	9. A	14. A	19. A	24. D
5. B	10. B	15. B	20. C	25. B

1. **The correct answer is D.** The service brake system applies and frees the brakes when the driver uses the brake pedal during normal driving. The emergency brake system uses components of the service and parking brake systems to stop the vehicle normally (choice A) as well as during an emergency (choice B). The parking brake applies and releases the parking brakes (choice C).

2. **The correct answer is C.** The governor control will allow the compressor to start pumping again at 100 psi. The governor control blocks the compressor from pumping air at 125 psi (choice A). The safety relief valve that safeguards the tank and the remainder of the system from too much pressure is set to open at 150 psi (choice B). The low-pressure warning devices will trigger an alarm at 80-85 psi on large buses and other vehicles (choice D).

3. **The correct answer is A.** The s-cam brake is the most common foundation brake. Although both are foundation brakes, the wedge brake (choice B) and the disc brake (choice C) are less common than the s-cam brake. The limiting valve (choice D) is found in older trucks and decreases the "normal" air pressure to the front brakes by half.

4. **The correct answer is B.** When the air pressure drops to a range of 20 to 45 psi, the spring brakes will engage completely from the lack of pressure being unable to hold the springs back.

5. **The correct answer is B.** The trailer will have the yellow malfunction lamps of the antilock braking system on the left side, either on the front or rear corner of it.

6. **The correct answer is C.** All vehicles with air brakes operating at the current time must have a low air pressure warning signal. Therefore, choices that indicate vehicles built after 2006 (choice A), vehicles built after 1998 (choice B), and only 90% of the vehicles operating with air brakes and on the road (choice D) are incorrect.

7. **The correct answer is A.** Since air is compressed in air brakes, it will take more time to run through the lines than hydraulic fluid. Air does not tend to seep through the air brake tube fittings if the fittings are in proper working condition (choice B). Air brakes use either drum or disc brakes, not various brake drums (choice C). Air brakes do not need heavier return springs (choice D).

8. **The correct answer is B.** A safety relief valve is fitted in the first tank where the air compressor pumps the air.

9. **The correct answer is A.** The modulating control valve is a dashboard control handle that can be used to apply the spring brakes steadily. The limiting valve (choice B) is found in older trucks and decreases the "normal" air pressure to the front brakes by half. The push-pull control knob (choice C) puts on the parking brakes. The wig wag (choice D) device releases a mechanical arm into the driver's view when the pressure in the system declines below 60 psi.

10. **The correct answer is B.** If a commercial vehicle's air brake system is working improperly, the malfunction lamp will light up yellow or amber.

11. **The correct answer is A.** Although the two brake systems are separate, the primary and secondary do both supply air to the trailer.

12. **The correct answer is B.** The presence of oil, grease, or any form of lubrication on the brake linings can lead to inconsistent braking—grabby, dragging, or pulsating brakes. Linings should not be loose (choice A), extremely thin (choice C), nor soaked with oil or grease (choice D).

13. **The correct answer is C.** The manual slack adjusters on s-cam brakes should be checked on level ground. They should not be checked on an incline (choice A), a decline (choice B), or on vehicles with the wheels removed (choice D).

14. **The correct answer is A.** Compounding the brakes is the result of stepping on the foot valve with the spring brakes applied. If too much pressure is applied, the brake parts can be damaged.

15. **The correct answer is B.** Emergency control braking is when drivers apply the brakes as hard as they can without locking the wheels. Stab braking is when drivers brake hard, release the brakes when the wheels lock, and reapply them when the wheels start moving (choice A). Truck and bus parking or emergency brakes must be held on by mechanical force (choice C). The emergency brake system uses components of the service and parking brake systems to stop the vehicle (choice D).

16. **The correct answer is B.** Foundation brakes are used at each of the vehicle's wheels.

17. **The correct answer is A.** The limiting valve drops the normal air pressure to the front brakes by half when the driver puts the control in the slippery position. Therefore, the limiting valve dropping the air pressure to the front brakes by a fourth (choice B), a third (choice C), and three-fourths (choice D) is incorrect.

18. **The correct answer is B.** The brake pedal is the mechanism that controls the air pressure that is applied to operate the brakes. The slack adjuster (choice A) uses an adjusting nut on the rear side of the brake drum to adjust the brakes. The limiting valve (choice B) is found in older trucks and decreases the "normal" air pressure to the front brakes by half. The linings (choice D) apply frictional forces to the drum that is attached to the wheel and decreases its speed while enhancing the control of the vehicle.

19. **The correct answer is A.** If applied when they are very hot, parking brakes can be damaged, but if they are applied wet during freezing conditions, they can freeze, inhibiting the driver from moving the vehicle.

20. **The correct answer is C.** The service line and the emergency line run between each of the combination vehicles, such as the tractor to trailer. Control line and the signal line (choice A) are additional names for the service line. The emergency line and the supply line (choice B) are the same line that controls the emergency brake on combination vehicles. The front line and the back line (choice D) do not represent anything for commercial vehicles.

21. **The correct answer is D.** On newer combination vehicles, the trailer air supply control is a red eight-sided knob. Therefore, it is not a red four-sided knob (choice A), a yellow four-sided knob (choice B), nor a yellow eight-sided knob (choice C).

22. **The correct answer is B.** Perception Distance + Reaction Distance + Brake Lag Distance + Braking Distance = Total Stopping Distance.

23. **The correct answer is A.** About 32 feet is added to the stopping distance of an air brake lag distance done on dry pavement. Therefore, adding about 22 feet (choice B) and 10 feet (choice C) of air brake lag distance at 55 mph is not sufficient, while adding 45 feet (choice D) is too much.

24. **The correct answer is D.** When on a steep downgrade, the brakes should be used in combination with the slow-down action of the engine in low gear; however, brakes should not be applied until the driver has reduced the vehicle's speed to the "safe" speed, 45mph, and then should gradually apply the brakes until the driver reaches 5 mph below the safe speed. Since the "safe" speed is 45 mph while traveling on a steep downgrade, 60 mph (choice A), 55 mph (choice B), and 30 mph (choice C) are incorrect.

25. **The correct answer is B.** Since the linings' chemical changes reduce friction and cause expansion of the brake drums, the shoes and lining need to move farther to make contact with the drums, causing the brakes to fade, not overheat.

NOTES

AIR BRAKES PRACTICE TEST 2

25 Questions - 60 Minutes

> **Directions:** This test consists of a combination of true/false and multiple-choice questions. Only one answer is correct for each question.

1. Pumping air into the air storage reservoirs (tanks) is done by the

   A. V-belt.

   B. tank drains.

   C. air compressor.

   D. wig wag device.

2. Having small amounts of water and compressor oil in the compressed air is good for the air brake system.

   A. True

   B. False

3. The gauge that indicates how much air pressure is being directed to the brakes is the

   A. supply pressure gauge.

   B. low pressure gauge.

   C. safety relief valve.

   D. application gauge.

4. After the initial pressure drop, the maximum leakage rates per minute are

   A. 2 psi for single vehicles and 3 psi for combination vehicles.

   B. 1 psi for single vehicles and 3 psi for combination vehicles.

   C. 3 psi for single vehicles and 4 psi for combination vehicles.

   D. 3.5 psi for single vehicles and 10 psi for combination vehicles.

5. When a driver applies the disc brakes in an air brake system, a stop light switch activated by the disc brake pressure turns on the brake lights.

   A. True

   B. False

6. Manually draining the safety valve of moisture is the solution to the issue of a safety valve releasing air.

   A. True

   B. False

7. The emergency brake system uses parts of the

   A. service and parking brake systems to stop the vehicle.

   B. parking brake and governor control to slow the vehicle.

   C. air compressor and service brake system to stop the vehicle.

   D. parking brake and brake pedal to slow the vehicle.

8. The slack adjuster will need to be adjusted after the driver pulls hard on it and finds that its free play is more than

   A. 3/4 inch.

   B. 1/4 inch.

   C. 1/2 inch.

   D. 1 inch.

9. If the air compressor is gear driven, the belt's condition and tightness should be checked.

   A. True

   B. False

10. While driving under usual conditions, the spring brakes are typically held back by

    A. bolts.

    B. brake linings.

    C. air pressure.

    D. springs.

11. If properly installed, automatic slack adjusters should not need either manual adjustment or checks.

    A. True

    B. False

12. In a dual air system, allowing time for the air compressor to build pressure will let the warning light and buzzer shut off when air pressure in both the primary and secondary systems climb greater than

    A. 100 psi.

    B. 50 psi.

    C. 60 psi.

    D. 125 psi.

13. When the brakes are employed, brake shoes will press against the

    A. brake drum or disc.

    B. slack adjuster.

    C. s-cam.

    D. return spring.

14. The total stopping distance for the average driver in a vehicle with air brakes traveling 55 mph under good braking conditions and traction is over

    A. 250 feet.

    B. 300 feet.

    C. 450 feet.

    D. 600 feet.

15. A driver links the service and emergency air lines from the truck or tractor to the trailer, which means the glad hands are being used.

    A. True

    B. False

16. If the air compressor is belt driven, it will be checked during Step 2: The Engine Compartment Checks.

    A. True

    B. False

17. The service air line is connected to the

    A. signal line.

    B. control line.

    C. relay valves.

    D. hand valve.

18. Extreme use of the service brakes leads to overheating and results in

    A. proper modification of the s-cam.

    B. a better chance of contact between the brake drums and linings.

    C. increased stopping power.

    D. expansion of the brake drums.

19. If a truck has an alcohol evaporator, its function is to

   A. remove the requirement for daily tank draining.

   B. lower the danger of ice in the air brake valves during cold weather.

   C. clear the wet tank of alcohol that rests at the bottom.

   D. inhibit water from getting in the tanks.

20. If the antilock braking system fails, the driver is unable to operate the air brake system on the vehicle normally.

   A. True

   B. False

21. Air pressure build-up is tested during Step 7-Final Air Brake Check of the inspection procedure

   A. True

   B. False

22. The braking distance of a fully loaded tractor trailer increases at a rate of

   A. 2x as it moves up in speed.

   B. 6x as it moves up in speed.

   C. 8x as it moves up in speed.

   D. 4x as it moves up in speed.

23. The stopping distance will be increased on all of the following EXCEPT:

   A. Brake lag distance

   B. Effective braking distance

   C. Reaction distance

   D. Applied friction distance

24. The tractor protection valve maintains air in the trailer brake system should the tractor or truck separate or have a bad leak.

   A. True

   B. False

25. The dual air brake system is two separate systems that operate

   A. a set during day driving and another set that operates during night driving.

   B. brakes for the front axle and brakes for the back axle.

   C. one for each side of the vehicle.

   D. the brakes for attached trailers only.

Air Brakes Practice Test 2 Answer Key and Explanations

1. C	6. B	11. B	16. A	21. A
2. B	7. A	12. C	17. C	22. D
3. D	8. D	13. A	18. D	23. D
4. C	9. B	14. C	19. B	24. B
5. B	10. C	15. A	20. B	25. B

1. **The correct answer is C.** The air compressor pumps air into the air storage reservoirs (tanks). The v-belt connects the air compressor to the engine (choice A). Each air tank is outfitted with a drain valve in the bottom that drains the tanks (choice B) of water and oil. The wig wag device (choice D) releases a mechanical arm into the driver's view when the pressure in the system declines below 60 psi in older vehicles.

2. **The correct answer is B.** Since having small amounts of water and compressor oil in the compressed air can cause failures in the braking system, it is important to drain the air tanks daily.

3. **The correct answer is D.** Although not on all vehicles, the application gauge indicates how much air pressure is being applied to the brakes. The supply pressure gauge (choice A) reveals how much air pressure is in the air holding tanks. The low-pressure gauge (choice B) will signal before the air pressure is at 60 psi. The safety relief valve (choice C) safeguards the tank and the remainder of the system from too much pressure.

4. **The correct answer is C.** After the initial pressure drop, the maximum leakage rates per minute are 3 psi for single vehicles and 4 psi for combination vehicles. With a completely charged air system the maximum leakage rate should be less than 2 psi in one minute for single vehicles and less than three psi in one minute for combination vehicles (choice A). A maximum leakage rate of 1 psi for single vehicles, 2.5 psi for combination vehicles (choice B) indicates a normal loss of air for these vehicles with a completely charged air system. The air loss is too great with a 3.5 psi for single vehicles and

10 psi for combination vehicles and will require maintenance (choice D).

5. **The correct answer is B.** The air brakes, not the disc brakes, operate the brake lights in an air brake system, and it does this with an electric switch that works via air pressure.

6. **The correct answer is B.** The driver should not manually drain the safety valve of moisture, but they should have the governor and lines checked out by a mechanic when a safety valve is releasing air.

7. **The correct answer is A.** The emergency brake system uses parts of the service and parking brake systems to stop the vehicle in the event there is a brake system malfunction. Since the emergency brake system uses parts of the service and parking brake systems to stop the vehicle, using the parking brake and governor control to slow the vehicle (choice B), using the air compressor and service brake system to stop the vehicle (choice C), or using the parking brake and brake pedal to slow the vehicle (choice D) are not parts used by the emergency brake system.

8. **The correct answer is D.** When measuring the distance that the push rod travels (the "slack"), if it is 1 inch or more, the driver must adjust the brakes. Consequently, the slacks do not need to be adjusted if the slack is ¾ inch (choice A), ¼ inch (choice B), or ½ inch (choice C).

9. **The correct answer is B.** If the air compressor is belt driven, then the belt's condition and tightness should be checked.

10. **The correct answer is C.** The spring brakes are typically held back by air pressure. They are not held back by bolts (choice A), brake linings (choice B), or springs (choice D).

11. **The correct answer is B.** The automatic slack adjusters should not need manual adjustment but must still be checked as part of the pre-trip inspection.

12. **The correct answer is C.** In a dual air system, the warning light and buzzer should shut off when air pressure in both systems climbs greater than 60 psi. Before the driver can operate the vehicle, the air compressor should build to at least 100 psi (choice A) in both the primary and secondary systems. The warning light and buzzer should not shut off when air pressure is at 50 psi (choice B). The air compressor should stop pumping air pressure into both systems at about 125 psi (choice D).

13. **The correct answer is A.** The brake shoes will press against the brake drum or disc when the brakes are employed. The slack adjuster (choice B) uses an adjusting nut on the rear side of the brake drum to adjust the brakes. The s-cam (choice C) is the most common foundation brake that pulls the brake shoes away from one another and pushes them against the inside of the brake drum. The return spring (choice D) pulls the brake shoes away from the drum and allows the vehicle's wheels to roll easily.

14. **The correct answer is C.** Under good braking conditions and good traction, the total stopping distance for the average driver in a vehicle with air brakes traveling 55 mph is 450 feet. Therefore, the total stopping distance for the average driver in a vehicle with air brakes traveling 55 mph under good brake conditions and traction is NOT 250 feet (choice A), 300 feet (choice B), or 600 feet (choice D).

15. **The correct answer is A.** The glad hands are coupling devices that link the service and emergency air lines from the truck or tractor to the trailer.

16. **The correct answer is A.** Step 2-Engine Compartment Checks of the inspection procedure is where the condition and the tightness of the belt is checked.

17. **The correct answer is C.** The service line is connected to the relay valves which allow the trailer brakes to be applied more quickly. The signal line (choice A) and the control line (choice B) are other names given to the service line. The hand valve (choice D) controls the air that is carried from the service line to the relay valves and is used only when testing the trailer brakes.

18. **The correct answer is D.** Since extreme use of the service brakes leads to overheating, it will cause the brake drums to expand. Consequently, the rest of the brake system will be out of adjustment and unable to have a proper modification of the s-cam (choice A), no chance of contact between the brake drums and linings (choice B), and decreased stopping power (choice C).

19. **The correct answer is B.** The function of the alcohol evaporator is to lower the danger of ice in the air brake valves during cold weather. Regardless of the alcohol evaporator's function, the tank must be drained daily (choice A). Since the tank must be drained daily, it will clear the wet tank of residual water and oil that rests at the bottom, not alcohol (choice C). Since small amounts of water get into the tanks, alcohol evaporators only decrease the risk of the water becoming ice, not inhibit water from getting in the tanks (choice D).

20. **The correct answer is B.** Although the antilock braking system (ABS) has failed, the driver can operate the vehicle normally because it still has brakes, but the ABS system should be serviced as soon as possible.

21. **The correct answer is A.** Step 7-Final Air Brake Check of the inspection procedure is where the air pressure build-up is tested.

22. **The correct answer is D.** The braking distance of a fully loaded tractor-trailer increases at a rate of 4x as it moves up in speed; so, if a driver doubles

their speed, they need four times the braking distance. Increasing at a rate of 2x as it moves up in speed (choice A) is not a sufficient braking distance, while increasing at 6x (choice B) and 8x (choice C) as it moves up in speed is not necessarily needed.

23. **The correct answer is D.** There is no such thing as applied friction distance. However, considering brake lag distance (choice A), effective braking distance (choice B), and reaction distance (choice C) will increase the stopping distance.

24. **The correct answer is B.** The tractor protection valve maintains air in the tractor or truck brake system should the trailer separate or have a bad leak.

25. **The correct answer is B.** The dual air brake system is two separate systems that operate brakes for the front axle and brakes for the back axle. Hence, they are not systems set to operate exclusively during day driving or night driving (choice A), for each side of the vehicle (choice C), or for attached trailers only (choice D).

NOTES

COMBINATION VEHICLES PRACTICE TESTS ANSWER SHEET

Practice Test 1

1. Ⓐ Ⓑ Ⓒ Ⓓ
2. Ⓐ Ⓑ
3. Ⓐ Ⓑ
4. Ⓐ Ⓑ Ⓒ Ⓓ

5. Ⓐ Ⓑ
6. Ⓐ Ⓑ Ⓒ Ⓓ
7. Ⓐ Ⓑ Ⓒ Ⓓ
8. Ⓐ Ⓑ Ⓒ Ⓓ

9. Ⓐ Ⓑ Ⓒ Ⓓ
10. Ⓐ Ⓑ Ⓒ Ⓓ
11. Ⓐ Ⓑ Ⓒ Ⓓ
12. Ⓐ Ⓑ

13. Ⓐ Ⓑ
14. Ⓐ Ⓑ Ⓒ Ⓓ
15. Ⓐ Ⓑ Ⓒ Ⓓ
16. Ⓐ Ⓑ Ⓒ Ⓓ

17. Ⓐ Ⓑ Ⓒ Ⓓ
18. Ⓐ Ⓑ Ⓒ Ⓓ
19. Ⓐ Ⓑ
20. Ⓐ Ⓑ Ⓒ Ⓓ

Practice Test 2

1. Ⓐ Ⓑ
2. Ⓐ Ⓑ
3. Ⓐ Ⓑ
4. Ⓐ Ⓑ

5. Ⓐ Ⓑ Ⓒ Ⓓ
6. Ⓐ Ⓑ Ⓒ Ⓓ
7. Ⓐ Ⓑ Ⓒ Ⓓ
8. Ⓐ Ⓑ

9. Ⓐ Ⓑ Ⓒ Ⓓ
10. Ⓐ Ⓑ Ⓒ Ⓓ
11. Ⓐ Ⓑ Ⓒ Ⓓ
12. Ⓐ Ⓑ Ⓒ Ⓓ

13. Ⓐ Ⓑ Ⓒ Ⓓ
14. Ⓐ Ⓑ Ⓒ Ⓓ
15. Ⓐ Ⓑ Ⓒ Ⓓ
16. Ⓐ Ⓑ Ⓒ Ⓓ

17. Ⓐ Ⓑ Ⓒ Ⓓ
18. Ⓐ Ⓑ Ⓒ Ⓓ
19. Ⓐ Ⓑ
20. Ⓐ Ⓑ Ⓒ Ⓓ

ANSWER SHEET: PRACTICE TESTS

COMBINATION VEHICLES PRACTICE TEST 1

20 Questions - 60 Minutes

> **Directions:** This test consists of a combination of true/false and multiple-choice questions. Only one answer is correct for each question.

1. If a combination vehicle has a rearward amplification of 2.0 it means it

   A. is twice as likely that the trailer will roll over compared to the tractor.

   B. is twice as likely the tractor will roll over due to the increased weight.

   C. is twice as heavy as a bobtail tractor.

   D. requires twice the stopping distance in comparison with empty trailers.

2. A combination vehicle that measures 90 feet in length should follow nine seconds behind another vehicle when traveling at 25 miles per hour.

   A. True

   B. False

3. A car carrier is less likely to get stuck on a railroad crossing compared to a possum-belly livestock trailer.

   A. True

   B. False

4. Which type of trailer is especially prone to skidding?

   A. Those at maximum gross weight

   B. Those loaded unevenly

   C. Those loaded too high

   D. Those that are empty

5. The last trailers in a triple combination with equal length trailers has a rearward amplification of 3.0.

   A. True

   B. False

6. What color is the antilock braking system (ABS) malfunction lamp on trailers?

   A. Red

   B. Orange

   C. Green

   D. Yellow

7. Why should the trailer hand valve never be used when driving?

   A. It increases the chance of a rollover.

   B. It doesn't work when in motion.

   C. It overrides the service brakes.

   D. It increases the likelihood of a trailer skidding.

8. Which gear should the tractor be in when coupling it to a trailer?

   A. 1L

   B. 1H

   C. Neutral

   D. Reverse

9. What is a pintle hook used for?

   A. Connecting the service lines to the trailer

   B. Operating the landing gear

   C. Towing the trailer

   D. Pumping air into the service line

10. In a drawbar connection, a safety lock screw

    A. does not require the self-locking nut.

    B. secures the safety cover bar.

    C. is present in only one location.

    D. applies pressure to the ball cup.

11. What must be properly greased before coupling a trailer?

    A. Drawbar

    B. Fifth wheel plate

    C. Pintle hook

    D. Gooseneck

12. Combination vehicles need to add two seconds per 10 feet of vehicle length to their following distance when the speed is above 40 miles per hour.

    A. True

    B. False

13. Combination vehicles take longer to stop when empty.

    A. True

    B. False

14. The emergency pressure range for the air brake service line is usually _____ per most manufacturers.

    A. 45-60 psi

    B. 80-85 psi

    C. 20-45 psi

    D. 100-120 psi

15. How much space should be between the upper and lower fifth wheel?

    A. 12 inches

    B. 6 inches

    C. 1 inch

    D. No space

16. In what position should the rig be when uncoupling?

    A. The tractor should be at a 45-degree angle to the tractor.

    B. The tractor should be at a 90-degree angle to the tractor.

    C. The tractor should be in a straight line with the trailer.

    D. Angle is not important as long as there is clearance around it.

17. The proper turn technique for wide turns requiring the vehicle to go into another lane is called a(n)

    A. button hook.

    B. jug handle.

    C. jackknife.

    D. off-track.

18. Fully loaded combination vehicles are _____ times more likely to rollover compared to empty ones.

    A. ten

    B. five

    C. two

    D. three

19. The landing gear should be raised up enough to just clear the ground prior to putting the rig in motion.

   A. True
   B. False

20. The best method for backing up a combination trailer is

   A. in a straight line.
   B. toward the passenger side.
   C. toward the driver's side.
   D. dependent on the driver's preference.

Combination Vehicles Practice Test 1 Answer Key and Explanations

1. A	**5.** B	**9.** C	**13.** A	**17.** A
2. A	**6.** D	**10.** B	**14.** C	**18.** A
3. B	**7.** D	**11.** B	**15.** D	**19.** B
4. D	**8.** C	**12.** B	**16.** C	**20.** A

1. **The correct answer is A.** Rearward amplification refers to the increased rate of rollovers for trailers of combination vehicles based on length and distance from the tractor. A tractor is not two times more likely to roll over due to weight (choice B), but it does have an increased chance of rollover due to height and center of gravity. A combination vehicle may or may not be two times heavier than a bobtail (which is a tractor without a trailer attached), but it is not referred to as rearward amplification (choice C). The required stopping distance (choice D) is not referred to as rearward amplification.

2. **The correct answer is A.** The rate at which combination tractor-trailers should follow is one second per 10 feet of length for speeds under 40 miles per hour. Since this vehicle was 90 feet in length, they should follow at a distance of nine seconds.

3. **The correct answer is B.** Both a car carrier and a possum-belly livestock trailer are considered low-slung units that are at an equally increased risk of getting stuck on railroad tracks.

4. **The correct answer is D.** An empty trailer is at the highest risk for skidding due to a lack of weight. Brakes for combination vehicles are designed to stop extremely heavy weights and are very powerful. When the trailer is empty, the brakes can be too powerful, increasing the risk for skidding. Trailers that are loaded unevenly (choice B) or too high (choice C) are at an increased risk for rollover. A trailer that is at maximum gross weight (choice A) is at the lowest risk of trailer skid when compared to the other three choices.

5. **The correct answer is B.** The last trailer in a triple combination with equal length trailers has a

rearward amplification of 3.5, not 3.0, as the risk increases with distance and length.

6. **The correct answer is D.** The ABS malfunction lamp on trailers is yellow. The color red (choice A) indicates a problem with the coupling between the tractor and trailer. The color orange (choice B) is used to mark the side of the trailers to help others see it better at night. The color green (choice C) is used to indicate that all systems are working correctly.

7. **The correct answer is D.** The trailer hand valve should never be used when driving as it increases the likelihood of the trailer skidding—it only applies braking to the trailer and not to the entire vehicle. It does not directly increase the chance of a rollover (choice A) and does not override the service brakes (choice C). Although the trailer hand valve will work when in motion (choice B), it should never be used.

8. **The correct answer is C.** The tractor should be in neutral during the coupling process. If the tractor is in gear at all, whether it be 1L (choice A), 1H (choice B) or reverse (choice D), there is a risk of it jerking forward or backward unexpectedly should it accidentally slip out of gear.

9. **The correct answer is C.** A pintle hook is a type of hitch that connects and tows a trailer. Glad hands connect the service lines to the trailer (choice A). Operation of the landing gear (choice B) and the pumping of air into the service line (choice D) are both controlled in the cabin of the tractor through levers and buttons.

10. **The correct answer is B.** The safety lock screw secures the safety cover bar. The screw connects to the self-locking nut (choice A). There are safety lock screws on both sides of the safety cover bar

(choice C). The adjustment screw applies pressure to the ball cup (choice D).

11. **The correct answer is B.** The fifth wheel plate needs to be properly greased before coupling a trailer as it is the location where the hitch will be inserted. A drawbar (choice A), a pintle hook (choice C), and a gooseneck (choice D) are all types of hitches that do not need to be specifically greased like the fifth wheel.

12. **The correct answer is B.** Combination vehicles need to add one second per 10 feet of vehicle length, plus an additional second to the total time, not two seconds per 10 feet.

13. **The correct answer is A.** Because of the reduced weight, empty combination vehicles take longer to stop due to stiff suspension springs, an increase in locked wheels, and poor traction. The increased weight in a fully loaded combination vehicle provides better traction and more flexible springs, thus decreasing necessary stopping distance.

14. **The correct answer is C.** A pressure range of 20-45 psi is considered an emergency range and will cause the tractor protection valve and parking brake to pop out. Pressure that drops below 45-60 psi (choice A) results in improper air in the lines and a warning will be given. Many vehicles will provide a warning when the pressure reaches 80-85 psi (choice B). A pressure range of 100-120 psi (choice D) is optimal.

15. **The correct answer is D.** There should be no space between the upper and lower fifth wheel. The upper fifth wheel has the kingpin, and the lower fifth wheel has locking jaws that must lock completely around it, forming a tight seal. Any space can indicate a poorly coupled trailer, which can lead to it becoming dislodged or disconnected. Any space, whether 1 inch (choice C), 6 inches (choice B), or 12 inches (choice A) is too much for a safe coupling.

16. **The correct answer is C.** The tractor and trailer should be in a straight line to the trailer. Angle is very important (choice D) as having it at a 45-degree angle (choice A) or 90-degree angle (choice B) can actually damage the landing gear. This can sometimes be difficult given the area, but every effort to uncouple in a straight line is recommended.

17. **The correct answer is A.** A button hook turn is one in which the driver steers wide towards the end of the turn to ensure clearance of the curb while maintaining a close distance to avoid increasing the space on the passenger's side for passing cars. A jug handle turn (choice B) is when the driver steers wide at the beginning of the turn, which is too soon and allows a large gap on the passenger's side to form, which becomes open for passing cars. A jackknife (choice C) is not a type of turn at all, but rather when the trailer gets ahead of the tractor. Off-tracking (choice D) refers to the path wheels take during a turn.

18. **The correct answer is A.** A fully loaded combination vehicle is ten times more likely to rollover when compared to an empty one. This is due in part to the combination of height and weight of the fully loaded rig. Two times (choice C), three times (choice D), and five times (choice B) are all incorrect.

19. **The correct answer is B.** The landing gear should not only be raised up enough to clear the ground but should also be completely raised up to avoid getting stuck on things such as railroad tracks.

20. **The correct answer is A.** It is best to back up in a straight line, which requires the driver to position themselves effectively to back up straight if at all possible. When it is not possible to back up in a straight line, the next option is to back up towards the driver's side (choice C) as that side has the most visibility. The passenger side (choice B) is the worst way to back up as it has the poorest visibility. Which way to back up should never be based on driver preference (choice D) but rather on safety and layout of the area provided.

COMBINATION VEHICLES PRACTICE TEST 2

20 Question - 60 Minutes

Directions: This test consists of a combination of true/false and multiple-choice questions. Only one answer is correct for each question.

1. An empty combination vehicle is more likely to jackknife compared to a fully loaded one.

   A. True

   B. False

2. A combination vehicle with a total length of 80 feet should follow 8 seconds behind another vehicle when traveling at 45 miles per hour.

   A. True

   B. False

3. A trailer skid occurs when the brakes fail to engage.

   A. True

   B. False

4. Rearward amplification refers to the increased risk for a trailer to flip compared to, and possibly without also flipping, the tractor.

   A. True

   B. False

5. When a turn requires more space than your own lane, it is best to steer wide

   A. before you start the turn.

   B. if you feel the wheels contact the curb.

   C. mid-turn.

   D. as you complete the turn.

6. One thing to avoid when backing up combination vehicles is

   A. getting out of the cab.

   B. staying in the cab.

   C. asking for help.

   D. using both mirrors.

7. The purpose of the trailer hand valve is

   A. to operate the trailer brakes.

   B. to test the trailer brakes.

   C. to override foot brakes in an emergency.

   D. to brake by hand versus foot.

8. A 5-axle tractor-semitrailer with a length of 45 feet has a rearward amplification of 1.0.

   A. True

   B. False

9. What color is used to indicate the service line couplers?

   A. Red

   B. Green

   C. Blue

   D. Yellow

10. What must you do AFTER uncoupling the fifth wheel?

    A. Secure the tractor

    B. Lower the landing gear

    C. Chock the trailer wheels

    D. Disconnect the airlines

11. The last trailer in a triple combination has a rearward amplification of

    A. 1.5.

    B. 3.0.

    C. 3.5.

    D. 4.0.

12. Which takes longer to stop, an empty tractor/semitrailer or a full one?

    A. A full one due to the weight

    B. A full one due to lacking traction

    C. They take an equal distance to stop.

    D. The empty one due to lacking traction

13. Which of the following should you never do to recover from a skid?

    A. Release the service brakes

    B. Engage the trailer hand brake

    C. Resume braking after wheels grip

    D. Check mirrors to observe the trailer

14. How do you correct a drift?

    A. Apply a handbrake

    B. Pull forward and keep the steering wheel straight

    C. Turn the steering wheel in the direction of the drift

    D. Turn the steering wheel in the opposite direction of the drift

15. The trailer hand valve works the

    A. service brakes.

    B. trailer lights.

    C. trailer brakes.

    D. trailer couplings.

16. Which should occur first?

    A. Connect air lines to the trailer

    B. Supply air to the trailer

    C. Check the height of the trailer

    D. Lock the trailer brakes

17. What is the final step in coupling a pintle hook?

    A. Rotating the jack handle

    B. Insert the tethered lock pin through the latch and lock holes

    C. Push the latch closed

    D. Ensure the drawbar eye is over the horn of the pintle hook

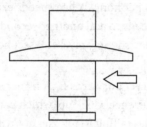

18. What part of the kingpin is the arrow in the image above pointing to?

    A. Base

    B. Shank

    C. Head

    D. Neck

19. The rearmost trailer has the highest rollover rate.

    A. True

    B. False

20. The purpose of the tractor protection valve is to

    A. keep air in the tractor brake system.

    B. keep entire brake system from losing air.

    C. keep tractor wheels from locking.

    D. keep the steering mechanism from locking.

Combination Vehicles Practice Test 2 Answer Key and Explanations

1. A	5. D	9. C	13. B	17. B
2. B	6. B	10. A	14. C	18. B
3. B	7. B	11. C	15. C	19. A
4. A	8. A	12. D	16. C	20. A

1. **The correct answer is A.** Empty combination vehicles are more likely to jackknife compared to fully loaded ones due to a decrease in traction because of the lighter overall weight of each trailer. Heavier trailers provide better traction.

2. **The correct answer is B.** The 1 second per 10 feet of vehicle length only pertains to speeds below 40 miles per hour. When speeds exceed this, the driver needs to add another second, which would mean they should travel at 9 seconds behind the other vehicle.

3. **The correct answer is B.** A trailer skid occurs when the wheels lock up, which can be due to the brakes failing to release, not when they fail to engage.

4. **The correct answer is A.** Rearward amplification refers to the increased risk of a trailer flipping compared to, and possibly without also flipping, the tractor. The amount of amplification is calculated by the total length of the combination vehicle combined with the number and size of trailers attached.

5. **The correct answer is D.** When a turn requires more than one lane to complete, it is best to steer wide as you complete the turn, which will reduce the gap on the passenger side that may allow small cars to drive into the right lane within your blind spot. Steering wide before you start the turn (choice A) increases the space on the passenger side of the tractor, which allows for cars to enter in an attempt to pass you or complete their own turn. Steering wide when you feel the curb (choice B) is too late. Steering wide mid-turn (choice C) is too soon and can impede your ability to recover back into your own lane quickly and without confusion to other drivers on the road.

6. **The correct answer is B.** A driver should never stay in the cab during the entire backing up process. Getting out of the cab (choice A) should be the first and foremost action before and during the backing up process as visibility is limited for combination vehicles. Asking for help (choice C) and using both mirrors (choice D) are also routine actions that every driver should do during every back up.

7. **The correct answer is B.** The purpose of the trailer hand valve is to test the trailer brakes. It is not to be used to operate the trailer brakes (choice A) when in motion. It should also never be used to override the foot brakes (choice C). It does not work as a simple conversion from braking by foot to braking by hand (choice D) and is only used to test the trailer brakes.

8. **The correct answer is A.** A 5-axle tractor trailer with a length of 45 feet is not an increased risk of rollover based on the fact that it is simply a standard size trailer hitched to a tractor. The rearward amplification increases when additional trailers are added, thus increasing both the length and the connection points.

9. **The correct answer is C.** Service line couplers are not always color coded, but when they are, service line couplers are blue. Red (choice A) is used to indicate the emergency lines. Green (choice B) and Yellow (choice D) are not used to color code couplers.

10. **The correct answer is A.** After uncoupling the fifth wheel, the driver must secure the tractor. Lowering the landing gear (choice B) chocking the trailer wheels (choice C) and disconnecting the airlines (choice D) should all happen well before uncoupling is complete.

11. **The correct answer is C.** The rearward amplification of the last trailer in a triple combination is 3.5. An example of a trailer with a rearward amplification of 1.5 (choice A) would be a Rocky Mountain Double. A rearward amplification of 3.0 (choice B) or 4.0 (choice D) is not currently possible given the design of trailers currently in use.

12. **The correct answer is D.** An empty tractor/semitrailer will always take longer to stop as it does not have the same level of traction that a full one does. The back part of the combination vehicle is not as connected to the ground; thus, it takes longer to stop. The weight of the full combination vehicle (choice A) is actually a benefit to it. The traction (choice B) is actually better in the fully loaded vehicle, thus it cannot take the same distance (choice C) for both of them to stop.

13. **The correct answer is B.** A trailer skid is caused by braking strongly, therefore releasing the brakes will fix it, not engaging additional brakes. Releasing the service brakes (choice A), resuming braking after wheels grip (choice C), and checking mirrors to observe the trailer (choice D) are all best practice when recovering from a skid.

14. **The correct answer is C.** To correct a drift, turn the steering wheel in the same direction as the drift. Applying the handbrake (choice A) can actually aggravate the drift. Pulling forward and keeping the steering wheel straight (choice B) may help but will not correct it. Turning the steering wheel in the opposite direction of the drift (choice D) may also lead to an increased drift.

15. **The correct answer is C.** The trailer hand valve directly works the trailer brakes. The service brakes (choice A) are controlled by the foot pedal in the cabin. The trailer lights (choice B) are connected to the service brakes. The trailer couplings are connections that link the tractor and the trailer and are not controlled by the trailer hand valve.

16. **The correct answer is C.** Checking the height of the trailer must occur first. Otherwise, the driver may not be able to properly connect the air lines (choice A), supply air to the trailer (choice B), or lock trailer brakes (choice D) due to too high or too low of a trailer position.

17. **The correct answer is B.** The final step in coupling a pintle hook is to insert the tethered lock pin through the latch and lock holes. This is a safety precaution. Rotating the jack handle (choice A) is done when uncoupling, not coupling. Pushing the latch closed (choice C) and ensuring the drawbar eye is over the horn of the pintle hook (choice D) both occur before inserting the lock pin.

18. **The correct answer is B.** The arrow is pointing to the shank, which is at the middle part of the kingpin. The base (choice A) is up at the top of the kingpin and the head (choice C) is the bottom part. There is no part labeled as the "neck" (choice D).

19. **The correct answer is A.** The trailer that is furthest away from the tractor has the highest rollover rate due to the crack-the-whip effect when changing lanes or turning.

20. **The correct answer is A.** The purpose of the tractor protection valve is to keep air in the tractor brake system in the event that the trailer becomes detached or disconnected. This allows the tractor to still brake independently. It does not keep the entire brake system from losing air (choice B), but rather locks off the air in a reservoir for the tractor specifically should a leak arise so that the tractor can stop. It does not affect the tractor wheels (choice C) or the steering mechanism (choice D).

DOUBLE AND TRIPLE TRAILERS PRACTICE TESTS ANSWER SHEET

Practice Test 1

1. Ⓐ Ⓑ
2. Ⓐ Ⓑ Ⓒ Ⓓ
3. Ⓐ Ⓑ
4. Ⓐ Ⓑ Ⓒ Ⓓ

5. Ⓐ Ⓑ
6. Ⓐ Ⓑ Ⓒ Ⓓ
7. Ⓐ Ⓑ Ⓒ Ⓓ
8. Ⓐ Ⓑ Ⓒ Ⓓ

9. Ⓐ Ⓑ Ⓒ Ⓓ
10. Ⓐ Ⓑ Ⓒ Ⓓ
11. Ⓐ Ⓑ
12. Ⓐ Ⓑ Ⓒ Ⓓ

13. Ⓐ Ⓑ Ⓒ Ⓓ
14. Ⓐ Ⓑ Ⓒ Ⓓ
15. Ⓐ Ⓑ Ⓒ Ⓓ
16. Ⓐ Ⓑ Ⓒ Ⓓ

17. Ⓐ Ⓑ Ⓒ Ⓓ
18. Ⓐ Ⓑ
19. Ⓐ Ⓑ Ⓒ Ⓓ
20. Ⓐ Ⓑ

Practice Test 2

1. Ⓐ Ⓑ Ⓒ Ⓓ
2. Ⓐ Ⓑ Ⓒ Ⓓ
3. Ⓐ Ⓑ Ⓒ Ⓓ
4. Ⓐ Ⓑ Ⓒ Ⓓ

5. Ⓐ Ⓑ Ⓒ Ⓓ
6. Ⓐ Ⓑ Ⓒ Ⓓ
7. Ⓐ Ⓑ Ⓒ Ⓓ
8. Ⓐ Ⓑ

9. Ⓐ Ⓑ
10. Ⓐ Ⓑ Ⓒ Ⓓ
11. Ⓐ Ⓑ Ⓒ Ⓓ
12. Ⓐ Ⓑ Ⓒ Ⓓ

13. Ⓐ Ⓑ Ⓒ Ⓓ
14. Ⓐ Ⓑ Ⓒ Ⓓ
15. Ⓐ Ⓑ
16. Ⓐ Ⓑ

17. Ⓐ Ⓑ Ⓒ Ⓓ
18. Ⓐ Ⓑ Ⓒ Ⓓ
19. Ⓐ Ⓑ Ⓒ Ⓓ
20. Ⓐ Ⓑ Ⓒ Ⓓ

Practice Test 3

1. Ⓐ Ⓑ Ⓒ Ⓓ
2. Ⓐ Ⓑ Ⓒ Ⓓ
3. Ⓐ Ⓑ
4. Ⓐ Ⓑ Ⓒ Ⓓ

5. Ⓐ Ⓑ
6. Ⓐ Ⓑ Ⓒ Ⓓ
7. Ⓐ Ⓑ Ⓒ Ⓓ
8. Ⓐ Ⓑ

9. Ⓐ Ⓑ Ⓒ Ⓓ
10. Ⓐ Ⓑ Ⓒ Ⓓ
11. Ⓐ Ⓑ
12. Ⓐ Ⓑ Ⓒ Ⓓ

13. Ⓐ Ⓑ Ⓒ Ⓓ
14. Ⓐ Ⓑ Ⓒ Ⓓ
15. Ⓐ Ⓑ Ⓒ Ⓓ
16. Ⓐ Ⓑ

17. Ⓐ Ⓑ Ⓒ Ⓓ
18. Ⓐ Ⓑ Ⓒ Ⓓ
19. Ⓐ Ⓑ
20. Ⓐ Ⓑ Ⓒ Ⓓ

DOUBLE AND TRIPLE TRAILERS PRACTICE TEST 1

20 Questions - 60 Minutes

Directions: This test consists of a combination of true/false and multiple-choice questions. Only one answer is correct for each question.

---

1. A safe speed on a curve for a combination vehicle does not necessarily equate to a safe speed for a set of doubles.

    A. True

    B. False

2. One of the most important things to consider when parking a double or triple is the

    A. incline of the parking area.

    B. ground material.

    C. distance around the vehicle.

    D. ability to pull straight through.

3. Converter dollies built on or after March 1, 1988 are required to have antilock brakes.

    A. True

    B. False

4. Where on the kingpin should the lockjaws close?

    A. The shank

    B. The head

    C. The neck

    D. The base

5. The correct order for shut-off valves on a double, starting from the first trailer is open, closed.

    A. True

    B. False

6. What is the easiest way to verify that a converter dolly has an antilock braking system?

    A. Ask your supervisor

    B. Check the owner's manual

    C. Locate the yellow lamp on the left side

    D. Look under the belly of the dolly

7. Where should the heaviest trailer be positioned in a triple?

    A. 1st position behind the tractor

    B. 2nd position between two trailers

    C. 3rd position at the end

    D. It does not matter.

8. What happens when you push the trailer air supply knob?

    A. It supplies air to the service air lines.

    B. It supplies air to the emergency air line.

    C. It cuts off air to the emergency air line.

    D. It cuts off air to the service air lines.

9. A converter dolly consists of a maximum of how many possible axles?

    A. 2

    B. 3

    C. 4

    D. 5

10. A double trailer that is _____ in length, traveling at a speed of 35 miles per hour, should have 8 seconds of space between it and the vehicle in front of it.

    A. 80 feet

    B. 80 yards

    C. 160 feet

    D. 16 yards

11. When coupling two trailers together, the driver should always couple the front of the second trailer first, and then connect the back of the front trailer next.

    A. True

    B. False

12. What is the next step after coupling the first trailer during a trailer-to-trailer coupling?

    A. Position the dolly to the nose of the second trailer

    B. Lower the dolly support

    C. Lock the pintle hook

    D. Secure dolly support in the raised position

13. How should the driver verify that air is flowing to all trailers?

    A. Drive slowly around the lot and test them

    B. Check the air gauges in the cab of the tractor

    C. Listen for a hissing sound

    D. Open the emergency line shut-off at the rear of the last trailer

14. Which states specifically ban triple trailers?

    A. Nevada and California

    B. Arizona and Nevada

    C. Washington and California

    D. Colorado and Nebraska

15. LCV stands for

    A. lengthened combination vehicle.

    B. long-haul combination vehicle.

    C. longer combination vehicle.

    D. lowriding combination vehicle.

16. When uncoupling a triple, the driver should uncouple which section first?

    A. The tractor from the first trailer

    B. The first trailer from the converter dolly

    C. The third trailer from the converter dolly

    D. The second trailer from the converter dolly

17. When emergency braking with double trailers, which method should be utilized?

    A. Pushing the brake strongly and holding it

    B. Engaging the parking brake

    C. Using controlled or stab braking

    D. Pulling up the Johnson Bar

18. When uncoupling a double trailer, the driver should not pull the tractor forward until both trailers and the converter dolly are uncoupled.

    A. True

    B. False

19. How many states allow triple trailers?

    A. 13

    B. 12

    C. 37

    D. 50

20. Before driving, it is important to inspect the pintle hook to make sure it is detached.

    A. True

    B. False

Double and Triple Trailers Practice Test 1 Answer Key and Explanations

1. A	5. A	9. A	13. D	17. C
2. D	6. C	10. A	14. C	18. B
3. B	7. A	11. B	15. C	19. A
4. A	8. B	12. C	16. C	20. B

1. **The correct answer is A.** Due to the length, weight, and increased rollover rate of doubles, a safe speed for a combination vehicle may or may not be safe for them when turning. It is important for the driver to remember the length and weight of the double or triple when turning. Slower is better.

2. **The correct answer is D.** When parking a double or triple, one of the most important things to consider is the ability to pull straight through. Combination vehicles of this size are not able to turn easily and without an extremely large area to do so. The incline of the parking area (choice A), the ground material (choice B) and the distance around the vehicle (choice C) are all important to note but are not a specific concern only related to doubles or triples.

3. **The correct answer is B.** Converter dollies built on or after March 1, 1998 are required to have antilock brakes. This is important information to remember as older dollies may or may not have antilock brakes. Without ABS, they are at increased risk for trailer skids.

4. **The correct answer is A.** The lockjaws should close on the shank, or middle of the kingpin. If it is around the head (choice B) or the base (choice D) the trailer could become uncoupled. There is no neck (choice C) on a kingpin.

5. **The correct answer is A.** The shut-off valves refer to the brake lines in the vehicle. The first trailer should always be open and the last should always be closed, thus trapping the air in the lines so the brakes can function.

6. **The correct answer is C.** The easiest way to verify that a converter dolly has ABS is to locate the

yellow lamp on the left side of the dolly. While asking a supervisor (choice A), checking the owner's manual (choice B) and looking under the belly of the dolly (choice D) are all options, they are not necessarily accurate or easy.

7. **The correct answer is A.** The heaviest trailer should always be positioned first, behind the tractor. It should not be sandwiched between two trailers (choice B) or at the last position (choice C) as these increase the risk of rollover. The position absolutely matters (choice D).

8. **The correct answer B.** Pushing the trailer air supply knob supplies air to the emergency air line. It does not cut off air to the emergency air line (choice C) unless it is popped out. It also does not affect the service line by supplying (choice A) or cutting off the air (choice D).

9. **The correct answer is A.** A converter consists of one or two axles at most. It cannot have 3 (choice B), 4 (choice C), or 5 (choice D).

10. **The correct answer is A.** A double trailer that is 80 feet in length, traveling at a speed of 35 miles per hour must have 1 second of space per every 10 feet of length. 80 feet equals 8 seconds of space at a speed under 40 mph. 80 yards (choice B) and 16 yards (choice D) are both too long. 160 feet (choice C) is also too long.

11. **The correct answer is B.** The rear of the front trailer should always be coupled first. This allows the trailer and the dolly to easily be moved into alignment with the stationary second trailer prior to coupling.

12. **The correct answer is C.** After coupling the first trailer, the next step is to lock the pintle hook. Securing the dolly support in a raised position

(choice D) occurs after locking the pintle hook. After this, you position the dolly to the nose of the second trailer (choice A) and then lower the dolly support (choice B).

13. **The correct answer is D.** To verify that the trailer brakes are working, open the emergency line shut-off at the rear of the last trailer after charging them. If air pressure is not present, which you will know if there is not a sound of air escaping, then something is malfunctioning with the brakes. Driving slowly around the lot (choice A) could be dangerous if there is no air pressure present. Checking the air gauges in the cab will not tell you if the trailer brakes are working (choice B). Though a hissing sound (choice C) can notify you that brakes are working, you will not be able to always tell if it is coming from all the brakes, so that option is also incorrect.

14. **The correct answer is C.** Washington and California both specifically ban triple trailers. Triple trailers are only allowed in 13 states, most of which are clustered in the western US. Nevada (choice A and B) allows them, as do Arizona (choice B), Colorado (choice D), and Nebraska (choice D).

15. **The correct answer is C.** LCV stands for longer combination vehicle, often referring to double and triple trailers. Choices B, C, and D are not what this abbreviation refers to.

16. **The correct answer is C.** When uncoupling triples, always start from the rear of the vehicle and work your way forward. This means uncoupling the third trailer from the dolly would be the first step. You would then move on to the second trailer (choice D) after removing the dolly from the back of it, then the dolly from the back of the first trailer, then uncouple the first trailer (choice B) from the tractor (choice A).

17. **The correct answer is C.** Both controlled and stab braking allow the driver to remain in control when braking suddenly or in an emergency. Pushing the brake strongly and holding it (choice A) is likely to cause a skid. Engaging the parking brakes (choice B) should never be done when the vehicle is in motion because it could cause a rollover. Pulling up on the Johnson bar (choice D) should never be done while the vehicle is in motion.

18. **The correct answer is B.** The driver should pull the vehicle forward slowly after uncoupling the second trailer from the dolly to allow the dolly to come out from underneath the trailer.

19. **The correct answer is A.** Triple trailers are only permitted in 13 states, all of which are clustered in the western half of the country. 12 (choice B), 37 (choice C), and 50 (choice D) are incorrect.

20. **The correct answer is B.** The pintle hook is a type of hitch and should always be latched, which the driver should verify during inspection.

NOTES

DOUBLE AND TRIPLE TRAILERS PRACTICE TEST 2

20 Questions - 60 Minutes

Directions: This test consists of a combination of true/false and multiple-choice questions. Only one answer is correct for each question.

---

1. What is a converter dolly?

    A. A type of hitch that connects a trailer to another trailer

    B. A coupling that has one or two axles and a fifth wheel to connect two trailers

    C. A dolly used to secure a trailer after it is uncoupled from the tractor

    D. A temporary staging dolly in place to assist in coupling two trailers

2. What is the correct order for the shut-off valves on a triple trailer rig, starting from the first trailer?

    A. Open, Closed, Closed

    B. Closed, Open, Closed

    C. Open, Open, Closed

    D. Open, Open, Open

3. Where should the lightest trailer be positioned in a triple rig?

    A. 1st position behind the tractor

    B. 2nd position between two trailers

    C. 3rd position at the end

    D. It does not matter.

4. A triple trailer 120 feet in length is traveling at a rate of 35 mph. How many seconds of space should be between it and the vehicle in front of it?

    A. 13 seconds

    B. 12 seconds

    C. 6 seconds

    D. 10 seconds

5. Where is the antilock brake lamp on a converter dolly?

    A. Front

    B. Left

    C. Right

    D. Rear

6. Which trailer do you couple first when using a converter dolly on a double rig?

    A. The back of the first trailer

    B. The front of the second trailer

    C. The front of the first trailer

    D. The back of the second trailer

7. How do you charge the trailer brakes?

    A. Use the Johnson bar

    B. Release the trailer shut-off valve

    C. Push the air supply knob in

    D. Pump the brake pedal after coupling

8. It is safe to assume that all trailers have spring brakes unless otherwise noted by the company during pick up.

    A. True

    B. False

9. Triple trailers are permitted in all 50 states.

    A. True

    B. False

10. A "pup" trailer ranges in length from

    A. 15-20 feet.

    B. 26-29 feet.

    C. 30-40 feet.

    D. 53-60 feet.

11. In what order should the following trailers be ordered behind the tractor?

    A. Lightest, heavier, heaviest

    B. Lightest, heaviest, heavier

    C. Heavier, heaviest, lightest

    D. Heaviest, heavier, lightest

12. Where is the ring hitch located?

    A. On the back of tractors

    B. On the back of trailers

    C. On the back of converter dollies and the front of trailers

    D. On the front of both converter dollies and trailers

13. How many total converter dollies are needed on a triple?

    A. It depends on the load.

    B. 3

    C. 2

    D. 1

14. When uncoupling the rear trailer in a triple, the driver should lower the landing gear of

    A. all three trailers.

    B. the second trailer.

    C. the third trailer.

    D. the second and third trailer.

15. The lightest trailer should be positioned in the 3rd position at the end of a triple rig.

    A. True

    B. False

16. The lockjaws should be engaged around the shank of the kingpin.

    A. True

    B. False

17. What causes the ring hitch on a dolly to fly up?

    A. The pintle hook being detached while the dolly is free of a rear trailer

    B. The pintle hook being detached while the dolly is still under a trailer

    C. The front trailer still containing its load

    D. The rear trailer still containing its load

18. The dolly should be _____ with the kingpin.

    A. in line

    B. parallel

    C. perpendicular

    D. at a 45-degree angle

19. Which of the following vehicles require a following distance of 11 seconds when traveling 45 miles per hour?

    A. A double trailer 110 feet in length

    B. A double trailer 100 feet in length

    C. A triple trailer 90 feet in length

    D. A triple trailer 110 feet in length

20. How many states ban double trailers?

    A. 4

    B. 2

    C. None

    D. 13

Double and Triple Trailers Practice Test 2 Answer Key and Explanations

1. B	**5.** B	**9.** B	**13.** C	**17.** B
2. C	**6.** A	**10.** B	**14.** C	**18.** A
3. C	**7.** C	**11.** D	**15.** A	**19.** B
4. B	**8.** B	**12.** D	**16.** A	**20.** C

1. **The correct answer is B.** A converter is a coupling with one or two axles and a fifth wheel used to connect two trailers. It is not a type of hitch (choice A) or a dolly used to secure a trailer after uncoupling (choice C) or temporarily during coupling (choice D).

2. **The correct answer is C.** The shut-off valves refer to the brake lines in the vehicle. They should be open for all trailers, except for the last as every trailer requires air for braking. If the second and third are both closed (choice A), there is no air in the third trailer for braking. If the first trailer shut-off valve is closed (choice B), there is no air in the second or third trailer even if the second trailer is open because air did not get past the first one. If all of them are open (choice D), the air is not secure in the line and is simply passing through and out the back.

3. **The correct answer is C.** The lightest trailer should be positioned at the end in the third position of a triple. It should not be in the first position (choice A) or the second position (choice B) as the order of the trailers is always based on weight. The position absolutely matters (choice D).

4. **The correct answer is B.** A vehicle of this size needs 12 seconds between it and vehicle in front of it. The amount of time needed between a combination vehicle and the car in front of it is calculated by speed. If the speed is below 40 miles per hour, the semi needs 1 second for every 10 feet of vehicle length. 13 seconds (choice A) would be correct if the speed was over 40 miles per hour as the timing adds an additional second at these speeds. 6 seconds (choice C) and 10 seconds (choice D) are too short and could lead to an accident should sudden stopping be required.

5. **The correct answer is B.** The antilock brake lamp on a converter dolly is located on the left side of the dolly. It is not located in the front (choice A) or the right (choice C). It is also not located on the rear (choice D) of the dolly.

6. **The correct answer is A.** When coupling two trailers using a converter dolly, the back of the first trailer is coupled first. The front of the second trailer (choice B) is then coupled. The front of the first trailer (choice C) should already be coupled to the tractor and does not involve a converter dolly. The back of the second trailer (choice D) would only be coupled with a dolly if the vehicle was carrying a third trailer.

7. **The correct answer is C.** To charge the trailer brakes, push the air supply knob in. Using the Johnson bar (choice A) tests the trailer brakes but does not charge them. Pumping the brake pedal (choice D) does not charge the brakes. The trailer shut-off valve (choice B) allows air to pass through the air brake system and does not inherently charge the brakes.

8. **The correct answer is B.** Assuming that all trailers have spring brakes is a dangerous and potentially fatal assumption. It is best practice to assume that every trailer does NOT have spring brakes and secure it using wheel chocks whenever you are unsure.

9. **The correct answer is B.** Triples are not permitted in the majority of states (37 do not allow them). Of the 13 that do, they are almost all clustered in the western half of the United States.

10. **The correct answer is B.** A "pup" trailer ranges in length from 26-29 feet and they are commonly used in double and triple combinations. 15-20 feet (choice A) is too short. 30-40 feet (choice C)

falls under a standard size trailer, and 53-60 feet (choice D) are longer trailers.

11. **The correct answer is D.** The heaviest trailer should always be closest to the tractor and the lightest should always be the last. Choices A, B, and C are all incorrect because the heaviest is not located closest to the tractor.

12. **The correct answer is D.** The ring hitch is located on the front of both converter dollies and some trailers. The pintle hook is located on the back of tractors (choice A) and trailers (choice B). Choice C is incorrect as it combines the location of both a pintle hook and a ring hitch.

13. **The correct answer is C.** Two converter dollies are needed on a triple as a converter dolly is specifically used to connect two trailers. The connection between the tractor and the first trailer does not require a dolly, so 3 (choice B) is incorrect. 1 (choice D) would only afford enough connections for a double, and the size of the load (choice A) does not dictate the number of dollies needed.

14. **The correct answer is C.** Lowering the landing gear of the third trailer allows some of the weight to be redistributed off the dolly and onto the trailer, thus making it easier to uncouple. You do not want to lower the landing gear of all three trailers (choice A) as this will not help with the weight and will not allow you to pull the rest of the rig forward when you need to. This is also true for lowering the landing gear of just the second trailer (choice B) or only the second and third trailers (choice D).

15. **The correct answer is A.** The positioning of trailers should always be heaviest in the front and lightest in the back to decrease the risk of rollover.

16. **The correct answer is A.** The shank is the middle part of the kingpin, and the lockjaws should always be engaged in this position. If the lockjaws are around the neck or the base, the coupling could detach.

17. **The correct answer is B.** The pintle hook being detached while the rear trailer is still on the dolly causes the dolly's ring hitch to fly up, which can cause serious injury. The rear trailer still containing its load (choice D) should not matter because the rear trailer should be removed from the dolly before the pintle hook is detached (choice A) in order to keep the ring hitch from flying up. The front trailer still containing its load (choice C) will not cause the ring hitch to fly up.

18. **The correct answer is A.** When coupling, the dolly should be in line with the kingpin. If it was parallel (choice B), it would be going the same direction, but not necessarily in line. If it was perpendicular (choice C), it would be at a 90-degree angle, which would not allow for coupling. The same is true at a 45-degree angle (choice D).

19. **The correct answer is B.** The formula for calculating following distance is 1 second per 10 feet of vehicle length for speeds below 40 miles per hour. For speeds greater than this you simply add an additional second. A vehicle that is 100 feet in length requires 10 seconds + 1 additional second for a speed of 45 miles per hour. Choices A and D do not account for the additional second and would need 12 seconds total, so they are incorrect. A vehicle measuring 90 feet in length (choice C) at a speed of 45 mph would need 10 seconds, not 11.

20. **The correct answer is C.** No state specifically bans double trailers, but they do have very clear guidelines on the total length of the double. As recently as 2009, 4 states (choice A) still had bans, but that has since been adjusted. 2 (choice B) is incorrect, and 13 (choice D) refers to the number of states that have triple bans, not double bans.

20 Questions - 60 Minutes

Directions: This test consists of a combination of true/false and multiple-choice questions. Only one answer is correct for each question.

1. What color is the lamp on the side of newer converter dollies equipped with ABS?

   A. Yellow

   B. Blue

   C. Red

   D. Green

2. Which of the following states allow triple trailers?

   A. Oklahoma

   B. Texas

   C. New York

   D. California

3. The best method for parking a double or triple is to pull straight through.

   A. True

   B. False

4. When inspecting the coupling of a converter dolly and the second trailer, how much space should be between the upper and lower fifth wheel?

   A. Between 1/2 and 3/4 of an inch

   B. At least 1 inch

   C. It depends on the weight of the load

   D. None

5. The trailer air supply knob supplies air to the emergency air line.

   A. True

   B. False

6. When verifying the height needed for the trailers prior to coupling, the rear trailer should be

   A. slightly above the center of the fifth wheel.

   B. slightly below the center of the fifth wheel.

   C. the same height as the center of the fifth wheel.

   D. dependent on the load.

7. On a double rig, the shut-off valves should be in the OPEN position on

   A. the first trailer only.

   B. both trailers.

   C. the first trailer and the dolly.

   D. the dolly only.

8. The heaviest trailer should be in the 2nd position in a triple.

   A. True

   B. False

9. When connecting a second trailer without spring brakes, what do you do after connecting the emergency line?

   A. Adjust the slack adjusters

   B. Chock the wheels

   C. Charge the trailer air tank

   D. Drive the tractor close to the trailer

PRACTICE TESTS

10. After visually checking the coupling, make sure to connect the safety chains, air hoses, and

    A. light cords.

    B. service lines.

    C. brakes.

    D. landing gear.

11. Converter dolly wheels can lock and cause a skid in a triple.

    A. True

    B. False

12. Every converter dolly has all the following brakes EXCEPT:

    A. Spring brakes

    B. Antilock brakes

    C. Service brakes

    D. Parking brake

13. What connects to the kingpin?

    A. The coupling

    B. The lockjaws

    C. The pintle hook

    D. The drawbar

14. Which of the following vehicles require a following distance of 11 seconds when traveling 45 miles per hour?

    A. A double trailer 110 feet in length

    B. A double trailer 100 feet in length

    C. A triple trailer 90 feet in length

    D. A triple trailer 110 feet in length

15. Which trailer is most likely to rollover in a set of triples?

    A. The first trailer connected to the tractor

    B. The second or third trailer

    C. The third trailer

    D. The second trailer

16. The antilock brakes on newer converter dollies provide fluctuating pressure on the brakes, thus decreasing the likelihood of trailer skids.

    A. True

    B. False

17. Which of the following should always be a part of a visual check of the coupling after it is connected?

    A. Adequate spacing between the upper and lower fifth wheel

    B. Locking jaws are not engaged

    C. No space is present between the upper and lower fifth wheel

    D. Kingpin is engaged around the locking jaws

18. What is the best position for uncoupling a double or triple?

    A. In a straight line on a small incline

    B. In a straight line on level ground

    C. At a slight angle on a small incline

    D. At a slight angle on level ground

19. All converter dollies have antilock braking systems (ABS).

    A. True

    B. False

20. Never detach the pintle hook while the dolly is under a trailer because

    A. the weight of the trailer can cause the ring hitch to break off.

    B. the weight of the trailer can cause the ring hitch to drop to the ground.

    C. the weight of the trailer can cause the ring hitch to be crushed.

    D. the weight of the trailer can cause the ring hitch to fly up.

Double and Triple Trailers Practice Test 3 Answer Key and Explanations

1. A	**5.** A	**9.** C	**13.** B	**17.** C
2. A	**6.** B	**10.** A	**14.** B	**18.** B
3. A	**7.** C	**11.** A	**15.** C	**19.** B
4. D	**8.** B	**12.** B	**16.** A	**20.** D

1. **The correct answer is A.** The lamp on the side of newer converter dollies equipped with ABS is yellow. There are no blue (choice B) or green lamps (choice D). The red lamps (choice C) are at the rear of some dollies, but not on most, and they are the brake lights, which do not tell you if there is ABS or not.

2. **The correct answer is A.** Oklahoma is the only state of the four that allows triple trailers. Texas (choice B), New York (choice C), and California (choice D) all do not allow the use of triples.

3. **The correct answer is A.** Due to the size and dramatically reduced turning radius, a double or triple should be parked in a location where it is possible to pull straight through.

4. **The correct answer is D.** There should be no space between the upper and lower fifth wheel as that indicates that the converter dolly is not connected to the trailer properly. Any gap, whether it is 1/2 inch (choice A) or over an inch (choice B) is unsafe. The weight of the load (choice C) does not affect the gap allowed.

5. **The correct answer is A.** The trailer air supply knob supplies air to the emergency line when it is pushed.

6. **The correct answer is B.** When coupling two trailers together, the rear trailer should be slightly below the center of the fifth wheel, as it will be slightly raised when the dolly is pushed underneath it. If it is the same height (choice C) or slightly above (choice A), it will not couple correctly and could damage the coupling device. The weight of the load (choice D) does not dictate the height of the trailer for coupling purposes.

7. **The correct answer is C.** On a double, the shut-off valves should be in the OPEN position on the first trailer and on the dolly (if the dolly has one equipped). If it is only open on the first trailer (choice A) and not the dolly, the air will not run into the second trailer. If it is open on both trailers (choice B), the air will not be trapped in the lines and the brakes will not work. If it is only open on the dolly (choice D), the brake system does not have a continuous line as the first trailer remains closed.

8. **The correct answer is B.** The heaviest trailer should be in the 1st position in a triple, directly behind the tractor. This decreases the likelihood of rollover as the farther away the heavier trailer is from the tractor, the higher the rollover risk.

9. **The correct answer is C.** After connecting the emergency line, charge the trailer air tank and then disconnect the line. This sets the emergency brakes, which is needed since the trailer does not have spring brakes. Adjusting the slack adjusters (choice A) should be done only if needed and is not part of every brake coupling. Chocking the wheels (choice B) should be done before connecting the emergency line, as well as driving the tractor close to the trailer (choice D).

10. **The correct answer A.** The safety chains, air hose, and light cords should all be connected after the coupling is inspected. The service lines (choice B), which are a part of the brake (choice C) system, are connected via the air hoses. The landing gear (choice D) does not get connected as it is part of the trailer at all times.

11. **The correct answer is A.** Any wheels can lock due to too much brake pressure (usually from braking

strongly), thus causing a skid. This includes the brakes on the converter dolly.

12. **The correct answer is B.** Every converter dolly does not have antilock brakes, especially if it is made prior to March 1, 1998. A yellow lamp on the left side of the dolly is there to indicate the presence of antilock brakes. All converter dollies should have a parking brake (choice D), which is also the spring brakes (choice A), as well as service brakes (choice C).

13. **The correct answer is B.** The lockjaws connect to the kingpin by engaging around the shank, or the middle of it. The coupling (choice A) is the broad term for entire mechanism that joins two trailers together. The pintle hook (choice C) and the drawbar (choice D) are both types of hitches that do not interact with a kingpin in their coupling style.

14. **The correct answer is B.** The formula for calculating following distance is 1 second per 10 feet of vehicle length for speeds below 40 miles per hour. For speeds greater than this you simply add an additional second. A vehicle that is 100 feet in length requires 10 seconds + 1 additional second for a speed of 45 miles per hour. Choices A and D do not account for the additional second and would need 12 seconds total, so they are incorrect. A vehicle measuring 90 feet in length (choice C) at a speed of 45 mph would need 10 seconds, not 11.

15. **The correct answer is C.** The third trailer is most likely to rollover due to the crack-the-whip effect and rearward amplification that occurs on longer combination vehicles. The first trailer (choice A) is least likely to rollover. The second trailer (choice

D) has an increased risk but not the same risk as the third trailer (choice B).

16. **The correct answer is A.** The antilock brakes on newer converter dollies are designed to distribute the braking pressure in fluctuations, thus preventing the wheels from locking up and reducing the risk of trailer skids.

17. **The correct answer is C.** There should be no space between the upper and lower fifth wheel. A visual inspection allows the driver to verify this. Any space (choice A) is dangerous and should be corrected. The lockjaws should always be engaged (choice B) around the kingpin, and not the other way around (choice D).

18. **The correct answer is B.** The best position for uncoupling a double or triple is in a straight line on level ground. Adding an incline (choices A and C) or adding an angle to the rig itself (choices C and D) both increase the likelihood of accidents from the trailers moving or falling.

19. **The correct answer is B.** All converter dollies have spring brakes, but they do not all have ABS, especially if they were made before March 1, 1998. If they are equipped, there is a yellow lamp on the left side to indicate it.

20. **The correct answer is D.** Detaching the pintle hook while the dolly is under a trailer is very dangerous because the weight of the trailer can cause the ring hitch to fly up. It does not cause the ring hitch to break off (choice A), drop to the ground (choice B), or become crushed (choice C).

TANKER VEHICLES PRACTICE TESTS ANSWER SHEET

Practice Test 1

1. Ⓐ Ⓑ Ⓒ Ⓓ   5. Ⓐ Ⓑ Ⓒ Ⓓ   9. Ⓐ Ⓑ Ⓒ Ⓓ   13. Ⓐ Ⓑ   17. Ⓐ Ⓑ Ⓒ Ⓓ

2. Ⓐ Ⓑ   6. Ⓐ Ⓑ Ⓒ Ⓓ   10. Ⓐ Ⓑ   14. Ⓐ Ⓑ Ⓒ Ⓓ   18. Ⓐ Ⓑ

3. Ⓐ Ⓑ Ⓒ Ⓓ   7. Ⓐ Ⓑ   11. Ⓐ Ⓑ Ⓒ Ⓓ   15. Ⓐ Ⓑ Ⓒ Ⓓ   19. Ⓐ Ⓑ Ⓒ Ⓓ

4. Ⓐ Ⓑ Ⓒ Ⓓ   8. Ⓐ Ⓑ   12. Ⓐ Ⓑ Ⓒ Ⓓ   16. Ⓐ Ⓑ Ⓒ Ⓓ   20. Ⓐ Ⓑ Ⓒ Ⓓ

Practice Test 2

1. Ⓐ Ⓑ Ⓒ Ⓓ   5. Ⓐ Ⓑ Ⓒ Ⓓ   9. Ⓐ Ⓑ Ⓒ Ⓓ   13. Ⓐ Ⓑ   17. Ⓐ Ⓑ Ⓒ Ⓓ

2. Ⓐ Ⓑ Ⓒ Ⓓ   6. Ⓐ Ⓑ   10. Ⓐ Ⓑ   14. Ⓐ Ⓑ Ⓒ Ⓓ   18. Ⓐ Ⓑ Ⓒ Ⓓ

3. Ⓐ Ⓑ   7. Ⓐ Ⓑ Ⓒ Ⓓ   11. Ⓐ Ⓑ Ⓒ Ⓓ   15. Ⓐ Ⓑ Ⓒ Ⓓ   19. Ⓐ Ⓑ Ⓒ Ⓓ

4. Ⓐ Ⓑ Ⓒ Ⓓ   8. Ⓐ Ⓑ   12. Ⓐ Ⓑ Ⓒ Ⓓ   16. Ⓐ Ⓑ   20. Ⓐ Ⓑ Ⓒ Ⓓ

Practice Test 3

1. Ⓐ Ⓑ Ⓒ Ⓓ   5. Ⓐ Ⓑ Ⓒ Ⓓ   9. Ⓐ Ⓑ   13. Ⓐ Ⓑ Ⓒ Ⓓ   17. Ⓐ Ⓑ Ⓒ Ⓓ

2. Ⓐ Ⓑ Ⓒ Ⓓ   6. Ⓐ Ⓑ Ⓒ Ⓓ   10. Ⓐ Ⓑ   14. Ⓐ Ⓑ   18. Ⓐ Ⓑ

3. Ⓐ Ⓑ   7. Ⓐ Ⓑ Ⓒ Ⓓ   11. Ⓐ Ⓑ Ⓒ Ⓓ   15. Ⓐ Ⓑ Ⓒ Ⓓ   19. Ⓐ Ⓑ Ⓒ Ⓓ

4. Ⓐ Ⓑ   8. Ⓐ Ⓑ Ⓒ Ⓓ   12. Ⓐ Ⓑ Ⓒ Ⓓ   16. Ⓐ Ⓑ Ⓒ Ⓓ   20. Ⓐ Ⓑ Ⓒ Ⓓ

TANKER VEHICLES PRACTICE TEST 1

20 Questions - 60 Minutes

Directions: This test consists of a combination of true/false and multiple-choice questions. Only one answer is correct for each question.

1. Which type of cargo requires a tank endorsement?

   A. Hazardous materials

   B. Liquids and gases

   C. Animals

   D. Cargo over 50,000 lbs. gross maximum weight

2. Bulkheads are smaller compartments within a large tank.

   A. True

   B. False

3. A liquid surge increases the risk of _____ on a tanker.

   A. trailer skids

   B. rollover

   C. locking wheels

   D. mechanical problems

4. What is the purpose of a baffled tank?

   A. To provide room for an outage

   B. To allow for expansion of liquid during warmer temperatures

   C. To help control the forward and backward distribution of liquid

   D. To lock in liquid into one compartment to decrease leaks

5. A higher center of gravity means the bulk of the weight is

   A. higher off the ground.

   B. closer to the tractor.

   C. stored in the top layer of bulkheads.

   D. closer to the ground.

6. The most important thing to check during the vehicle inspection of a tanker is/are

   A. vapor recovery kits.

   B. possible leaks.

   C. fluid levels in the tank.

   D. emergency shut-off systems.

7. Baffled tanks eliminate the possibility of side-to-side surges.

   A. True

   B. False

8. A full tank of oil is at a greater risk for surges compared to a partially full tank.

   A. True

   B. False

9. An outage is

   A. when the electrical components go out.

   B. the process of liquids expanding as they heat up.

   C. the loss of power on the hydraulics.

   D. the process of draining liquids from a tank.

10. Bulkheads will always have holes in them, creating a baffled tank.

    A. True

    B. False

11. All of the following are part of every tanker vehicle inspection EXCEPT:

    A. Intake valves

    B. Pipes

    C. Hoses

    D. Vapor recovery kits

12. When braking suddenly in a partially full tank, it is safest to

    A. press down slowly on the brakes.

    B. brake firmly.

    C. brake with a stabbing motion.

    D. brake depending on the stopping distance needed.

13. Empty tanks may take longer to stop than full ones.

    A. True

    B. False

14. Manholes should always be in the _____ position before driving.

    A. open

    B. closed

    C. latched

    D. unlatched

15. Which of the following types of valves should be a part of every tank inspection?

    A. Intake, outage, and cut-off valves

    B. Intake, discharge, and shut-off valves

    C. Intake, outage, and shut-off valves

    D. Intake, discharge, and cut-off valves

16. When deciding how much to load in the tank, the driver needs to know

    A. how much the liquid will expand.

    B. how much the liquid will evaporate.

    C. the high temperature for all regions the tank will travel through.

    D. the distance the tank will travel.

17. How are bulkheads different from baffled tanks?

    A. Bulkheads hold liquid, baffled tanks do not.

    B. Baffled tanks hold liquids, bulkheads do not.

    C. Baffled tanks with holes in them are inside bulkheads.

    D. Bulkheads with holes in them are inside baffled tanks.

18. It is important to know the weight of the liquid because not all liquids have the same weight.

    A. True

    B. False

19. A manhole cover is usually located on

    A. the top of the tank.

    B. the front of the tank.

    C. the back of the tank.

    D. both sides of the tank.

20. Openings in baffles are commonly located

    A. in the front.

    B. in the back.

    C. at the bottom.

    D. at the top and bottom.

Tanker Vehicles Practice Test 1 Answer Key and Explanations

1. B	**5.** A	**9.** B	**13.** A	**17.** D
2. A	**6.** B	**10.** B	**14.** B	**18.** A
3. B	**7.** B	**11.** D	**15.** D	**19.** A
4. C	**8.** B	**12.** C	**16.** A	**20.** D

1. **The correct answer is B.** A tank endorsement is specifically required for any trailer transporting liquids and gases. They do not need to be hazardous materials (choice A). Animal transport (choice C) and heavy cargo (choice D) do not require a tank endorsement.

2. **The correct answer is A.** Bulkheads are smaller compartments within a larger tank. They divide up the liquid into smaller amounts to reduce the amount of liquid shifting during transport.

3. **The correct answer is B.** Liquid surges increase the risk of rollovers on a tanker as they redistribute the weight suddenly to one side. Liquid surges do not increase the risk for trailer skids (choice A), locking wheels (choice C) or mechanical problems (choice D) to the same extent that they do to rollovers.

4. **The correct answer is C.** A baffled tank is specifically used to help control the forward and backward distribution of liquid, also called a surge. Baffled tanks are not used to provide room for an outage (choice A), allow for expansion of liquid (choice B), or lock in liquid into one compartment (choice D).

5. **The correct answer is A.** A higher center of gravity means that the bulk of the weight of the tank is higher off the ground, which makes it more dangerous to maneuver. The bulk weight is not closer to the tractor (choice B), stored in the top layer of bulkheads as there is only one layer of bulkheads (choice C), and it is not closer to the ground (choice D) as that would mean a lower center of gravity.

6. **The correct answer is B.** When inspecting a tanker, the most important thing to check for is

the possibility of leaks. Fluid Levels in the tank (choice C) may help to indicate a possible leak, but it is not the most important item to check as leaks can also be present through cracks, dents, and poor seals. Vapor recovery kits (choice A) and emergency shut-off systems (choice D) are important but are not present on all tankers.

7. **The correct answer is B.** Baffled tanks reduce the likelihood of a front-to-back surge, but side-to-side surges are still possible as they do not control this type of motion through the bulkheads.

8. **The correct answer is B.** Full tanks are at a lower risk for surges as the amount of available space within the tank is much lower compared to a partially filled tank.

9. **The correct answer is B.** Outage is the process of liquids expanding as they heat up. In commercial driving, an outage does not refer to any electrical or mechanical outages (choices A and C) or draining the liquid (choice D).

10. **The correct answer is B.** Bulkheads with holes in them create a baffled tank, but bulkheads are commonly solid, separating a larger tank into smaller compartments.

11. **The correct answer is D.** Vapor recovery kits fall under the category of special purpose equipment, which is not present on every tanker. Intake valves (choice A), pipes (choice B), and hoses (choice C) are all part of every tank inspection.

12. **The correct answer is C.** If a driver must brake suddenly in a partially full tank, it is safest to brake with a stabbing motion. Pressing down slowly (choice A) and braking firmly (choice B) can cause the vehicle to roll over or get pushed into traffic because of surging. The stopping

distance (choice D) does not affect the safest way to brake suddenly.

13. **The correct answer is A.** Empty tanks may take longer to stop than full ones because a full tank creates more friction and thus has better traction with its additional weight.

14. **The correct answer is B.** Manholes should always be in the closed position before driving. Open (choice A) manholes allow for leakage. Latched (choice C) and unlatched (choice D) do not refer to the position of the manhole.

15. **The correct answer is D.** Intake, discharge, and cut-off valves are part of every tank inspection. There is no outage valve (choices A and C), and a shut-off valve (choice B) pertains to the air brake system.

16. **The correct answer is A.** It is important that the driver knows how much the liquid will expand as certain liquids need more room and thus the tank will need more outage. The amount of evaporation (choice B), the regional weather (choice C), and the distance traveled (choice D) are not factors when deciding how much to load in the tank.

17. **The correct answer is D.** A baffled tank has bulkheads with holes in them. Both the bulkheads and the baffled tanks are used to hold liquid (choices A and B). A baffled tank is not inside a bulkhead (choice C).

18. **The correct answer is A.** All liquids do not have the same weight as each other because many liquids have different densities. Assuming they all have the same weight and density can also lead to an improper outage calculation.

19. **The correct answer is A.** A manhole cover is almost always located on the top of the tank. They are not located on the front (choice B), back (choice C), or both sides of the tank (choice D).

20. **The correct answer is D.** The openings in baffles are commonly located at both the bottom and top. They are not located in the front (choice A) or back (choice B) as that would not allow for proper drainage. They are not solely located at the bottom (choice C).

NOTES

TANKER VEHICLES PRACTICE TEST 2

20 Questions - 60 Minutes

Directions: This test consists of a combination of true/false and multiple-choice questions. Only one answer is correct for each question.

1. A tank endorsement is required if the aggregate rated capacity of the liquid or gas being transported is

   A. 119 gallons or more.

   B. 120 gallons or more.

   C. 1,000 gallons or more.

   D. 999 gallons or more.

2. A surge in a tank is related to which of the following?

   A. Increased air pressure

   B. Expanding liquid due to temperature increase

   C. Movement of the liquid in tanks

   D. Trapped liquid in hoses

3. Another name for an unbaffled tank is a smooth-bore tank.

   A. True

   B. False

4. Which type of tank would be preferred for transporting potable water?

   A. Baffled tank

   B. Rough-bore tank

   C. Unbaffled tank

   D. Bulkhead

5. Which has a higher risk for liquid surges, a baffled tank or an unbaffled tank?

   A. A baffled tank because it does not have bulkheads

   B. An unbaffled tank because it does not have bulkheads

   C. An unbaffled tank because it has bulkheads

   D. A baffled tank because it has bulkheads

6. The amount of liquid a tank can carry is determined by the available volume in the tank.

   A. True

   B. False

7. It is important to pay special attention to this on a smaller tank:

   A. fluid levels.

   B. surging.

   C. weight distribution.

   D. outage.

8. Retest markings give the date of the last retest.

   A. True

   B. False

9. The following are important areas to inspect for leaks on a tank EXCEPT:

   A. Dents

   B. Cracks

   C. Valves

   D. Dollies

10. Bulkhead tanks are at a higher risk for weight distribution problems during loading and unloading compared to tanks without bulkheads.

    A. True

    B. False

11. Stopping distance for a tanker vehicle _____ on wet roads.

    A. doubles

    B. triples

    C. quadruples

    D. doesn't change

12. If a driver knowingly carries liquids or gases in a leaking tank, they can

    A. be fined up to $55,000 for a first offense.

    B. be held responsible for cleanup of the leak.

    C. lose their commercial driver's license.

    D. be jailed for up to 6 months.

13. The shut-off valve is part of every tank inspection.

    A. True

    B. False

14. Which of the following is most helpful in controlling a surge or weight shift?

    A. Use hard pressure when braking

    B. Turn and switch lanes smoothly

    C. Keep the tank partially full

    D. Use unbaffled tanks

15. Skids on tanker trailers are more likely to cause

    A. rollovers.

    B. jackknifing.

    C. uncoupling of the trailer.

    D. locked wheels.

16. A tanker endorsement is required for all drivers transporting tanks, even if they are empty.

    A. True

    B. False

17. Another term for stab braking is

    A. periodic braking.

    B. pumped braking.

    C. firm braking.

    D. air braking.

18. Manhole covers are present on

    A. tankers that transport liquids.

    B. tankers that transport gases.

    C. special tankers.

    D. all tankers.

19. Improperly calculating outage can cause

    A. rollovers.

    B. surges.

    C. leaks.

    D. skids.

20. Which statement is true?

    A. Manhole covers can connect to the intake valves.

    B. Intake valves can connect to the manhole covers.

    C. Intake valves are not related to manhole covers.

    D. Manhole covers and intake valves have the same diameter.

Tanker Vehicles Practice Test 2 Answer Key and Explanations

1. C	**5.** B	**9.** D	**13.** B	**17.** A
2. C	**6.** B	**10.** A	**14.** B	**18.** D
3. A	**7.** C	**11.** A	**15.** B	**19.** C
4. C	**8.** B	**12.** B	**16.** B	**20.** B

1. **The correct answer is C.** A tank endorsement is required if the aggregate rated capacity of the liquid or gas being transported is 1,000 gallons or more. A tank endorsement is also required if the individual tank's rated capacity is 120 gallons (choice B) or more. 119 gallons (choice A) and 999 gallons (choice D) are both too low.

2. **The correct answer is C.** A surge is due to the movement of liquid in tanks. The liquid moves suddenly from one side to the other, causing a surge, which can in turn unintentionally move the vehicle. Increased air pressure (choice A), expanding liquid due to temperature (choice B), and trapped liquid in hoses (choice D) are not related to a surge.

3. **The correct answer is A.** An unbaffled tank does not have anything inside to slow down the flow of liquid (such as bulkheads). This is usually due to sanitation regulations as it is hard to clean baffled tanks due to all the parts and surfaces on the inside.

4. **The correct answer is C.** An unbaffled tank is most commonly used to transport liquid food products that require a high level of sanitation, like potable water. A baffled tank (choice A) has extra bulkheads and tubes that make it harder to sanitize. A rough-bore tank (choice A) and bulkhead (choice D) are not types of transportation tanks.

5. **The correct answer is B.** An unbaffled tank is at a higher risk for liquid surges because it does not have bulkheads, which divide up and slow down the flow of liquid. A baffled tank (choices A and D) has bulkheads and is at a lower risk for surges. An unbaffled tank does not have bulkheads, so choice C is incorrect.

6. **The correct answer is B.** The amount of liquid a tank can carry is determined by the amount the liquid will expand during transit, the weight of the liquid, and the legal weight limits.

7. **The correct answer is C.** Pay special attention to weight distribution on a smaller tank because unloading and loading liquids can put too much strain on the front or rear of the vehicle. Fluid levels (choice A), surging (choice B), and outage (choice D) are all important to pay attention to on tanks, but increase in risk on the larger tanks, not the smaller ones.

8. **The correct answer is B.** Retest markings inform the driver what type of test or inspection was performed.

9. **The correct answer is D.** Leak inspection should always be done on all areas that come in contact with the liquids. Dollies are used to hitch trailers together and therefore do not need to be inspected for possible tank leaks. Dents (choice A), cracks (choice B), and valves (choice C) should be checked with every inspection.

10. **The correct answer is A.** Bulkhead tanks divide up the liquid into what is equivalent to smaller tanks within a larger tank. Because of this it is important to load or unload the liquids with weight distribution in mind. If too much is left on the front or back axles, it can cause damage. Tanks without bulkheads do not have this problem as there is nothing to divide up the weight, so the liquid is naturally evenly distributed.

11. **The correct answer is A.** Stopping distance doubles on wet roads. It does not triple (choice B) or quadruple (choice C) unless the tank is on a steep grade and driving at excessive speeds. Stopping

distance definitely increases on wet roads (choice D) because traction decreases.

12. **The correct answer is B.** A driver who knowingly carries liquids or gases in a leaking tank can be held responsible for cleanup of the leak. A first offense is not fined up to $55,000 (choice A) but $75,000 if it is hazardous materials. They will not lose their license (choice C) or be jailed (choice D) for their first offense.

13. **The correct answer is B.** The cut-off valve, not the shut-off valve, is part of every tank inspection.

14. **The correct answer is B.** Surges, also sometimes referred to as weight shifts, occur when the flow of the liquid is distributed too quickly from front to back or side to side. Turning and switching lanes smoothly decreases this. Using hard pressure when braking (choice A), keeping the tank partially full (choice C), and unbaffled tanks (choice D) are all contributors to surges.

15. **The correct answer is B.** Skids on tanker trailers are likely to cause jackknifing because of the weight of the tank coupled with the surge of the liquid. Skids on tanker trailers are not more likely to cause rollovers (choice A) or uncoupling (choice C). Locked wheels (choice D) are what cause the skids in the first place.

16. **The correct answer is B.** Drivers that transport only empty tanks do not need the tanker endorsement.

17. **The correct answer is A.** Stab braking is also called periodic braking. Rather than pumping the brakes (choice B) or using a firm brake (choice C), stab braking is when the driver presses on the brakes completely in a stabbing motion, which can also be thought of as periodic. Air braking (choice D) refers to any braking that uses air.

18. **The correct answer is D.** Manhole covers are present on all tankers. They can be used for loading and unloading cargo as well as in emergency situations to gain quick access to the tank. Choices A, B, and C are incorrect because they only mention one type of tanker.

19. **The correct answer is C.** Improperly calculating outage can cause leaks as not enough outage will fail to account for expansion of the liquid in the tank. Outage does not directly affect rollovers (choice A), surges (choice B), or skids (choice D).

20. **The correct answer is B.** Intake valves can connect to manhole covers. Some covers have openings for intake and discharge valves (choices A and C). Intake valves are not the same size in diameter (choice D) as the manhole cover.

 NOTES

TANKER VEHICLES PRACTICE TEST 3

20 Questions - 60 Minutes

Directions: This test consists of a combination of true/false and multiple-choice questions. Only one answer is correct for each question.

1. Which type of liquid should never be transported in a baffled tank?

   A. Milk

   B. Diesel

   C. Oil

   D. Industrial Chemicals

2. Smaller tanks within a large liquid tank are called

   A. baffled tanks.

   B. unbaffled tanks.

   C. bulkheads.

   D. cargo heads.

3. A tractor transporting 1,500 gallons of water is not required to have a tank endorsement because it is not a hazardous material.

   A. True

   B. False

4. One major reason a tanker is at an increased risk for rollover is because of liquid surges.

   A. True

   B. False

5. What is one design that helps to decrease surges in a tank?

   A. Bulkheads with baffled tanks inside

   B. Baffled tanks with bulkheads inside

   C. Baffled tanks with holes drilled in them

   D. Bulking tanks with holes drilled in them

6. Which of the following poses an increased risk for a tanker to lurch forward?

   A. Highway driving

   B. Mountain driving

   C. Stop-and-go traffic

   D. Poor weather

7. What is the purpose of baffled tanks?

   A. To reduce the likelihood of combustion of volatile liquids

   B. To reduce the likelihood of powerful liquid surges

   C. To reduce the likelihood of leaks

   D. To reduce the stress placed on the front and back axles of the tanker

8. Which tank would be the easiest to drive down a hill with switchbacks?

   A. A half full tank of water

   B. A full tank of water

   C. A half full tank of oil

   D. A partially full tank of oil

9. It is important to fill the tank completely to maximize efficiency and decrease surges.

   A. True

   B. False

10. It is considered a crime to carry gases or liquids in a leaking tank.

    A. True

    B. False

11. Which of the following is true about the center of gravity of a tanker?

    A. It is lower than a passenger vehicle.

    B. It is equal to a passenger vehicle.

    C. It is higher than a passenger vehicle.

    D. Its center of gravity depends on the maximum weight of the tank.

12. Within the first 50 miles of the trip, the vehicle should be stopped to

    A. refill fuel.

    B. allow brake air pressure to increase.

    C. check the tank and vehicle for any leaks, loose valves, or manhole covers.

    D. check that the brakes are working.

13. If wheels in the front of a tanker trailer cause a skid, the tanker will

    A. jackknife.

    B. roll over.

    C. drive straight even if you turn the wheel.

    D. create a side-to-side surge.

14. It is more dangerous to transport dry cargo than liquid cargo because of weight distribution.

    A. True

    B. False

15. All of the following are examples of special purpose equipment EXCEPT:

    A. Vapor recovery kits

    B. Built-in fire extinguishers

    C. Intake and discharge valves

    D. Grounding and bonding cables

16. The most important items to check for in addition to the standard items during a tanker inspection are

    A. possible leaks.

    B. brakes.

    C. valve seals.

    D. intake and discharge valves.

17. What are the three things to consider when deciding how much liquid to fill the tank with?

    A. How much the liquid will expand, how much it weighs, and the legal weight limits for that liquid

    B. How much the liquid will expand, how much it will contract, and the legal weight limits for that liquid

    C. How much the liquid will contract, how much it weighs, and how viscous it is

    D. How much the liquid will contract, how viscous it is, and the legal weight limits for that liquid

18. Surges occur when the flow of the liquid is distributed too quickly from front-to-back or side-to-side.

    A. True

    B. False

19. Manhole covers are used for all of the following EXCEPT:

    A. Gaining access to sanitize the inside of a tank

    B. Connecting valves to the tank

    C. Quick release of cargo during an emergency

    D. Monitoring outage in the tank

20. Unbaffled tanks are also referred to as

    A. bore tanks.

    B. smooth bore tanks.

    C. rough bore tanks.

    D. divided tanks.

Tanker Vehicles Practice Test 3 Answer Key and Explanations

1. A	**5.** B	**9.** B	**13.** C	**17.** A
2. C	**6.** C	**10.** A	**14.** B	**18.** A
3. B	**7.** B	**11.** C	**15.** C	**19.** D
4. A	**8.** B	**12.** C	**16.** A	**20.** B

1. **The correct answer is A.** Milk should never be transported in a baffled tank due to sanitation needs. A baffled tank has many compartments, thus increasing the possibility of improper sanitation before filling. Diesel (choice B), oil (choice C), and industrial chemicals (choice D) are all commonly transported in baffled tanks to reduce the likelihood of a surge.

2. **The correct answer is C.** Bulkheads are the smaller tanks within a larger liquid tank. A baffled tank (choice A) is the name of the larger liquid tank that has bulkheads, but there are holes in the bulkheads to allow liquid to pass through. An unbaffled tank (choice B) is a large tank that is not divided. Cargo tanks (choice D) are not specifically related to tanks in commercial driving.

3. **The correct answer is B.** A tank endorsement is not specifically for hazardous materials. It is for all types of liquids and gases that are in large quantities.

4. **The correct answer is A.** Tankers are at an increased risk for rollover because of liquid surges, which occur when partially filled tanks have a sudden movement of the liquid. This sudden movement from one side to the other causes a large weight shift, which can lead to a rollover.

5. **The correct answer is B.** Baffled tanks with bulkheads inside help to decrease surges in a tank. Bulkheads are located within the baffled tank and not the other way around (choice A). Baffled tanks do not have holes drilled in them (choice C), rather the bulkheads do. Bulking tanks (choice D) do not exist for a tanker.

6. **The correct answer is C.** Stop-and-go traffic can affect the tank as stopping suddenly can cause the liquid in the tank to surge forward, which can lead to the vehicle lurching forward. Highway driving (choice A), mountain driving (choice B) and poor weather (choice D) are all dangerous at times, but do not cause a specifically higher risk for tanks over traditional semi-trailer combinations.

7. **The correct answer is B.** The purpose of baffled tanks is to reduce the likelihood of powerful liquid surges by dividing the liquid into smaller tanks called bulkheads. They do not reduce combustion (choice A), leaks (choice C), or stress on the axles (choice D).

8. **The correct answer is B.** A full tank of water would be the easiest of the choices provided because a full tank does not allow room for more powerful liquid surges. A half-full tank of water (choice A) or oil (choice C) allows for powerful surges as half of the tank is empty. A partially full tank of oil (choice D) also allows for an increase in surge, although the total weight is lower, so the risk is not as high as the half-full options.

9. **The correct answer is B.** A tank should never be filled completely full because liquids will expand when heated, and a full tank may increase the likelihood of leaks post expansion.

10. **The correct answer is A.** Carrying gases or liquids in a leaking tank is a crime and the driver will receive a citation, be prevented from driving, and may also be responsible for cleanup of the leak.

11. **The correct answer is C.** The center of gravity of a tanker is higher than a passenger vehicle, thus making it more prone to a rollover. It is not lower (choice A) or equal (choice B). It also doesn't directly relate to the maximum weight (choice D) of the tank.

12. **The correct answer is C.** Within the first 50 miles of a trip of transporting liquids/gases in a tanker, the driver should stop and check for any leaks, loose valves, or manhole covers as well as the standard inspection after the first 50 miles of the trip. Fuel levels (choice A) and brake inspection/testing (choices B and D) should be done during the vehicle inspection before driving.

13. **The correct answer is C.** When front wheels lock up and skid, they force the tanker forward even if the wheel is turned. It does not always cause a jackknife (choice A) as that is more common when the back of the trailer skids. It does not cause a rollover (choice B) or side-to-side surge (choice D), which most commonly result from turning too quickly.

14. **The correct answer is B.** It is more dangerous to transport liquids due to higher chances of leaks, surges, and other hazards.

15. **The correct answer is C.** Intake and discharge valves are not special purpose equipment as they are present on all tanks. Vapor recovery kits (choice A), built-in fire extinguishers (choice B), and grounding and bonding cables (choice D) are all examples of special purpose equipment that is present on only certain types of tanks.

16. **The correct answer is A.** After standard items, the most important tanker specific items for inspection are possible leaks. Valve seals (choice C) and intake and discharge valves (choice S) are included in the leak inspection. Brakes (choice B) are part of a standard inspection on all commercial trucks and trailers.

17. **The correct answer is A.** How much a liquid will expand, how much it will weigh, and what the legal weight limit is for that liquid are the three things that must be considered when deciding how much liquid to fill the tank with. How much the liquid will contract (choices B, C, and D) and how viscous it is (choices C and D) are not considerations that will be made when deciding how much to fill the tank.

18. **The correct answer is A.** It's important to remember that surges not only occur front-to-back but also side-to-side. Baffled tanks help to break up the liquid with bulkheads and decrease the intensity of front-to-back surges, but side-to-side ones are still possible.

19. **The correct answer is D.** Manhole covers do not monitor outage as that is calculated before loading. They do allow access to the inside of the tank (choice A), connect valves to the tank (choice B), and allow for quick release during emergencies (choice C).

20. **The correct answer is B.** Unbaffled tanks are also referred to as smooth bore tanks as there is nothing inside to slow down the flow of liquids. Bore tanks (choice A), rough bore tanks (choice C), and divided tanks (choice D) are not actual names used in commercial driving.

NOTES

HAZARDOUS MATERIALS PRACTICE TESTS ANSWER SHEET

Practice Test 1

1. Ⓐ Ⓑ Ⓒ Ⓓ	7. Ⓐ Ⓑ	13. Ⓐ Ⓑ Ⓒ Ⓓ	19. Ⓐ Ⓑ Ⓒ Ⓓ	25. Ⓐ Ⓑ
2. Ⓐ Ⓑ Ⓒ Ⓓ	8. Ⓐ Ⓑ Ⓒ Ⓓ	14. Ⓐ Ⓑ	20. Ⓐ Ⓑ Ⓒ Ⓓ	26. Ⓐ Ⓑ Ⓒ Ⓓ
3. Ⓐ Ⓑ Ⓒ Ⓓ	9. Ⓐ Ⓑ	15. Ⓐ Ⓑ	21. Ⓐ Ⓑ Ⓒ Ⓓ	27. Ⓐ Ⓑ Ⓒ Ⓓ
4. Ⓐ Ⓑ	10. Ⓐ Ⓑ Ⓒ Ⓓ	16. Ⓐ Ⓑ Ⓒ Ⓓ	22. Ⓐ Ⓑ	28. Ⓐ Ⓑ
5. Ⓐ Ⓑ Ⓒ Ⓓ	11. Ⓐ Ⓑ	17. Ⓐ Ⓑ Ⓒ Ⓓ	23. Ⓐ Ⓑ Ⓒ Ⓓ	29. Ⓐ Ⓑ
6. Ⓐ Ⓑ Ⓒ Ⓓ	12. Ⓐ Ⓑ Ⓒ Ⓓ	18. Ⓐ Ⓑ	24. Ⓐ Ⓑ Ⓒ Ⓓ	30. Ⓐ Ⓑ Ⓒ Ⓓ

Practice Test 2

1. Ⓐ Ⓑ Ⓒ Ⓓ	7. Ⓐ Ⓑ	13. Ⓐ Ⓑ Ⓒ Ⓓ	19. Ⓐ Ⓑ Ⓒ Ⓓ	25. Ⓐ Ⓑ Ⓒ Ⓓ
2. Ⓐ Ⓑ Ⓒ Ⓓ	8. Ⓐ Ⓑ Ⓒ Ⓓ	14. Ⓐ Ⓑ Ⓒ Ⓓ	20. Ⓐ Ⓑ	26. Ⓐ Ⓑ Ⓒ Ⓓ
3. Ⓐ Ⓑ Ⓒ Ⓓ	9. Ⓐ Ⓑ Ⓒ Ⓓ	15. Ⓐ Ⓑ	21. Ⓐ Ⓑ	27. Ⓐ Ⓑ Ⓒ Ⓓ
4. Ⓐ Ⓑ	10. Ⓐ Ⓑ Ⓒ Ⓓ	16. Ⓐ Ⓑ	22. Ⓐ Ⓑ Ⓒ Ⓓ	28. Ⓐ Ⓑ
5. Ⓐ Ⓑ Ⓒ Ⓓ	11. Ⓐ Ⓑ	17. Ⓐ Ⓑ Ⓒ Ⓓ	23. Ⓐ Ⓑ	29. Ⓐ Ⓑ
6. Ⓐ Ⓑ Ⓒ Ⓓ	12. Ⓐ Ⓑ Ⓒ Ⓓ	18. Ⓐ Ⓑ Ⓒ Ⓓ	24. Ⓐ Ⓑ Ⓒ Ⓓ	30. Ⓐ Ⓑ Ⓒ Ⓓ

Practice Test 3

1. Ⓐ Ⓑ Ⓒ Ⓓ	7. Ⓐ Ⓑ Ⓒ Ⓓ	13. Ⓐ Ⓑ Ⓒ Ⓓ	19. Ⓐ Ⓑ	25. Ⓐ Ⓑ Ⓒ Ⓓ
2. Ⓐ Ⓑ Ⓒ Ⓓ	8. Ⓐ Ⓑ	14. Ⓐ Ⓑ Ⓒ Ⓓ	20. Ⓐ Ⓑ Ⓒ Ⓓ	26. Ⓐ Ⓑ Ⓒ Ⓓ
3. Ⓐ Ⓑ Ⓒ Ⓓ	9. Ⓐ Ⓑ Ⓒ Ⓓ	15. Ⓐ Ⓑ Ⓒ Ⓓ	21. Ⓐ Ⓑ	27. Ⓐ Ⓑ
4. Ⓐ Ⓑ	10. Ⓐ Ⓑ Ⓒ Ⓓ	16. Ⓐ Ⓑ Ⓒ Ⓓ	22. Ⓐ Ⓑ Ⓒ Ⓓ	28. Ⓐ Ⓑ
5. Ⓐ Ⓑ Ⓒ Ⓓ	11. Ⓐ Ⓑ Ⓒ Ⓓ	17. Ⓐ Ⓑ	23. Ⓐ Ⓑ	29. Ⓐ Ⓑ
6. Ⓐ Ⓑ Ⓒ Ⓓ	12. Ⓐ Ⓑ Ⓒ Ⓓ	18. Ⓐ Ⓑ	24. Ⓐ Ⓑ Ⓒ Ⓓ	30. Ⓐ Ⓑ Ⓒ Ⓓ

HAZARDOUS MATERIALS PRACTICE TEST 1

30 Questions - 60 Minutes

Directions: This test consists of a combination of true/false and multiple-choice questions. Only one answer is correct for each question.

1. The column in the Hazardous Materials Table that shows a material's hazard class or division, or the entry "Forbidden," is

    A. column 3.

    B. column 5.

    C. column 8.

    D. column 4.

2. Flammable and combustible liquids are a Class

    A. 6 material.

    B. 4 material.

    C. 8 material.

    D. 3 material.

3. The personnel responsible for checking that the shipper has correctly named, labeled, and marked the HazMat is the

    A. shipping company.

    B. carrier.

    C. driver.

    D. manufacturer.

4. Drivers who have a HazMat endorsement and are transporting certain hazardous materials over certain routes may require an additional written exam.

    A. True

    B. False

5. Marine pollutant bulk packages are required to show a

    A. red triangle with a fish and an "X" through the fish.

    B. black triangle with a turtle and an "X" through the turtle.

    C. yellow triangle with a fish and an "M" through the fish.

    D. white triangle with a fish and an "X" through the fish.

6. Spills exceeding the RQ (Reportable Quantity) must be reported to the

    A. HHS and TSA.

    B. DMV and TSA.

    C. DOT and EPA.

    D. DOT and DMV.

7. Since some hazardous materials cannot be loaded together with other hazardous materials, the forbidden combinations are listed in the Hazardous Waste Manifest.

    A. True

    B. False

8. Drivers should never transport a package labeled poison if they are hauling

    A. porous products.

    B. food products.

    C. fuel.

    D. fireworks.

9. A driver transporting HazMat in a tank with an aggregate rated capacity of 1,000 gallons will need the X endorsement.

   A. True

   B. False

10. The identification markings of a product on a tank are required to be

    A. white 3.9" numbers on red panels.

    B. orange 3.9" numbers on black panels.

    C. green 3.9" numbers on orange panels.

    D. black 3.9" numbers on orange panels.

11. The Class 9 Miscellaneous placard does not have to be displayed on a vehicle hauling Class 9 in a domestic transportation, but drivers may display them if they wish.

    A. True

    B. False

12. After the material is accepted by the primary carrier, shippers are required to keep a copy of shipping papers, or an electronic image of them, of hazardous waste for a period of

    A. 2 years.

    B. 3 years.

    C. 1 year.

    D. 6 months.

13. A Class 7 radioactive material package with a transport index of 0.9 and a maximum surface radiation level of 70 millirems per hour would require a

    A. Yellow II label.

    B. White I label.

    C. Yellow III label.

    D. Yellow I label.

14. A copy of Federal Motor Carrier Safety Regulations (FMCSR), Part 401 must be given to each driver transporting Division 1.1, 1.2, or 1.3 explosives by the carrier.

    A. True

    B. False

15. A driver should never continue driving with hazardous materials leaking from the vehicle to find a phone, truck stop, or assistance.

    A. True

    B. False

16. Oxidizers are a Class

    A. 2 hazardous material.

    B. 5 hazardous material.

    C. 3 hazardous material.

    D. 7 hazardous material.

17. On portable tanks with capacities of more than 1,000 gallons, the letters of the shipping name must be at least

    A. one inch tall.

    B. two and a half inches tall.

    C. two inches tall.

    D. one and a half inches tall.

18. Radioactive Yellow II or Yellow III labeled packages with a total index of 2.3 should not be left near people or animals longer than 2 hours.

    A. True

    B. False

19. Drivers must have an approved gas mask on hand when they are

    A. carrying chlorine.

    B. carrying an inhalation hazard cargo.

    C. carrying toxic materials.

    D. carrying corrosive materials.

20. All of these lists are used by drivers, shippers, and carriers to find out if a material is regulated as hazardous EXCEPT:

    A. The list of hazardous substances and reportable quantities

    B. The poison inhalation list

    C. The hazardous materials list

    D. The EPA dangerous materials list

21. If a driver is hauling both Explosives 1.1 and 1.3, the placard to be used is

    A. Explosives 1.1.

    B. Explosives 1.3.

    C. Dangerous.

    D. Explosive 1.1-3a.

22. Unless it is empty, according to 49 CFR 173.29, it is illegal to move a cargo tank with open valves or covers.

    A. True

    B. False

23. If transporting hazardous materials, drivers of placarded vehicles must stop

    A. 5 to 10 feet from the closest rail of a railroad.

    B. 15 to 50 feet from the closest rail of a railroad.

    C. 15 to 50 yards from the closest rail of a railroad.

    D. 5 to 10 yards from the closest rail of a railroad.

24. In completing the Uniform Hazardous Waste Manifest, a driver must

    A. sign the manifest only if traveling into another state.

    B. sign the manifest only if a witness is present.

    C. sign by hand.

    D. have it stamped by the shipper.

25. If operating a pump, a driver must turn off the engine before loading or unloading any flammable liquids.

    A. True

    B. False

26. Bulk packaging is a single container with a capacity of

    A. less than 120 gallons.

    B. less than 135 gallons.

    C. greater than 119 gallons.

    D. greater than 150 gallons.

27. When drivers are fueling their placarded vehicle, they must always be

    A. within 5 feet of the pump with a fire extinguisher.

    B. by the pump's emergency power shut-off.

    C. at the front, driver-side corner of the vehicle.

    D. at the nozzle, managing the fuel flow.

28. An inflexible or flexible portable packaging, other than a cylinder or portable tank, intended for mechanical handling is an Intermediate Bulk Container (IBC).

    A. True

    B. False

29. Charged storage batteries cannot be loaded with Division 1.1 materials.

    A. True

    B. False

30. On the Uniform Hazardous Waste Manifest, the name and EPA registration number of the shippers, carriers, and

    A. Poison Control Center must appear.

    B. drivers must appear.

    C. Transportation Safety Board must appear.

    D. destination must appear.

Hazardous Materials Practice Test 1 Answer Key and Explanations

1. A	6. C	11. A	16. B	21. A	26. C
2. D	7. B	12. B	17. C	22. A	27. D
3. C	8. B	13. C	18. A	23. B	28. A
4. B	9. A	14. B	19. A	24. C	29. A
5. D	10. D	15. A	20. D	25. B	30. D

1. **The correct answer is A.** Column 3 shows the material's hazard class or division, or the entry "Forbidden." Column 5 (choice B) illustrates the packing group, in Roman numerals, assigned to a material. Column 8 (choice C) indicates the section numbers that reveal the packaging requirements for each hazardous material shown in a three-part column. Column 4 (choice D) records the identification number for each proper shipping name.

2. **The correct answer is D.** Flammable and combustible liquids are a Class 3 hazardous material. Toxic or infectious substances are a Class 6 hazardous material (choice A). Flammable solids are a Class 4 hazardous material (choice B). Corrosives are a Class 8 hazardous material (choice C).

3. **The correct answer is C.** The driver is responsible for checking that the shipper has correctly named, labeled, and marked the HazMat. The shipping company (choice A), carrier (choice B), and the manufacturer (choice D) have other responsibilities in ensuring that the hazardous materials are made and transported in a safe manner.

4. **The correct answer is B.** Drivers who have a HazMat endorsement and are transporting certain hazardous materials over certain routes may require an additional permit or exemption.

5. **The correct answer is D.** A white triangle with a fish and an "X" through the fish is shown on marine pollutant bulk packages. However, a red triangle with a fish and an "X" through the fish (choice A), a black triangle with a turtle and an "X" through the turtle (choice B), and a yellow triangle with a fish and an "M" through the fish

(choice C) are NOT shown on marine pollutant bulk packages.

6. **The correct answer is C.** Reporting any spills exceeding the RQ (Reportable Quantity) must be done to the DOT and EPA.

7. **The correct answer is B.** Because some hazardous materials cannot be loaded together with other hazardous materials, the forbidden combinations are listed in the Segregation and Separation Chart.

8. **The correct answer is B.** Since poisons can be transmitted in any form, drivers should never transport them if they are hauling food products. As long as they are in line with transportation regulations, drivers can still transport porous products (choice A), fuel (choice C), and fireworks (choice D).

9. **The correct answer is A.** To drive a tank vehicle that hauls HazMat materials in an aggregate rated capacity of 1,000 gallons or more, a driver must have the X endorsement (a combination of the HazMat and tanker endorsements).

10. **The correct answer is D.** The rules require black 3.9" numbers on orange panels to be the identified marking of a product on a tank. Therefore, white 3.9" numbers on red panels (choice A), orange 3.9" numbers on black panels (choice B), and green 3.9" numbers on orange panels (choice C) are incorrect.

11. **The correct answer is A.** Although drivers may display them if they wish, the Class 9 Miscellaneous placard is not required to be displayed on a vehicle hauling Class 9 in domestic transportation.

12. **The correct answer is B.** A copy of hazardous waste shipping papers, or electronic images of

them, are required to be kept by the shipper for a period 3 years after the material is accepted by the primary carrier. A copy of the shipping papers for hazardous materials (not waste) are kept for a period of 2 years (choice A). Copies of the shipping papers for both hazardous materials and waste are not kept for a period of 1 year (choice C) or 6 months (choice D).

13. **The correct answer is C.** Since the proper label to attach to a package of Class 7 radioactive material is based on the transport index and the maximum surface of the package, a package with a transport index of 0.9 and a maximum surface radiation level of 70 millirems per hour would require a Yellow III label. Based on this information a Yellow II label (choice A), a White I label (choice B), or a Yellow I label (choice D) are not the proper labels to affix to this package.

14. **The correct answer is B.** If drivers are transporting Division 1.1, 1.2, or 1.3 explosives, then the carrier must supply them with a copy of Federal Motor Carrier Safety Regulations (FMCSR), Part 397.

15. **The correct answer is A.** Drivers should never continue operating a truck with hazardous materials leaking from the vehicle to find a phone, truck stop, or assistance.

16. **The correct answer is B.** A Class 5 hazardous material is an oxidizer. A Class 2 hazardous material (choice A) is a flammable gas. A Class 3 hazardous material (choice C) is a flammable liquid. A Class 7 hazardous material (choice D) is a radioactive material.

17. **The correct answer is C.** On portable tanks with capacities of more than 1,000 gallons, the letters of the shipping name must be at least two inches tall. On portable tanks with capacities of less than 1,000 gallons the letters of the shipping name must be at least one-inch tall (choice A). Therefore, the letters of the shipping name that are two and a half inches tall (choice B) and one and a half inches tall (choice D) for portable tanks with capacities of more than 1,000 gallons are incorrect.

18. **The correct answer is A.** People or animals should not be exposed longer than 2 hours to a radioactive Yellow II or Yellow III labeled package with a total index of 2.3.

19. **The correct answer is A.** Since chlorine in sufficient concentration can irritate the mucous membranes, the respiratory tract, and the eyes, carrying chlorine requires that the drivers have an approved gas mask on hand. If drivers are carrying an inhalation hazard cargo (choice B), carrying toxic materials (choice C), or carrying corrosive materials (choice D), they are not required to have an approved gas mask on hand.

20. **The correct answer is D.** Since there is not an EPA dangerous materials list that the drivers, shippers, and carriers are mandated to refer to, they do not reference the EPA to find out if a material is regulated as hazardous. Drivers, shippers, and carriers do, however, refer to the list of hazardous substances and reportable quantities (choice A), the poison inhalation list (choice B), and the hazardous materials list (choice C) to find out if a material is regulated as hazardous.

21. **The correct answer is A.** Using Explosive placard 1.1 comprises all the explosives listed under this Division. Therefore, a separate placard for Explosives 1.3 (choice B) is not required if the driver is hauling both Explosives 1.1 and 1.3 simultaneously. Although a driver who is hauling both Explosives 1.1 and 1.3 can use a "Dangerous" (choice C) placard along with the Explosives placard(s), it cannot be used in lieu of them. Since there is no Division Explosive 1.1-3a (choice D) on the HazMat Placard Table, it is not an option.

22. **The correct answer is A.** If a cargo tank is empty with open valves or covers, according to 49 CFR 173.29, it can be moved. However, it is illegal to move a cargo tank with open valves if it contains any amount of load.

23. **The correct answer is B.** Drivers of placarded vehicles that are transporting hazardous materials are required to stop 15 to 50 feet from the closest rail of a railroad. They are not to stop 5 to 10 feet

from the closest rail of a railroad (choice A), 15 to 50 yards from the closest rail of a railroad (choice C), or 5 to 10 yards from the closest rail of a railroad (choice D).

24. **The correct answer is C.** A driver must sign, by hand, when completing the Uniform Hazardous Waste Manifest. A driver cannot sign the manifest only if traveling into another state (choice A), sign the manifest only if a witness is present (choice B), or have it stamped by the shipper (choice D).

25. **The correct answer is B.** A driver may run the engine while loading or unloading any flammable liquids if, and only if, needing to operate a pump.

26. **The correct answer is C.** In a single container, the bulk packaging has a capacity greater than 119 gallons. Therefore, it is not defined as a capacity of less than 120 gallons (choice A), less than 135 gallons (choice B), or greater than 150 gallons (choice D).

27. **The correct answer is D.** Drivers must always be at the nozzle, managing the fuel flow when fueling their placarded vehicle. They must not always be within 5 feet of the pump with a fire extinguisher (choice A), by the pump's emergency power shut-off (choice B), nor at the front, driver-side corner of the vehicle (choice C).

28. **The correct answer is A.** An Intermediate Bulk Container (IBC) is an inflexible or flexible portable packaging, other than a cylinder or portable tank, intended for mechanical handling.

29. **The correct answer is A.** According to the Do Not Load Table, charged storage batteries cannot be loaded in the same vehicle with Division 1.1 materials.

30. **The correct answer is D.** The name and EPA registration number of the shippers, carriers, and destination must appear on the manifest.

NOTES

HAZARDOUS MATERIALS PRACTICE TEST 2

30 Questions - 60 Minutes

> **Directions:** This test consists of a combination of true/false and multiple-choice questions. Only one answer is correct for each question.

1. The objective of the hazardous material rules is to contain the hazardous products and
   - **A.** convey the risk of cargo.
   - **B.** deter people from carrying it.
   - **C.** create revenue for companies.
   - **D.** manage the drive time for operators.

2. Explosives are a Class
   - **A.** 3 HazMat.
   - **B.** 5 HazMat.
   - **C.** 1 HazMat.
   - **D.** 8 HazMat.

3. The common reference for Hazardous Materials Regulations is
   - **A.** 49 CFR 171 – 180.
   - **B.** 39 CFR 128 – 188.
   - **C.** 19 CMR 130 – 180.
   - **D.** 29 CFR 160 – 190.

4. The hazardous material name is known as the shortened term, HazMat, and is the only written name/term used on road signs or in government regulations.
   - **A.** True
   - **B.** False

5. Shippers are instructed on how to package hazardous materials safely, and drivers are instructed on how to load, transport, and unload these materials through the
   - **A.** "communication rules."
   - **B.** "packaging rules."
   - **C.** "confinement rules."
   - **D.** "containment rules."

6. When drivers apply for or renew a HazMat endorsement, they must submit to a background check through the
   - **A.** Federal Bureau of Investigation.
   - **B.** Food and Drug Administration.
   - **C.** Department of Defense.
   - **D.** Transportation and Security Administration.

7. Placards are regulatory signs that display certain types or quantities of hazardous materials on the truck.
   - **A.** True
   - **B.** False

8. If a driver is involved in an accident and cannot speak, the best way to communicate the risk to the fire department or police personnel is to
   - **A.** write notes to them.
   - **B.** point them to the information on the placards.
   - **C.** have accessible, properly filled shipping papers.
   - **D.** ensure the shipping papers are displayed in plain sight.

9. The personnel responsible for reporting accidents and incidents containing hazardous materials to the correct government agency is the

   A. carrier.
   B. driver.
   C. shipper.
   D. manufacturer.

10. A HazMat driver cannot park a vehicle within

    A. 300 feet of a fire.
    B. 500 feet of a fire.
    C. 400 feet of a fire.
    D. 350 feet of a fire.

11. The United States Transportation and Security Administration's Emergency Response Guidebook (ERG) lists the chemicals and their ID numbers assigned to them.

    A. True
    B. False

12. The Hazardous Materials Table lists the materials

    A. in numerical order.
    B. alphabetically using label codes.
    C. alphabetically via symbols.
    D. alphabetically via hazard class.

13. The letters that will precede the identification number are

    A. "AN" or "NU."
    B. "BA" or "LN."
    C. "NA" or "UN."
    D. "AB" or "UN."

14. The column in the Hazardous Materials Table that records the additional and specific requirements that apply to the materials listed on it is

    A. column 1.
    B. column 5.
    C. column 7.
    D. column 8.

15. A government approved place for parking vehicles loaded with explosives is called a cargo heater.

    A. True
    B. False

16. Although a bulk package and the vehicle transporting a bulk package contain only the residue of a hazardous material, it must be placarded.

    A. True
    B. False

17. The floor liner for explosives cannot have any of these EXCEPT:

    A. Nonmetallic material
    B. Steel or iron
    C. Nails or screws
    D. Cracks or holes

18. Drivers who transport route controlled radioactive materials must have received special training by the carrier within the last

    A. 4 years.
    B. 3 years.
    C. 2 years.
    D. 1 year.

19. Placarded vehicles require a fire extinguisher with an Underwriters Laboratories (UL) rating of _____ in the power unit.

    A. 10 B:C
    B. 20 A:C
    C. 5 B:C
    D. 10 A:C

20. The basic description of hazardous materials on the shipping papers contains the identification number, proper shipping name, hazard class or division, and the packing group, if any.

    A. True
    B. False

21. Class 4 materials are solids that act in response to water, heat, and air or can even react suddenly.

    A. True
    B. False

22. It is necessary to ground a trailer

    A. only when unloading any flammable-filled cargo tanks.
    B. only when filling it with corrosives.
    C. only when filling it with explosives.
    D. when filling or unloading any flammable liquid tanks and maintaining the ground until the filling hole is closed.

23. Some bulk packages only have to be placarded on the two opposite sides of the vehicle, or they can display labels instead of being placarded.

    A. True
    B. False

24. Placard Table 1 hazardous materials must be placarded

    A. if the entire amount transported is 1,001 lbs. or more not including packaging.
    B. whenever any amount is transported.
    C. if the entire amount transported is 1,001 lbs. or more including packages.
    D. if the entire amount transported exceeds 500 lbs.

25. If the truck contains explosives, oxidizers, or flammables, no one can smoke within

    A. 45 feet of the vehicle.
    B. 35 feet of the vehicle.
    C. 50 feet of the vehicle.
    D. 25 feet of the vehicle.

26. An identification number or hazard class name may not be used to describe

    A. corrosives.
    B. an RQ of a hazardous material.
    C. non-hazardous material.
    D. anthrax.

27. The most common cargo tanks for liquids are

    A. MC306.
    B. MC331.
    C. MC332.
    D. MC320.

28. To transport placarded radioactive materials, a driver must choose the safest route.

    A. True
    B. False

29. It is acceptable for drivers to proceed over rail-road tracks when confident that no train is coming, assured they can clear the tracks without stopping, and be able to shift gears while crossing the tracks.

    A. True
    B. False

30. All drivers must be prepared to do the following EXCEPT:

    A. Determine if a material in the regulation is considered hazardous
    B. Be trained and tested every three years in transporting HazMats
    C. Know how to identify and react to possible security threats
    D. Have a commercial driver's license (CDL) with a hazardous materials endorsement

Hazardous Materials Practice Test 2 Answer Key and Explanations

1. A	6. D	11. B	16. A	21. A	26. C
2. C	7. B	12. D	17. A	22. D	27. A
3. A	8. C	13. C	18. C	23. A	28. B
4. B	9. A	14. C	19. A	24. B	29. B
5. D	10. A	15. B	20. A	25. D	30. A

1. **The correct answer is A.** Conveying the risk of cargo and containing the hazardous products are the objectives of the hazardous materials rules. The objectives are not to deter people from carrying it (choice A), create revenue for companies (choice C), or to manage the drive time for operators (choice D).

2. **The correct answer is C.** Explosives are a Class 1 HazMat. A Class 3 HazMat (choice A) is a flammable and combustible liquid. A Class 5 HazMat (choice B) is an oxidizing substance. A Class 8 HazMat (choice D) is a corrosive.

3. **The correct answer is A.** The Hazardous Materials Regulations is commonly referenced as 49 CFR 171 – 180. The following reference type numbers: 39 CFR 128 – 188 (choice B), 19 CMR 130 – 180 (choice C), and 29 CFR 160 – 190 (choice D) are not connected to a factual Hazardous Material Regulation.

4. **The correct answer is B.** Although the hazardous material name is known as and seen on road signs as the shortened term, HazMat, it is also termed in government regulations as HM.

5. **The correct answer is D.** "Containment rules" instruct shippers on how to package hazardous materials safely and instruct drivers on how to load, transport, and unload these materials. Therefore, "communication rules" (choice A), "packaging rules" (choice B), and "confinement rules" (choice C) are not the correct terms to use.

6. **The correct answer is D.** To acquire an original or renewed hazardous materials endorsement, drivers must pass a Transportation Security Administration (TSA) background check. The background

check is NOT completed through the Federal Bureau of Investigation (choice A), the Food and Drug Administration (choice B), or the Department of Defense (choice C).

7. **The correct answer is B.** Placards are warning signs that display certain types or quantities of hazardous materials on the truck.

8. **The correct answer is C.** Having accessible, properly filled shipping papers is the best way to communicate the risk to the fire department or police personnel when the driver is involved in an accident and cannot speak. Writing notes to them (choice A), pointing them to the information on the placards (choice B), and ensuring the shipping papers are displayed in plain sight (choice D) are not efficient ways to communicate the risk.

9. **The correct answer is A.** The carrier is responsible for reporting accidents and incidents containing hazardous materials to the correct government agency. Therefore, the driver (choice B), the shipper (choice C), and the manufacturer (choice D) are not responsible for reporting accidents and incidents containing hazardous materials to the correct government agency.

10. **The correct answer is A.** Unless safeguards are taken to ensure a safe passage, a HazMat driver cannot park a vehicle within 300 feet of a fire. According to the regulations, they can, however, park within 500 feet of a fire (choice B), 400 feet of a fire (choice C), and 350 feet of a fire (choice D).

11. **The correct answer is B.** It is the United States Department of Transportation's Emergency Response Guidebook (ERG) that lists chemicals and the ID numbers assigned to them.

12. **The correct answer is D.** The hazardous materials table lists the materials alphabetically via hazard class by shipping the correct name. It is not listed in numerical order (choice A), alphabetically using label codes (choice B), or alphabetically via symbols (choice C).

13. **The correct answer is C.** The letters "NA" or "UN" will come before the identification number. However, "AN" or "NU" (choice A), "BA" or "LN" (choice B), and "AB" or "UN" (choice D) are not letters that will precede the identification number.

14. **The correct answer is C.** Column 7 records the additional and specific requirements that apply to the materials listed on it. Column 1 (choice A) of the hazardous materials table lists one of the 6 different symbols affecting the shipping method(s). Column 5 (choice B) illustrates the packing group, in Roman numeral numbers, assigned to a material. Column 8 (choice C) indicates the section numbers that reveal the packaging requirements for each hazardous material shown in a three-part column.

15. **The correct answer is B.** Safe haven is a government approved place for parking vehicles loaded with explosives.

16. **The correct answer is A.** Whether a bulk package and the vehicle transporting the bulk package contains any hazard material residue, it must be placarded.

17. **The correct answer is A.** When transporting Division 1.1, 1.2, or 1.3 materials, the floor liner must be either a nonmetallic material or a non-ferrous metal. Therefore, floor liners cannot contain steel or iron (choice B), nails or screws (choice C), or cracks or holes (choice D).

18. **The correct answer is C.** Drivers must have received special training by the carrier within the last 2 years if transporting route controlled radioactive materials. Therefore, 4 years (choice A), 3 years (choice B), and 1 year (choice D) are incorrect.

19. **The correct answer is A.** The power unit of a placarded load are required to be equipped with a fire extinguisher that has an Underwriters Laboratories (UL) rating of 10 B:C or more. Therefore, 20 A:C (choice B), 5 B:C (choice C), or 10 A:C (choice D) are incorrect rating options for placarded vehicles that require a fire extinguisher.

20. **The correct answer is A.** The identification number, proper shipping name, hazard class or division, and the packing group, if any, is the basic description of hazardous materials listed on the shipping papers.

21. **The correct answer is A.** Since Class 4 materials are solids that react to water, heat, and air or can even react suddenly, it is best to keep these hazardous materials in an enclosed vehicle with sufficient ventilation.

22. **The correct answer is D.** When filling or unloading any flammable liquids into tanks, maintain grounding. Although trailers are not cargo tanks, it is important to ground them when filling or unloading flammable-filled cargo tanks (choice A). A trailer does not just need to be grounded when filling it with corrosives (choice B) but also when unloading it. A trailer does not just need to be grounded when filling it with explosives (choice C) but also when unloading it.

23. **The correct answer is A.** Some bulk packages need only to be placarded on the two opposite sides of the vehicle, or they can display labels instead of being placarded.

24. **The correct answer is B.** Whenever any amount of hazardous material in Placard Table 1 is transported, they must be placarded. Hazardous materials listed on Placard Table 2 must be placarded if the entire amount transported is 1,001 lbs. or more, not including packaging (choice A), or if the entire amount transported is 1,001 lbs. or more, including packages (choice C). Since any amount of hazardous materials on Placard Table 1 must be placarded, if the entire amount transported exceeds 500 lbs. (choice D), it will be placarded anyway.

25. **The correct answer is D.** No one can smoke within 25 feet of the vehicle if it contains explosives, oxidizers, or flammables. Although it is not

a good idea to smoke around any of these trucks containing any hazardous materials, it is not against regulations if a person smokes within 45 feet (choice A), 35 feet (choice B), or 50 feet of the vehicle (choice C).

26. **The correct answer is C.** An identification number or hazard class name may not be used to describe a non-hazardous material. However, an identification number or a hazard class name may be used to describe corrosives (choice A), an RQ of a hazardous material (choice B), or anthrax (choice D).

27. **The correct answer is A.** The most common cargo tanks for liquids are MC306. Cargo tanks MC331 (choice B) and MC332 (choice C) are used for gases, with MC331 being the most common. MC320 (choice D) is not a cargo tank.

28. **The correct answer is B.** To transport placarded radioactive materials, a carrier must choose the safest route.

29. **The correct answer is B.** Although drivers can proceed over railroad tracks when confident that no train is coming and be assured that they can clear the tracks without stopping, they should never shift gears while crossing the tracks.

30. **The correct answer is A.** The decision on whether the material meets a definition of a hazardous material in the regulations is based on the shipper, not the driver. However, drivers must be prepared to be trained and tested every three years in transporting HazMats (choice B), know how to identify and react to possible security threats (choice C), and have a commercial driver's license (CDL) with a hazardous materials endorsement (choice D).

NOTES

HAZARDOUS MATERIALS PRACTICE TEST 3

30 Questions - 60 Minutes

Directions: This test consists of a combination of true/false and multiple-choice questions. Only one answer is correct for each question.

---

1. A Class 7 HazMat material is a(n)

   A. corrosive.

   B. explosive.

   C. toxic substance.

   D. radioactive material.

2. Whether a material is deemed hazardous is based on its characteristics and the decision of the

   A. carrier.

   B. shipper.

   C. scientist.

   D. driver.

3. Propane and helium fall under HazMat Class

   A. 4.

   B. 1.

   C. 2.

   D. 9.

4. HazMat shipping paperwork must be kept in the glove compartment while a driver is operating the vehicle and on the passenger seat of the truck when out of the vehicle.

   A. True

   B. False

5. The personnel responsible for making sure the placards are attached to the trailer is the

   A. carrier.

   B. shipping company.

   C. manufacturer.

   D. driver.

6. To receive a CDL HazMat endorsement, drivers must pass a written test and know the following about transporting them EXCEPT:

   A. Recognizing what the hazardous materials are

   B. Safely monitoring the loading of the shipments

   C. Correctly placarding the vehicle in accordance with the guidelines

   D. Safely hauling the shipments

7. In order for first responders to detect hazardous materials, they use an identification number with a

   A. two-digit code.

   B. single digit code.

   C. four-digit code.

   D. six-digit code.

8. The letter "D" in column 1 of the Hazardous Material Table indicates that the proper shipping name is suitable for describing materials for domestic hauling but may not be suitable for international transport.

   A. True

   B. False

9. The following are authorized abbreviations EXCEPT:

   A. N.O.S. (Not Otherwise Specified)

   B. Psi (pounds per square inch)

   C. IBC (Intermediate Bulk Container)

   D. M.C.L (Minimum Contaminant Level)

10. The three primary lists that drivers, shippers, and carriers use to identify hazardous materials are all of these EXCEPT:

    A. Section 172.101, the Hazardous Materials Table

    B. Appendix A to Section 172.101, the List of Hazardous Substances and Reportable Quantities

    C. Appendix B to Section 172.101, the List of Marine Pollutants

    D. Appendix C to Section 172.101, the List of Air Pollutants

11. The column in the Hazardous Materials Table that demonstrates the danger warning label(s) that shippers must put on the packages of hazardous materials is

    A. column 3.

    B. column 6.

    C. column 1.

    D. column 4.

12. A transport index relates to products that are

    A. overweight.

    B. liquid.

    C. corrosive.

    D. radioactive.

13. The placard that must be used with an inhalation HazMat load is

    A. Reportable Quantity.

    B. Flammable.

    C. Dangerous.

    D. Poison.

14. If hauling hazardous materials, a driver must stop and check any dual tires at least once every

    A. 1 hour or 40 miles.

    B. 2 hours or 100 miles.

    C. 4 hours or 200 miles.

    D. 3 hours or 150 miles.

15. The term "RQ" classifies the material's

    A. Reference Qualifier.

    B. Regulatory Qualifier.

    C. Reportable Quantity.

    D. Regulatory Quantity.

16. A portable tank vehicle endorsement is required for tanks with a capacity of

    A. any amount.

    B. less than 1,000 gallons.

    C. over 1,000 gallons.

    D. over 5,000 gallons.

17. It is the job of the driver to find out if permits are needed or if special routes must be used when transporting HazMats in some states and counties.

    A. True

    B. False

18. The best description of a cargo tank is bulk packaging permanently attached to a vehicle.

    A. True

    B. False

19. Cargo heaters are prohibited when loading cargo from Class 1, Class 2.1, and Class 3 hazardous materials.

    A. True

    B. False

20. So that the relief valve is in the vapor space, cylinders can be loaded in a

    A. rolling position.

    B. horizontal position.

    C. diagonal position with the relief valve to the right.

    D. diagonal position with the relief valve to the left.

21. Drivers who park a truck carrying explosives in any place other than a specified safe haven must have a qualified person within sight of the vehicle at all times.

    A. True
    B. False

22. The person responsible for watching an unattended HazMat truck is required to have it in clear view and stay within a maximum of

    A. 50 feet of the vehicle.
    B. 25 feet of the vehicle.
    C. 100 feet of the vehicle.
    D. 75 feet of the vehicle.

23. A truck carrying explosives has crashed with another vehicle and should not be pulled apart until 30 minutes has passed and the shipper's loading foreman is present.

    A. True
    B. False

24. While transporting Explosives 1.1, 1.2, or 1.3, a driver must have _____ in their possession.

    A. extra HazMat labels
    B. a written route plan
    C. the carrier's insurance policy
    D. the paperwork to request a gas mask

25. Since placards must be readable from all four directions, they must be sized at least

    A. 250 mm square.
    B. 9.25 inches square.
    C. 200 mm square.
    D. 7.87 inches square.

26. When there is a spill of hazardous materials, drivers may have to call

    A. CHEMTREC.
    B. the National Response Center.
    C. the Poison Control Center.
    D. the Local Emergency Planning Committee.

27. A specified packaging that is following standards of packaging follows the standards of the United Nations recommendations.

    A. True
    B. False

28. If a substance in the Hazardous Materials Table is written in italics, it means it is its proper shipping name.

    A. True
    B. False

29. Placards should be placed on the vehicle before drivers start operating the vehicle, not before they load it.

    A. True
    B. False

30. Of the following HazMat classes, the most dangerous is

    A. Division 6.1.
    B. Division 6.2.
    C. Division 6.3.
    D. Division 6.4

Hazardous Materials Practice Test 3 Answer Key and Explanations

1. D	6. B	11. B	16. C	21. A	26. B
2. B	7. C	12. D	17. A	22. C	27. A
3. C	8. A	13. D	18. A	23. B	28. B
4. B	9. D	14. B	19. A	24. B	29. A
5. D	10. D	15. C	20. B	25. A	30. A

1. **The correct answer is D.** Radioactive materials, such as uranium, are a Class 7 hazardous materials. Corrosives (choice A) are a Class 8 hazardous material. Explosives (choice B) are a Class 1 hazardous material. Toxic substances (choice C) are a Class 6 hazardous material.

2. **The correct answer is B.** The decision as to whether the material meets a definition of a hazardous material in the regulations is based on the shipper and on the material's characteristics. The carrier (choice A), scientist (choice C), and the driver (choice D) do not make these decisions.

3. **The correct answer is C.** HazMat Class 2 identifies gases such as propane and helium. HazMat Class 4 (choice A) identifies flammable solids such as white phosphorus. HazMat Class 1 (choice B) identifies explosives such as dynamite and flares. HazMat Class 9 (choice D) identifies miscellaneous HazMat such as polychlorinated biphenyls (PCB).

4. **The correct answer is B.** HazMat shipping paperwork must be kept in a pouch on the driver's door, in plain sight and within direct reach while the seat belt is fastened while driving, or on the driver's seat when out of the vehicle.

5. **The correct answer is D.** The driver is responsible for making sure the placards are attached to the trailer. Therefore, the carrier (choice A), the shipping company (choice B), and the manufacturer (choice C) are not responsible for making sure the placards are attached to the trailer.

6. **The correct answer is B.** Drivers must safely load the shipments, not monitor the loading of the shipments. Drivers are responsible for recognizing

what hazardous materials are (choice A), correctly placarding the vehicle in accordance with the guidelines (choice C), and safely hauling the shipments (choice D).

7. **The correct answer is C.** First responders use an identification number with a four-digit code to detect hazardous materials. Therefore, a two-digit code (choice A), a single digit code (choice B), and a six-digit code (choice D) are not used as identification numbers to detect hazardous materials.

8. **The correct answer is A.** The letter "D" in column one of the hazardous material table does indicate that the proper shipping name is suitable for defining the materials for domestic hauling but may not be suitable for international transport.

9. **The correct answer is D.** The abbreviation M.C.L. is not an authorized abbreviation. However, N.O.S. (Not Otherwise Specified) (choice A), psi (choice B), and IBC (intermediate Bulk Container) (choice C) are authorized abbreviations.

10. **The correct answer is D.** Appendix C to Section 172.101, the List of Air Pollutants, is not a list used by drivers, shippers, and carriers to identify hazardous materials. However, Section 172.101, the Hazardous Materials Table (choice A), Appendix A to Section 172.101, the List of Hazardous Substances and Reportable Quantities (choice B), and Appendix B to Section 172.101, the List of Marine Pollutants (choice C) are the three primary lists that drivers, shippers, and carriers use to identify hazardous materials.

11. **The correct answer is B.** Column 6 demonstrates the danger warning label(s) that shippers must put on the packages of hazardous materials. Column

3 (choice A) shows the material's hazard class or division, or the entry "Forbidden." Column 1 (choice C) of the hazardous materials table lists one of the 6 different symbols affecting the shipping method(s). Column 4 (choice D) records the identification number for each proper shipping name.

12. **The correct answer is D.** Since the transport index conveys the degree of control needed during transportation, it relates to products that are radioactive. It does not relate to products that are overweight (choice A), liquid (choice B), or corrosive (choice C).

13. **The correct answer is D.** A Poison placard must be used with an inhalation HazMat load. A Reportable Quantity (choice A) is not a placard, but the amount of a hazardous material that has to be discharged into the environment before the EPA requires notice of this release to go to the National Response Center. An inhalation HazMat load does not need to use a Flammable (choice B) or a Dangerous (choice C) placard.

14. **The correct answer is B.** A driver must check any dual tires at least every 2 hours or 100 miles if hauling hazardous materials. Therefore, it is not necessary to stop and check the dual tires at 1 hour or 40 miles (choice A) if hauling hazardous materials. It is against regulations to wait and check the dual tires at 4 hours or 200 miles (choice C) or at 3 hours or 150 miles (choice D) if hauling hazardous materials because those intervals are too long.

15. **The correct answer is C.** The term "RQ" classifies the material's Reportable Quantity if spilled. It is not the Reference Qualifier (choice A), the Regulatory Qualifier (choice B), nor the Regulatory Quantity (choice D).

16. **The correct answer is C.** A portable tank endorsement is required for tanks with a capacity of 1,000 gallons or more. No tank endorsement is required for capacities of any amount (choice A) or an amount less than 1,000 gallons (choice B). Over 5,000 gallons (choice D) is much higher than the required amount.

17. **The correct answer is A.** Drivers carry the responsibility to find out if permits are needed or if special routes must be used when transporting HazMats in some states and counties.

18. **The correct answer is A.** Bulk packaging that is attached to a vehicle is the best description of a cargo tank.

19. **The correct answer is A.** Class 1 (explosives), Class 2.1 (flammable gas), and Class 3 (flammable liquids) prohibit the use of cargo heaters, as well as the automatic cargo heater and air conditioner units.

20. **The correct answer is B.** Although they should be vertically loaded and held in an upright position, if the relief valve is designed to be in the vapor space, cylinders may be loaded in a horizontal position. Cylinders may not be loaded in a rolling position (choice A), a diagonal position with the relief valve to the right (choice C) or a diagonal position with the relief valve to the left (choice D).

21. **The corrects answer is A.** A truck carrying explosives must always be within sight of a qualified person when parking in any place other than a specified safe haven.

22. **The correct answer is C.** When responsible for watching an unattended HazMat truck, a person must have a clear view and stay within 100 feet of the vehicle. Therefore, the person being within 50 feet (choice A), 25 feet (choice B), or 75 feet of the truck (choice D) is not the maximum distance.

23. **The correct answer is B.** A truck carrying explosives that has crashed with another vehicle should not be separated from said vehicle until the explosives are 200 feet away from the vehicles and any occupied buildings.

24. **The correct answer is B.** A driver must have a written route plane in their possession while transporting Explosives 1.1, 1.2, or 1.3. They are not required to have extra HazMat labels (choice A), the carrier's insurance policy (choice C), or paperwork to request a gas mask (choice D).

25. **The correct answer is A.** Since placards are put on the front, rear, and both sides of the vehicle, they

must be readable and sized at 250 mm (9.8 inches) square. Sizing them at 9.25 inches square (choice B), 200 mm square (choice C), and 7.87 inches square (choice D) does not meet the required regulated measurements.

26. **The correct answer is B.** Drivers may have to call the National Response Center to report the spill. Drivers do not have to call CHEMTREC (choice A) because it is intended to give emergency personnel technical information; however, drivers can call them, and they are in close relation to the National Response Center. Drivers do not have to call the Poison Control Center (choice C) or the Local Emergency Planning Committee (choice D) because employers or shippers will be in communication with these agencies or committees.

27. **The correct answer is A.** The required specifications of standard packaging conform to the standards of the United Nations recommendations.

NOTES

28. **The correct answer is B.** When a substance in the Hazardous Materials Table is written in italics, it means that the proper shipping name is NOT what is written in italics; just those in regular type are correct.

29. **The correct answer is A.** Before drivers operate the vehicle, and not before they load it, is when drivers should place placards on the vehicle.

30. **The correct answer is A.** Division 6.1 Poison/Toxic Material is the most dangerous in these classes and must be placarded whenever any amount is transported. Although dangerous, Division 6.2 (choice B) hazardous materials are not the most dangerous. There are no Division 6.3 (choice C) or Division 6.4 (choice D) in this Class.

PASSENGER TRANSPORT PRACTICE TESTS ANSWER SHEET

Practice Test 1

1. Ⓐ Ⓑ Ⓒ Ⓓ   5. Ⓐ Ⓑ   9. Ⓐ Ⓑ Ⓒ Ⓓ   13. Ⓐ Ⓑ Ⓒ Ⓓ   17. Ⓐ Ⓑ

2. Ⓐ Ⓑ   6. Ⓐ Ⓑ   10. Ⓐ Ⓑ Ⓒ Ⓓ   14. Ⓐ Ⓑ Ⓒ Ⓓ   18. Ⓐ Ⓑ Ⓒ Ⓓ

3. Ⓐ Ⓑ   7. Ⓐ Ⓑ   11. Ⓐ Ⓑ Ⓒ Ⓓ   15. Ⓐ Ⓑ   19. Ⓐ Ⓑ Ⓒ Ⓓ

4. Ⓐ Ⓑ Ⓒ Ⓓ   8. Ⓐ Ⓑ Ⓒ Ⓓ   12. Ⓐ Ⓑ   16. Ⓐ Ⓑ Ⓒ Ⓓ   20. Ⓐ Ⓑ Ⓒ Ⓓ

Practice Test 2

1. Ⓐ Ⓑ   5. Ⓐ Ⓑ   9. Ⓐ Ⓑ Ⓒ Ⓓ   13. Ⓐ Ⓑ Ⓒ Ⓓ   17. Ⓐ Ⓑ

2. Ⓐ Ⓑ   6. Ⓐ Ⓑ Ⓒ Ⓓ   10. Ⓐ Ⓑ   14. Ⓐ Ⓑ Ⓒ Ⓓ   18. Ⓐ Ⓑ

3. Ⓐ Ⓑ   7. Ⓐ Ⓑ   11. Ⓐ Ⓑ   15. Ⓐ Ⓑ   19. Ⓐ Ⓑ Ⓒ Ⓓ

4. Ⓐ Ⓑ Ⓒ Ⓓ   8. Ⓐ Ⓑ   12. Ⓐ Ⓑ   16. Ⓐ Ⓑ Ⓒ Ⓓ   20. Ⓐ Ⓑ Ⓒ Ⓓ

Practice Test 3

1. Ⓐ Ⓑ   5. Ⓐ Ⓑ Ⓒ Ⓓ   9. Ⓐ Ⓑ Ⓒ Ⓓ   13. Ⓐ Ⓑ   17. Ⓐ Ⓑ Ⓒ Ⓓ

2. Ⓐ Ⓑ Ⓒ Ⓓ   6. Ⓐ Ⓑ   10. Ⓐ Ⓑ Ⓒ Ⓓ   14. Ⓐ Ⓑ Ⓒ Ⓓ   18. Ⓐ Ⓑ Ⓒ Ⓓ

3. Ⓐ Ⓑ   7. Ⓐ Ⓑ Ⓒ Ⓓ   11. Ⓐ Ⓑ   15. Ⓐ Ⓑ Ⓒ Ⓓ   19. Ⓐ Ⓑ Ⓒ Ⓓ

4. Ⓐ Ⓑ Ⓒ Ⓓ   8. Ⓐ Ⓑ Ⓒ Ⓓ   12. Ⓐ Ⓑ   16. Ⓐ Ⓑ Ⓒ Ⓓ   20. Ⓐ Ⓑ

PASSENGER TRANSPORT PRACTICE TEST 1

20 Questions - 60 Minutes

Directions: This test consists of a combination of true/false and multiple-choice questions. Only one answer is correct for each question.

1. A driver must have a passenger endorsement on a CDL to operate a bus with any number of passengers aboard UNLESS the passenger is

   A. a CDL trainer.

   B. a family member.

   C. over 25.

   D. under 18.

2. Household pets can be transported on a passenger bus as long as they are crated.

   A. True

   B. False

3. The standee line is a 1-inch thick line that designates where standing passengers are allowed to stand while the bus is in motion.

   A. True

   B. False

4. The interior mirrors of the bus are used to

   A. expand peripheral vision.

   B. monitor passengers.

   C. check for blind spots.

   D. see behind the bus.

5. The majority of bus accidents occur at intersections.

   A. True

   B. False

6. The nose swing refers to the front of the bus.

   A. True

   B. False

7. A driver must stop the bus 10-20 feet before a railroad crossing.

   A. True

   B. False

8. The standee line is _____ in width.

   A. 1 inch

   B. 2 inches

   C. 3 inches

   D. 4 inches

9. The total weight of any 1 class of hazardous materials on a passenger transport bus may not exceed

   A. 200 pounds.

   B. 500 pounds.

   C. 100 pounds.

   D. 1,000 pounds.

10. During an emergency, passengers can exit via

    A. the roof hatches.

    B. any window.

    C. any door.

    D. any window or door.

11. Which of the following is allowed on a bus?

    A. Tear gas

    B. Gasoline

    C. Car batteries

    D. Oxygen tanks

12. A coupling device is present on all buses.

    A. True

    B. False

13. What safety device is in place to ensure the bus does not accidentally move while passengers are boarding?

    A. The interlock system

    B. The parking brake

    C. The air brakes

    D. The idle

14. If a driver with a Class A CDL takes the passenger endorsement in a Class B vehicle, the restriction code on their license will be

    A. E.

    B. M.

    C. N.

    D. V.

15. Every bus must have spare electrical fuses in the emergency kit.

    A. True

    B. False

16. What must the driver always do during the post inspection?

    A. Fill out the vehicle inspection report

    B. Fuel up

    C. Sweep out the passenger space

    D. Clean the windshield

17. Excessive speed on a turn when a bus has good traction is likely to cause the bus to slide off the road.

    A. True

    B. False

18. What must the driver always wear when the bus is in motion?

    A. Uniform

    B. Name tag

    C. Seatbelt

    D. Reflective gear

19. A bus must stop at least _____ feet before a drawbridge.

    A. 50

    B. 15

    C. 25

    D. 10

20. All of the following are part of the vehicle inspection EXCEPT:

    A. Parking brake

    B. Odometer

    C. Seats

    D. Tires

Passenger Transport Practice Test 1 Answer Key and Explanations

1. A	5. A	9. C	13. A	17. B
2. B	6. A	10. D	14. B	18. C
3. B	7. B	11. D	15. B	19. A
4. B	8. B	12. B	16. A	20. B

1. **The correct answer is A.** A passenger endorsement on a CDL is not needed if it is on a CLP and the only passenger being transported on the bus is a CDL trainer. This allowance permits new drivers the opportunity to train on the bus before scheduling their passenger endorsement exam. If a CDL trainer is present then other trainees can also be on board, and federal/state auditors and inspectors can also be transported. A passenger endorsement is needed for any other type of passenger transport, including family members (choice B), people over 25 (choice C), and minors (choice D).

2. **The correct answer is B.** Household pets can never be transported on a bus, even if they are crated. The only permitted animals are documented service animals.

3. **The correct answer is B.** The standee line is a 2-inch thick line, not 1-inch. However, its purpose is correctly stated in the question as it is used to designate where standing passengers are allowed to stand while the bus is in motion.

4. **The correct answer is B.** The interior mirrors are used to monitor passengers for safety and compliance. This includes adherence to rules (no eating, smoking, etc.), checking for disruptive behavior, and ensuring safety. The exterior side mirrors are used to expand peripheral vision (choice A). The rearview mirror in some buses is used to see behind the bus (choice D), but not all buses have them as many buses do not have back windows. It is the responsibility of the driver to look over their shoulder to check for blind spots (choice C) as the interior mirrors will not help with this.

5. **The correct answer is A.** Buses have reduced visibility on either side and have a wider turning radius compared to compact cars. In addition, their stopping distance is extended due to the weight of the vehicle. Other drivers are often unaware of this and do not allow for more space and time for buses to navigate intersections.

6. **The correct answer is A.** The nose swing refers to the front of the bus, also called the nose (similar to the nose of an airplane). The rear of the bus is referenced as the tail.

7. **The correct answer is B.** 10 feet is too close to a railroad crossing. A driver must stop between 15-50 feet before crossing a railroad crossing depending on visibility.

8. **The correct answer is B.** The standee line is 2 inches in width. 1 inch (choice A) is too thin and 3 inches (choice C) and 4 inches (choice D) are too wide for the application that it is used for.

9. **The correct answer is C.** The total weight of any one class of hazardous materials may not exceed 100 pounds. 200 pounds (choice A) and 1,000 pounds (choice D) are both incorrect. 500 pounds (choice B) refers to the total combined weight for all classes of hazardous materials allowed on a bus.

10. **The correct answer is D.** During an emergency, a passenger can exit by any means necessary, including all windows and doors as they all have safety features that allow passengers to release them manually if needed. The roof hatch (choose A) may not release completely and thus is not a possibility on all buses. Any window (choice B) and any door (choice C) excludes the other possibility and is therefore incorrect.

11. **The correct answer is D.** Oxygen tanks are permitted on a bus and can be within the passenger space if they are medically prescribed for one of the passengers. Tear gas (choice A) is always

prohibited as it is a Class 2.3 hazardous material. Gasoline (choice B) and a car batteries (choice C) are also prohibited as they are common hazards that are not clearly labeled and can be dangerous to passengers.

12. **The correct answer is B.** A coupling device is only present on a bus that is connected to something behind it, such as another bus, a trailer, etc.

13. **The correct answer is A.** The interlock system is specifically designed to engage the brakes whenever the rear door is open so that the bus does not accidentally move when passengers are boarding. The parking brake (choice B) can be used for this purpose but is not specifically designed for this purpose. Air brakes (choice C) and the idle (choice D) do not pertain to this topic specifically and are thus incorrect.

14. **The correct answer is B.** Restriction codes for taking tests in lower class vehicles vary depending on the class. For Class A CDL drivers taking tests in Class B vehicles, the code is M. For Class A or B CDL drivers taking tests in Class C vehicles, the code is N (choice C). A restriction code of E (choice A) refers to a test completed with an automatic transmission vehicle. A restriction code of V (choice D) refers to a medical restriction.

15. **The correct answer is B.** Spare electrical fuses are only required if the bus does not have circuit breakers. In the instance that the bus is equipped with circuit breakers, spare fuses are not required.

16. **The correct answer is A.** A driver must fill out the vehicle inspection report during the post inspection, so the mechanic is notified of any needed repairs and the next driver is prepared for any defects before driving. Although it is best practice to fuel up (choice B), sweep out the passenger space (choice C), and clean the windshield (choice D), these actions are not as important as completion of the vehicle inspection report.

17. **The correct answer is B.** A bus with good traction is more likely to roll over when using excessive speed on a turn as the traction creates a pivot point. A bus with poor traction would be more likely to slide due to a lack of grip on the road.

18. **The correct answer is C.** Regardless of whether the passengers have seatbelts or not, every driver has a seatbelt and is required to wear it whenever the bus is in motion. Company policies may also add requirements that include a uniform (choice A), nametag (choice B), and reflective gear (choice D), but they are not mandatory outside of the company's policies.

19. **The correct answer is A.** A bus must stop AT LEAST 50 feet before a drawbridge to ensure it is safe to cross. 10 feet (choice D) 15 feet (choice B) and 25 feet (choice C) are all too close.

20. **The correct answer is B.** It is not necessary to inspect the odometer during your routine vehicle inspections. However, the parking brake (choice A), seats (choice C), and tires (choice D) must all be inspected during routine vehicle inspections as defects could cause a safety risk.

NOTES

PASSENGER TRANSPORT PRACTICE TEST 2

20 Questions - 60 Minutes

> **Directions:** This test consists of a combination of true/false and multiple-choice questions. Only one answer is correct for each question.

1. Only 3 passengers are permitted to stand in front of the standee line on a bus.

   A. True

   B. False

2. All operating railroad crossings are protected by flashing lights.

   A. True

   B. False

3. All Class 3 flammable liquids are forbidden on a bus.

   A. True

   B. False

4. How many passengers can stand in front of the standee line when the bus is in motion?

   A. 0

   B. 5

   C. 3

   D. 10

5. The interlock system releases when the rear door closes.

   A. True

   B. False

6. A bus can only transport a combined total weight of _____ for all classes of hazardous materials.

   A. 200 pounds

   B. 1,000 pounds

   C. 100 pounds

   D. 500 pounds

7. The vehicle inspection should always include the exterior of the vehicle but does not need to include the interior of the bus if no passengers are expected to board.

   A. True

   B. False

8. Buses are not required to stop at a railroad crossing if the tracks run parallel to the vehicle, down the middle of the road.

   A. True

   B. False

9. All of the following are part of a vehicle inspection of any type of bus EXCEPT:

   A. Emergency equipment

   B. Horn

   C. Coupling devices

   D. Steering mechanism

10. Luggage may be stored in overhead bins or secured under passenger seats on buses that are traveling long distances.

    A. True

    B. False

11. A person who needs reminders to take prescription medicine is permitted to bring a service dog aboard a bus.

    A. True

    B. False

12. The "design speed" used in developing a highway factors in all vehicles, including buses.

    A. True

    B. False

13. Where can explosives be transported on a bus?

    A. Anywhere as long as they are clearly labeled

    B. They can never be transported on a bus

    C. In a location separated from the passengers

    D. In a designated overhead bin

14. A bus must stop at least _____ feet before a railroad crossing.

    A. 5

    B. 10

    C. 15

    D. 20

15. The interlock system is used to apply the brakes any time the roof hatches are open.

    A. True

    B. False

16. A passenger endorsement is required for _____ or more passengers, including the driver, in most states.

    A. 5

    B. 10

    C. 16

    D. 20

17. The nose swing and tail swing move together in the same direction during a turn.

    A. True

    B. False

18. Bad traction can cause a bus to slide off the road during a turn if excessive speed is used.

    A. True

    B. False

19. Which of the following is NOT a prohibited practice for passenger transport?

    A. Allowing passengers to stand while the bus is in motion

    B. Fueling when passengers are on board

    C. Talking with passengers while driving

    D. Pushing a disabled bus with riders on board

20. What will happen if the roof hatch is locked in a partly open position?

    A. Passengers can be hurt if the bus rolls over

    B. The height clearance is increased

    C. The emergency exit options decrease

    D. The air conditioning no longer works

Passenger Transport Practice Test 2 Answer Key and Explanations

1. B	**5.** A	**9.** C	**13.** C	**17.** B
2. B	**6.** D	**10.** A	**14.** C	**18.** A
3. B	**7.** B	**11.** A	**15.** B	**19.** A
4. A	**8.** A	**12.** B	**16.** C	**20.** B

1. **The correct answer is B.** The standee line designates the area where no passengers may stand. Therefore, zero passengers are permitted to stand in front of it.

2. **The correct answer is B.** Never assume that a railroad crossing is nonoperational just because it is devoid of flashing lights. Depending on the location and age of the crossing, flashing lights may or may not be present. Follow all traffic laws regarding railroad crossings even if flashing lights are not present.

3. **The correct answer is B.** Class 3 flammable liquids, except for gasoline, are permitted on a bus as long as they are properly labeled and have a combined weight of less than 100 pounds.

4. **The correct answer is A.** No passengers are ever permitted to stand in front of the standee line when the bus is in motion. Therefore 5 (choice B), 3 (choice C), and 10 (choice D) are all incorrect.

5. **The correct answer is A.** The interlock system works by applying the brake any time the rear door is open, thus preventing the bus from moving when passengers are boarding. However, it should never be used as a parking brake as it automatically releases when the rear door is closed.

6. **The correct answer is D.** The combined total weight for all hazardous materials cannot exceed 500 pounds. 200 pounds (choice A) and 1,000 pounds (choice B) are both incorrect. 100 pounds (choice C) refers to the weight restrictions for an individual class and not the total combined weight across multiple classes.

7. **The correct answer is B.** The vehicle inspection should always include the entire vehicle, both inside and out, regardless of whether or not passengers are expected during that particular day. This ensures that every component is inspected and a report is filed if repairs are needed.

8. **The correct answer is A.** Railroad crossings present in the middle of a road do not have the same rules as traditional perpendicular crossings. Drivers do not need to stop at crossings that go down the middle of the road.

9. **The correct answer is C.** Coupling devices are not always present as they are used to join two pieces of equipment together. Emergency equipment (choice A), the horn (choice B), and the steering mechanism (choice D) are all present on every bus.

10. **The correct answer is A.** Although luggage may be stored in overhead bins or secured under passenger seats, it can never be left in aisles or doorways once the bus is in motion. This includes any emergency exit doorways or bathroom areas. This is to protect the safety of all aboard and keep the walkways clear in case of emergency.

11. **The correct answer is A.** Any person with a legally acknowledged disability is permitted to bring their service animal aboard any vehicle, including buses.

12. **The correct answer is B.** The "design speed" refers to the speed used to determine the design of the roadway, including the grades and angles of turns. However, it is designed based on small, personal cars with good traction that are driving on dry pavement. Roadways are not intentionally designed for larger, heavier vehicles, including buses. It is important to be aware of this when driving on frontage roads, country roads, and side streets.

13. **The correct answer is C.** Explosives can be transported as long as they are separated from the passengers. They are not prohibited (choice B); however, they cannot be anywhere in the bus with passengers (choice A) or in a designated overhead bin (choice D) as they must be separated from passengers, unless it is small arms ammunition clearly labeled "ORM-D".

14. **The correct answer is C.** A bus must stop AT LEAST 15 feet before a railroad crossing. The specific distance is 15-50 feet depending on visibility. 5 feet (choice A) and 10 feet (choice B) are too close. 20 feet (choice D) is not close enough to be the least distance.

15. **The correct answer is B.** The interlock system is used to apply the brakes any time the rear door is open. It automatically releases the brake when the rear door is shut. The roof hatches do not affect the interlock system in any capacity.

16. **The correct answer is C.** In the majority of states, a passenger endorsement is required for vehicles that carry 16 people, including the driver. A passenger endorsement is not needed for a vehicle with 5 passengers (choice A). Only in California is a passenger endorsement required for 10 passengers (choice B). No state allows the transport of more than 16 passengers without a passenger endorsement, therefore 20 (choice D) is wrong as well.

17. **The correct answer is B.** The nose swing (referring to the front of the bus) and the tail swing (referring to the back of the bus) actually move in opposite directions during a turn. The nose swing turns in while the tail swing turns out.

18. **The correct answer is A.** Poor traction is likely to cause the bus to slide off the road, rather than roll over. This is due to the limited grip on the road combined with the force on the bus from the speed.

19. **The correct answer is A.** Passengers are allowed to stand on the bus while it is in motion as long as they are behind the standee line. Fueling when passengers are onboard (choice B) is prohibited, barring an emergency. Talking with passengers while driving (choice C) is listed as a prohibited practice for passenger transport vehicles, as is pushing a disabled bus with riders onboard (choice D).

20. **The correct answer is B.** When the roof hatch is locked in a partly open position, it adds inches onto the height of the bus, thus increasing the clearance needed for bridges, parking garages, etc. Choices A, C, and D are all incorrect.

 NOTES

PASSENGER TRANSPORT PRACTICE TEST 3

20 Questions - 60 Minutes

Directions: This test consists of a combination of true/false and multiple-choice questions. Only one answer is correct for each question.

---

1. Any driver of a 12-passenger van must have a passenger endorsement in order to operate the vehicle.

   A. True

   B. False

2. Which of the following are prohibited from being transported on a passenger van or bus?

   A. Tear gas

   B. Medical oxygen

   C. Oxidizers

   D. Corrosives

3. One way to help prevent theft and vandalism on a long-distance bus is to shut the door after letting early passengers board before the scheduled departure time.

   A. True

   B. False

4. Any standing passengers on a bus must remain behind the

   A. border line.

   B. standing line.

   C. standee line.

   D. designated passenger line.

5. Buses are required to stop at all railroad crossings EXCEPT for when:

   A. The traffic signal is green.

   B. The railroad crossing lights aren't blinking.

   C. The railroad crossing bar is raised up.

   D. There are no trains coming.

6. The air hose couplings should be inspected on every bus before operating it.

   A. True

   B. False

7. All hazardous materials must be labeled with which shape?

   A. Square

   B. Diamond

   C. Circle

   D. Triangle

8. At each stop it is important to announce all of these EXCEPT:

   A. Bus number

   B. Next departure time

   C. Location

   D. Arrival time

9. Once a driver receives a passenger endorsement, the following code is added to their license:

   A. P

   B. PE

   C. C

   D. A

10. To receive a passenger endorsement, a driver must complete

   A. 10 hours of driving with passengers.

   B. a written test.

   C. a written test and a skills test.

   D. service with an instructor.

11. Emergency reflectors can be either 3 reflective triangles or 3 liquid flares. Only one option is needed, not both.

    A. True

    B. False

12. Roof hatches may never be locked in a partly open position.

    A. True

    B. False

13. A full vehicle inspection must occur every time a new driver operates the bus.

    A. True

    B. False

14. An example of a Class 1 explosive that is allowed on a bus within the same space as passengers is

    A. fireworks.

    B. dynamite.

    C. small arms ammunition.

    D. nitroglycerine.

15. Any driver that drives a CDL passenger vehicle nationally must be at least _____ years old.

    A. 16

    B. 18

    C. 21

    D. 25

16. How often should the tires of a bus be checked during periods of hot weather?

    A. Every 2 hours or 100 miles

    B. Every 3 hours or 120 miles

    C. Every hour or 60 miles

    D. Every 4 hours or 120 miles

17. What must be open in order for the interlock system to engage?

    A. Driver door

    B. Emergency door

    C. Rear door

    D. Roof hatch

18. What is present on some buses, but not on others?

    A. Emergency exit signs

    B. Seatbelts

    C. Fire extinguishers

    D. Lights

19. When does a bus need to stop at a drawbridge?

    A. Any time it approaches one

    B. When there is a control attendant present

    C. When the traffic light is green

    D. When there is no signal

20. An interlock system is an appropriate substitute for the parking brake.

    A. True

    B. False

Passenger Transport Practice Test 3 Answer Key and Explanations

1. B	**5.** A	**9.** A	**13.** A	**17.** C
2. A	**6.** B	**10.** C	**14.** C	**18.** B
3. B	**7.** B	**11.** A	**15.** C	**19.** D
4. C	**8.** D	**12.** B	**16.** A	**20.** B

1. **The correct answer is B.** A passenger endorsement is not needed in 12-passenger vans that are below 26,0001 GWD and used for personal use. Although some states have lower passenger numbers (California requires a passenger endorsement for passenger vehicles with 10 or more passengers), it is coupled with the type of use—for profit, for hire, business or government use, etc. Families are excluded from this if the weight is lower and the seating is less than 16 passengers including the driver.

2. **The correct answer is A.** Tear gas is a Class 2 poison gas that is expressly prohibited from transport aboard a passenger vehicle, including buses and vans. Although medical oxygen (choice A), oxidizers (choice B), and corrosives (choice D) are all hazardous materials, they can be transported as long as their independent weight does not exceed 100 pounds and their combined weight does not exceed 500 pounds.

3. **The correct answer is B.** Allowing passengers to board early, regardless of whether you are a short-distance or long-distance route, can actually increase your risk of theft and vandalism. The best practice is to never allow anyone to board prior to the scheduled boarding time.

4. **The correct answer is C.** Any standing passengers must remain behind the standee line. The other terms (border line, choice A; standing line, choice C; designated passenger line, choice D) are not used in the commercial driving license arena.

5. **The correct answer is A.** Buses are not required to stop at railroad crossings when the traffic signal is green. A bus must stop at a railroad crossing even if the lights aren't blinking (choice B), the crossing

bar is raised up (choice C), and there are no visible trains coming (choice D).

6. **The correct answer is B.** Air hose couplings are only present with a trailer or semi-trailer. Therefore, they will not be a part of the vehicle inspection on all buses, as most are not connected to another vehicular component such as a trailer.

7. **The correct answer is B.** Hazardous materials must be clearly labeled with a diamond. In addition, the diamond will be a different color depending on the class of hazardous material present. Square (choice A), circle (choice C), and triangle (choice D) are all incorrect and do not reference hazardous material contents on a container.

8. **The correct answer is D.** It is not necessary to announce the arrival time; although if time permits, it can help passenges that are connecting with other modes of transportation. The bus number (choice A), next departure time (choice B), and location (choice C) are all necessary parts of the announcement that help passengers at each stop, as they provide vital information.

9. **The correct answer is A.** The code P refers to a passenger endorsement. PE (choice B) is not a valid license code. C (choice C) refers to a Class C CDL license. A (choice D) refers to a Class A CDL license.

10. **The correct answer is C.** The passenger endorsement requires both a written test and a skills test. There are no required hours of driving with passengers (choice A), and service with an instructor (choice D) is unnecessary as many CDL drivers receive this endorsement after already finishing school. Although a written test (choice B) alone is all that is required for some endorsements, this is not true for the passenger endorsement.

11. **The correct answer is A.** Either of these options are permitted as emergency reflectors in the emergency kit. Both together are not necessary.

12. **The correct answer is B.** It is permitted to lock the roof hatch in a partly open position to allow fresh air to circulate. However, it is not always permitted to keep roof hatches locked in this position, and when they are locked open then you must be aware that your vehicle's height has increased.

13. **The correct answer is A.** Not only are daily inspections required, but a new vehicle inspection must be completed any time a new driver comes aboard.

14. **The correct answer is C.** Small arms ammunition is permitted within the passenger space as long as it is clearly labeled "ORM-D". Fireworks (choice A), dynamite (choice B), and nitroglycerine (choice D) are not permitted to be stored in the same space as passengers.

15. **The correct answer is C.** The national age requirement for CDL drivers is 21 years of age. In Idaho you can be 16 (choice A) and apply for a seasonal CDL license but not to transport passengers. The CDL must be used for farming purposes within the state. All states except New York and Hawaii allow for CDL licenses at age 18 (choice B) for intrastate purposes but not for passenger endorsements. 25 (choice D) is usually connected to insurance requirements, not restrictions related to passenger endorsements.

16. **The correct answer is A.** The tires of a bus should be checked every 2 hours or 100 miles during periods of hot weather. Every hour or 60 miles (choice C) is too frequent and unnecessary. Every 3 hours (choice B) or every 4 hours (choice D) are too infrequent and may cause the driver to miss damage or other safety hazards due to the extreme heat.

17. **The correct answer is C.** The rear door where the passengers board must be open for the interlock system to engage and ensure the brakes are locked so the bus will not move. The driver door (choice A), emergency door (choice B), and the roof hatch (choice D) do not directly affect the interlock system.

18. **The correct answer is B.** Some buses have seatbelts, but not all of them do. However, all buses have some type of emergency exit sign (choice A), fire extinguisher (choice C), and lights (choice D).

19. **The correct answer is D.** When there is no signal present, a driver is required to stop the bus at the drawbridge. When there is a control attendant present (choice B) the bus must follow their instructions, which may or may not include stopping. When the traffic light is green (choice C), the bus is permitted to go without stopping first, therefore buses do not always need to stop (choice A).

20. **The correct answer is B.** The interlock system should never be used in place of the parking brake as it only engages when the rear door is open. Should the rear door close, the bus will no longer be secure and could move suddenly.

SCHOOL BUSES PRACTICE TESTS ANSWER SHEET

Practice Test 1

1. Ⓐ Ⓑ
2. Ⓐ Ⓑ Ⓒ Ⓓ
3. Ⓐ Ⓑ Ⓒ Ⓓ
4. Ⓐ Ⓑ Ⓒ Ⓓ

5. Ⓐ Ⓑ Ⓒ Ⓓ
6. Ⓐ Ⓑ
7. Ⓐ Ⓑ
8. Ⓐ Ⓑ Ⓒ Ⓓ

9. Ⓐ Ⓑ Ⓒ Ⓓ
10. Ⓐ Ⓑ Ⓒ Ⓓ
11. Ⓐ Ⓑ Ⓒ Ⓓ
12. Ⓐ Ⓑ

13. Ⓐ Ⓑ
14. Ⓐ Ⓑ Ⓒ Ⓓ
15. Ⓐ Ⓑ Ⓒ Ⓓ
16. Ⓐ Ⓑ Ⓒ Ⓓ

17. Ⓐ Ⓑ Ⓒ Ⓓ
18. Ⓐ Ⓑ Ⓒ Ⓓ
19. Ⓐ Ⓑ Ⓒ Ⓓ
20. Ⓐ Ⓑ

Practice Test 2

1. Ⓐ Ⓑ Ⓒ Ⓓ
2. Ⓐ Ⓑ
3. Ⓐ Ⓑ Ⓒ Ⓓ
4. Ⓐ Ⓑ Ⓒ Ⓓ

5. Ⓐ Ⓑ Ⓒ Ⓓ
6. Ⓐ Ⓑ Ⓒ Ⓓ
7. Ⓐ Ⓑ
8. Ⓐ Ⓑ Ⓒ Ⓓ

9. Ⓐ Ⓑ Ⓒ Ⓓ
10. Ⓐ Ⓑ
11. Ⓐ Ⓑ Ⓒ Ⓓ
12. Ⓐ Ⓑ Ⓒ Ⓓ

13. Ⓐ Ⓑ Ⓒ Ⓓ
14. Ⓐ Ⓑ Ⓒ Ⓓ
15. Ⓐ Ⓑ Ⓒ Ⓓ
16. Ⓐ Ⓑ Ⓒ Ⓓ

17. Ⓐ Ⓑ Ⓒ Ⓓ
18. Ⓐ Ⓑ
19. Ⓐ Ⓑ Ⓒ Ⓓ
20. Ⓐ Ⓑ Ⓒ Ⓓ

SCHOOL BUSES PRACTICE TEST 1

20 Questions - 60 Minutes

Directions: This test consists of a combination of true/false and multiple-choice questions. Only one answer is correct for each question.

1. The first 10 feet from the front bumper is the MOST dangerous area at the front of the bus.

   A. True

   B. False

2. The blind spot of the flat mirrors of a bus

   A. is present along the side of the bus on the driver's side only.

   B. extends 10 feet from the front bumper.

   C. extends 10 feet from each side of the bus.

   D. is located at the rear bumper and directly in front of and below each flat mirror.

3. How should the driver properly position the overhead inside rearview mirror of a school bus?

   A. Position the mirrors in order to see the left and right sides of the bus, the back tires touching the ground, and a distance of 200 feet (or 4 bus lengths) behind the bus.

   B. Position the mirror so that the heads of the students directly behind the driver's seat are visible.

   C. Position the mirror so that the back window is barely visible.

   D. Position the mirror in order to see the heads of the students directly behind the driver's seat, the rest of the students on the bus, and the back window visible in the mirror's top section.

4. Most bus fatalities of students occur

   A. during accidents as passengers in the front half of the bus.

   B. during accidents as passengers in the back half of the bus.

   C. when moving around unrestrained when the bus is in motion.

   D. when they are loading and unloading from the bus.

5. To prepare for leaving after unloading students on the route, what must the driver do?

   A. Close the door before pulling away from a stop

   B. Ensure that the parking brake is on

   C. Keep the alternating flashing red lights on

   D. Activate the right turn signal

6. A safe stop includes removing the key from the ignition switch.

   A. True

   B. False

7. The safest way to ensure all students have properly exited the bus is to do a headcount as they exit.

   A. True

   B. False

8. What potential mechanical or operational problems should be inspected during a post-trip walkthrough of a school bus?

   A. Tire pressure

   B. Stop signal arms, mirror systems, and flashing warning lamps

   C. Cracked or damaged windows or doors

   D. Windshield wipers

9. During an emergency evacuation, a "safe place" should be how many feet away from the road?

   A. At least 100 feet away from the road

   B. At least 25 feet from the road

   C. At least 150 feet from the road

   D. At least 250 feet from the road

10. When must a driver stop the bus BEFORE a crossbuck sign?

    A. When visibility is reduced

    B. When students are on the bus

    C. When there is no painted white line on the road

    D. When there is oncoming traffic present

11. At a crossing, the driver should remain

    A. 15 feet away but within 10 feet of the closest rail.

    B. 25 feet away but within 50 feet of the closest rail.

    C. 50 feet away but within 15 feet of the closest rail.

    D. 15 feet away but within 50 feet of the closest rail.

12. If a serious problem is present on the bus, it should be dealt with immediately by instructing uninvolved students to move to the front of the bus to ensure their safety.

    A. True

    B. False

13. When handling behavior problems on the bus, the driver may request that the offender move to a seat near them.

    A. True

    B. False

14. Which of the following statements is true regarding antilock braking systems (ABS)?

    A. ABS braking systems prevent skids due to overbraking.

    B. ABS braking systems decrease the stopping time.

    C. ABS braking systems do not prevent skids due to overbraking.

    D. ABS braking systems do not affect steering control.

15. When braking in a vehicle with an antilock braking system (ABS), the driver should

    A. brake normally.

    B. brake sooner and hold the brake down longer.

    C. brake lightly.

    D. increase pressure on the brakes as you slow down.

16. An antilock braking system (ABS) may

    A. prevent turning skids.

    B. prevent brake-induced skids.

    C. increase the life of the regular brakes.

    D. decrease steering control.

17. All of the following describe the use of strobe lights on a school bus EXCEPT:

    A. Strobe lights are mounted on the roof of the bus.

    B. Strobe lights on a bus are white.

    C. Strobe lights should be used when the driver's visibility is limited.

    D. Strobe lights are used to increase visibility in the cab.

18. All of the following describe strong winds EXCEPT:

    A. They can move a bus sideways.

    B. They can push a bus off road.

    C. They can affect ABS.

    D. They can tip a bus over.

19. All of the following are true regarding the backing of a school bus EXCEPT:

    A. It is highly discouraged to back a school bus.

    B. Backing should never be done if students are outside of the bus.

    C. The chance of collision is increased when backing a bus.

    D. A lookout can complicate the backing up process.

20. A school bus is permitted to drive through a railroad crossing if the traffic light on the other side of the crossing is green.

    A. True

    B. False

School Buses Practice Test 1 Answer Key and Explanations

1. A	**5.** A	**9.** A	**13.** A	**17.** D
2. D	**6.** B	**10.** C	**14.** A	**18.** C
3. D	**7.** B	**11.** D	**15.** A	**19.** D
4. D	**8.** B	**12.** B	**16.** B	**20.** B

1. **The correct answer is A.** The danger zone from the front bumper of the bus may extend as far as 30 feet. The most dangerous area is the initial 10 feet of this danger zone.

2. **The correct answer is D.** The flat mirrors of a school bus have a blind spot located immediately in front of and below each mirror that spans 50–150 feet (or, depending on the width and length of the school bus, as far as 400 feet) behind the bus from the rear bumper. It is not present only on the driver's side (choice A), nor does it only extend 10 feet from either the front bumper (choice B) or the sides of the bus (choice C).

3. **The correct answer is D.** The overhead inside rearview mirror should always be positioned for the driver to see all students, including the tops of the heads of the students located directly behind the driver's seat (choice B) and the window at the back of the bus in the top section of the mirror (choice C). Choice A is incorrect because this option describes the appropriate adjustment for the flat mirrors of a bus.

4. **The correct answer is D.** Most student fatalities occur when they are loading and unloading from the bus. In fact, more students are killed during this procedure than during transport even if they are in the front half of the bus (choice A), the back half of the bus (choice B), or moving around unrestrained (choice C).

5. **The correct answer is A.** The door of the school bus should be closed before the driver pulls away from a stop. The parking brake should be released (choice B) and the alternating flashing red lights should be turned off (choice C). The left turn signal should be activated (choice D) and all mirrors

should be checked before the driver safely enters the flow of traffic.

6. **The correct answer is B.** A safe stop does not always include removing the key from the ignition switch as it depends on whether the driver is at the school or at a designated bus stop.

7. **The correct answer is B.** Accessories, clothing, and even parts of a student's body can become entangled or caught on the handrail or in the door of a school bus as they exit. This can cause injury and even death. The driver should monitor all students closely as they exit the bus and confirm that all students are in a location of safety before moving the school bus.

8. **The correct answer is B.** Potential mechanical or operational problems of items exclusive to school buses should be prioritized during a post-trip inspection. These items include the stop signal arms, mirror systems, and flashing warning lamps of the school bus. Tire pressure (choice A), cracked or damaged windows or doors (choice C), and the proper functioning of windshield wipers (choice D) should be checked if they are involved in a special situation or problem.

9. **The correct answer is A.** When determining a "safe place," students should be led at least 100 feet away from the road and in the same direction as oncoming traffic. 25 feet (choice B) is not far enough away to ensure safety. 150 feet (choice C) and 250 feet (choice D) are more than far enough and at times may be too far for emergency personnel to locate.

10. **The correct answer is C.** A crossbuck sign indicates that there is a railway crossing and that the driver should yield to any oncoming train(s). When there is no painted white line on the road,

a bus must stop before the sign instead of at the painted line. Inclement weather (choice A), students (choice B), and oncoming traffic (choice D) do not affect whether to stop the bus before the crossbuck sign.

11. **The correct answer is D.** At a crossing, the driver should remain 15 feet away but within 50 feet of the closest rail in order to have the clearest view of the railroad tracks. 25 feet away (choice A) and 50 feet away (choice C) are too far away for a quality view. Being 10 feet away from the closest rail (choice A) is too close for a clear view of the tracks.

12. **The correct answer is B.** If a serious problem is present on the bus, it should be dealt with after all uninvolved students are safely off the bus.

13. **The correct answer is A.** Handling serious problems on the bus should always be aligned with the school's disciplinary procedures. It is appropriate for the driver of a school bus to request that a student who is misbehaving move to a seat near the driver in order to try to alleviate the problem.

14. **The correct answer is A.** ABS aids the driver in avoiding wheel lockups and helps them to maintain control of the vehicle. While ABS can help the driver to stop more immediately, this is not always the case (choice B). ABS does, however, better enable the driver to avoid obstacles when braking by allowing them to maintain control of the steering and move around the obstacle (choice D). ABS also assists in preventing skids during overbraking (choice C).

15. **The correct answer is A.** When braking in a vehicle with ABS, the driver should brake as they normally would. The braking force applied should be enough to safely stop and to stay in control of the vehicle; additional pressure (choices B and D) is not needed. Braking lightly (choice C) could be dangerous as ABS requires the same pressure as older brakes.

16. **The correct answer is B.** Brake-induced skids should be prevented by ABS, but the system will not prevent skids that are the result of turning too fast or the spinning of the drive wheels (choice A). ABS is not a replacement for normal or poorly maintained brakes (choice C). ABS does help the driver to avoid wheel lockups and to maintain control of the vehicle (choice D).

17. **The correct answer is D.** Strobe lights increase visibility outside of the bus but not inside the cab. Not all buses are equipped with strobe lights, but they can be located on the roof of buses that are (choice A). The white strobe lights (choice B) should be used when the driver's visibility is limited (choice C). This may include being unable to see clearly in front of, behind, or beside the bus.

18. **The correct answer is C.** ABS is not directly affected by high winds, although braking in general can be difficult and somewhat unpredictable in these situations. Because the sides of a school bus can be compared to the sails of a sailboat, strong winds can easily move a bus sideways (choice A) and push it off the road (choice B). Extreme high winds can even tip a bus over (choice D).

19. **The correct answer is D.** Using a lookout is the preferred method when backing is necessary. The backing of a school bus is dangerous. Because of this, it is highly discouraged to back a school bus (choice A). Backing should only be conducted if there is no other choice. If the driver must back a school bus, it should never be done when students are outside of the bus (choice B). Backing is not only dangerous, but also increases the risk of collision (choice C).

20. **The correct answer is B.** A school bus must stop at all railroad crossings before proceeding, even if the traffic light is green.

SCHOOL BUSES PRACTICE TEST 2
20 Questions - 60 Minutes

Directions: This test consists of a combination of true/false and multiple-choice questions. Only one answer is correct for each question.

1. When should the driver make sure each mirror is adjusted properly on a school bus?

    A. After operating a school bus

    B. While operating a school bus

    C. Before operating a school bus

    D. It is not important to adjust the mirrors of a school bus properly.

2. The convex mirrors of a school bus can be found above the flat mirrors on the outside of a bus.

    A. True

    B. False

3. Where are the crossover mirrors located?

    A. Below the flat mirrors on the outside of the bus

    B. On each side of the bus at the front left and right corners

    C. On each side of the bus at the back left and right corners

    D. At the rear bumper and directly in front of and below each flat mirror

4. All of the following statements are true regarding the blind spots of the overhead inside rearview mirror EXCEPT:

    A. The overhead inside rearview mirror has two blind spots.

    B. The overhead inside rearview mirror has one blind spot.

    C. The overhead inside rearview mirror has a blind spot immediately behind the driver's seat.

    D. The overhead inside rearview mirror has a blind spot that starts at the back bumper and can span as far as 400 feet or more behind the bus.

5. When stopping at an official school bus stop, which of the following should the driver do?

    A. Stop the school bus completely with the front bumper at least 5 feet away from students waiting at the official bus stop

    B. Put the transmission in "Park"

    C. Only activate the alternating red lights when traffic is close to the bus

    D. Decide if the stop bar extension is needed

6. How far away from the side of the bus should a driver instruct the students to walk when unloading from the bus?

    A. 10 feet

    B. 5 feet

    C. 15 feet

    D. 25 feet

7. It is safe for a student to retrieve a dropped object near the outside of the bus as long as it is more than 10 feet away from the passenger doors.

   A. True
   B. False

8. All of the following should be considered by the driver when deciding to evacuate a school bus EXCEPT:

   A. The smell of leaking fuel
   B. Danger of fire
   C. Student behavior
   D. Location of the bus

9. Which of the following does NOT apply to a passive crossing?

   A. It is not controlled by a traffic device.
   B. The driver is not required to stop.
   C. It is marked with a circular yellow sign.
   D. Such a crossing does not determine if the driver should proceed.

10. All active crossings utilize some type of traffic control device.

    A. True
    B. False

11. All of the following should be considered by the driver in order to prevent a tail swing EXCEPT:

    A. The length and width of the school bus
    B. Mirror adjustment
    C. Pre-trip inspection
    D. The number of students on the bus

12. If the bus stalls or becomes trapped on the railroad tracks, the driver should immediately

    A. call for help.
    B. assess the distance of the oncoming train.
    C. reverse the bus.
    D. evacuate everyone from the bus and away from the railroad tracks.

13. When faced with a potentially dangerous behavioral problem on the bus while loading and unloading, the driver should

    A. ignore the problem.
    B. issue a verbal warning to the student(s).
    C. pull over and handle the situation.
    D. wait until arriving at the destination to ensure safe transport.

14. The Department of Transportation requires that all vehicles with air brakes (such as buses and trailers) have antilock braking systems if they were built on or after March 1,

    A. 1978.
    B. 1998.
    C. 1968.
    D. 1988.

15. What color is the ABS lamp on a school bus?

    A. Red
    B. Yellow
    C. Blue
    D. Green

16. At railroad tracks, a bus driver should avoid which of the following?

    A. Changing gears on a manual transmission when crossing
    B. Opening the service door
    C. Using the parking brake when stopped
    D. Crossing a set of parallel tracks without stopping

17. The tail swing of a school bus can be up to

    A. 5 feet.
    B. 2 feet.
    C. 3 feet.
    D. 10 feet.

18. When it comes to antilock braking systems (ABS), it is important to remember that a safe driver is the vehicle's best safety feature.

    A. True
    B. False

19. When approaching a bus stop, the driver should turn on the turn signal to indicate the bus is pulling over

    A. 1-3 seconds ahead of time.
    B. 3-5 seconds ahead of time.
    C. 4-6 seconds ahead of time.
    D. 7-10 seconds ahead of time.

20. An advance warning sign

    A. is circular and yellow with black markings.
    B. is circular and red with white markings.
    C. includes markings that warn not to pass on a two-lane road, an "X" and the letters "RR."
    D. is a white stop line on the pavement in front of the tracks.

School Buses Practice Test 2 Answer Key and Explanations

1. C	5. B	9. B	13. C	17. C
2. B	6. A	10. A	14. B	18. A
3. B	7. B	11. D	15. B	19. B
4. B	8. C	12. D	16. A	20. A

1. **The correct answer is C.** Before operating a school bus, the driver should always adjust the mirrors properly. Choice D is incorrect as it is essential that the driver properly adjust the mirrors of a school bus in order to observe any object, traffic, or students in the danger zone around a school bus. Adjusting mirrors while operating a school bus (choice B) may prevent the driver from safely monitoring danger zones from the time of initial operation. Adjusting mirrors after operating a school bus (choice A) can be dangerous as the driver will not be able to monitor danger zones properly during transportation.

2. **The correct answer is B.** The upper flat mirrors of a school bus can be found above the convex mirrors of a school bus. Therefore, the convex mirrors of a school bus are located below the flat mirrors on the outside of the bus.

3. **The correct answer is B.** The crossover mirrors are located on each side of the school bus at the front left and right corners. The convex mirrors, and not the crossover mirrors, are positioned below the upper flat mirrors (choice A) while the back of the bus lacks mirrors (choice C). Choice D is incorrect as it describes the blind spot area of flat mirrors.

4. **The correct answer is B.** The overhead inside rearview mirror has two blind spots. The two blind spots of this mirror (choice A) are located immediately behind the driver's seat (choice C) with the second and largest blind spot starting at the back bumper and spanning as far as 400 feet or more behind the bus. Only acknowledging one blind spot (choice B) can be dangerous as the driver is missing the second one.

5. **The correct answer is B.** The transmission of a school bus should be placed in "Park" when coming to a full stop. If a "Park" shift is not available, the bus should be put in neutral and the parking brake should be used at each stop. While the school bus should come to a complete stop, the front bumper should be at least 10 feet away from students waiting at the official bus stop (Choice A). The driver should also activate the alternating red lights when traffic is safely at a distance (choice C), and the stop arm should always be extended (Choice D) when approaching the stop.

6. **The correct answer is A.** Students should walk at least 10 feet away from the side of the bus when unloading. 5 feet (choice B) is not far enough and can result in being within the blind spot of the driver. 15 feet (choice C) and 25 feet (choice D) are too far and may be dangerous depending on where the students are unloading.

7. **The correct answer is B.** Students should never retrieve a dropped object outside the bus without expressly informing the driver as the student can drop out of sight when picking up the object, thus making it unsafe.

8. **The correct answer is C.** If a serious problem results from the inappropriate behavior of a student, the student should only be put off the bus at school or at their designated bus stop. Evacuation should be considered if the driver smells leaking fuel (choice A), if there is fire or the danger of fire (choice B), or if the school bus is at risk of being hit by another vehicle or vehicles (choice D).

9. **The correct answer is B.** Drivers are required to stop at passive crossings and follow proper procedures for crossing. Passive crossings do not include a traffic control device (choice A) and are marked

with a circular yellow sign (choice C). Determining whether to proceed is the responsibility of the driver (choice D). The driver should determine the safety of the crossing by making sure the tracks are not being used by a train and that there is enough space to proceed.

10. **The correct answer is A.** Active crossings have an installed traffic control device that conducts traffic. They can be recognized by flashing red lights with bells, flashing red lights without bells, and flashing red lights with gates and bells.

11. **The correct answer is D.** The number of students on the school bus is not significant when avoiding a tail swing. The driver should know the dimensions of the school bus in order to calculate their bus's tail swing (option A). The tail swing of a school bus can be up to 3 feet. Appropriate mirror adjustment is critical in preventing tail swing as the driver must monitor them before and during each turn (option B). A pre-trip inspection of the bus should include ensuring that the windows, windshield, and mirrors are clean while also adjusting the mirrors appropriately before operating the school bus (choice C) as visibility is key in the prevention of a tail swing.

12. **The correct answer is D.** If the bus stalls or becomes trapped on the railroad tracks, the driver should evacuate everyone off of the bus and the railroad tracks immediately. They should be led at an angle from the bus, far away from the railroad tracks and in the direction of the oncoming train. While assistance may be necessary (choice A), evacuation is the first priority in the situation of a trapped or stalled bus on the tracks. Assessing the distance of a train (choice B) could lead to injury or death as this takes away from the time to evacuate. Attempts to move the bus can be dangerous and jeopardize the safety of the driver and the students (choice C).

13. **The correct answer is C.** A potentially dangerous problem should be handled as soon as possible, thus the driver should pull over as soon as possible to handle it. It should not be ignored (choice A), nor should the driver simply issue a verbal

warning (choice B) or wait until arriving at the final destination (choice D) as someone may get hurt during that time.

14. **The correct answer is B.** The Department of Transportation has required that all vehicles with air brakes built since March 1, 1998 have ABS.

15. **The correct answer is B.** The ABS lamp on a school bus is yellow. Red (choice A), blue (choice C), and green (choice D) lights are not related to the antilock braking system.

16. **The correct answer is A.** When crossing railroad tracks, drivers should use a low gear when crossing and refrain from shifting gears. Improper shifting can lead to a stall and thus endanger the driver and passengers. Opening the service door (choice B) before crossing the tracks allows a driver to hear oncoming trains more clearly. When coming to a stop before tracks, the driver will place the vehicle in neutral then use the parking brake (choice C) while making sure the tracks are clear. When two sets of tracks are present (choice D), a driver will ensure that both sets of tracks are clear then cross them one after another.

17. **The correct answer is C.** The tail swing of a school bus occurs during turning movements and can be up to 3 feet. 2 feet (choice B) is too small. 5 feet (choice A) and 10 feet (choice D) are too large for a tail swing of a bus.

18. **The correct answer is A.** ABS should not be considered an addition to a vehicle's normal brakes, and operating a vehicle with ABS should not change the way a driver normally brakes. Safe driving should always be conducted so that the driver may never need to use a vehicle's antilock braking system.

19. **The correct answer is B.** The turn signal should be used 3-5 seconds ahead of the turn to indicate that the bus is pulling over for the designated bus stop. 1-3 seconds (choice A) is not enough notice. 4-6 seconds (choice C) and 7-10 seconds (choice D) are too far in advance and may be ignored by other drivers.

20. **The correct answer is A.** Advance warning signs, which are circular and yellow with black markings, are positioned before railroad-highway crossings and warn the driver to slow down, look and listen, and to anticipate having to stop as there could be an approaching train. It is not red with white markings (choice B). Choice C is incorrect as it describes pavement markings, which have the same function as advance warning signs. Pavement markings may include a white stop line on the pavement in front of the tracks (choice D). This line signals that the bus should be stopped before the line with the front bumper of the bus behind the line.

NOTES

APPENDIX

Glossary of CDL Terms

APPENDIX

GLOSSARY OF CDL TERMS

The following is a glossary of basic terms, acronyms, and initialisms you will encounter in this book as well as in your state CDL manual and entry-level driver training programs. These terms form a core knowledge base both for the CDL exams and the everyday tasks of a commercial driver. They are arranged in alphabetical order.

A

Antilock braking system (ABS): A current standard on trailers and converter dollies made after March 1, 1998. ABS will not increase the stopping distance or braking power, but it can help keep the wheels from locking.

B

Baffled tank: A tank divided by bulkheads with holes that allow the flow of liquid but reduce the strength of surges. Baffled tanks cannot be used to transport all liquids due to sanitation concerns.

Bobtail: Any tractor that does not have an attached trailer.

Brake lag: The natural lag on all air brakes. On average, brake lag is 1 second from the time the driver presses the pedal to the time the brakes engage.

Braking distance: The distance traveled during the time it takes from the brakes engaging to the truck arriving at a complete stop.

Bulkhead: An insert placed into a tank that separates it into smaller tanks. Bulkheads allow the liquid to be better distributed and reduce the risk created by front-to-back surges.

Button hook turn: A type of right turn where the driver turns wide through the turn, which allows the truck to go straight forward and then turn widely into the other lane mid-turn.

C

Combination vehicle: A vehicle that consists of either a truck or a tractor pulling a trailer. This can be a straight truck with a trailer or a tractor-trailer with one, two, or three trailers.

Commercial driver's license (CDL): A license specifically for working drivers that allows them to operate commercial vehicles with or without trailers.

Commercial learner's permit (CLP): A permit acquired by passing the CDL general knowledge exam. The permit must be held for at least 14 days before a physical skills test can be completed. Although, that timeline may vary by state. The permit allows a driver to operate a commercial vehicle under the supervision of a qualified trainer, supervisor, test administrator, or regulator.

Controlled braking: The practice of braking as hard as possible without locking the wheels up.

Converter dollies: The equipment used to connect one trailer to another for double or triple combination vehicles. They can either have one or two axles on them depending on the model.

Convex mirrors: Mirrors located below the flat mirrors in a school bus. They are used to give a wide angled view of traffic, the left and right sides of the bus, and of students that may be on either side of the bus.

Crossover mirrors: Mirrors mounted on both front corners of a school bus. They provide a view of the danger zone in front of the bus, an area not visible when looking directly out of the windshield.

D

Danger zones: The areas surrounding a school bus where students are more likely to get hit. Danger zones include the first ten feet from the front, back, and both sides of the bus.

Double/triple trailer: An alternative name for a combination vehicle that has two or three trailers. May also refer to the endorsement specific for this type of vehicle.

Drawbar: A common style of coupling used for heavy duty towing. Drawbars create a solid connection between the truck and trailer by tightening down on the connection point of the trailer.

Dry bulk cargo: Cargo that comes in a tank and has a higher center of gravity than most loads.

E

Emergency brake: The springs that are held back by the air pressure built up by the air brakes. Also called spring brakes.

Endorsement: An added component that can be placed on a commercial driver's license (CDL) that expands what a driver can and cannot transport.

F

Fifth wheel: A common style of coupling used for Class A vehicles. A fifth wheel is a U-shaped hitch that interacts with the kingpin of a trailer, offering greater stability and control for the load.

Flat mirrors: Mirrors mounted on the windshield of a school bus, either at the sides or on the front. They should be adjusted to ensure a visual distance of 4 buses (or 200 ft.) from the back of the bus.

Following distance: The amount of space needed between the commercial vehicle and the vehicle in front of it.

G

Gooseneck: A common style of coupling named for the craning feature of its design. Goosenecks work by reaching over into the bed of a truck or reaching the coupling point of a tractor if the trailer is very low to the ground.

Gross Vehicle Weight (GVW): The true weight of a vehicle, including its load.

Gross Vehicle Weight Rating (GWVR): The maximum weight rating for a vehicle, including its load, that is given by the manufacturer.

Gross Combination Weight (GCW): The same as the GVW but for a combination vehicle (a vehicle with a trailer).

Gross Combination Weight Rating (GCWR): The same as the GWVR but for a combination vehicle (a vehicle with a trailer).

H

Hazardous materials (HazMat): Any kind of cargo that poses a risk to health, safety, and property when being transported. HazMat are heavily regulated to help keep their transportation as safe as possible. Regulations for HazMat can be found in 49 CFR Parts 100–185.

Header boards: Also called headache racks. Used to protect the driver in case there is a crash or other emergency that can throw cargo forward.

J

Jug handle turn: A type of right turn where the driver turns wide at the beginning of the turn, thus thrusting the nose of the vehicle into the other lane before completing the turn.

L

Long combination vehicle (LCV): A tractor with a double or triple trailer.

O

Outage: The amount of expansion a liquid will experience when it is heated.

Overhead inside rearview mirror: An interior overhead mirror on a school bus. It should always be positioned for the driver to see all students, including the tops of the heads of the students located directly behind the driver's seat, and the window at the back of the bus.

Oversized cargo: Any cargo that is over-length, over-width, or overweight. This type of cargo requires special permits to transport, is usually restricted to certain times it can be transported, and sometimes requires police or pilot vehicle escort.

P

Parking brake: The button or lever that operates the emergency (spring) brakes when the air pressure is released and the vehicle is not in motion. Located inside the cab.

Passenger endorsement: An endorsement that can be added to a CDL that enables the driver to transport passengers in a vehicle used for profit or hire. The exact quantity of passengers that necessitates the endorsement is state-dependent; however, federal law requires the endorsement for vehicles designed to carry 16 people or more, which includes empty seats and the driver. Individual states may require this endorsement for fewer passengers. This endorsement does not apply to school bus operation.

Perception distance: The distance traveled during the time it takes for your brain to recognize a hazard after seeing it. The average perception time is 1 ¾ seconds.

Physical skills test: The portion of the CDL exam that requires direct interaction with the commercial vehicle. It is typically broken up into three smaller segments: pre-trip inspection, basic controls, and driving (on-road). All of the segments combined generally take around 2 hours to complete.

Pintle hook: A common style of coupling hitch often used in heavy duty towing applications. They are a hinged hook on the back of a truck or trailer that clamps around a circular connection point on the front of a trailer or dolly.

Pup trailers: Trailers that range in length from 26 to 29 feet. They can be used in a single configuration but are also common in combination configurations.

R

Reaction distance: The distance traveled during the time it takes a driver to react after recognizing a hazard. The average reaction time is ¾ second.

Rearward amplification: The compacted risk a vehicle has towards a crack-the-whip effect, determined by the total length of a vehicle. The longer the length, the higher the risk.

Refrigerated cargo: Cargo that is temperature sensitive and must be transported in a refrigerated trailer.

Rollover: An accident where the truck flips onto its side, top, or even completely rolls over.

S

Service brakes: The brakes that engage when the driver presses the brake pedal, operating using air pressure. They are also called the air brakes.

Stab braking: The practice of applying the brakes hard enough to lock the wheels, releasing the brakes to let the wheels roll free, and braking hard again. This type of braking is often used when there is a need for quick stopping, such as a drop in pressure, a possible collision, or a steep downgrade.

Staging: The process of organizing trailers prior to coupling. In general, the heaviest trailer should go first behind the tractor and the lightest trailer should go last.

Standee line: A two-inch thick line on the floor of a bus that designates where passengers can stand. Passengers are never allowed to be in front of the standee line while the vehicle is in motion.

Stop light switch: An electrical switch that turns on the brake lights when the air brakes are engaged in order to notify those behind you that you are braking.

Stopping distance: The amount of space needed to completely stop the vehicle. The formula for calculating stopping distance is perception distance + reaction distance + braking distance.

Strobe lights: School buses may have strobe lights mounted on the roof. They are bright white and should be used when the driver's visibility is limited and they are unable to see clearly in front of, behind, or beside the bus.

Surge: A phenomenon that occurs when a partially filled tank experiences a sudden shift in the liquid. Surges most commonly occur from front-to-back due to braking but can also occur from side-to-side because of sudden steering.

T

Tanker: The name for the endorsement that permits a driver to transport liquids and gaseous materials in tanks. Tanker may also refer to the vehicle itself.

Tie-downs: A method of securing cargo that is commonly used on flatbeds or similar cargo areas that have no side walls. There should be one tie-down for every ten feet of cargo, and at least two tie-downs on any cargo less than ten feet.

U

Unbaffled tank: A standard single tank that has no divisions. They are also often called smooth bore tanks because they have no bulkheads or baffling inside.

notes

notes

notes

notes

notes

notes

notes

notes

notes

notes

notes

notes

notes